**A Reader's Guide to
Fifty European Novels**

A Reader's Guide to
Fifty European Novels

by Martin Seymour-Smith

Heinemann – London
Barnes & Noble – Totowa, New Jersey

Heinemann Educational Books Ltd

LONDON EDINBURGH MELBOURNE AUCKLAND HONG KONG
SINGAPORE KUALA LUMPUR NEW DELHI IBADAN NAIROBI
JOHANNESBURG KINGSTON PORT OF SPAIN

©Martin Seymour-Smith 1980

First published 1980 by Pan Books as
An Introduction to Fifty European Novels
in the Pan Literature Guides Series
First published in this casebound edition 1980

British Library CIP Data
Seymour-Smith, Martin
A reader's guide to fifty European novels.
– (Reader's guide series).
1. Fiction – History and criticism
I. Title   II. Series
809.3   PN3451

ISBN 0-435-18812-7

ISBN (USA) 0-389-20138-3

Published in Great Britain by
Heinemann Educational Books Ltd
22 Bedford Square, London WC1B 3HH
Published in the U.S.A. 1980 by
Barnes & Noble Books

Printed and bound in Great Britain by
Richard Clay (The Chaucer Press) Ltd,
Bungay, Suffolk

to Charles and Nora Sisson
who don't need any part of this but do have my
gratitude for the many years of their friendship
and generosity

Contents

Introduction

The selection of novels in this book is the result of con-
sultation between Andrew Mylett, the General Editor of
this series, some teachers of foreign literatures at universities, the publishers, and myself. The selection does not
represent the *best* European novels, or my favourite European novels (or, probably, anyone else's), though most of
the best are included. The exercise is in the main historical; our aim is to provide, by the means of dealing
with fifty individual titles, an outline of the development
of the novel in Europe since Rabelais.

Movements, topics, important and influential critics,
and writers who could not be represented individually are
included in the index, which is fully cross-referenced.
The reader should thus be able, with the minimum of
fuss, to discover information about such movements as
naturalism; such concepts as phenomenology, 'the superfluous man', or Jansenism; such novelists as Rousseau;
such philosophers as Husserl; such critics as Conor
Cruise O'Brien.

The full plots or stories of some novels cannot be given
in the space allowed: in these cases an outline has been
given. The reader may therefore be curious to know why
so much space has been allotted to Goethe's *Wilhelm
Meister*. The reason is practical: people will read and
enjoy much of Rabelais, nearly all of Cervantes, much of
Proust. I doubt if they will read *Wilhelm Meister*,

although they will undoubtedly try. Though flawed, the book is extremely important: Goethe anticipated all the themes of modern fiction, and this novel is highly relevant to almost all the German novels which followed it, and to some others too.

The method usually followed in this *Literature Guide* has been to devote one section to the author's biography seen against the historical background; a second to an outline of the novel or novels; and a third to exegesis. I have varied this approach when appropriate: it would have been unwise, for example, to consider *Cousine Bette* or *Germinal* outside literary contexts – the larger enterprises of which they form part.

In writing a book on European Literature, titles prove something of a problem. It seemed best, for this book, to use the form by which the novel is most popularly known in English.

The chapter bibliographies are skeletal: further reading can be pursued through the general books (and through the bibliographies supplied in them) listed in the General Bibliography (p. 515).

I am grateful to Miranda Britt, Bernadino Ochino, and my wife for their invaluable assistance and advice; and to the publishers, many of whose staff studied my initial selections and sensibly amended them.

François Rabelais

Rabelais was famous in his lifetime, but modern scholarship has unearthed only enough facts to give an outline of his career. He was born about 1494 at a small farm, La Devinière, near Tours. His father was a lawyer. Nothing is known of his childhood education, but in his youth he became a Franciscan friar at Fontenay-le-Comte, Bas-Poitou. He had humanist connections and before long joined the less strict Benedictine Order. He remained, however, indebted to his strict Franciscan training: both to the sermons he studied and to the notion of original sin so stressed by the Franciscans.

In 1527 he abandoned the cloister, and in 1536 was able, by a technicality, to become a lay priest; by that time he had become famous not only as a writer but also as a man of wide learning: Greek, architecture, warfare, equitation, theology – he was a true Renaissance Man. He qualified in medicine in 1530 at Montpellier, and received his doctorate in 1537. There are stories of his skill as a demonstrative anatomist and even as a 'miraculous' healer. He published *Pantagruel* in 1532 under the anagram (of his own name) of Maître Alcofribas Nasier; *Gargantua*, the First Book of the complete work, followed in 1534 after a visit to his home.

By this time Rabelais had gained the attention of wealthy and influential patrons, particularly Cardinal Jean du Bellay; he was able to use them to protect him from prison or the stake for the rest of his life. In 1546 he was able to publish a work (the Third Book) under his own name; but despite his protectors, trouble was to attend him until almost the end of his life. This, it must be emphasized, was in no sense unusual for a curious and open-minded public man in the France of his era.

Rabelais probably had one or even two bastard children; these were legitimized in the usual fashion of the time. There is no evidence of his having been more or less promiscuous than any other of his contemporaries. From the time he became famous, in the early 1530s, his most relentless enemies were the ferocious Catholic orthodoxists of the Sorbonne whose aim was to root out any hint of heresy. For his part, Rabelais was happy to remain within the fold of the Roman Catholic Church – even though on what would today be called its left wing. All his books (Third Book, 1546; Fourth Book, 1548, completed 1552) were condemned with monotonous regularity by the Sorbonne, but he was only in serious danger when the Court, for reasons of its own, happened to be out of sympathy with his reformist position. Thus, during the 1540s he had to go into exile at Metz, where he perhaps lived in the Jewish quarter and practised as a doctor, and to go to Rome with his protector du Bellay. But he seems to have been fairly safe from 1549, and was installed as the curate of Saint-Martin-de-Meudon, near Paris, and at another benefice, Saint-Christophe-de-Jambet. Probably these were sinecures. Tradition has it that he died in Paris in the April of 1553.

Rabelais was the author, compiler or editor of many books: popular almanacs, editions of medical textbooks by such as Galen and Hippocrates, and probably some stage farces and revisions of popular works. There is a disputed Fifth Book of *Gargantua and Pantagruel*, issued (1564) after Rabelais' death: the first sixteen chapters appeared in 1562 as *L'Isle sonante* [*The Ringing Island*]. Certainly it is based on Rabelais, and Rabelais experts consider it to be 'essentially authentic'. But it contains some editorial additions, and is imaginatively inferior.

Gargantua and Pantagruel
[Gargantua, Pantagruel, Tiers Livre, Quart Livre]

SUMMARY Only an outline of *Gargantua and Pantagruel* can be provided: so full is it of characters and exotic details. The Second Book, *Pantagruel*, the first to be written, got its title from the summer drought of 1532: Pantagruel was the 'little demon' of thirst of the fifteenth-century mystery plays (particularly of Simon Grébon's *Actes des Apôtres*) who put salt down drunkards' throats. Thus Pantagruel, only to be seriously developed in the Third and Fourth Books, becomes a character who induces thirst: thirst for everything – death, drink, illusorily deathless lust – that life can offer. This Second Book is the slightest section of the work which none the less originated in it. It is probable that a visit Rabelais made to his home at La Devinière around 1532–3 prompted him to take up a theme then much in the air at Lyons – the legend of Gargantua – and to combine it with his tale of Pantagruel. When he arrived, there was a row going on over river rights between aristocrats and their well-to-do neighbours, who were headed by his own father. The details of this row he slotted (as the Picrocholine episode) into his adaptation of the Gargantua legend, a full version of which had appeared in Lyons in 1532 as the *Grandes Chroniques*. Rabelais might possibly have had a hand in the revision of this anonymous popular book, but he certainly did not write it.

The First Book (written second) tells the story of Pantagruel's father, Gargantua. It is more deliberately naturalized than the rest of the work. This is so in spite of Gargantua's giantism, a feature that is largely dropped in Books Three and Four. The giant Gargantua – born after an eleven-month period of gestation from his mother Gargamelle's ear shouting 'Give me a drink! Give me a drink! Give me a drink!' – shows his genius early: for example, he discovers that the softest lavatory paper is a goose's neck. He is educated in an old-fashioned and pedantic manner, which is learnedly satirized – as are the Sorbonne reactionaries. Incorporated into the account of Gargantua's education is much satire on contemporary university life in Paris. Later follows Gargantua's invaluable help to his father, Grandgousier, in defence of his lands against Picrochole; and the eventual foundation of the Abbey of Thélème where the rule is *Do what thou wilt* – but whose programme is subtler and less purely vitalistic than used to be assumed, particularly by readers of Urquhart's version of Rabelais.

In Book Two, Pantagruel, born in the terrible drought that has been mentioned, is introduced as the son of Gargantua and Badebec ('open-mouthed'). This is somewhat more conventional and strictly topical, though it lays the foundations for the Third and Fourth Books. It recounts the gigantic Pantagruel's incredible childhood feats, and introduces Panurge, who is originally based on some of the Greek writer Lucian's studies of rogues but (in Book Two) is none the less nearer to a *picaresque* rascal whose crooked eloquence and high intellectual capacity usually disguise his profound psychological disturbance. In the succeeding Books, Panurge is transformed into Rabelais' most subtle and puzzling creation. The narrative of Book Two is concerned with another war: this time against the Dipsodes in Far Eastern Utopia (Rabelais borrowed the word from More, whose work influenced him profoundly). There are further satirical descriptions of university life.

With Book Three, the most self-contained of the four, an entirely new note is introduced. Pantagruel's hugeness is more or less dropped, and the substance becomes markedly more Rabelais' own, although the learned and topical allusions continue to abound: the final two books are more clearly the work of a cohesive imagination. Panurge, who in the Second Book had some measure of dignity, retains his intellectual capacities, but is turned into a more fantastic, caricaturized and, indeed, symbolic figure: a cowardly but complex buffoon who belongs to the long line that produced Shakespeare's Falstaff. He has become a wasteful prince who ponders whether he should marry, and worries that if he does he will be cuckolded. Having failed to find a satisfactory solution to his dilemma, he decides to consult the Oracle of the Holy Bottle 'near Cathay in Upper India'. The Third Book, mostly taken up with learned discussion presented with great liveliness and skill, ends as Pantagruel, Panurge and their followers set off on their voyage. The last chapters contain some of Rabelais' most enigmatic writing: the eulogy to the herb *pantagruelien*, which is hemp.

Book Four concerns the voyage; its nautical language and geography are accurate and authentic. In contrast to Book Three, it is more colloquial and less erudite. The oracle has not been reached by the end – in Book Five the answer it gives is a bottle of wine, which is likely to accord with Rabelais' enigmatic plans.

CRITICAL COMMENTARY The reader must not expect consistency from one book to another, as in each book the author was doing something different; though his characters have the same names they do not have entirely the same shapes. There is cohesion, but not the kind of planned cohesion that the post-Renaissance reader expects. Rabelais wrote for and commented upon his times; he is one of the founding fathers of modernist fiction, but had no notion of fictional coherence as this was to be understood by his successors, particularly those of the eighteenth and nineteenth centuries. (The wheel has come full circle in the sense that many twentieth-century writers, too, would like to be rid of such a notion.)

The adjective *Rabelaisian* is still often taken to mean 'hearty, bawdy, coarse, cloacal, buffoonish'. Nothing could be further from the truth. Part of the responsibility must lie with Sir Thomas Urquhart, the gifted and roaring Cavalier, whose famous translation was made at the very time when the concept of 'smut' was being invented by the Puritans. Urquhart's Rabelais is good literature on its own account – it even has features, of smaller proportions, in common with Rabelais; but it is not always Rabelais – rather a jolly mid-seventeenth-century English view of him. This did not emerge until scholarly work began on Rabelais in France at the beginning of this century. But in Rabelais' time 'smut' did not exist as such: coarseness was an important and ever present component of everyday speech.

Although his genius is quintessentially a comic one, Rabelais was subtle, perhaps uniquely erudite, and a careful writer. He is always laughing. *Pantagruelism*, so much discussed throughout his work, may certainly be rendered as 'humour', although in itself it is one of the profoundest definitions of humour ever attempted. But if Rabelais has one special subject, then this is education: education in the broadest possible sense.

Rabelais, like Montaigne, is basically a critic of the immediate fifteenth-century past and its intrusion into the sixteenth-century present.

He is also one of the initiators of our own world. Like Erasmus before him and Montaigne after him, he introduces into literature an element of constructive scepticism, or open-mindedness, which justifies his insatiable curiosity. Without wishing to follow Luther into Protestantism, he questions the validity of the two dominant mutually opposing fifteenth-century spiritual ideas: the notion that punctilious external observance will ensure salvation; and the belief that an internal self-realized image will bring about the same result. The questions being asked by Rabelais are (and he was one of the first to ask them): does meaning or absolute truth exist? And if it does, what is it?

Rabelais' work is an attempt to solve the problem, and it approaches this by taking only one thing for granted (and that with much laughter): that literature has a status. Literature is no longer anonymous, in the sense that it had been for centuries past. Rabelais employs his own text to explore the possibility of entertaining and searching for *the meaning of meaning* at the same time. We cannot read *Gargantua and Pantagruel* as a nonsense narrative, but neither can we read it as an esoteric treatise in comic wrapping: the wrapping is too monstrously corrugated. True, he begins Book One by saying that his readers may 'all too readily assume that there is to be found inside [his book] nothing but mockeries, pranks, and hilarious concoctions, seeing that the sign hung out in front ... is, without further enquiry, commonly received with jest and derision'. He then exhorts the reader to 'break the bone and suck the substantific marrow'. This has led many Rabelais scholars to assume that he is an allegorical writer in the Platonic tradition. He is actually amongst the earliest mockers of it: his contemporaries could enjoy the pagan Homer or Ovid, and then interpret them in absurdly allegorical terms; they would not admit that they were involving themselves in a false process of Christianization. Rabelais finds this funny. He scorns no knowledge, but is robust and full of common sense. His message, though probably less thoroughly sceptical than that of Montaigne, would, stated openly, have cost him his life. Thus the 'Enigma in the Form of a Prophecy' at the close of Book One, which Gargantua claims reveals 'the progress and carrying on of the divine truth', is no more than a 'description of a set at *tennis* in dark and obscure terms'.

Throughout he reminds the reader that this story is his invention: it is not 'true' – that is, separate from the real world outside.

In the Third Book the subject of the *Querelles des Femmes* (The 'Woman Question', which embraced the whole matter of the status of Women from the serious to the absurd), which was raging in France in the decade of its publication, is not really as important as the fatal attitude of Panurge, who cannot decide to get married because he is certain that if he does he will be cuckolded. Rabelais dedicated the book to Marguerite of Navarre, the great 'feminist' of the time; but he clearly regarded the literary battle going on around him as ridiculously characterized on both sides by didacticism and pompous dogma. *Pantagruelism*, the exercise of humour and humanity in the profoundest sense, consists, as G. D. Josipovici has well stated, in 'ceasing to ask this type of question [if I am married will I be cuckolded and beaten?]'.

Rabelais is concerned not to confuse *things* with their *names*. Language is not the invention of God, he seems (surprisingly) to be saying: no secret meaning lies hidden in words. Language is the invention of men: words are flexible.

Rabelais' style is colloquial in a manner that looks forward to that of the influential twentieth-century French novelist Louis-Ferdinand Céline. He has been taken up in the twentieth century because his work is the first emphatic reminder of the fact that fiction is fiction, the real world is the real world, and there is a difference. Like so many of his twentieth-century successors, he tries to discover the world through a thoroughgoing sensuality.

This most massively erudite of all works of fiction is in its essence one of the most modest: it continually calls into question the possibility of giving a coherent account of the world. It reminds the reader that all books are subjective, that no narrators can be *omniscient*. It is one of the most resolutely anti-mystical works ever written. But Rabelais does not ignore the power of men's wishes. *Gargantua and Pantagruel* describes them with wisdom, but dissolves them into laughter.

BIBLIOGRAPHY

Translations: T. Urquhart and P. Motteux, *The Heroic Deeds of Gargantua and Pantagruel* (1653–94), 1937; W. F. Smith, *Five Books*, 1893; S. Putnam, 1929; J. M. Cohen, *Gargantua and Pantagruel*, 1955. The problem of which translation to choose is difficult. Urquhart is in the best English (Motteux's continuation is 'hack' work), but is an only sometimes inspired adaptation. Smith is prolix but has accurate and excellent notes. Samuel Putnam's *The Essential Rabelais* (*The Portable Rabelais* in USA) is a selection with good linking commentaries, and is the best introduction.

Texts: A. Lefranc's *Édition critique* (1912) is the fullest. More easy of access, and good, are the editions of J. Boulenger, 1934, and P. Jourda, 1962.

Criticism: S. Putnam, *François Rabelais*, 1930; J. Plattard, *La Vie et l'œuvre de Rabelais*, 1932 – standard; M. A. Screech, *The Rabelaisian Marriage*, 1958; M. Tetel, *Rabelais*, 1967 – in French.

Lazarillo de Tormes (Anonymous)
[La Vida de Lazarillo de Tormes, y de sus fortunas y adversidades]

This short Spanish novel, always known by its short title
Lazarillo de Tormes, has been attributed to Diego
Hurtado de Mendoza (1503–75), to a 'converso' (converted Jew) resentful of his vulnerability to genealogical
inquiry, to an Erasmian, and to others. Good reasons
have been adduced for the first and third of these attribu-
tions, without being conclusive. The novel appeared in
three separate editions in 1554; internal evidence shows
that it was written in 1539, and there may be an earlier
lost text, perhaps a manuscript which was circulated. It
was an immediate success, and another author published
an inferior sequel in 1555. The Inquisition tried, not
altogether successfully, to ban it in 1559. There were
soon translations: into French in 1560, English in 1586,
German (expurgated) in 1617. But the romances of
chivalry and the pastoral novels outstripped it in popularity until the end of the century, when Mateo Alemán
published the first part of his *Guzmán de Alfarache*
(1599).

SUMMARY Lazarillo (diminutive of Lázaro) consists of a
short prologue and seven *tratados* (chapters). Lázaro, son
of a miller sent to the war for stealing grain (and subsequently killed) tells his own story. His mother is kept
by a Negro, and gives Lázaro a 'little black brother'.
When the Negro is caught stealing from his master and

his mother thus loses his support, she sends the boy Lázaro out into the world.

His first master is a blind beggar who is especially skilful at getting money out of women: he will say prayers for them, or prescribe quack remedies. He is mean, cunning and cruel, and Lázaro learns from him that the world is a hard place, in which one has to use one's wits to earn a living. Lázaro is able to steal from him, owing to his blindness; but he is often too sharp for the boy. Eventually Lázaro tricks him into jumping into a pillar, whereupon he leaves him.

His next master is a priest, a curate who is so mean with him that he nearly starves. For a time he manages to feed himself, by an ingenious ruse, from a chest where the priest hoards the bread offerings from the church; he is eventually discovered and thrown out.

Reaching Toledo, he falls into the service of an *escudero*, a country squire, who is desperately poor and hungry but is too proud to work. This new master is obsessed only with keeping up appearances, with *honour*. Lázaro is hungrier than ever. He manages to beg some food, and even to feed the *escudero,* whose 'honour' obliges him to pretend that he has eaten (he picks his teeth in public) and is not hungry. Lázaro takes pity on him, even though he does his 'dirty work' for him while he 'swaggers': he is better than the two previous masters. But this master leaves him: two people pay him advance rent for the house he is living in, and when he takes their doubloon to 'change' it he takes the opportunity to flee the town.

The next episode is told in a few lines of text. Lázaro's fourth master is a friar of the Order of Mercy, who is devoted to worldly affairs and spends all his time visiting people. Lázaro leaves him because he cannot stand running around – and for other reasons that he prefers, he tells us, not to mention (did the friar try to seduce him?).

The fifth master is a pardoner, a seller of papal indulgences (a type long before satirized, as the Pardoner, by Chaucer in his Prologue to the *Canterbury Tales*). He is ignorant, but is an adept salesman; to similarly ignorant clergy (whose help he needs to sell his indulgences) he can talk nonsense which sounds like Latin. We do not hear anything of the boy Lázaro's own experiences with him except that he was often kind to him at the expense of other priests; instead we are given two examples of his ingenuity in selling his (probably forged) indulgences when people were not eager for them.

In the highly condensed sixth *tratado* Lázaro, previously a boy, appears as a 'well set-up young man'. He takes on the task of mixing colours for a painter of tambourines. Then a priest gives him a job as water carrier: this is his first step towards respectability, for he begins to make money. He sticks at it for four years, carefully saving. Eventually he is able to buy decent second-hand clothes and an old sword.

In the concluding chapter, again short, he achieves what he regards as success. First he works for a constable on the basis that it would be useful to get in with the law; but he abandons this as too dangerous. In his quest for an easy life and a good pension he realizes that he must join the civil service. He becomes a town crier: he announces the prices of wines and follows criminals to their punishment, proclaiming their sins. He gets a corrupt finger in a number of pies. The Archpriest of St Salvador's hears about him, and arranges for him to marry his mistress as a cover for himself. He tells Lázaro not to worry about gossip, but to look after his own affairs. The blind man, his first master, had prophesied that he would be lucky with wine, and that he would have much to do with ropes (gallows) and horns (cuckold's). We leave him at the height of good fortune, and well satisfied.

CRITICAL COMMENTARY *Lazarillo* is properly regarded as the first picaresque novel. Although Alemán's *Guzmán* was the first novel whose hero is actually called a *pícaro*, it is clear that he, Quevedo (whose picaresque novel *El buscón* [*The Swindler*], was written about 1608 and published in 1626) and others regarded *Lazarillo* as their precursor.

The origins of the word *pícaro* (picaroon) are not clear. Its first recorded use is in 1525, where it means 'scullion'. At least ten years before the publication of *Lazarillo* it carried the pejorative connotation of 'dishonest'. The nearest English word is 'delinquent'. Some believe that *pícaro* is a corruption of Picard – the Picards were French mercenaries employed by the government and hated by the people for their trickery and treachery. There are other hypotheses. But the *picaros* were a recognized type in the sixteenth century: urchins, errand boys, personal servants (like Lázaro), adventurers. They were thought of as lazy and living off their wits – but not as violent or especially criminal.

The picaresque novel as a conscious genre crystallized in Spain, with Alemán's *Guzmán*. It spread to England (Nashe's *Unfortunate Traveller*, 1594), to France (where it flowered in Le Sage's *Gil Blas*, 1715), to Germany as the *Schelmenroman* (*Schelm* means 'rascal'), and elsewhere. After it became more widely established – Defoe's *Moll Flanders* (1722) and certain of Fielding's and Smollett's novels marked its development in England – critics began to try to trace it to its origins. They found candour, interest in rogues, accounts of plebeian life and other characteristics of the picaresque novel in various very early works, though never all together (Petronius' *Satyricon* is an obvious early precursor); they also rightly found picaresque elements in the mediaeval fables, especially in the stories of the crafty fox Reynard. There is one sixteenth-century precursor of *Lazarillo*; the Italianized Spanish priest Francisco Delicado published, in Venice in

1528, *Retrato de la loçana andaluza*, generally known as *La lozana andaluza* [*The Lusty Andalusian*], considered by some to be the most obscene book in Spanish literature.

The picaresque novel proper has all or some of the following characteristics: it is the biography, or more often 'autobiography', of a social delinquent of low birth; it is episodic – having no plot; it is likely to be satirical, even if it contains moralizing elements; the *picaro* attracts the reader's sympathy – whether, conventionally, he 'ought' to or not; the *picaro* is not a serious criminal; there is emphasis not on character development but on luck. The central character may be man, woman or animal (for example in Cervantes' *Coloquio de los perros* [*Dogs' Colloquy*]).

The genre first emerged in Spain partly though not wholly because of the nature of Spanish society at that time, which certainly provided excellent material: Spain, with its hypocritical priests, hoards of beggars, mountebanks and poverty-stricken *hidalgos* (men of high birth pretending to be financially secure), was not as different from the rest of Europe as was previously supposed. But in Spanish Catholicism there is a strong element of anti-clericalism – if only because Spaniards expect too much of their priests. The Spanish concepts of honour and of keeping up appearances are peculiar to the nation, at least in their persistent strength, and intelligent Spaniards were led to criticize them. It is a matter of the Spanish temperament in confrontation with more or less universal social conditions; a matter of a peculiar, often ambiguous irony combined with an undisguised admiring envy of the irresponsibility and 'roguery' of an *anti-hero*.

Such envy would be natural to proud, tense men of intelligence and imagination. The Spanish imagination is exceptionally intricate, having within it a yearning for the direct and coarse – the Spanish picaresque novels are direct, coarse and brutal. A complex tension is then set up, as the simple and episodic story-form is retained but embellished anew by the involute imagination which sets, if involuntarily, to work again. The result is curiously ambiguous.

Lazarillo puzzles its readers. Although universally regarded as delightful, adroit, artfully artless, skilful in its concise and vivid portrayals of types, the best sixteenth-century Spanish novel, it initially raises doubts as to whether it is comedy, satire or morality. It is in fact all three, and more.

The miserliness of the priest, the absurd pride of the *escudero*, the tricks of the pardoner: these and other episodes are, of course, sheerly comic, and should first be taken as comedy.

The increasing ingenuity and resourcefulness of Lázaro – who incidentally often shows signs of compassion – is, at the primary level of storytelling, a matter for simple admiration. We are glad when he has good luck: he has not seriously harmed anyone; he has shown courage and the ability to look after himself in adversity; and he saves prudently for four years in order to seek advancement. All the people with whom he comes into contact are inferior to him. This also is straightforward enough.

But there are problems. The clergy are satirized (without hatred), and the moral question of their outward piety as contrasted with their inner degradation is therefore inevitably raised. At one point an unmistakably Erasmian scorn for scholasticism is displayed – when people ask the pardoner whether indulgences are valid for 'children still in their mothers' wombs'.

Again, the 'God' to whom Lázaro himself frequently appeals seems to be 'luck' rather than the Christian God. Lázaro is educated by villains, hypocrites and fools (the stupidity of the *escudero's* pursuit of 'honour' is fully and explicitly exposed); but, though he gains a sort of 'honour', a position, he ends up as a moral villain (using his post to earn money corruptly), a hypocrite (pretending his wife is faithful) and a fool (Spaniards despise cuckolds as fools who can't control their women). How are we, then, to view this 'admirable' hero?

The text shows literary skill of a high order; for all the author's unquestionable originality, he borrowed some of his material (including one of the pardoner's frauds) from literary sources, and he transmuted more from oral tradition. Lázaro stood, in popular proverbs, for a victim of starvation and servant of many masters.

Is the author a cynical pessimist, demonstrating how a crooked environment *must* form a crooked individual, or is he an unobtrusively stern moralist? R. O. Jones regards the novel as an unequivocal – though subtly ironic – demonstration of Lázaro's moral destruction at the hands of his 'masters'. Other readers regard ambiguity as the work's chief strength. Who can withhold sympathy from Lázaro? He foreshadows such similarly ambiguous characters as Hašek's Sergeant Švejk (1921–3), who passively manipulates an evil and mad society by pretending to agree with its 'values' and thus gains a curious kind of moral stature.

We are told nothing of his inner life; but it is clear that Lázaro sees through the *escudero*'s stupidity and the pardoner's wickedness. He never admires his masters, although he does sometimes admire their ingenuity. While the sense of ambiguity remains, we are entitled – on the strength of a text that is simple, racy, lucid, and yet cryptic – to guess that Lázaro possesses a morally valid, ironic stance: an awareness of his situation which is at least superior to the active wickedness or hypocrisy or foolishness of the other characters. The question is whether Lázaro *knows himself*, as some critics think, or whether he does not, as others think. The balance seems to be tilted towards the former conclusion, on the grounds of the tersely expressed wisdom that Lázaro acquires between boyhood and manhood. Ultimately it is a question for the individual reader to decide for himself. It is certainly raised, and in the course of one of the most pithy texts ever written.

BIBLIOGRAPHY

Translations: D. Rouland, *Lazarillo de Tormes*, 1576; J. Crofts, 1924; J. M. Cohen, *Lazarillo de Tormes*, 1962; M. Alpert, *Lazarillo de Tormes*, 1969.

Text: R. O. Jones, 1963, is the most convenient. See also J. Caso González, 1967. The text is a collation of the three editions of 1554.

Criticism: M. Bataillon, *El Sentido de Lazarillo de Tormes*, 1954, and *Novedad y Fecundidad del Lazarillo de Tormes*, 1968. On the picaresque novel, with sections on *Lazarillo*: S. Miller, *The Picaresque Novel*, 1967; A. A. Parker, *Literature and the Delinquent*, 1967.

Miguel de Cervantes Saavedra

Miguel de Cervantes Saavedra was born in Alcalá de Henares, east of Madrid, in 1547; he died in Madrid in 1616. Like Rabelais, with whom he may justly be called the father of modern fiction, he was influenced by the humanism of Erasmus – although he absorbed this at second hand, through his teacher Juan López de Hoyos.

Few certain facts are known of his early life. Probably he was educated in Jesuit colleges at Córdoba where his father, an unsuccessful surgeon, moved, and later at Seville. He finally studied under López de Hoyos at the City School of Madrid in 1568. At this time he began to write. Late in 1568 he had a duel, whereupon he fled to escape having his hand cut off: his opponent, whom he wounded, had more influence than he.

By 1569 he was in Rome serving in the household of Cardinal Acquaviva. Here he gratefully and lastingly absorbed Italian culture. In 1570 in Naples he became a soldier in the service of Spain. At the Sea-battle of Lepanto (1571) his left hand was smashed and permanently crippled.

In 1575, while on his way home to Spain, he was captured by pirates and sold into slavery, in which, despite four 'Quixotic' efforts to escape, he spent five years before being ransomed by the Trinitarian friars. His behaviour while in captivity in Algiers was exemplary and resourceful.

Back in Spain, he tried to devote himself to a literary life. By now Philip II had replaced the more flamboyant Charles V on the throne of Spain. Although Cervantes deserved preferment – he already had some reputation as a poet – he found it hard to come by. He undertook some missions, wrote plays – then much in demand in Madrid – and published an (uncompleted) novel in the pastoral tradition, *La Galatea* (1585). But he never attained solvency. He had an illegitimate daughter, Isabel (1584); and in the same year married Catalina de Salazar y Palacios, a girl eighteen years younger than himself. This marriage was supposed to have been a failure; but there is now good reason to suppose it was not. Catalina asked, in a will made four years after his death, to be buried where Miguel was buried; earlier she had spoken of the love and good company they had had together.

Cervantes was forced to take various petty official jobs, since he could not make a living as a playwright. He became a tax collector and, through no fault of his own, went to prison for a time (1592; 1597–8). On his travels he saw much that would later be incorporated into *Don Quixote*. He probably began the novel in jail in Seville in 1597–8; the first part was published in 1605, the second in 1615. From 1600, freed at last from bureaucratic squalor, he was able to devote himself to writing. He wrote much poetry and drama, none of which is altogether successful, though his daringly satirical sonnet on the death of Philip II (1598) is more than able. Besides *Don Quixote* his most important work is *Novellas ejemplares* (1613), twelve varied stories, some of which are revolutionary in form and content.

Cervantes' three greatest contemporaries were the poet Luis de Góngora, the prolific playwright and poet Lope de Vega, and Francisco de Quevedo. These three fought amongst themselves, but Cervantes took no part in their battles. He did however have differences with Lope, but they did not prevent him from admiring him.

His last years were easier. He lived in Valladolid until about 1606, and then in Madrid. *Don Quixote* brought him fame if not money – and the Count of Lemos and the Archbishop of Seville became his patrons. He had not often had the company of his wife in his years as travelling tax collector; now, it is likely, he enjoyed this. He also had his full share of trials. The affairs of his illegitimate daughter gave him trouble, and eventually she estranged herself from him. His health began to fail and, feeling that he should not 'trifle with the life to come', he turned to religion for support. He was always busy with writing, and was spurred to finish the second part of *Don Quixote* by the discovery that an unknown writer calling himself Avellaneda had published a spurious continuation – and had attacked Cervantes in his preface.

Just before Cervantes died in Madrid in April 1616 he finished the romance *Persiles y Sigismunda*, an imitation of Heliodorus. He was buried in the brown habit of the Franciscans.

Don Quixote
[El ingenioso hidalgo Don Quijote de la Mancha]

SUMMARY Like Fielding's *Joseph Andrews*, *Don Quixote* is an example of an original masterpiece that grew out of a satirical intention. A character originally intended to be an absurd chivalric caricature takes on a life of his own. (The same may be said of some of the characters in Wyndham Lewis' *The Apes of God* and of Pirandello's madman Henry IV in the play of that name: the twentieth century has returned, wittingly or unwittingly, to Cervantes as it has to Rabelais). *Don Quixote* is full of detail, and incorporates several *inset* episodes. Here only a brief outline is given.

Alonso Quijano is a simple-minded and elderly country gentleman with an enormous library of chivalric romances. As the novel begins, he has taken leave of his senses in a way not uncommon in either Cervantes' age or our own: he has become obsessed with his reading and, resisting the efforts of his village priest and housekeeper, takes its (mostly) false and cheapened world as fact; he changes his name to Don Quijote (this old-style *j* is now *in English*) written with an *x*) de la Mancha, and is knighted by the keeper of a wretched inn which he envisages as a castle.

He is mad when possessed by his *idée fixe* of knight errantry; but sane, kind and moderate when not. Thus madness and sanity coexist in him. He finds a beloved to idealize; he calls her Dulcinea del Toboso; she is in fact an ugly peasant girl called Aldonza Lorenzo. He goes forth into the world to right its wrongs. But, thrashed by some merchants whom he has challenged to battle, he returns home. Still deaf to the advice of his neighbours, he makes plans to go forth once again. As his squire he chooses the squat, commonsensical, aspiritual, proverb-making Sancho Panza (*panza*: paunch), who acts as foil to him throughout the rest of the book. As his horse he chooses Rocinante, an ex-carthorse as ill equipped as himself to deal with high and noble adventure.

The middle section of the work shows Don Quixote's febrile imagination engaged in fruitless action against reality. He charges windmills, believing them to be giants; mistakes sheep for soldiers; takes slaves to be gentlemen in misfortune.

Ultimately he believes himself to have been taken seriously by a duke and duchess, whose intention, however, is mainly to have sport at his expense. After losing a duel with the Knight of the White Moon – actually one of his own sceptical neighbours – he returns home, falls ill, and dies both penitent and sane.

All the apparently extraneous material may easily be seen as well adjusted to the main plot: the miniature pastoral story of Grisóstomo and Marcela, the adventure story of the captive, the Italianate 'El curioso impertinente' ['Fretful Curiosity'], and the literary criticism.

CRITICAL COMMENTARY The germ of most later literary concerns, and most particularly those of the twentieth century, is to be found in Cervantes. *Don Quixote* fuses two traditions: the idealist-chivalric and the cynical-picaresque. But the book, although vividly realistic, is neither idealistic nor cynical. It transcends all genres, and its success helped fiction to an enjoyment of a new prestige – it was still, in Cervantes' time, regarded as an inferior form to poetry.

This novel is one of the first examinations of the relationship between appearance and reality, between nobility and stupidity, between moral virtue and the need to compromise in a world that is a mixture of good and evil. Don Quixote is sublime in his faith, but certainly absurd; Sancho Panza is greedy and deceitful – but he cannot be disloyal to his master, whom he reveres, esteems and loves.

Like all great works, *Don Quixote* has been interpreted in many different ways, including some that exist only in the eye of the humourless beholder. Because its author's approach was both conservative and sceptically open-minded, the book has a multitude of mutually reinforcing meanings. It is, for one thing, an inimitable picture of the Spain of Cervantes' time. It is, too, an allegory of the Spanish character. Cervantes was one of the few Spanish writers to be able to see the comic and lovable as well as the tragic side of this. Although it should be read, initially, in the light of Cervantes' own literary background, *Don Quixote* speaks equally to us today. None of the technical problems that trouble modernist writers is absent from it. 'A book like *Don Quixote*,' wrote Erich Auerbach, 'dissociates itself from its author's intention and leads a life of its own.'

It slashes the absurdities and affectations of the badly written chivalric romances of the period into ribbons, though inspired by the same noble spirit, expressed in as noble language, that engendered them; it educates the amoral *picaresque* into awareness. It dragged a nearly moribund Spanish literature screaming into the seventeenth century of new scientific knowledge, humanism and moveable type – even while warning it of the results of arrogance and hubris.

Until the eighteenth century *Don Quixote* was seen as farce. The eighteenth century viewed it as satire on those who refused to live by the precepts of common sense. But the romantics discovered in Don Quixote a *wise fool,* a sacred madman or an idealist misunderstood and brought down by an unpoetic and materialistic world. Some modern critics see the novel as literary criticism: as an embodied *theory of the novel.* The nineteenth-century critics went too far: they saw the pathos and dignity in Don Quixote, but went against Cervantes' intentions and the spirit of the text in suggesting his madness is heroic. Don Quixote is often *better* than the other characters, and he is usually more dignified than those who set up situations to exploit his *idée fixe.* But his madness is not presented as superior *in itself.* Sometimes the sane seem madder than he; but his own madness, is none the less regrettable, even though comic. This is not to say that the world of supposedly sane men is really sane. Don Quixote's madness has positive overtones: it reflects Cervantes' nostalgia for a better, past age – even if he does satirize *bad* chivalric romances – and at the same time it symbolizes the madness of the world, differently formed and varied though this is.

The ostensible genre of *Don Quixote* is undoubtedly comedy. We need not, with the example of Shakespeare's or Verdi's Falstaff before us, take this to mean that it is in some way inferior. The comic, funny though it must be, is as *serious* as the tragic. There can be little in literature as serious – and moving – as the description of the death of Don Quixote.

What is usually called the *literary criticism* in *Don Quixote* is, as one might expect, wholly unacademic. It is inventive and creative, qualities in which Cervantes firmly believed. Within the novel there are three main accounts of the knight: there is his own, which until he is dying is mad; there is the account by the fictional 'Cide Hamete Benengeli'; and there is (in the second published part) 'Avellaneda's' spurious continuation, of which Cervantes, with characteristic good humour, makes brilliant use. We shall see that Cervantes questions the validity of fiction as fruitfully as it ever has been questioned.

Don Quixote thirsts, as a good knight errant should, for fame and commemoration in print. He becomes famous, and so does Sancho – foil to him in that while Don Quixote projects fantasies on to reality Sancho is limited by his inability to see beyond surface appearances. Sancho is delighted, but the knight's fame is not of the sort *he* desires. Part I showed him up as a man seeking to be what he could not be; in Part II he and Sancho are influenced by this failure. Just as he rationalizes his disappointment when he meets the ugly Dulcinea (II, 10) by immediately assuming that she is enchanted to appear thus to him, so – with the logic of the madman – he clings to the belief in himself that is recorded in Part I.

'Cide Hamete Benengeli' is a fictional Arab scholar and magician whose account of the adventures of Don Quixote and Sancho Panza has been 'translated by a Moor'; there are other 'sources', also invented by the author. Cervantes points, by his special use of this old device, of piling invention on invention, to the unlikelihood of Don Quixote's existence; paradoxically, he relies on his own creative energy to contradict this and make him credible. Looked at another way, Cide Hamete may have been 'invented', not (so to say) by Cervantes, but by Don Quixote himself, who assures himself at the beginning that the 'sage' (later Cide) who will write of his adventures will do so in an appropriate manner: the 'knight invents an enchanter-chronicler' (writes E. C. Riley) 'and proceeds to believe in him'. In other words, Don Quixote's world is essentially a literary fantasy – implying perhaps, that literature is itself somehow *unreal*. Cervantes is not solemn about this problem, and blames the Arab, the 'dog of an author', if the story is faulty!

'Avellaneda', an imaginary poor writer, gives Cervantes further opportunity to question his own fiction and to confuse the reader. Are there rogues about who are pretending to be Don Quixote and Sancho? They themselves are certain that this is so. Thus Cervantes deals with the question of human identity three centuries before the modern master of the subject, Luigi Pirandello.

While he draws attention to the illusory nature of fiction, Cervantes claims superior status for his own. It is superior to that of 'Avellaneda' because, leaving aside the other's clumsiness and inferiority as a writer, it embodies within itself this very awareness of its own illusoriness. Therefore *Don Quixote* does live, is 'real', its art has a function. Here Cervantes looks forward to Flaubert, although he does not go as far in asserting that art is superior to life. Art for him is *recreation* – but also *re-creation* – as W. J. Entwhistle has pointed out.

BIBLIOGRAPHY

Translations: T. Shelton, *Don Quixote* (1612–52), 1923; S. Putnam, *Don Quixote*, 1949; J. M. Cohen, *Don Quixote*, 1950. Shelton's contemporary translation is in some ways nearer to Cervantes than any other. There are many versions, including those by Motteux and Smollett. Of the recent versions Putnam's is racier than, and as accurate as, Cohen's, though he has slightly abridged the text.

Text: F. Rodríguez Marín, ten volumes, 1947–9.

Criticism: W. J. Entwhistle, *Cervantes*, 1940; E. C. Riley, *Cervantes' Theory of the Novel*, 1962; R. L. Predmore, *The World of Don Quixote*, 1967, and *Cervantes*, 1973.

Honoré d'Urfé

Honoré d'Urfé was born near Lyon in 1567. He took part, on the Catholic side, in the Wars of Religion under Henri IV. When the Catholic *Ligue* was dissolved in 1596 he was forced to retire to the territories of the Duke of Savoy, to whom he was related through his mother. Here he lived in exile until his death, as a result of the military operations in the war between Savoy and Genoa, in 1625. In 1600 he married Diane de Châteaumorand, the ex-wife of his brother, the poet Anne d'Urfé.

D'Urfé wrote plays and dramatic poems such as *Sireine*, but it is for the immensely long (5,000 pages) *L'Astrée* that he is best known. This was immensely successful in its time and is frequently regarded as the first French novel (as distinct from romance); it exercised an influence for a century, and was loved by such as La Rochefoucauld, Rousseau and La Fontaine. It was published as follows: Part I (1607), Part II (1610), Part III (1619) – Parts IV and V were published posthumously in 1627, edited by Balthazar Baro, d'Urfé's secretary; the conclusion was written up from the author's notes.

L'Astrée

SUMMARY *L'Astrée* is set in the region of Forez, which lies between Lyon and Clermont-Ferrand. The river, the

Lignon, is a small one. D'Urfé knew the region intimately from his boyhood. The framework of the novel is pastoral; but much semi-autobiography, history (some eighty *histoires* [tales from history] are interpolated, and are indexed volume by volume), adventure, chivalry and discussion are grafted on to this. The work is interspersed with madrigals and sonnets. The prose is for the most part fluent and straightforward; but there are many conceits. The plot is not taken very seriously, and is followed only inconsequentially.

The time is the fifth century: we are in an idealized Gaul. The district of Forez is represented, initially, as being free from barbarian invasions: 'good and ancient families' decide to live as shepherds. Its ruler is Queen Amasis. The hero, Céladon, is a shepherd, as is his beloved Astrée. Astrée, also called Dike (meaning Justice: one of the most important concepts in the book), was the daughter of Zeus and Themis. When, in mythology, men became evil, she became the constellation of Virgo. As the book begins, Céladon has been dismissed by Astrée: a jealous rival has persuaded her that he is in love with someone else. In despair, he throws himself into the river. Astrée swoons on the bank, and her parents are so distraught over her grief that they die. Unknown to Astrée, Céladon has been rescued by three nymphs from the Queen's court, led by Princesse Galathée. They take him to court and care for him and attempt to seduce him; he virtuously escapes to a mournful cavern where he pines for Astrée. He writes an anonymous letter to her, and she sets out to find him. Eventually, disguised as a Druid's daughter (which Astrée also is), Céladon becomes her close friend. War comes to Forez through the traitor Polémas, and Céladon is wounded in the defence of his country. When he reveals himself to Astrée, he is again repulsed. In the subsequent adventures there are many tests of Céladon's constancy. Eventually the hero decides to do away with himself: he goes with the other characters to the Fountain of Truth where liars are eaten by lions. Céladon's constancy is proved when he is spared, and Astrée accepts him at last. The long story ends – and there is no reason to suppose that Baro falsified his master's intentions – with marriage and general rejoicing.

There are many inset tales, including the love affair between Sylvandre and Diane, and the story of the sensual Hylas, who advocates infidelity, and who therefore acts as a counterweight to the (for the modern reader) somewhat numbing virtuousness of the whole. There are many other tales of different kinds of lovers. Facts, sometimes a ghostly presence, lie behind most of the fictions; for example, Astrée and Céladon are certainly idealized portraits of d'Urfé and his wife, and Henri IV probably appears as Euric. Yet d'Urfé's admirers wrote (1624) to tell him that 'We have, not long since, changed our real names ... to those in your works which we judged to be the most appropriate and suitable to the humour, actions, history, supposed resemblance, and parentage of each and every one of us.' Thus the *roman à clef* is in a sense turned on its head – aptly illustrating the wide influence of *L'Astrée*.

CRITICAL COMMENTARY *L'Astrée* is the culmination of the pastoral tradition. It possesses elements of originality, but should be considered initially in its historical context. The chief features of this are the popularity of the pastoral mode, and the movement known as *Préciosité* and its home, the *salons*, the chief of which was the Hôtel de Rambouillet.

The pastoral ancestors of *L'Astrée* are Italian and Spanish. In 1573 Tasso's dramatic poem *Aminta* had appeared, and soon after it Guarini's drama *Il pastor fido* (1590). The Neapolitan Sannazaro's pastoral romance *Arcadia* had appeared as early as 1504. In 1559 the Spaniard Montemayor's *Diana*, cast like *L'Astrée* in a mixture of prose and verse, had been published. All of these works had rejected military adventuring (although d'Urfé had himself been a soldier, and although there is war in *L'Astrée*, there is little or no emphasis on physical valour) and substituted for it the investigation of sexual tension. The settings were invariably rural, the age golden. The classical inspiration came from such writers as Theocritus and the Virgil of the country poems.

The French movement known as *Préciosité* originally arose as a reaction to what was felt to be the coarseness and barbarous forms of expression employed in the court of Henri IV. It aimed at good manners, good taste and delicacy. Unfortunately, as the nineteenth-century critic Ferdinand Brunetière said, it 'degenerated too quickly into a spirit of narrowness and of affectation'. Its parallels may be found in the English *euphuism*, the Spanish *Gongorism*, and the Italian *Marinism*. Originally it sought for lucidity and precision, but it became increasingly involute, and the metaphors tended to become over-involved: such a mixture may be found in *L'Astrée*. But on the whole, despite some tedious and artificial episodes, the novel is clearly written and can still engage the reader's attention for long periods. It is a work of considerable charm. It was assiduously studied at the Hôtel de Rambouillet, particularly by Mme Lafayette, upon whose *Princess de Clèves* it exercised considerable influence.

The Hôtel de Rambouillet, standing on the site of the present Palais-Royal, was the Paris house of the Marquise de Rambouillet and was the breeding-ground of *Préciosité*. It flourished in the first half of the seventeenth century. Here the leading writers and thinkers of the day met and discussed – at an elevated level – every subject of literary and topical interest.

The philosophy of d'Urfé is unrelentingly neo-Platonic. The virtues are loved because they are beautiful – as Platonic *forms*, eternal and unchanging essences. To love women should be like loving God; and women's love of men is like that of God. But this basic philosophy does not prevent *L'Astrée* from accommodating many different types of character. Indeed, its most original feature is the introduction into French literature of a dynamic psychological element. There is true psychological realism in the portraiture of a number of the characters, most particularly in that of the sinister Hylas. *La Princesse de Clèves*, though an infinitely greater novel, could hardly have been written without the example set by d'Urfé: *L'Astrée* stands as a vital signpost pointing towards the highest qualities in the French novel.

BIBLIOGRAPHY

Translation: *The History of Astraea. The First Part*, 1620; 'A Person of Quality' [John Davies], *Astraea. A Romance*, three volumes, 1657–8. This adaptation has unfortunately never been reprinted; a modern selection is called for.

Text: H. Vaganay (ed), 1925–8.

Criticism: O. C. Reure, *Honoré d'Urfé*, 1910; M. Magendie, *Du Nouveau sur L'Astrée*, 1927, and *L'Astrée, Analyse et extraits*, 1928.

Hans Jakob Christoffel von Grimmelshausen

Grimmelshausen, son of a Protestant innkeeper-baker, was born in Gelnhausen about 1621. Few exact details of his life are known. His grammar-school education was interrupted when he was abducted (1634–5) by Croat forces in the seething turmoil of the Thirty Years' War. He found himself first on one side, then on the other. In the last stages he fought as a musketeer for the Imperial troops, and ended as a regimental clerk. It was probably then that he began writing, though he did not take it up seriously until 1665. In 1649 he married, and at some – not determined – time he became at least a nominal Roman Catholic. He held various jobs – pub keeper, bailiff, steward, horse dealer, magistrate. From 1667 he was the agent of the Bishop of Strasbourg in Renchen, where he died in 1676. He was not a systematically educated man, but picked up a great deal of knowledge, both literary and popular; and he had some literary contacts. Although he wrote the greatest seventeenth-century German novel, Grimmelshausen was an odd-man-out in that he was not a member of a learned profession, and had not received an academic education. Apart from *Simplicissimus* (1669), which was published under an anagram of his own name (he was not identified as its author until 1838), he wrote both courtly and popular tales, which gained him some reputation. He also wrote *continuations* of *Simplicissimus* (as did others, for it was an instant success). But although one of the sequels gave Brecht the theme for *Mother Courage*, none of his other work is of comparable interest.

Simplicissimus
[Der Abenteuerliche Simplicissimus Teutsch]

SUMMARY *Simplicissimus* begins in the middle of the Thirty Years' War and ends just after the peace of 1648. It is written in the first person: an old man reviews his past. An unnamed boy of ten, living with his supposed parents, peasants in the Spessart (a forest region east of Hanau), is carried off by marauding troops. He is a simpleton, believing for example that a man on a horse is a single creature – the 'wolf' of whom his father has told him. He judges only by appearances. He escapes and finds refuge in the forest with an old hermit, who calls him Simplicius and gives him a rudimentary education and some religious instruction. After a time the old man dies; Simplicius finds himself in the anti-Imperial fortress at Hanau. Here, cast in the role of fool, he is made to wear donkey's ears and jester's costume. On the advice of a priest, who had been the old hermit's friend, he conceals what little wisdom he has. Soon he is showing a ready wit and some ingenuity. But his behaviour is still generally stupid. There is much bawdy and repulsive physical detail; this is a true representation of behaviour in those times.

Simplicius is taken prisoner by Croats, but escapes when he becomes involved in a witches' sabbath, during which he is magically transported. He now falls into the hands of Imperial troops in Westphalia. At first, because a prisoner from Hanau remembers him, he is forced to remain in his jester's role. But he soon encounters friends: Herzbruder and his son. The older man (later murdered) advises him; the younger becomes his fast friend. He also encounters the villainous Olivier, who successfully discredits the younger Herzbruder by a trick, and thus obtains the promotion which is the latter's due.

It is not long before Simplicius, who has developed a cunning resourcefulness, reaches the height of his fortunes. He becomes famous as the 'huntsman of Soest', a brave, daring, wily and dangerous warrior; he accumulates a good deal of booty. He meets an idealistic madman called Jupiter; and he succeeds in outwitting and humiliating another 'huntsman' – one who pretends that he himself is the 'huntsman of Soest'.

He is captured by the Swedes, into whose favour he soon insinuates himself. He indulges in some erotic exploits (begetting six bastards), and then falls in love. His desire is further inflamed when his beloved, daughter of a retired officer, refuses to yield to him. Caught in bed with her – but before he has seduced her – he is forced to marry her. Having appeased his father-in-law's wrath, he goes to Cologne to collect the small fortune which he had previously deposited with a Cologne merchant.

But this merchant has become bankrupt, and has vanished. Simplicius lodges with a miserly attorney who promises to help him to recover his money as soon as possible. The attorney inveigles him into making a journey to Paris, where he is obliged to prostitute himself to a number of anonymous ladies of high rank.

Then Simplicius' luck changes for the worse. He contracts smallpox, which ruins his looks. He returns to Germany as beggar and mountebank. He becomes a soldier again, and re-encounters young Herzbruder and Olivier. He hates Olivier (the rival 'huntsman', he learns, was none other than he) but cooperates with him in his wicked deeds. Old Herzbruder had once prophesied that Olivier would perish, and that Simplicius would avenge his death. This prophecy is fulfilled when the two men are attacked by soldiers. With Herzbruder, who has lost his testicles in a fierce battle, Simplicius makes a pilgrimage and becomes converted to Catholicism. But this conversion has been prompted by fear of the devil, not by faith: Simplicius is not led into more virtuous ways. Herzbruder dies, poisoned by jealous rivals, and leaves his property to Simplicius. Subsequently the latter meets his 'father', still alive and in good health. He is told that he is really the son of a noble lady (who died in bearing him) and of the old hermit of Spessart – an ex-captain. His real name is Melchior Sternfels von Fuchsheim (another anagram of the author's name).

Simplicius contracts an unwise marriage (his first wife has died after bearing him a son), and deceives his drunkard wife, who also deceives him, but who soons dies.

After this, in the most impressive sustained passage in the book, Simplicius visits the centre of the earth by entering the Mummulsee (a mountain lake in the Black Forest). He is introduced to the water spirits, who know nothing of eternity but have very long lives and prevent the earth from disintegrating by providing it with all its water. He tells the king of this world that all on earth is good, and that the earth is not about to end. For vouchsafing this information he is rewarded with a stone which will provide a benign spring – but because he has lied this gift brings him no good.

He rejoins the army, travels to Moscow, where he survives pressure from the Tsar to join the Orthodox Church, and turns to making gunpowder instead. He then has a series of adventures in Asia (told in very short compass and hardly necessary to the book). Finally he returns to his books: he becomes a scholar, renounces the world, and embraces the eremitic life that had been taken up by his real father. The book ends with a long quotation, a *farewell to the evil world*, from the Spaniard Antonio de Guevara (?1481–1545), inquisitor, devotional author, father-confessor to Charles V and at the last himself a hermit. (In Book VI, added in 1669, he is once again tempted by the world. Eventually he is wrecked on an island, where he remains as a hermit. This is the first 'Crusoe' story in German.)

CRITICAL COMMENTARY *Simplicissimus* combines, in an often near colloquial style designed for the *ordinary man*, a vivid and scarifying picture of the horrors of war with imaginative depth and an eclectic, at times visionary, religious morality. Technically, it is a German picaresque novel (*Schelmenroman*) with Baroque traits; it has been described as 'popular Baroque' and its author has been said to have belonged to the 'plebeian fringe of the Baroque'; its irony and stylistic subtlety were innovatory in German fiction. Largely forgotten in the eighteenth century, the novel's virtues were rediscovered in the nineteenth, and have been recognized ever since. Grimmelshausen shows a 'more subtle understanding of the nature of fiction and illusionism, of the sovereignty of the fictional writer, than ... any German contemporary' (Roy Pascal). *Simplicissimus* may need preliminary identification in terms of categories, but it soon becomes apparent that it combines Baroque with anti-Baroque in a remarkably successful and original manner – and that therefore, like all great novels, it eventually transcends categories. Grimmelshausen was able to express humanity and zest for life; other contemporary German prose writers were not. However, Simplicissimus is a complex work: the critics who have called it, variously, 'metaphysical', 'contrapuntal', 'realistic', 'a representation of the pilgrimage of the Christian soul ... a symbolic statement of the nature of existence itself', are none of them wrong. It is all these.

In the sixteenth century German fiction was written in various narrative forms; the romance, the fable, and the story with a moral are but three examples. Then came the European post-Renaissance period which, only much later, came to be known as the Baroque (approximately late sixteenth century to early eighteenth century, when

48   Hans Jakob Christoffel von Grimmelshausen

it gave way to *rococo*). The term has since been the subject of much controversy; certainly the special characteristics which critics have seen in it are revealed more
clearly in architecture, music and painting than in literature. It is important to realize that no writer later described as Baroque thought of himself as such – even
though the word, of uncertain origin, had been used
(most often to mean *absurd* or *grotesque*) a few times in
individual works. What we now call Baroque, never un-
controversially, differed considerably from country to
country. In general terms one can say no more than that
Baroque resulted from the attempt to express contemporary anxieties (intensified by the Reformation) in traditional form; Baroque can be paradoxical, fantastical,
can contrast the mundane with the exotic – and much
else.

In Germany the Baroque at first asserted itself in a
complicated *poetics*, which at least in its theory was
strongly moralistic in tone. The fictional modes of the
pre-Baroque era gave way to a form more like the modern
novel: a single narrative which, though it might incorporate various of the older modes, aimed at a wholeness,
a coherence. One kind of earlier seventeenth-century
novel – courtly, pastoral, lofty – approximated to the
Baroque; the other, more picaresque and plebeian, was
not so near. It was Grimmelshausen who first successfully
combined the two.

Simplicissimus has four major sources. The first is undoubtedly the metaphysical, paradoxical spirit inherent
in the German Baroque, as seen in such highly artificial
pastoral novels as the *Adriatische Rosemund* (1645),
which was influenced by *L'Astrée*. Grimmelshausen himself wrote two such (indifferent) examples in the genre
– probably for the market. The second source is the
Spanish picaresque novel as most notably typified by
Lazarillo de Tormes and Alemán's *Guzmán de Alfarache* (1599). The German translations of these deleted

anti-clerical passages and added a dull, moralizing element. Grimmelshausen's third source, 'Soldatenleben', the last part of a novel by J. M. Moscherosch (1601–69), made some advance: though the narrator is an educated man, his descriptions of the fierce troops with whom he becomes involved are more realistic and empathetic than anything preceding them. Grimmelshausen's fourth source is popular material: folk-tales, legend, tall stories, chap-books, almanacs, lives of saints, the untutored knowledge of the common people – which, although he does not always take it seriously, he knows to contain wisdom gained from hard experience, as well as nonsense.

Grimmelshausen was an enlightened man for his period and especially so in his particular context. The pilgrimage of the Christian soul is an important aspect of his book (Bunyan's *Pilgrim's Progress* was written soon after); it nevertheless anticipates the *Bildungsroman* (apprenticeship novel) because of its (admittedly sporadic) concern with psychological growth. There are many sly and shrewd psychological asides, and some interest is shown in purely individual characteristics.

Despite the remarks of one of his translators, it is clear that Grimmelshausen did not believe in witchcraft, alchemy or 'magic'. Even the great Mummulsee episode is prefaced by a witty warning that it is not to be taken literally: it is 'like a "masquerade" or thing in mummery'.

He uses *Fremdwörter*, foreign words (frowned on by the rigid linguistic purists of the time), to prompt the reader to reflection: to show that there is more than one way of considering a thing – that, in our terms, there are *many realities*. Though nominally a Catholic when he wrote *Simplicissimus*, Grimmelshausen is inclined to an eclectic Christianity: that of one who has absorbed the terrible lesson of the Thirty Years' War. Simplicius' 'conversion' is made in fear. But before it he is allowed to remark to a priest that he will not commit himself to Protestantism or Catholicism until one of them can 'bring me enough proof that they possess the ... only redeeming religion'. However, the king of the water spirits, who may be presumed to know everything, gives a strongly anti-Calvinist, even Catholic, explanation of creation.

Three visionary episodes in the novel are important. The first is a purely Baroque-style emblem, though it is more sharply critical of affairs than other contemporary German examples. The ignorant young Simplicius dreams of a tree which represents the social hierarchy disturbed by violent turmoil: at the top sit noble officers, beneath them are other officers, and so on to the roots – those of 'low esteem' who bear the weight of the whole. The pattern is destroyed by greed for money, which leads to atrocious acts; many fall to the ground.

The vision of the madman Jupiter ironically demonstrates that truths can only be expressed by lunatics: his diagnosis of the terrible state of Germany is correct, but his remarkably misguided solution is a 'hero': no modern reader can fail to see Hitler as this 'hero'.

The Mummulsee episode is the most poetic. The water spirits, who have long lives but are not immortal (their 'reasoning souls ... will disappear when [they] die' and are a 'link between you [ie, men] and all other living creatures in the world'), who have 'knowledge of the will of God', and who 'cannot sin and are therefore not subject to ... the wrath of God', are a strange invention; whether Grimmelshausen drew on legend or other sources or not, his own presentation of their nature is highly original. Their king wants to know whether the world is about to end because of the collapse of the Christian faith. Simplicius' lying account of how excellent things are there (itself a fine piece of irony) is an inversion of Jupiter's savage diagnosis. The moral, as the king implies, is that man's only hope is to renounce the world and so gain salvation (denied to him and his people) after death. But the very existence of these enigmatic creatures who serve mankind poses at least the notion that man's spiritual condition may not, after all, be immortal – that Christianity itself may be an illusion. For in this realm we have a community who know of God's will, and yet are denied his grace. Grimmelshausen's attitude – or perhaps we should say that of his text – therefore tends towards ambiguity, and wavers towards scepticism. His ending, the quotation from Guevara, is a perfectly conventional *farewell to the world*, tacked on for extra-literary reasons.

Grimmelshausen is no Rabelais or Cervantes. His context, in any case, restricted him. But he is a genial, humanitarian and subtle writer who still, in the English-speaking countries, deserves more attention than he has obtained. The primary need is for a complete first-rate translation into English.

BIBLIOGRAPHY

Translations: A. T. S. Goodrick, *The Adventurous Simplicissimus* (1912), 1924; W. Wallich, *The Adventures of Simplicissimus*, 1962; H. Weissenborn and L. Macdonald, *Simplicius Simplicissimus*, 1964; G. Schulz-Behrend, *Simplicius Simplicissimus*, 1965. The first two are abridged (bowdlerized), though Wallich's is the best of all; the third is in dull and clumsy prose; the fourth is in American colloquialese and also slightly abridged.

Text: J. H. Scholte (ed), 1939.

Criticism: K. C. Hayens, *Grimmelshausen*, 1933.

Marie-Madeleine de Lafayette

Marie-Madeleine, Comtesse de Lafayette, *née* Pioche de la Vergne, was born in 1634. Her father had been tutor to the nephews of Cardinal Richelieu. She was brought up in the house of Anne of Austria. At the age of twenty-one she married an army officer eighteen years her senior. She bore him two sons, but separated from him – amicably – in 1659, and went to live in Paris while he looked after his estate in the Auvergne. She had many friends – the sister of Charles II of England, Mme de Sévigné, the outspoken, intelligent and influential letter writer, and, above all the aphorist La Rochefoucauld, who had been a leading member of the cult of *Préciosité* and who shared her house during the last fifteen years of his life. In Mme de Lafayette's lifetime it was not permitted to women to acknowledge authorship of literary works: none of her principal works therefore appeared under her own name. These are of relatively high quality, but are eclipsed by her masterpiece.

The extent to which her works were group products has been much debated. It is impossible to solve this problem; but the influence of La Rochefoucauld on *La Princesse de Clèves* (1678) is evident.

Mme de Lafayette died in 1693.

La Princesse de Clèves

SUMMARY *La Princesse de Clèves* has a simple plot. The background is that of the Court, ostensibly that of Henri II (1547-9); this provides the most transparent of disguises for the contemporary Court of the late seventeenth century, which is the object of the author's subtle and unobtrusive criticism. Life in this Court was magnificent – but only superficially so:

Never had a Court had so many lovely women and so many striking men: and it seemed as though Nature had taken pleasure in pouring forth all her bounties on the greatest princes and on the greatest princesses.

But the *soul* of the Court was ambition as well as gallantry; people were not bored or idle, but only because they 'were always taken up with pleasure or intrigues'. The ladies envied one another, and all were members of cliques. Into this atmosphere, where 'there was a kind of agitation without disorder, which made it highly agreeable but also highly dangerous for a girl', there arrives the young Mlle de Chartres. She is soon pressed by her mother, a widow, into a marriage of convenience with the Prince of Clèves. The young woman respects her new husband, but does not love him; she grants him his conjugal rights, but he is deeply – indeed, almost pathologically – disturbed by the sexual passion that her inability to give herself completely to him arouses within him. The virtuous, innocent and helpless Princess is not equipped to deal with this dangerous situation. Her mother has given her an education which, however well meaning, has been shallow, hypocritical, conformist. The Princess has an almost *existentialist* bent towards self-authenticity. She possesses an integrity of which her neighbours are unaware.

When the Duc de Nemours, already well experienced

in *affaires*, falls in love with her she reciprocates his feelings; but she remains faithful to her husband.

The crucial point in the plot – it was something of an innovation, and was widely discussed – is the scene in which the Princess tells her husband that she is in love with someone (she does not disclose his name), and tacitly begs for his help. In order to restore her previous tranquillity she would need to leave the Court. But her confession is disastrous. Her mother, who has known of the situation, dies; soon after, so does the Prince, now further lacerated by doubts of his wife's fidelity and sexual jealousy.

Nemours renews his suit; even he, product of the Court, has suffered much for his so unusually unrequited love, and even he has developed morally through suffering. But the Princess refuses him: first she is violently hostile to him as the agent of the Prince's destruction, and then becomes crushed by melancholy. She has been destroyed. She tells Nemours that she must be 'guided by the stern rules which duty imposes' on her. She retires to a convent where, after a few years, she dies. There is no note whatever of Christian reconciliation: the convent is simply a refuge for a psychologically ruined woman.

There are a number of interposed episodes: for example, that of Anne Boleyn in the second part. All these are intended to illustrate the lack of moral seriousness prevailing at Court.

CRITICAL COMMENTARY Mme de Lafayette fully sympathized with the Princess in her predicament and in her final decision to refuse Nemours, when it would have been perfectly feasible to marry him. As narrator she is not quite omniscient: she assumes close familiarity with all her characters, but absolute knowledge only of the Princess. *La Princesse de Clèves* marks a new departure in French, indeed European, fiction. The style is economic, lucid, balanced; despite the digressions – which are necessary to illustrate the nature of the corruption of the Court—it is the first wholly psychological study in fictional form. It is a psychological portrait-in-depth of a woman set in a realistic, unidealized *milieu*. Whatever the influence of La Rouchefoucauld – and this was considerable – it is evident that the essential brilliance of the novel comes from Mme de Lafayette herself. As she once said, if La Rochefoucauld had given her *l'ésprit* she had 'reformed his heart'.

Mme de Lafayette had learnt much from and admired the fiction that was popular in her youth; but she completely broke with it. She deeply admired *L'Astrée*, which at one time she read every afternoon with La Rochefoucauld, but d'Urfé's artifices and preciosities are absent from her work. The popular works of Gomberville (?1600–74) and La Calprenède (?1610–?63) and of her friend Mme de Scudéry (1607–1701), a leading light of the *Préciosité* movement and an influence on Mme de Lafayette – all these are, in contrast to *La Princesse de Clèves*, what a critic has described as 'gaudy pretentious romances'.

La Princesse de Clèves is a sensitive and imaginative critique of society and education. Extemporizing on rather than drawing from the fiction of its time and the drama of Corneille and Racine, it imparts for the first time in the French novel a sense of actual life. It has been described as being about *passion*; but more precisely it concerns romantic love (which it sees as excessive, disruptive, deadly and destructive), and the conflict between personal desire and *bienséance* (propriety). For the first time in fiction an unmistakably feminine intelligence makes itself felt. As with Corneille and Racine, a common human predicament is combined with an ostensibly historical setting to produce a timeless objectivity.

There has been relatively little argument about the merits of *La Princesse de Clèves*, particularly because of its early position in the history of the European novel. It influenced French novelists at least as late as Gide, and it is arguable that, at least, in one sense, it dominated the French novel until the advent of Flaubert. *Manon Lescaut* is clearly an attempt to achieve its pellucid morality; and Stendhal always regarded it as a paradigm of fiction.

BIBLIOGRAPHY

Translations: T. S. Perry, *La Princesse de Clèves*, 1892; H. Ashton, 1927; N. Mitford, 1950. Ashton's translation is incomparably superior.

Text: K. B. Kettle (ed), 1967.

Criticism: H. Ashton, *Madame de La Fayette*, 1922 – standard; É. Magne, *Madame de Lafayette en ménage*; M.-J. Durry, *Madame de Lafayette*, 1962 – in French.

Antoine-François (Abbé) Prévost

Antoine-François Prévost (1697–1763) is also known as the Abbé Prévost d'Exiles and hence, for short, the Abbé Prévost. This title of Abbé need not mislead us. The son of a provincial official of Hesdin in Artois, Prévost led an adventurous as well as industrious life. He was a Jesuit novice, a soldier, and then a Benedictine priest. When he became converted to Protestantism he was forced to fly abroad (1728). For the next six years he lived in Holland and in England, where he led a hazardous existence: frequently forced to move from place to place because of the large debts he had incurred, and even serving a jail sentence in England for forgery. He was eventually able to return to France and to re-enter the Benedictine Order. Between 1740 and 1742 he had once again to go into exile as he was under suspicion of having written satiric pamphlets. The rest of his life was only comparatively quiet: he was harassed by his many mistresses and also by his creditors, whom he could only partially hold off despite an enormous wage-earning output of fiction, journalism and translation.

A few critics have preferred his *L'Histoire d'une Grecque moderne* (1741) and *Mémoires d'un honnête homme* (1745) as more mature than his acknowledged masterpiece, *Manon Lescaut*; but it is still *Manon* for which he is generally famed.

Manon Lescaut is the seventh volume of a long

picaresque adventure story entitled *Mémoires et aventures d'un homme de qualité* (vols 1–4, 1728; vols 5–7, 1731). Its six predecessors have been forgotten, and have not been reprinted in modern times. An English translation of the whole work appeared in 1738. Prévost was much influenced by his experiences of England, and particularly by the English novelist Samuel Richardson, the whole of whose *Clarissa Harlowe* and *Sir Charles Grandison* he translated.

Manon Lescaut was first separately reprinted in 1733; it was banned, and of course at once achieved popularity. The revised form of 1753, with an additional episode, is the text usually preferred, although Prévost added some moralizing elements. There was a further revision in 1759.

Manon Lescaut

[Histoire du Chevalier des Grieux et de Manon Lescaut]

SUMMARY The only link *Manon Lescaut* has with its six predecessors is that the Chevalier des Grieux tells his story to the Man of Quality of the seven-volume title. It is otherwise an entirely separate work. The action is set in a Parisian high-society ruled by money and deceit.

The Chevalier, seventeen years old, is studying for the priesthood. By chance he meets the fourteen-year-old Manon Lescaut in a tavern. She tells him that she is being forced into a convent against her will; he falls in love with her, and they run off together. Thenceforth the story essentially portrays the destruction of the Chevalier's moral being by his passion for this agreeable, gentle but amoral child.

Soon after the elopement, des Grieux is carried home by his father. Manon has become M de B.'s mistress owing to their shortage of money. Believing that she has been concerned in his discovery, des Grieux is able to forget her and resume his studies. But after a year she seeks him out – he once again succumbs – and they once more flee. Soon they are penniless, and the Chevalier takes to gambling, while she becomes a prostitute. True to her erratic and unpredictable form, she refuses a prince's offer of marriage and declares her love for des Grieux.

Both land up in prison; in escaping, the Chevalier kills a man. After he has effected her escape, she once again leaves him. He discovers her, and she is about to go away with him (and her lover's money) again, when they are arrested. After some intrigue, the Chevalier finds himself on a ship bound for Louisiana: Manon has been deported, and he is determined to accompany her. They plan to marry, but the hitherto complaisant Governor of Louisiana is persuaded by his son, who has fallen in love with Manon, to forbid the marriage. Des Grieux wounds the governor's son, and the couple try to escape from Louisiana. Manon dies and the Chevalier, having buried her, lies down on her grave to await his own death. After being found he is tried for and acquitted of her murder; he then goes back to France and (Prévost implies) to a better life.

CRITICAL COMMENTARY Martin Turnell writes of Gide's 'luke-warmness' about *Manon Lescaut*, although Gide, in 1913, had included it in his list of the ten best French novels. It has always been the subject of controversy. In his prefatory avis to the reader, Prévost argued his novel as a *moral lesson*. His intentions have been doubted: it must be remembered that eighteenth-century French writers operated under a touchy censorship (novels were still disapproved of); and in any case a writer's intentions are not always consonant with the effects he achieves.

Clearly, in view of Prévost's difficult and 'immoral' life,

des Grieux is to a certain extent a projection of himself; but this is hardly a profitable way to examine *Manon Lescaut*.

Prévost alternated in his life between what may be described as passionate and adventurous episodes, and periods of contemplation. *Manon Lescaut* is based on *La Princesse de Clèves* at least in the sense that passion is seen as disruptive. But times had changed between 1678 and 1731. *La Princesse de Clèves* is a serenely virtuous novel, such as could only have been written by a woman. It acknowledges *feeling*, but presents us with a heroine who is heroically able to reject it.

By the time Prévost came to write, *sensibilité* had become, at least in many minds, a virtue. It could be urged against the negative view of the novel (held by a minority of critics) that *Manon Lescaut* represents (whatever the vagaries of its author's life, or his intentions in the book) a remarkably objective investigation into the problem of the exaltation of *sensibilité* – and moreover one which creates convincing characters. Des Grieux is made to reveal himself with consummate mastery.

The eighteenth-century French *sensibilité* is markedly different from the term *sensibility* as understood in English today. For Prévost, *l'homme sensible* is at least ostensibly virtuous: he indulges himself in pity, grief, public tears, and because of his soft-heartedness he is both *grand* and *noble*. Today we might well consider him not only sentimental but also hysterical and self-indulgent; it is certainly a fault that his style is so hyperbolic. This system of values, seen by the imaginatively detached Prévost as a part of himself and as a prevailing tendency, is both an anticipatory (intuitive) reaction to – and a cause of – the Enlightenment enshrinement of Reason, which was building up. There is certainly little of the spirit of the Enlightenment in Prévost; but it must be remembered that Diderot wrote in praise of the Abbé's beloved Richardson, and that neither seems to have discerned the squalid pornographer beneath the mercantile English virtuist.

There is a despairing ambiguity at the heart of *Manon Lescaut*. It seems as though the author would have liked passion, *sensibilité*, to prevail; but his intelligence cannot allow this. By virtue of this severe conflict we are given a novel of profound psychological depth: the action springs from character. The role of chance is markedly reduced (as it had been in *La Princesse de Clèves*). *Manon Lescaut* has many purely objective merits: the portrait des Grieux gives of himself and, above all, the Manon that we see through his sexually inflamed *sensibilité* – one of the most subtle and sympathetic depictions of a whore in literature. Manon is genuinely loving, even rewarding in her sexual personality; she can give herself, as many 'moral' and 'virtuous' women cannot; but she is incapable of living without material comforts. Her *ennui*, beautifully conveyed, is classic. She is one of the earliest beautiful psychopaths in European fiction. Prévost uses his impassioned character des Grieux as a lens for the reader to see her (he only puts a foot wrong in the episode of the prince, which he added to the 1553 edition). Only genteel distaste, one suspects, can deny the author this achievement of portraiture.

As for des Grieux, the narrator, it is sometimes implied that he expresses his creator's intentions. This may be the case, but it cannot be proved from the text. His *altruism* functions in the story as a brilliant and ironic foil to what the majority of Prévost's readers must have felt as being the fatal, entrapping *egotism* of Manon. This apparent altruism, however, is no more than a ploy – not only for socially disruptive activity (this might be excused, in the corrupt context of the times) but also for selfishness and betrayal. We are forced to ask the question: does the Chevalier *love* Manon, or does he merely wish to *possess* her? This perceptive analysis is the great merit of Prévost's novel. Furthermore, he may be argued to have anticipated *realism* in the nineteenth-century sense; for, by trying to give authenticity to his narrative – setting it in a real Paris, and depicting the pressures of poverty – he brings his reader into the everyday world. This was admittedly part of the *memoir* convention, in which novelists pretended that their stories were true. But Prévost exploited the device for more than convenience, by raising the question, in a novel undoubtedly influenced by Jansenism, of whether des Grieux' love is *natural* or *sinful*. This ambiguity is at the heart of the book.

BIBLIOGRAPHY
Translation: L. W. Tancock, 1949.

Texts: M. E. I. Robertson (ed), 1943; G. Matoré (ed), 1953 (of the 1731 text); M. Allem (ed), 1959; C. King (ed), 1963 (of the 1759 text); F. Deloffre and R. Picard (eds), 1965.

Criticism: H. Roddier, *L'Abbé Prévost*, 1955 – in French.

Voltaire
(François-Marie Arouet)

François-Marie Arouet, known as Voltaire, was born in 1694 in Paris. He was the son of a wealthy notary. He was educated by the Jesuits, but early and decisively came under the influence of the circle of Le Temple, the main Parisian centre of free thought in the late seventeenth and early eighteenth centuries. In his early twenties he emerged as a pungent satirist, and spent almost a year in the Bastille (1717–18) as a result. Here he wrote his tragedy *Oedipe* (1718), the performance of which established him as a major writer. After his release he entered a period of success: he was popular in high society, patronized by the Court, and became rich through shrewd speculation. A quarrel with a courtier caused his reimprisonment in the Bastille – from where he was quickly allowed to go to England (1726). He stayed for almost three years, learned English, and met Swift, Pope and other leading literary and political figures.

In 1749, after publishing the scandal-making *Lettres philosophiques* (1734), he decided to accept the invitation of Frederick the Great, with whom he had been corresponding for fifteen years, to visit the Prussian Court. He was there for three increasingly unhappy years. He retired to Geneva (1755), and then to Ferney (1760), just inside France, and issued the first edition of his *Dictionnaire philosophique*, to which he continued to add for the rest of his life.

Voltaire had published his first philosophical *conte*, *Zadig*, in 1747. In his final phase he continued to pour out plays, poems and *contes*; these last have emerged as his most enduring work. He also attacked what he called *L'infâme*. The Voltairean *infâme* is not God (whose existence Voltaire, philosophically a disciple of Locke, thought he had proved), Jesus Christ or even the Church; it is intolerance, injustice, stupidity, privilege, superstition wherever encountered – but Voltaire, who was a Deist but not a Christian, often found it emanating from the Church.

In 1778 he went to Paris with the last of his many plays, *Irène*, and was rapturously received; but the excitement proved too much. He died before he could return home.

Voltaire is the epitome of the eighteenth-century Enlightenment, and may be regarded as in part its creator. His contradictions are those of his age. He was vastly energetic, and yet physically frail; dynamic and excitable, and yet subject to fits of depression which caused him to withdraw from the world for long periods; personally optimistic and yet (finally) pessimistic about the future of humanity; as full of love and loyalty as of hate and despair. There is no questioning the genuine passion of his advocacy of freedom, justice and tolerance; but he had little or no insight into how society could achieve these goals.

Voltaire is known as a *philosophe*, and it is important to understand the distinction between this term and *philosopher* in the Anglo-Saxon sense. The French *philosophe*, of whom Voltaire is the paradigm, approached the subject of life in a free and sceptical spirit. The dogmatism we associate with the rigours of philosophy (and theology) is absent. Voltaire's clarity is nowhere more apparent than in his wit, which emerges most sharply and satisfyingly in the best of his *contes*.

In his *Encyclopédie* Voltaire defined the *conte* as 'an

incredible narration, in prose or verse, of which the chief virtue consists in the variety and the truth of its representations, its elegance and joking quality, its vivacity and fitness of style, its piquant contrasting of occurrences ... Its end is less to instruct than to entertain.' This last remark is characteristically ironic: Voltaire's intention in his *contes* is not only to entertain but to instruct. The *conte* is *philosophique* (rather than philosophical): it has a message. Its immediate roots are in Swift's *Gulliver's Travels*; but it also reaches back to the adventurous and incident-packed *picaresque* novel, and to Boccaccio's *Decameron*, to works populated by types rather than by characters. This form allowed Voltaire to exercise his considerable narrative skills, his profound wit and his energetic argumentativeness. Psychological insight, which he lacked, was not needed. His invention had just the scope it required. Furthermore, the form brought out his stylistic qualities of conciseness, precision, brevity and simplicity; here his neo-classical preoccupations do not hinder him. He is at his most relaxed.

Among the best of the *contes* are *Micromégas* (1752), which uses a 'science-fiction' framework to reveal the insignificance of mankind in the universe, and *L'Ingénu* (1767), which satirizes both Catholic conventionalism and abuse of power generally. But it is in *Candide* (1759) that the essential, mature Voltaire is seen most fully.

Candide

SUMMARY *Candide*, which is subtitled 'Optimism', was published anonymously, with the claim that it was a German translation by 'M le Docteur Ralph'. Candide combines 'unaffected simplicity' with 'sound judgement'. He is the bastard of the sister of Baron Thunder-ten-tronckh; she would not marry his father because of his

poverty. He is brought up in the Westphalian household
of the Baron. His tutor is the philosopher Pangloss, the
mainspring of whose existence and thought is the dictum, *All is for the best in this, the best of all possible
worlds.* Candide is forcibly ejected when the Baron
catches him kissing his daughter Cunégonde behind a
screen. He is pressed into service in the Bulgarian army,
deserts, but is caught and nearly beaten to death; he
takes part in a savage battle and witnesses the atrocities
committed in its wake. Once again he escapes, this time
successfully, and becomes friendly with the Anabaptist,
Jacques. He re-encounters Pangloss who, although suffering from syphilis, a rotted nose, black teeth and covered
in sores, is still an optimist (syphilis, he considers, 'is
indispensable in this best of worlds'). Pangloss tells him
that the Baron has been killed and his daughter ravished
and murdered by the Bulgarian troops. Jacques cures
Pangloss and sets out with him and Candide for Lisbon.
Within sight of Lisbon they are caught in a storm, and
Jacques is drowned.

As soon as they reach shore they are caught in the
famous earthquake (1755: 30,000 perished). Candide is
nearly killed. They meet the Grand Inquisitor, whom
the ever-optimistic Pangloss informs that the earthquake
has been a manifestation of the rightness of things. The
university has decided that the staging of a magnificent
auto-da-fé will be the surest way to avoid further earth-
quakes. Three men are slowly burned, while Pangloss is
hanged for heresy; Candide is flogged for having listened
to him. On the same day there is another earthquake.
Candide is rescued from his distress by an old woman,
who cares for him and brings him to Cunégonde, who
has indeed been raped, but who has survived: she has
been sold as a concubine, passing eventually into the
joint hands of the Grand Inquisitor and a rich Jew.
Having witnessed the *auto-da-fé*, she believes Pangloss
to have deceived her with his doctrines. The couple are

about to make love when they are interrupted by the Jews, whom Candide kills. The Grand Inquisitor arrives, and Candide kills him also. He, the old woman and Cunégonde then run away to Cadiz, where a fleet and army are being assembled to subdue the Paraguayan Jesuits; Candide impresses its general so much that he gains command of a company of infantry.

On the voyage the old woman, the bastard of Pope Urban X, tells her own sad story. She ends by suggesting to her listeners that if they can find even one passenger 'who has not often cursed his life and told himself that he is the most miserable man alive' then they can throw her into the sea.

When they arrive at Buenos Aires Cunégonde is seized by the Governor; Candide is forced to flee, since a Spanish magistrate is pursuing the murderer of the Grand Inquisitor. He joins the Jesuit rebels, amongst whom he finds Cunégonde's brother, who manages to combine the roles of priest and colonel. Accompanied by his halfbreed servant, Cacambo, he is forced to flee again into the forests when he kills Cunégonde's brother, who has struck him on hearing that he aspires to marry her. He visits Eldorado, a Utopia where everyone is virtuous. But he pines for Cunégonde and so, having acquired much treasure, sends Cacambo to pay a ransom to the Governor of Buenos Aires for Cunégonde, while he sails for Venice in the company of a Manichaean philosopher, Martin; this philosopher – in contrast to Pangloss – believes that the material world is ruled by an evil spirit. The ship visits France, where Candide is swindled, and then England, where he sees Admiral Byng being executed: in this country, he is told, it is good to kill an Admiral from time to time 'so as to encourage the others'. Finally he reaches Venice, only to discover that Cunégonde has been captured by pirates and sold as a slave in Turkey.

He goes immediately to Constantinople, and successfully ransoms her. She has become extremely ugly. Candide now finds two slaves on a galley: they are Cunégonde's brother and Pangloss – neither had been thoroughly killed. Candide does not now wish to marry Cunégonde; but her brother is so set against the match that he determines to go through with it. He arranges for her brother to be sent back to the galleys, and marries Cunégonde and settles down on a little farm with the still optimistic Pangloss, Martin, Cacambo and the old woman. His wife grows uglier every day; the old woman is useless and fouler-tempered than her mistress; Cacambo curses all the time because he has to grow and sell vegetables; Pangloss is miserable because he is not the leading professor in a German university. Only Martin is patient: he knows that a man is badly off wherever he is. Eventually they go to consult a famous dervish: they want to know 'why such a strange animal as man was ever made'. After being told that it is none of their business, the best advice they get is 'Keep your mouth shut!' Pangloss continues in his optimism: if what had happened had not happened, he tells Candide, 'you would not be here eating candied fruit and pistachio nuts.' Candide does not argue with Pangloss, and the book ends with his famous motto: *'Il faut cultiver notre jardin'* ['We must cultivate our garden'].

CRITICAL COMMENTARY There is much satire in *Candide*. But behind the tissue of allusion, behind the comedy, the bawdy and the good spirits, lies a more serious purpose. An activist who wishes to – in the famous phrase – change the hearts and minds of men, Voltaire reaches an imaginative level which gives his work literary as well as historical permanence. This is all the more remarkable because of the author's lack of interest in psychological detail. *Candide* is one of the most concise, laconic and beautifully paced pieces of fiction ever written, but it never pauses to consider states of mind except in the most general manner.

There are many topical allusions: the Bulgars and the Abars – two Scythian tribes – stand for the Prussians and the French respectively; the Jesuits had established such kingdoms in Paraguay as Voltaire describes; the English Admiral Byng was actually executed; and so on – the picturesque framework aside, most of what Voltaire describes is based on fact. That these facts are remarkable is of course grist to his mill – nor, indeed, can he be accused of exaggeration.

Pangloss's doctrine of the best of all possible worlds is not a fair representation of the optimistic philosophy of Leibniz (1646–1716), and Voltaire knew this; but it was a perfectly fair representation of a popular distortion of it, such as is expressed in Pope's complacent 'whatever is, is right' (Voltaire's own marginal note to this reads: 'What can I hope if all is right?'). Evil in *Candide* is seen in a number of increasingly subtle ways. First, it exists at the cosmic level, as the Lisbon earthquake: natural disaster. Voltaire, a deist, did not believe in 'Providence'; continually in his writings he attacked the view of a God who 'had his eye on' humanity, an Old Testament figure giving rewards or punishing various sets of people. He believed that man was prey to evil events and that the best thing he could do was not to think about them. If mankind would cultivate its garden, there might be less cruelty, intolerance and, not least, optimistic stupidity such as that of Pangloss. Much of the human evil in *Candide* is seen as residing in these characteristics: in behaviour in war, or in the irrational behaviour of the inhabitants of Lisbon after the earthquake. Jacques, more subtly, is seen as too benevolent for his own or anyone else's good. The character who comes nearest to being Voltaire's own spokesman in *Candide* is Martin. The conclusion of the novel, in which Candide expresses his belief in the necessity of cultivating one's garden, is an echo of Martin's own advice: to work without arguing is the only way to make life bearable. Martin is made a Manichaean to show his acceptance of the fact that evil is eternally coexistent with good.

And so, it might reasonably be asserted, Voltaire is a thoroughgoing pessimist. But there is another element, reminding us that this gibing cynic had written: 'Oh God! Reveal to us that we must be human and tolerant.' Technically, *Candide* is innovatory because it moves so fast – frame following frame to create a cinematographic illusion. More important, it is a grateful recognition of human resilience and capacity to endure suffering with courage. This, some readers may feel, is better than a Panglossian optimism whose function is no more than to abet mankind's capacity for self-deceit.

BIBLIOGRAPHY

Translations: J. Butt, 1947; N. Cameron, 1947; R. Aldington (1927), 1959. Cameron's is the best.

Texts: A. Morize (ed), 1913; R. Pomeau (ed), 1963; C. Thacker (ed), 1968.

Criticism: H. N. Brailsford, *Voltaire*, 1935 – the best short introduction; W. H. Barber, *Voltaire's 'Candide'*, 1960; G. Lanson, *Voltaire* (1906), 1965 – in French; V. W. Topazio, *Voltaire*, 1967.

Denis Diderot

Denis Diderot (1713–84) was born at Langres in Champagne, where his father was a master cutler. He was educated by Jesuits there from 1723 until 1732, when he went to Paris. He was intended for the Church, but persuaded his father to allow him to become a law student. Little is known about his activities between 1733 and 1740, except that he was able to combine a bohemian existence with a course of intensive study of mathematics, classical philosophy and science. It was at this time, also, that he began to frequent the theatre, his lifelong love. In 1741 he met Antoinette Champion, whom he married secretly two years later – after defeating his father's plans to incarcerate him in a monastery. The marriage turned out a failure. Now he began to translate for a living, and in 1745 had become famous enough for his learning for the publisher Le Breton to approach him with a plan to translate Chambers' *Cyclopaedia* into French; this turned into the brilliant *Encyclopédie* (1751–72). Diderot, at first with d'Alembert, presided over this until its completion. Many contributions to it are his own.

For the rest of his life Diderot poured forth a huge mass of every kind of writing: translations, novels (his first was the anonymous Oriental tale *Les Bijoux indiscrets* of 1784), many plays, dialogues, criticism and philosophical works.

Like all the bold-minded Frenchmen belonging to the

period of the Enlightenment, Diderot was harrassed by the authorities. This is why many of his later works, from the late 1750s onwards, were not published in his lifetime. For example, his brilliant and prophetic *Le Neveu de Rameau*, written in about 1761, was not published in France until 1823; but Goethe translated it into German in 1805. Two other famous novels are *Le Rêve de d'Alembert* [*D'Alembert's Dream*], 1769, and *Jacques le fataliste* (written about 1773, published 1796). His life was quieter in his last twenty years; he found much solace with his mistress Sophie Volland, a highly intelligent woman whom he first met in 1755. He spent the winter of 1773-4 in St Petersburg at the Court of Catherine the Great, to whom he bequeathed his library.

Diderot, with Voltaire and Rousseau, is one of the three great figures of the Enlightenment. He is also the deepest, subtlest, most learned and most attractive. He was not, like Voltaire, a deist; but his rejection of Christianity and his philosophical atheism did not conceal or seriously interfere with his passionate search for clues to buttress his conviction of the unity of all things, in which he believed with an intensity that may fairly be described as religious. He was a sceptic, but not negatively so: he insisted upon open-mindedness only in order to establish truth. He was as subject to that peculiarly French phenomenon of the eighteenth century, *sensibilité*, as he was to the dictates of reason. He was one of the earliest and most brilliant of 'futurologists', anticipating many modern scientific discoveries, ranging from embryology through physiology to psychology.

It is in his fiction, however, that Diderot most effectively exercises his imagination. He wrote in a hurry, and none of his novels is unflawed. *Le Neveu de Rameau*, *Le Rêve de d'Alembert* and *Jacques le fataliste* are works wider in philosophical scope; but it is nevertheless in *La Religieuse* (written 1760, published 1796) that Diderot's purely novelistic skill most clearly emerges.

La Religieuse

The group of friends and devotees of the *Encyclopédie* included a well liked liberal Catholic, the Marquis de Croismare. In 1758 this excellent man lent his support to a nun, Marguerite Delamarre, who had decided, in her mid-forties, to appeal to be released from her vows. Tragically, she lost her case.

Soon after this Croismare decided to leave Paris. Diderot and others played a practical joke on him in order to secure his return. They invented a young nun, Suzanne Simonin, and pretended that she was in the same case as the unfortunate Marguerite Delamarre. Diderot wrote letters purporting to be from her to the Marquis, and they were sent on to him from Versailles, through another member of the group in whose house they pretended the young woman was hidden. Croismare offered to employ her, and it was decided to kill her off. Only eight years later did Croismare learn the truth.

But it was not only this joke that caused Diderot to compose – throughout the summer of 1760 – his most sustained fiction. First, there was the appalling fate of Marguerite Delamarre: forced into vows by her parents at an age when she was quite incapable of understanding their consequences, she was now condemned by a cruel, absurd but inevitable decision to spend the rest of her life in misery. Secondly, Diderot's father had tried to arrange to send him into a monastery when his own heart was set on marriage. Thirdly, and perhaps decisively, his own sister had died mad in a convent.

La Religieuse had only a very small circulation until 1796, when the first trade edition appeared.

SUMMARY *La Religieuse* opens with a short paragraph explaining that it consists of letters written to the Marquis de Croismare. The narrator, Suzanne Simonin, first describes her unhappy early life. More beautiful and intelligent (as she blandly claims) than her two sisters, she remains unloved. She later makes clear that she is illegitimate, a fact of which her advocate father has only a suspicion. Her mother's unkindness towards her is seen by Suzanne as resulting from the former's own shame; Suzanne is to atone for her wretched and whining mother's 'sin' by her abstemious life. This is indeed precisely what her mother tells her: that she possesses nothing, and never will. But the mother hopes to have cleared her conscience before she dies – by saving the girl's dowry (in this case the price of entrance to a nunnery) secretly. Suzanne is made by her mother to feel responsible for the scandal and disgrace. She can never marry. If she will not agree to be shut up in a convent – to which she vehemently objects – she will prolong her mother's grief and remorse until her dying day.

She is forced to agree to become a postulant at Sainte-Marie. The Mother Superior is sympathetic to her, but powerless to help. When the time comes for her to pronounce her final vows, Suzanne courageously – and with typical obstinacy – refuses to do so, and makes a scandal. She now has to become a postulant at Longchamp; the Mother Superior here, Mme de Moni, is a good and sympathetic woman, sincere and much worried over the advisability of Suzanne's taking final vows. (The character of Mme de Moni makes it abundantly clear that Diderot, although himself no Christian, does not intend to attack Christianity.) Suzanne herself never loses her faith; she merely does not wish to become a nun.

Dazed by her experiences, not recollecting what she has done, understanding 'no more about the ceremony of my profession than about my baptism', 'what you would call physically absent', she takes her final vows.

Soon after this step her nominal father, the Mother Superior – her only real friend – and her mother all die. From the last she receives a small sum of money with the note that the giver's conscience has prevented her bequeathing a larger sum.

Now a new and more sinister Mother Superior succeeds: Sainte-Christine. She is strict, rigid, narrow, superstitious and puritanical. Under her rule Suzanne – having attempted rebellion against the new harsh order – is tormented both physically and mentally. But one nun befriends her, and through her she is able to get herself transferred to another convent, although failing in her appeal to be released from her vows despite the help of the lawyer M Manouri. Her sufferings until the very day she leaves Longchamp for Arpajon are described in vivid detail.

The Mother Superior of Arpajon is not named. With the possible exception of Suzanne herself, she is Diderot's most convincing creation. She is an eccentric lesbian, whom Suzanne eventually drives mad when she refuses her demands: but that is not before she has been seduced. In his two descriptions of their physical encounters Diderot is more clinical than any other novelist had yet been; there is a magnificently accurate description, from the viewpoint of the supposedly innocent Suzanne, of the Mother Superior's orgasm. Suzanne's confessor tells her that what she has been doing is evil, and that she must desist. Without understanding why (so she tells us), she obeys him; the Mother Superior becomes insane. The confessor is replaced by Dom Morel, a reluctant priest; he suggests that they escape together, which they do – Suzanne sustaining a bad fall. No sooner are they in the carriage on their way to freedom than he assaults her; the cab driver intervenes. It is clear from the 'notes for what apparently [Suzanne] meant to use in the rest of her tale', with which the book concludes, that she eventually succumbs to Dom Morel in a brothel. Later he is recaptured.

La Religieuse has, deliberately, no ending: Suzanne

works for a laundress, living in a state of continual alarm lest she be captured – her escape has become the talk of the town – and she ends by appealing to the Marquis to employ her in his household.

CRITICAL COMMENTARY While *La Religieuse* was certainly written to redress a wrong, it contains a substantial element of pure fiction. The portrait of the lesbian prioress, not without compassion, is the most complete part of Suzanne's narrative. She is not merely illustrative of Diderot's (factually correct) thesis that convent life can produce sexual and mental disturbance. She contrasts strongly with the genuinely saintly and sympathetic Mme de Moni. Suzanne's selfish and stupid mother is a sketch made vivid by only a few deft strokes of the pen; the character of her legal father, although only incidental to the story, makes a surprisingly strong impact. Diderot's interest in psychology is evident on every page.

La Religieuse is a subtler work than may first appear. It is, certainly, a moving story of a young girl in a fearful predicament. It was intended as such, and succeeds as such. But more should be recognized if we are to do it justice.

In the introduction to his translation L. W. Tancock is aware of the novel's other dimensions, yet he censures it on wholly realist criteria. He suggests that it is flawed because:

in order to give sustained interest Suzanne has to be subjected to a series of trials of increasing severity. But this very fact that she must be afflicted afresh with new and more acute fear and anguish means that she must remain throughout the innocent victim in spite of the manifest presence around her of evil and perversion, and this with her obvious intelligence and in a tale told retrospectively by a narrator perfectly aware of the end ... in spite of all her experience, including having been accused of masturbation or homosexual practices, she is completely innocent ... it is stretching credibility to breaking point to make Suzanne quite unaware of the meaning of her Superior's behaviour ...

What Tancock writes immediately after this gives a valuable clue as to why this is a wrong judgement:

One is tempted to compare these passages with the classical method of so much frankly pornographic literature: narration by a young girl of what somebody did to her in terms combining innocence with extreme accuracy of physical description.

This is an acute observation. For the technique of *La Religieuse* is, in part, *pornographic*. It is also somewhat more cunningly humorous than perhaps even Tancock recognizes, achieving its effects on two or even more levels. It should not be forgotten that Suzanne is supposedly writing to the Marquis de Croismare, whom she has described as both 'a man of the world' and 'elderly'. Not even a paragon of innocence could have failed to bear in mind that she could not afford to offend her correspondent's sensibility: after all, it is to him alone that she looks for succour. Now even as excellent and elderly a gentleman as the Marquis has his 'sensual' susceptibilities and it does not need to be emphasized that one of the chief features of pornography is a succulently innocent young girl.

Of course it is 'stretching credibility' to suggest that Suzanne is innocent. Since she states that she has been seduced, and since (as Tancock has written) she is aware of the end of her story, it is evident that she is now perfectly knowledgeable about all aspects of sex. Diderot does not intend us to think that she is innocent. But he does intend us to think that she wishes to persuade the Marquis of her innocence, and thus to titillate him – perhaps to become his mistress. In her postscript she writes that she has noticed:

that without the slightest intention I have shown myself
in every line, certainly as unhappy as I was, but much more
attractive than I am ... Supposing the Marquis ... were to
persuade himself that I am addressing myself not to his
charity but to his lust, what would he think of me? This
thought worries me. In reality he would be quite mistaken if
he ascribed to me in particular an instinct common to all
my sex. I am a woman, and perhaps a bit coquettish, who can
tell? But it is a result of our nature, and not of artifice on
my part.

Diderot's subtlety has eluded his translators and most
other critics, who fuss about his chronology as if Suzanne
were really innocent and were supposed to be writing
truthfully. As Suzanne makes clear, in her concluding
words quoted above, there is no necessity for the reader
to think the worse of her for being deceitful.

BIBLIOGRAPHY
Translation: L. W. Tancock, *The Nun* (1972), 1974.

Texts: H. Bénac (ed) in *Diderot: Oeuvres romanesques*,
1951; J. Parrish (ed), 1963.

Criticism: Georges May, *Diderot et 'La Religieuse'*, 1954
– in French; L. G. Crocker, *The Embattled Philosopher*
(1954), 1965.

Johann Wolfgang von Goethe

Johann Wolgang [von: acquired in the 1780s] Goethe was born at Frankfurt-am-Main in 1749 of well-to-do parents. He was educated privately and then at the University of Leipzig (1765–8), where he studied law. In Strasbourg Goethe met the Protestant parson Johann Herder (1744–1803), the acknowledged leader of the *Sturm und Drang* ['storm and stress'] writers, and the literary disciple of the 'irrationalist' Johann Hamann (1730–88); he later believed poetry to be the 'mother-tongue of the human race'. Goethe's career as a serious writer had begun. In 1755 he accepted an invitation from Duke Carl August of the small state of Weimar to live at his court. Apart from travels he remained there for the rest of his life. He filled political positions, and was in charge of the state theatre.

Goethe was an inveterate womanizer, forever searching for the *Ur-Frau*. Among the many women in his life, the most important was the non-intellectual Christiane Vulpius (1765–1816), with whom he lived from 1789 until her death. He married her in 1806. *Die Leiden des Jungen Werthers* [The Sufferings of Young Werther] is based on an earlier romantic episode in his life with Charlotte Buff and a friend called Kestner.

It is usual to divide Goethe's life into three periods: *Sturm und Drang*; the *classical* period of his friendship with the critic, dramatist and poet Friedrich Schiller

(1759–1805); and a final, more syncretic period in which he absorbed romantic and Oriental elements. *Werther* belongs to the *Sturm und Drang* period. Part of *Wilhelm Meister* (*Wilhelm Meisters Theatralische Sendung* [*Wilhelm Meister's Theatrical Mission*], written *c*. 1775–6, published 1911) belongs to the period of friendship with Schiller, who persuaded him to take up an early draft. The second part of *Wilhelm Meister* (incorporated in the revised and extended *Wilhelm Meisters Lehrjahre* [*Wilhelm Meister's Apprenticeship*], 1795–6) belongs to a last phase, when Goethe's powers were weakening.

Goethe's *classicism* was not reactionary; all his work may be seen as a continuing modification and development from *Sturm und Drang*. He was an immensely prolific writer: there are twenty finished plays beside *Faust*, a large body of poetry, fiction, autobiography, translations, and aesthetic and scientific works – parts, as he said, of a 'great confession'.

Young Werther

SUMMARY *Die Leiden des Jungen Werthers* [*The Sufferings of Young Werther*] which first brought Goethe international fame, consists of letters supposedly written by young Werther (the name connotes 'worthy one') within a sparse narrative framework. The letters are 'written' over a period lasting from May of an unspecified year until December the following year. The first batch (May–January) are to 'Wilhelm'; only one is to Charlotte ('Lotte'). Werther describes how, living a simple and rural life, he falls in love with his cousin Charlotte. She is engaged to Albert, who is staid and chides Werther for his extravagant behaviour and unorthodox ideas.

In late October Werther leaves the district to take up an appointment with an ambassador (whom he dislikes).

But in January he begins to write to Charlotte. When he hears of her marriage to Albert he writes to them jointly, making his position abundantly clear. He resigns his post and by September is living near Charlotte again. He turns to *Ossian* in place of Homer: *Ossian* carries him to 'pathless wilds, surrounded by impetuous whirlwinds'. He has a 'fearful void' in his heart, and by October is contemplating what sort of 'void' his death would cause in the family to which he considers himself 'everything'. He acknowledges that he alone is the cause of his woe; this woe is that he has lost 'that active sacred power which created worlds' around him. The November landscape reflects his distracted mood. He envies a particular madman, who does not know that the source of his madness lies in his 'own distracted heart'; Albert later informs him that the man was made mad by his passion for Charlotte. At this point the letters cease: the final section of the novel is entitled 'The Editor to the Reader'; it does, however, incorporate fragments purportedly written by Werther.

The narrator treats the case as one of importance: we must pay 'particular attention' to all that Werther wrote; he was 'not of the common order'. Albert's friends think that Werther is 'unhappy and unjust in his ideas', whereas they discern no change in Albert. The narrator implies that he disagrees, and goes so far as to suggest that Albert is wrongly unwilling to 'share his rich prize with another, even for a moment, and in the most innocent manner'. Albert censures Werther to Charlotte, and wants to end their friendship with him. Charlotte, for her part, determines to 'keep Werther at a distance'. Her hesitations are caused by 'friendly pity'. She asks him to be discreet, and to find another woman. He returns home and writes to her: 'It is all over ... I am resolved to die.' This letter, composed in fragments, is found in his room after his death. Charlotte 'knew how severely [Werther] would suffer from their separation'. Albert leaves on business.

Charlotte sits regretting that Werther cannot be a 'brother': 'His absence threatened to open a void in her existence which it might be impossible to fill.' Unexpectedly he arrives. Eyes swimming in tears, he reads her some of his own translations from *Ossian*. At the end of his recital Werther flings himself at her feet; their warm cheeks touch; 'Werther!' she cries, at the third attempt attaining the 'firm voice of virtue'. Werther remains prostrate for half an hour, recovers, says *adieu*, and runs to the town gate. After scaling an impossible summit (he hangs his hat on it) in wind and rain he returns home. In the morning he finishes his letter to Charlotte, in which he reaffirms his intention of killing himself. He writes a note to Albert asking for the loan of his two pistols 'for a journey'. Charlotte becomes more agitated when Albert, receiving Werther's note, says to her: 'Give him the pistols. I wish him a pleasant journey.' Despite her suspicions, she does not intervene, feeling a 'sort of compulsion'. Werther receives the pistols with 'transports of delight': they were given to his servant by Charlotte herself. He writes another note saying goodbye to Wilhelm – and one to Albert expressing his sorrow and instructing him to 'make that angel happy' – finishes his letter to Charlotte (informing her among other things that he wishes to be buried in the clothes he was then wearing (the famous yellow trousers and blue coat, 'rendered sacred by your touch') and shoots himself. He dies a few hours later. Albert is unable to attend the funeral. 'Charlotte's life was despaired of. The body was carried by labourers. No priest attended.'

CRITICAL COMMENTARY *Young Werther* is not altogether to twentieth-century taste. It is not enough to assert that it 'rings true' because of autobiographical echoes and because Werther's character is 'utterly consistent'. Although it is written with fluency and economy, most modern readers would be inclined to agree that it is 'preposterous'. Certainly it has its farcical side; it would be disingenuous to ignore this, for to see it as farce is not only a modern reaction. *Young Werther* was parodied as well as imitated all over Europe, and Goethe himself wrote: 'From the sorrows of Werther, and yet more from his joys, may the good Lord deliver us.' Does the novel 'appeal to us still'? Hardly. But we cannot ignore it, and we cannot judge it without understanding something of its background and of Goethe's many-sided personality.

Sturm und Drang is usually taken to begin with Goethe's drama *Götz von Berlichingen* (1773) and to end either with Goethe's withdrawal from the movement (1775) or, belatedly, with Schiller's *Kabale und Liebe* [*Intrigue and Love*] (1782–3). It was given its name from the play *Sturm und Drang* (1776), by F. M. Klinger (1752–1831).

While the movement gained much of its impetus from the young Goethe's dynamic personality, it had its forerunners: notably in Hamann and Herder; in certain aspects of the thought of Gotthold Lessing (1729–81) – although he was also representative of *Aufklärung* [Enlightenment] thinking; and in Shakespeare, Rousseau, *Ossian* and the English pre-romantics. For the first time in German literature a group of youthful writers emerged with ideals in common; *Sturm und Drang* put emphasis on the irrational, on the values of madness, on the uncorrupted peasantry, on folk poetry and on the *Kraftkarl* (the 'strong man') and on his opposite, the brooding introspective wanderer, such as Werther. The landscape in their work is magnificent or idyllic; men in flowing robes with flowing hair pass through desolate windswept gorges. *Sturm und Drang* was short lived, but played a vital part in the development of German romanticism in the 1790s, when a group of writers gathered around the Schlegel brothers (A. W., 1767–1845, and F., 1772–1829) at Jena (near Weimar). Intimately linked with this movement was the unique *Weimer classicism* of Christoph

Wieland (1732–1813), Goethe, Schiller and Herder. Weimar classicism is a synthesis of *Aufklärung* and *Sturm und Drang* elements; Goethe came to accept that man must evolve according to universal laws – this position is indicated by, among other works, *Wilhelm Meisters Lehrjahr*. 'Social integration', for Goethe, is now 'placed above self-assertion'.

Young Werther has been viewed as a young man's aggressively brilliant and yet 'preposterous' expression of *Sturm und Drang*, as a tragic illustration of the inevitable fate of an *unstable* character (ie, as a criticism of *Sturm und Drang* attitudes), as an ironic farce, and as a mostly unsatisfactory mixture of all the foregoing. The last view is the nearest to the truth; each of the others has its merits.

Sturm und Drang may have been exaggerated and have had 'Ossianic' elements that now seem quaint, but it was as necessary in Germany as it was inevitable. Goethe's narrator, with his sympathy for Werther and his animosity towards Albert, is clearly representative of the movement. *Young Werther* was not lacking in enthusiastic readers who were tired of the limitations rationalism tried to impose upon them; it captured a European mood. Werther's behaviour did not seem as strange to all its readers as it seems today. But Goethe's text could be taken as a warning against romantic excess, surrender to melancholy and over-intensity. For him it was perhaps therapeutic: he had just painfully renounced his love for a woman because she was betrothed to his friend (whom she married), and was still full of that enthusiasm which rationalism discouraged. Only later would he see its funny side. Yet when he reissued the novel in 1887 it had the original prologue, praising Werther; this may indicate a mature, ironic perspective.

What are the qualities of *Young Werther* as a novel? It is, rather curiously, not boring. Pre-romantics outside and inside Germany held it up as a model. However preposterous, it gives an absorbing account of a certain climate of thought, one which owed much to Pietism, the Protestant movement originating in Germany in the seventeenth century with Jakob Spener (1635–1705). With its roots in earlier mysticism, Pietism is important in German life and literature, reacting against mechanically observed dogma and Lutheran scholasticism and rigidity; the movement put emphasis on inner fervour, self-examination, submission to providence, and recognition of the spiritual worth of humble people. As a movement it became diversified, but in Goethe's time it profoundly influenced the thinking of many Germans. In its extremist form it even came to seek emancipation from the specifically Christian God. Goethe himself felt its influence strongly: through his mother and then (1769) through Susanna von Klettenberg (1723–74). Werther's attitudes are certainly related to the effects of Pietism – from which no German writer was immune.

But *Young Werther* suffers from a fatal imbalance. It has not worn well; it is more of an historical document than a work of art. Werther is hardly to be pitied: he is not tragic; he is a self-righteous, humourless and destructive prig; he attacks 'ill humour' in others, but practises something much worse. The novel can only be said to point up his vicious egoism in as much as it is farcical. It has been claimed that – unlike his Nietzschean successor, Knut Hamsun's Nagel of *Mysteries* – Werther is 'basically a study in pathological sensibility'. If so intended, then it is unsuccessful: it is not tragic because the narrator fails to give a clear portrait of any of the characters amongst whom Werther moves. All are seen through his own eyes or through those of the narrator – who takes his part. Albert appears as a cipher; he is unfairly diminished; never revealed: the staid, moderate foil to Werther's subjectivist need to dramatize himself. Charlotte herself is not more than a figure in this drama. It is implied that so divine a creature *must* really love so noble a man as Werther, that she has been mistaken in choosing the dull Albert; and, indeed, apparently Werther is not content with anything less than self-destruction in order to destroy her and so prove his point. But she is given no special characteristics, and Werther's view of her is sentimental, even hysterical. Werther's end may more correctly be seen as an over-dramatized example of *Sturm und Drang* revenge-suicide than as a deliberate demonstration of the terrible results of excess.

Of all novels of major historical importance *Young Werther* has the least intrinsic merit – as distinct from promise.

Wilhelm Meister's Apprenticeship

Goethe wrote the first draft of the first five books of *Wilhelm Meisters Lehrjahre* [*Wilhelm Meister's Apprenticeship*] between 1777 and 1785 under the title *Wilhelm Meisters theatralische Sendung* [*Wilhelm Meister's Theatrical Mission*]. In this earlier version, which was discovered in 1910 and published in 1911, the themes of self-realization through the theatre and the creation of a German national theatre – an ambition of many intellectuals – are paramount. But the *Apprenticeship* shows a considerable development in Goethe's thinking. It is a difficult book – and one which gets more difficult as it proceeds.

SUMMARY Wilhelm is the son of a prosperous merchant who wants him to follow in his footsteps. The older Meister is a partner with Werner, whose good-natured philistine son acts as friendly foil to the protagonist. Wilhelm has become passionately fond of the theatre; a rebellious if somewhat passive and unexpectedly prudent young man, he is enjoying an affair with Mariane, an actress who is financially supported by another suitor.

Wilhelm is about to propose marriage when he imagines he discovers her infidelity. He diligently pursues commerce, burning his poems in disillusionment. He is at this stage suffering like Werther, in a more subdued manner: he intends to cure himself.

He visits a town in the course of a business trip. Here he attends a performance of acrobats, and encounters Mignon, a child, 'young, dark, black-haired', dressed as a boy, he decides that she is a girl. Wilhelm had rejected the theatre; now he begins to preach its potential usefulness to the State. The obsession with *Hamlet* which pervades the book now comes into full view: Wilhelm meets an actor – whom 'for the present, we shall call Laertes'; Laertes' companion is the coquettish actress Philine. (Goethe uses all the eighteenth-century novelists' tricks designed to sustain interest: introduction of characters to be named later, cryptic references, inset stories. Motifs from *Hamlet* abound; the effect of these is for the time being puzzling – for some readers they remain impenetrable.)

Wilhelm *buys* the ill treated Mignon from the manager of the acrobats, and she becomes devoted to him, serving him and his out-of-work actor friends, flitting mysteriously in and out of the narrative. Soon afterwards the Harper arrives on the scene. With his flowing beard and robe and his mixture of joyous and 'harsh, cold, jarring' ballads, this minstrel is apparently a figure straight out of *Sturm und Drang*. Wilhelm looks upon him as a 'helping spirit'.

Remaining in the town against his better judgement, reluctantly fascinated by Philine, affected by Mignon's strange behaviour towards him (she begs him to be her 'father' and clings to him in a markedly sexual fashion), Wilhelm finances the troupe of his greedy friend, the cheat Melina, who obtains permission to play at the castle of a Count, knowledgeable in theatrical matters, and his Countess. A Baron now arrives: he is devoted to the German theatre, and wishes Melina's company to play a long five-act piece he has written. There follows satire on bad plays and the vanity of actors. But Wilhelm decides to associate himself with them: he has left home 'to study men', he wants to be amongst people of rank and, most vehemently, he wants to be near the Countess, who has indicated that she is interested in him. The performance at the Count's castle is for the pleasure of a Prince, shortly expected. When the company arrives at the castle Wilhelm encounters Jarno, rumoured to be the Prince's natural son, and much disliked by the Baron for his literary pretensions. Wilhelm feels an 'inclination' towards him, though he notices that he is 'cold and repulsive'. There are many odd happenings – notably the manner in which events appear to be determining that the ever-passive Wilhelm shall have a relationship with the Countess. She secretly assists him in the composition of a play in honour of the Prince, and insists that he act the part of leader of the peasants in it. The play is performed, and is well received.

As a result of a trick initiated by Philine and the Baroness, the Count sees Wilhelm's reflection in a mirror in his room; he believes it to be his own, a premonition of death, and later joins a Pietist sect. Wilhelm finally falls into an embrace with the Countess, who then tells him, 'Fly, if you love me!' War causes the removal of the nobility, and therefore of Melina's disorderly troupe. The Harper now begs Wilhelm to let him go: he has a 'horrid secret' and misfortune flies to overtake him, injuring all connected with him. 'I am secure while with you,' he adds mysteriously, 'but you are in peril.' Wilhelm refuses, and remains with the troupe in its search for a suitable town in which to establish itself. He becomes manager, by election, in place of Melina. His ambition is now to present *Hamlet*, with himself in the main role. But the company is set upon by robbers, and Wilhelm is wounded. As he lies in the lap of Philine the 'fair Amazon' approaches; he has never seen anyone so noble or lovely. It transpires that the company in which she travels had been the object of the robbers' attentions. She eventually leaves, and Wilhelm, with Mignon, the Harper and Philine, returns to the village whence the company had fled. They have lost almost everything: money, props, wardrobe. Wilhelm is looked after, at the expense of the 'fair Amazon', at a parson's home. When he has recovered he tries to find her, but without success. He determines to escape his 'inactivity' (yet another allusion to *Hamlet*) and to look for Serlo, the theatre-manager whose company he had been about to join when he thought to marry Mariane.

Serlo is a Shakespearean, and wants to present *Hamlet* – if he could find a prince. Wilhelm expounds to him his interpretation of the play. The kernel of it is that Shakespeare intended to 'represent the effects of a great action [to put the disjointed times right] laid upon a soul unfit for the performance of it'. Hamlet is 'lovely, pure, noble and most moral', but lacks the 'strength of nerve which forms a hero'. Wilhelm is thinking of himself, the more so when he later adds that while the hero has no plan the 'piece is full of plan'. Wilhelm's imagination is leading him towards the stage and a contract with Serlo; his reason leads him away. Serlo's sister Aurelia (interested in the role of Ophelia) mystifies him by her behaviour; she confesses her love for a man whom she calls Lothario, widely travelled, a distinguished soldier – and when Wilhelm promises to consecrate his life to any woman to whom he shall declare love, she cuts him on the hand, 'dividing the life-lines' with a sharp dagger. Aurelia ails, and Mignon takes charge of the little boy, Felix, whom most take to be hers. Wilhelm receives news of his father's death (this event again connected with the *Hamlet* theme). Werner, soon to marry Wilhelm's sister, writes asking him to come home to help settle his father's estate at a good profit. But

Wilhelm refuses. On the condition that *Hamlet* shall be played in its entirety he signs up as a member of Serlo's company. Wilhelm is in difficulty about who shall play the ghost of Hamlet's father; in his room he finds a strangely written note promising him a miracle.

At last the play is performed, and a ghost – hitherto missing – does appear. Wilhelm cannot identify him, and even thinks he resembles his own father; his performance is enhanced, and he triumphs. But there are hints of the supernatural or of conjuring: the ghost sinks into the ground like a real ghost, and flames appear when it moves in the cellarage; the unknown actor disappears, but a veil he has left where he sank into the ground is inscribed with the words: 'For the first and last time! Fly! Youth! Fly!' And that night when Wilhelm goes to bed he feels himself 'encircled with soft arms' which he cannot push away. On the next night the Harper sets the house on fire and tries to kill the child, Felix; Mignon, however, warns Wilhelm, and all are saved. It is generally agreed that the Harper is showing signs of insanity, and he is put into the care of a parson.

Philine suddenly distances herself from Wilhelm, and soon disappears with an officer dressed in red. From the clergyman who is looking after the Harper Wilhelm discovers that, while the Count has joined the Herrnhuters (a Pietist sect, distrustful of doctrine, founded at the Saxon village of Herrnhut in 1722), his wife (the Countess) while embracing a certain young man (of course Wilhelm) has been pierced in the breast by a diamond-studded portrait of her husband, and now believes herself to be suffering from cancer. Wilhelm is deeply upset.

Aurelia sickens and dies, but not before the clergyman-physician has given her a manuscript called 'Confessions of a Beautiful Soul' which Wilhelm reads to her (forming Book VI of the novel). She charges Wilhelm to go to Lothario, who has made her so unhappy, to wish him every happiness (before reading the manuscript she had wanted to hurt this 'faithless man' with news of her death). Wilhelm sets off, leaving Serlo and Melina free to spoil the troupe by turning it into a bad operatic company. Serlo, without true artistic integrity, is fond of music; Melina wants profit.

The 'Confessions', for the details of which Goethe owed much to Susanna von Klettenberg, is a Pietist and feminist 'inset story'. It is the autobiography of a woman who values God above her lover (Narciss); she also refuses to give up her independence of thought – and this is as significant as her essentially private piety. She becomes a 'young and pious canoness' and, rejecting the notion that good can be found on earth, awaits death cheerfully. She half-starves herself, but yet feels (perhaps paradoxically) spiritual 'weakness and misery'; of *sin* she knows, as yet, nothing. Her 'Invisible Leader' (it is not absolutely clear if he is synonymous with 'God') then permits her to change her life: she turns to another man, the middle-aged Philo. Though she finds him wanting, she feels the more drawn to him because of it; she realizes that she is no better. For a decade she had practised 'more than mere virtue'; but 'horrors' had lain hidden at the bottom of her soul ... No moral system can give her solace – only intercourse with her 'Invisible Friend'. She discovers a new, powerful faith in the contemplation of Christ on the cross: a mystical, rapturous experience. Her rejection of outward forms intensifies, and she is led to the work of Count Zinzendorf (1700–60, an influential, heterodox Herrnhuter who proclaimed a 'religion of the heart' which depended on an emotional, intimate relationship with Jesus Christ). She becomes associated with the Herrnhuters of her district, but is disillusioned when Pietism becomes fashionable and leads to violent and immoderate debates. She is now led to appreciate art (particularly Italian architecture), literature and music, and to see the 'finger of the Deity' in them. At the death of her aged father she passes from 'strictest obedience' to the 'greatest freedom': dining out, pleasure jaunts, walks. But her health, never good, deteriorates, and she begins to feel her soul 'thinking separately' from her body. She devotes herself to the supervision of the (Rousseauist) education of her nephews and nieces; and ends her story by declaring: 'There is no danger I should ever become proud of what I myself can do or can forbear to do; I have seen too well what a monster might be formed and nursed in every human bosom, did not higher influence restrain us.'

Books VII and VIII, which complete the *Apprenticeship*, increasingly emphasize the theme of character formation. Many characters are reintroduced, the narrative becomes excessively concentrated. Wilhelm journeys to Lothario's house, discovers that Lothario is a baron and the brother of the Countess, and re-encounters Jarno (Lothario's attendant) and an Abbé who had once accompanied him, 'Laertes' and others on a boating trip.

Wilhelm, still in search of his Amazon, meets Theresa in the course of a mission he performs for Jarno. She soon presents herself to him dressed as a 'handsome hunter-boy', and tells him of her love affair with Lothario, which ended when Lothario discovered that he had been her dissolute mother's lover.

Wilhelm discovers that Mariane is dead, that she had never been unfaithful while his lover, and that Felix is his own child. He resists attempts from the public to get him to act again, and concentrates his attention on fathoming the 'mysteries' of the men – Jarno, the Abbé, Lothario – with whom he means to join himself. At the end of Book VII he is initiated into their secret band, the Watchmen of the Tower; his apprenticeship is ended. But much tribulation lies before him. Mignon has been with Lothario's sister, who sends for Wilhelm because Felix is ill. Wilhelm dreads meeting the Countess – but

Lothario has two sisters, and this one is none other than Natalia, the Amazon ... He had meanwhile sent Theresa a letter proposing marriage (a mistaken move because it arose from 'reason'). Natalia's aunt proves to be the author of the 'Confessions' of Book VI; Natalia resembles her and was educated – with Lothario and the Countess – by the Abbé under her supervision. Wilhelm learns that Mignon is Italian, and that she has been sick with jealousy since the night when, after his first performance as Hamlet, he was visited by an unknown woman. He soon learns, too, that the Watchmen of the Tower, of whom he has become a part, albeit a small one, take 'certain charge of proceedings, of the destiny of certain people, and contrive to guide them'. They have sometimes been guiding him, as in the matter of the ghost of Hamlet's father. When he sees Natalia Wilhelm regrets having proposed to Theresa. But Theresa writes to him accepting his proposal. Now Jarno tells him that Lothario has discovered that she is not the daughter of the woman who had been his love, and that he therefore seeks her hand. Theresa, not believing in Lothario, resists this and visits Wilhelm, who is with Natalia. She embraces him warmly; Mignon falls dead. Wilhelm becomes confused and irritated by the apparently cruel or pointless activities of the Watchmen of the Tower, especially when Jarno informs him that what had been in 'deep earnest' is now viewed 'with a smile'; this, however, turns out to be no more than an acknowledgement of the fact that young men like *hocus pocus* and secrets – the Watchmen have merely infused some humour into their still serious enterprise as they have become older and more experienced in life. They realize that 'Thought expands, but lames; action animates, but narrows.' No one has yet been advanced to the status of 'Master' [*Meister*].

In this last book there is a series of revelations. Philine's servant Friedrich, who had been jealous of Wilhelm, turns out to be brother to Lothario, Natalia and the Countess. He tells Wilhelm that his night visitor after the *Hamlet* was Philine.

Theresa, Wilhelm realizes, had merely the attraction of a daughter for him. Asked to accompany a Marchese, one of the Watchmen, as an interpreter, he now protests his love for Natalia, which is 'serene and clear'; he determines to go on his travels, though in the company of his son Felix rather than as interpreter. Solemn obsequies are said for Mignon – who has always desired to return to Italy (Goethe's own crucial journeys there in 1786–8 are relevant). The Countess arrives, now evidently a convinced Pietist, in simple attire, much altered. From a tragic tale told by the Abbé it emerges that the Marchese (whom Wilhelm had held back from accompanying) is the brother of the Harper, whose name is Augustin. The tale has further revealed that Mignon was the fruit of an incestuous union between the Harper and his sister, Sperata. When he discovered the relationship he justified it: 'Were there not noble nations which admitted marriage with a sister? Name not your Gods!' The impact of this knowledge upon Wilhelm is decisive: he put himself at the disposal of the society of Watchmen of the Tower. The Harper himself now arrives, cured, shorn of his beard and dressed 'with some attention to the mode'; but he is terrified of Felix. He discovers the manuscript of his own story, cuts his throat, and dies. The Apprenticeship ends abruptly with Wilhelm's betrothal to Natalia.

The continuation of 1821, which was revised in 1829, the *Wanderjahre* (subtitled 'Die Entsagenden' ['The Renunciants']) is shorter but less organized than its predecessor. There are many tales, some of which are, almost impudently, left unfinished. At its beginning Wilhelm has left Natalia. G. H. Lewes wrote that he found in it 'almost every fault a work can have ... unintelligible ... tiresome ... fragmentary ... dull ... often ill-written'.

This is a matter for the judgement of the reader, who may or may not agree with some romantics' view of it: that it 'judges itself'. In his sequel Goethe develops his ideas on many subjects, and Wilhelm finds out that his real vocation is that of surgeon. Each 'renunciant' has devoted himself to a particular craft: his specialization has symbolic meaning, but it also enables him to function as a necessary cog in the social machine.

CRITICAL COMMENTARY The Apprenticeship is truly original. But its sources, though combined by Goethe with astonishing and daring versatility, were all well known to the contemporary public – even if they did not comprehend his combination of them. Today the uninitiated reader is likely to find the novel even more wayward and strange than it actually is, despite its important influence on later German fiction.

Wilhelm Meister's Apprenticeship is the paradigmatic German *Bildungsroman* (apprenticeship novel). A *Bildungsroman* is sometimes, though wrongly, called an *Erziehungsroman* (education novel); a *Künstlerroman* deals with the development of an artist. (The blanket term is *Entwicklungsroman* [development novel], the novel dealing with the evolution of the personality.) The first true *Bildungsroman* was the *Agathon* (1766–98) of Wieland, in that it was semi-autobiographical and tried to establish an ideal of a balanced personality; the influence of Wieland's 1777 revision of this novel on Goethe is evident. But Goethe, while accepting Wieland's conclusion that a man can only become a harmonious being by coming to terms with his dual – rational/ sensuous – nature, gives his protagonist that special passivity that characterizes the hero of *Bildungsroman* proper.

Wilhelm Meister combines picaresque, realist, Pietist, 'Gothic', ironic, Enlightenment and romantic elements. Wilhelm is not a *picaro*, but the presentation of his earlier adventures owes something to the picaresque method, and some of those he encounters (eg, Melina) are simply rogues with their eyes to the main chance. The novel is not realist, but there are vivid scenes, and some of Wilhelm's sexual predicaments are analysed with a strictly realistic exactitude. However, the complaint that the 'reader used to the masterpieces of French realism quickly gives up in despair at the vacuum in which Goethe's characters seem to exist' is justified. Wilhelm and the others seem to be floating in an ambiguous Utopian mist, which clears only in ironic or down-to-earth instants so short as to make us wonder if they were not delusions. This mixture of magic and realism is often delightful; but when the head clears a residue of puzzlement remains.

The Pietist influence is strong, as the 'Confessions' show. This is most apparent in Goethe's emphasis on the necessity for tolerance, and on *feeling* as the indispensable basis of religious belief. Goethe was ambivalent in his view of Count Zinzendorf's Pietism, and possibly not sure to what extent it fitted in with his own main tenet: that there can be no harmonious individual or society without reconciliation between the sensual and the rational sides of human nature. Zinzendorf had travelled widely, founding Herrnhut communities as far away as America; this is reflected in the end of the *Apprenticeship* and throughout the *Wanderjahre*, even though the latter is structurally really little more than a concatenation of *novellen* in various stages of composition. But the connection of the Watchmen of the Tower with Freemasonry (Goethe was a Freemason for much of his life) is hardly Pietist in nature, for Freemasonry was identified with the spirit of the *Aufklärung* and of Deism. The one certain element in the work, in fact, is its insistence on the necessity for exploration and unification of the divided self – and it may well be that this is the least satisfactory aspect of it. It is odd that the nation which invented and exploited the ambitious, optimistic *Bil-*

dungsroman, with its originally passive hero, should also be the nation that produced the figure of Hitler ...

Yet the *Bildungsroman* is not only a symptom of the German weakness for over-systematization; it also owes much to Rousseau's *Émile* (1762). The personality and all the writings of Jean-Jacques Rousseau (1712–78) had, in fact, as profound an influence on Goethe as on anybody. Allowing for the difference between the dates of their births, and between a Swiss of French ancestry and a German, there are certain resemblances between the two men: both are supreme egotists, both are 'rationalist emotionalists', both are complex and self-contradictory, and both tend to offer themselves as 'whole or not at all'. The difference is that Rousseau was at times half-mad; Goethe was not. *Émile*, written in the form of a novel, tries to envisage a form of education by which an individual, moved by *amour-soi*, (self-respect) may take no harm from the process of becoming a *civic* man. Émile is taught by example; acts are to be followed by their natural consequences (an important motif in the *Lehrjahre*); he does not hear of 'God' until he has grown up. Rousseau's insistence that each person should have his particular specialization, while will give him his proper place in an organic society, influenced Goethe and his contemporaries – though the misogyny of the crypto-paranoid last book of *Émile* did not affect Goethe. Book VI of the *Apprenticeship* is a feminine *Bildungsroman* set within a masculine one. The Rousseauist influence, combined with Pietist notions about providence, is seen clearly in an early conversation between Wilhelm and the Abbé: 'Fate,' says the Abbé, 'is an excellent, but most expensive schoolmaster. In all cases, I would rather trust to a human tutor. Fate, for whose wisdom I entertain all imaginable reverence, often finds in Chance, by which it works, an instrument not over manageable. At least the latter very seldom seems to execute precisely and accurately what the former had determined.'

Rousseau, successful in the theatre (as an opera composer: *Le Devin du village*, 1752) and worried by it, had written (1758) against the introduction of the theatre into Geneva, and had preferred, sanctimoniously and absurdly, 'innocent' open-air spectacles. In the *Sendung*, the original draft left unpublished until 1911, Goethe believed implicitly in the theatre; in the *Apprenticeship* he changed his mind somewhat, but he still lacks Rousseau's puritanism. Rousseau would have approved of his picture of the vanity and irresponsibility of Serlo's troupe, and of Wilhelm's departure from it. But Goethe himself never explicitly rejects the theatre; he uses it increasingly allegorically, on the Shakespearean premise that all the world's a stage.

From the end of Book VI *Wilhelm Meister* becomes hard to follow; much is both inexplicable and bathetic. Yet the argument that the prose is, overall, both enchanted and enchanting is a strong one, and is reinforced by the experience of many modern readers. Its faults embody many indeed most, of the faults of German literature and of the German character; it is in this light that it may best be viewed. As a whole it is a failure, whereas the best of Goethe's poetry is not. But it is an invaluable adjunct to *Faust*, Goethe's presentation of whose central character critics were surely justified in taking as an embodiment of the German people; and, if it does not 'judge itself', it certainly demonstrates the nature of a certain kind of failure much in evidence in the German mentality.

It is not, perhaps, to the advantage of *Wilhelm Meister* to judge it as the paradigmatic *Bildungsroman* – and then to test the form itself; but this is how it has been judged, and not unnaturally. Goethe certainly first intended the work as an illustration of how a man might cultivate himself and achieve a harmonious and balanced personality without ceasing to *be himself*. All his friends in Weimar were obsessed with one or another

aspect of the same problem. Yet Goethe is always ambivalent. Are we, for example, to take the Watchmen of
the Tower (*Turmgesellschaft*) absolutely seriously, or is
Goethe sometimes laughing at them? The certificate of
apprenticeship which Wilhelm is given after his initiation has been taken with great solemnity by some critics;
but surely Goethe was aware that this collection of evasive mystical clichés ('Art is long, life short, judgement
difficult ... To act is easy, to think is hard,' and so on)
is a cheapjack document. None of the members, with
the possible exception of the Abbé, is demonstrably wise
in his behaviour. Goethe, to his credit, wanted to reconcile the ideal and the real. But he fails.

The *Wanderjahre* is in certain respects a weak and
unconvincing work. Wilhelm is all but abandoned; the
psychological reasons that lead him to take up surgery,
to achieve himself in the community, remain obscure.
Nor is it clear what the 'fully cultivated' Wilhelm is
actually like. When he achieves 'equilibrium' he is a
cipher. One may claim that by the end of the *Apprenticeship*, Wilhelm is a *better* person: *he* has learned to
dedicate himself to meaningful activity – the proper
management of his estates, dedication to his son Felix.
Schiller stated in a letter of 1796, that Wilhelm 'steps
out of an empty and vague ideal into a definite, active
life ...' But the nature of Wilhelm's relationship with
Natalia (never explained by Goethe) is oddly arbitrary.

It is really the figure of Mignon that tends to undermine defences of the novel based on its efficacy as a
Bildungsroman (but neither can these deal satisfactorily
with the Wilhelm–Natalia relationship). Such defences
maintain that Wilhelm learns from his mistakes and
from his capacity for being influenced by others, that he
is 'open' in his attitude towards life, and that he is able
to engage himself actively in the present. They see the
book, as they must, as essentially didactic – and lay
stress on Goethe's *classicism*.

But Mignon is in no sense a classical figure: she is romantic, mysterious, ambiguously sexed, *Italian* – and she plays no discernible part in Wilhelm's education. She is out of place, and in killing her off Goethe failed to do justice to his apprehension of her magical qualities and her power. She is supposed to be sick, unhealthy; Goethe could justifiably feel that she and her father must be removed, in order that Wilhelm's 'healthy' development may be highlighted. But he had not dealt with the reasons for which sickness (including the anthropologically mysterious sickness of incest) is attractive. Yet the book is imbued with a sense of this; it is evident that Goethe is fascinated by decadence. One of the reasons – yet another paradox – why the book, once the reader has familiarized himself with its formidable ins-and-outs, is appealing lies in the portrayal of Mignon, even if she is not integrated into it. It is easy to remark that the emotional climate inhabited by Mignon and her father 'is not to be regarded as the general tendency of the novel or its "meaning"'. So Goethe – who said (1825) in relation to *Wilhelm Meister* that 'man reaches a happy goal, guided by a higher hand' – would like us to think. The *classical* defence of the novel depends on our taking it as a wholly didactic work but, as such, some readers feel it is merely tiresome and *unattractive*. While it is true that Wilhelm does not abandon himself to the dark strange world of Mignon and her father, it is also true that as soon as they are removed he becomes a less interesting, or more conventional (or of course simply inexplicable) figure. Goethe chose here to ignore the details of this dark world (which he called in a note 'madness of discordant relationships') in favour of the one-sided, 'harmonious' life of service led by Wilhelm in the *Wanderjahre*.

Werther had been an immature book; but Goethe was still not going, here at any rate, to try to define the irrational. One may feel that the serene narrator, the man with so excellent an idea of the Weimar-classical face he must present to the world, is the 'most important character in the book'. In advancing this thesis Roy Pascal adds that the narrator is not the real Goethe, but a somewhat 'avuncular' idealization. There may therefore be substance in the romantic poet Novalis' insistence that the *Apprenticeship* is a 'pilgrimage to the patent of nobility', a *'Candide* aimed against poetry'. Samuel Butler even wondered if it were a hoax.

Despite certain badly written passages (such as the notorious one in which Mignon laments Wilhelm's decision to abandon the theatre), this is an irresistibly fascinating book. But as we shall see, filled as it is with anticipations of future procedures (including perhaps hoaxes), the wisdom of its parts is not reflected in the whole.

BIBLIOGRAPHY

Translations: R. D. Boylan, *The Sufferings of Young Werther* – in *Works*, 1848–90; W. Rose, *The Sorrows of Werther*, 1929; B. Q. Morgan, *The Sorrows of Young Werther*, 1957; T. Carlyle, *Wilhelm Meister*, 1824–7; R. D. Boylan, *Wilhelm Meister* – in *Works*; R. O. Moon, *Wilhelm Meister*, 1947.

Texts: E. L. Stahl (ed), *Die Leiden des jungen Werthers*, 1942. *Wilhelm Meister* in *Werke*, 1948–60.

Criticism: G. H. Lewes, *The Life of Goethe*, 1864; R. Gray, *Goethe*, 1967; George Eliot, 'The Morality of Wilhelm Meister', reprinted in T. Pinney (ed), *Essays*, 1963.

Pierre-Ambroise-François Choderlos de Laclos

Laclos was born in 1741 at Amiens, of a modestly placed family. He took up a military career and spent the first twenty-odd years of it in provincial garrison towns. His political and literary attitudes were doubtless affected by the fact that his lack of social standing hindered his chances of promotion. In his late thirties he began to rebel. For an entry in an essay competition of 1786 he wrote on the defence theories of the military tactician Sébastien Vauban who, although he had died in 1703, was still regarded as the foremost authority on the subject. Laclos' trenchant criticisms of his theories lost him his commission.

Meanwhile in 1779 he had written *Les Liaisons dangereuses*, which reflected his liberal concerns in a more imaginative manner. This was published, as by 'Monsieur C— de L—' in 1782, and immediately caused a scandal. Everybody read this supposedly disgusting book, but few acknowledged the fascination it held for them. It was in the library of Marie Antoinette – in a plain binding.

Laclos' connection with the revolutionary nobleman Louis Philippe Joseph, Duc d'Orléans, reveals an important side of his character. Louis Philippe (1747–93) was always a revolutionary, and was disliked at the Court of Louis XIV not only for his politics but also for his debauchery. He published his *Délibérations* in 1788;

these, in the writing of which Laclos played a major role, asserted that the *tiers état* actually *was* the nation. With the Revolution Louis Philippe led the forty-seven noblemen who joined the *tiers état*. Later he became disillusioned; but he voted for the death of the King. Subsequently (1792), with the abolition of titles, he changed his name to Philippe Egalité. Laclos went to prison with him during the Terror, but escaped the guillotine – which Egalité did not. His son became Louis Philippe, King of France.

Another side of Laclos' character, less well documented, is seen in his devotion to his wife and family. He married Solanges du Perré in 1786, two years after she had borne him a child. His later letters give unequivocal evidence of his belief in the moral efficacy of domestic happiness; and there is no need to doubt the sincerity of his intentions – which were not fulfilled – to write a new novel which would demonstrate that true virtue could be discovered only in family life.

In 1800 Laclos went back to the army as one of Napoleon's brigadier generals. After serving with the army of the Rhine and in Italy, he died in Taranto in 1803. In 1824 the Paris Court commanded the destruction of his famous work as 'dangerous' – a nice reflection of his own description of it in its title. In the nineteenth century Baudelaire alone drew attention to its excellence. It was not rediscovered until our own century.

Les Liaisons dangereuses

SUMMARY *Les Liaisons dangereuses* is cast in the epistolary form made popular by Richardson – whom Laclos, like Diderot – and Rousseau in his *Julie, ou La nouvelle Héloise* – profoundly admired. It consists of 175 letters; two more were excluded from editions published in the author's lifetime.

The chief characters, the manipulators, are the Marquise de Merteuil and the Vicomte de Valmont. They were once lovers, but Valmont broke off the relationship – for which the Marquise secretly hates him. Mme de Volanges is arranging the marriage of her innocent daughter Cécile to the Comte de Gercourt. Gercourt's agreement to this plan is the mainspring of the action: it enables the Vicomte and the Marquise to revenge themselves upon him. For he has offended them both: he has abandoned the Marquise for another woman, who has therefore left the Vicomte. The Marquise is the stronger character, but she has a willing ally in the Vicomte. By a series of cunning manoeuvres on the part of both, the Vicomte succeeds in seducing Cécile, who is forced into a convent after she has miscarried a child. Meanwhile the Marquise seduces – and then forces into a renunciation of the flesh – the young man with whom Cécile has been in love, the Chevalier Danceny.

The Vicomte succeeds in the difficult task of seducing the high-principled, and married, Présidente de Tourvel. The Marquise de Merteuil, although she cannot bring herself to settle permanently with the Vicomte – any more than he can with her – is still enough obsessed with him, as he with her, to manifest signs of jealousy; for Valmont falls in love with the Présidente. Here the Marquise shows her strength of character by playing on his feelings for her – and on his vanity. By ensuring that he abandons the Présidente, she assures that the latter will die of grief and shame.

Inevitably, the two intriguers quarrel. Ironically it is their one virtue, their feelings for each other, that causes their downfall. The Marquise provokes a duel between Valmont and Cécile's former beloved, Danceny – and the Vicomte is killed. She, however, is doomed to live with total defeat: stripped of her possessions by a lawsuit, exposed by Danceny for the intriguer she is (Valmont shows him her letters), disfigured by smallpox, she is forced to seek miserable refuge in Holland.

CRITICAL COMMENTARY The style of *Les Liaisons dangereuses* is lucid, forceful and simple. Laclos improved considerably on the technique of the two novelists he used as his models: Richardson and Rousseau. In Laclos' admirably economical novel every letter counts; indeed, the letters themselves are part of the intricate plot, since each one gives rise to others. There are relatively few clumsinesses and inconsistencies: certainly not enough to rob the novel of its status as a major technical triumph.

The book caused a social outrage, and was regarded as 'pornographic' (it still is by some). Actually Laclos is positively *anti-pornographic*. To be thus, indeed, is part of his purpose: his two main characters try to distance themselves not only from the emotional complications caused by sexual relationships, but also from sensuality. This gives 'them' (Laclos) a special status as narrators: a function different from their wickedness.

For them love is a game: a strategy. Laclos makes his intentions clear by reviving the old tradition of speaking of love in terms of war. For the Marquise, especially, sexual intrigue is a matter of dissociation from all forms of morality. But her calculated evil-doing is strongly motivated. It arises from her resentment – that of an intelligent person – at society's treatment of women as inferior beings. Emancipation from morality is also Valmont's ideal, one that he finds it impossible to realize once he becomes embroiled with the Présidente.

There is in this novel, as in so much good fiction, an ambiguity. For, depraved and cynical though the two chief characters may be, we are unable completely to dislike them. A reader who went through the novel without tending to identify with them (particularly with Valmont) would be a rigid moralist quite incapable of appreciating any fiction. Their opinion of themselves as intellectually superior is correct – although this opinion is also *dangerous* to them. *Les Liaisons dangereuses* is as much a critique of the hypocritical and heartless pre-Revolutionary aristocracy as a whole as it is a story of the schemes and downfall of two *immoralistes*. It is clear that Laclos, a supporter of the Revolution (at the beginning), detested and despised this society.

With the exception of Cécile and the Présidente, the other characters are by no means paradigms of virtue. It might even be claimed that the Marquise and her ally are merely carrying the exploitatory sexual mores of their time to a logical conclusion: they are therefore more honest and more intelligent. Laclos did not want to carry this point too far, but he was aware of it.

Finally it should be noted that Laclos wrote three essays on the subject of the education of women. The claim that his novel has an ending which implies 'that a revolution in the attitude of men is essential in the emancipation of women' is justified, as the reader of these essays will discover. He was an early feminist, for he saw that although women are 'equal' they are also subordinated. He also saw that this led some of them to tragic ruthlessness. How did the Marquise become the woman she is? She has herself been a victim of the marriage game: a gifted woman, she has been forced into a career of heartless intrigue by frustration. Her rejection of the prevailing mores, while unjustifiable, was caused by the fact that society allowed her no function adequate to her intellect. The famous Letter 81 is an early document in the history of the emancipation of women.

This by no means implies that the Marquise is a heroine, or that she is a good woman, but it is eloquent testimony to Laclos' insight into the feminine temperament, and offers clear indication of the presence of a theme that, in this most elegant and accomplished of all novels-in-letters, is often ignored.

BIBLIOGRAPHY

Translations: Richard Aldington, *Dangerous Acquaintances*, 1924; P. W. K. Stone, *Les Liaisons dangereuses*, 1961.

Text: in *Oeuvres complètes*, 1943.

Criticism: D. Thelander, *Laclos and the Epistolary Novel*, 1963; L. Versini, *Laclos et la tradition*, 1968.

Benjamin Constant
(de Rebecque)

Benjamin Constant was born in 1767 in Lausanne, of a Swiss family whose Calvinist forbears had been forced to leave France at the time of the Revocation of the Edict of Nantes (1685). He later took French citizenship. His childhood was, as he tells us in his *Journaux intimes* and in the so-called *Cahier rouge*, disturbed and unhappy. His father took him to England, where he stayed long enough to learn the language; he was educated at universities in Scotland and Germany. He held the post of Chamberlain at the Court of Brunswick while still a young man. At the age of twenty-two he married a German woman, the apparently repulsive Wilhelmina von Cramm: this ended in separation in 1793 and divorce two years later. His famous liaison with Mme de Staël lasted from 1794 until 1811, and was not even interrupted by his second marriage to the already twice divorced Du Tertre, née Hardenberg, in 1808.

During the 1790s he was mostly in France; but he went into temporary exile (with Mme de Staël) in 1803 when he offended Napoleon. He had been expelled from the Tribunate in the previous year. However, his later and notorious attack on Napoleon, in 1813, did not prevent him from taking office during the Hundred Days. In 1815 he went to London, where, in 1816, he published *Adolphe*, which he had written (almost certainly) in 1806 – as an episode for inclusion in a longer and never finished novel.

After his return to France in 1818 he became successful both as leader of the liberal opposition in the Chamber and as a brilliant political journalist. The year
before his death in 1830 he became President of the
Council. His *De La Religion considérée dans sa source, ses
formes et ses dévelopments* (1824–31) was a pioneering
work by a pioneering spirit. Advocating a spirit of eclectic tolerance, it regards religious feeling in men as inera-
dicable and functional – but takes a historicist and
relativist view of particular manifestations. It is a book
that has not had its due.

Constant is a supreme example of the man who is so
much a child of his age that he looks eccentric and 'outside' it. He possessed extraordinary powers of intellectual analysis. In him the dichotomy between head and
heart seems absolute; indeed, the predicament supplies
him with his subject matter in both his great novel and
in his more directly autobiographical writings. He was a
gambler, an arch-womanizer and an egotist; but he was
also an immensely hard thinker, hard worker and dedicated liberal politician.

He had a turbulent sex life. The only lover who
made him happy was his first, an older woman who seduced him when he was eighteen. The most important
women in his subsequent life were almost invariably
older than himself. Mme de Charrière, whose lover he
may or may not have been, seems to have reinforced his
natural introspection and cynically tinged scepticism.
Mme de Staël, with whom he maintained a correspondence even after their final break in 1811, tormented him
by exacerbating him both in person and in absence. But
it was chiefly his proneness to sophisticated self-analysis
that caused his unhappiness.

Adolphe

SUMMARY *Adolphe* is a short novel, what the French call

a *récit*. Its action extends over four years, and the author's selective genius and capacity for compression are alone sufficient to give it the status of a technical masterpiece. There is scarcely a *plot*, in the accepted sense; a *récit* is in any case strictly a *recital*, or account of events, with the added sense, perhaps, of 'musical solo' – though we classify it as a novel in practice, as it is nearer to this than to a short story. The essence of *Adolphe* lies in the depth of psychological self-analysis of the hero (the narration is in the first person) and in its pellucid presentation.

Adolphe, twenty-two years old, has just graduated with marked success from the University of Göttingen. He has had a mistress, who died before his eyes. His father, a member of the government of one of the many small kingdoms of which Germany was then constituted, is 'a man of the world' who feels that his son should educate himself through travel. He sends him to another small kingdom to learn court life. When there, he discovers a woman called Ellénore. She is the mistress of a Count; the mother of his two bastards, she is generally regarded as having lost her charms. Adolphe, bored, disturbed and confused, decides that he will seduce her. He imagines that he has fallen in love with her, but his account reveals that he is in no such state. He succeeds in his project, soon realizing that his feelings for her are of pity rather than love. But he cannot leave her, and overstays his time at the Court. Finally he does leave; unfortunately she quarrels with the Count whose mistress she is, and so has good reason to follow him back to his home town. He discovers that his father is arranging to have her expelled; once again confused, he decides to follow her.

They go to Bohemia, and afterwards to Warsaw. He finds the affair increasingly tiresome; but he is still unable, owing to his scruples, to end it. Eventually Ellénore finds out that, tired of her, he is making arrangements to abandon her. She dies broken hearted.

CRITICAL COMMENTARY *Adolphe* is one of the first great novels of psychological analysis. Prévost analysed, but never to this extent. The form of the novel harks back to Mme de Lafayette's *Princesse de Clèves* in that the protagonist is at odds with a corrupt society. But Constant is more specific: romanticism was setting in. His hero does not, like Des Grieux, tell his story to another, discreetly preserving a formal supposition that it might not be true; he tells it, quite candidly, to the reader.

It has been mistakenly stated that Adolphe is the victim of 'the romantic *mal du siècle*'. The term *mal du siècle* is used to characterize the romantic generation: the state of mind that suffers from boredom, lack of purpose and energy, too vague passionateness, excessive imagination, disenchantment, and amorality. But what Adolphe has to tell us (for he tells it to us in the first person) has absolutely nothing to do with this *malaise*: he is far too exact. Exactitude had no part in the *mal du siècle* mood, which is perhaps most fully exemplified in the poet/dramatists Alfred de Musset and Alfred de Vigny. This mood is certainly romantic, and in *Adolphe* Constant *is* describing a partially romantic state of mind; but the analysis supplied by the first-person narrative is positively anti-romantic: it anticipates, by many years, the reaction against romanticism.

The novel is frequently described as 'repulsive'. But if the criticism is justified, then it is equally justifiable to condemn as 'repulsive' the way many men think about women.

Furthermore, there is a tendency to confuse Adolphe with Constant. This is explicable because the novel has obvious autobiographical elements. At one time Constant expressed his intention of writing a novel about himself; and his later denials that Adolphe had anything to do with him were not taken seriously. The material he used was based on three of his own relationships: first was that with Mme de Charrière, and with the decisive influence she exercised on him; the second affair he had with a woman called Anna Lindsay, whom he stole from another man; the third and most important relationship was that with Mme de Staël. It is the consensus of opinion that in *Adolphe* Constant examines his affair with Mme de Staël within the framework of the one with Anna Lindsay. However, all fiction is ultimately autobiographical; we cannot necessarily accuse Constant of Adolphe's deficiencies, for he distances himself from his narrator. Adolphe at one point remarks *'Je ne veux pas ici me justifier'* ['I don't want to justify myself here']. Since he does to a certain extent justify himself – by implying that his deficiencies have been caused by his environment – there is a certain disingenuousness in his claim. But it is a misreading and a misunderstanding to consider Constant himself disingenuous. By all means, when we read the *Journeaux intimes*, which are candidly autobiographical, let us accuse Constant of any fault we wish. But the accusation in the case of *Adolphe* is simply irrelevant.

The timeless quality of *Adolphe* is partly achieved by the device of giving names – and even then no surnames – to only two of the characters, Adolphe and Ellénore. Either Constant gives the other characters no names at all (for example, the woman based on Mme de Charrière is simply *'une femme'*) or he gives them initials.

Although Adolphe is undoubtedly an inhabitant of the Europe of about 1800, he also achieves a kind of universality. The 'modernness' of *Adolphe* is due in large part to its examination of two predicaments which, notwithstanding social change, are still with us. These are: the tragic and paradoxical manner in which introspection distorts love, turning it into something that is uglier than it should be; and the difficulties encountered by the innocent and inexperienced spirit in a corrupt society.

Adolphe's father represents contemporary social practice. He is a casual libertine who does not object to using women, but who profoundly objects to the sort of scruples which might lead a man to feel that he should not desert them. It amuses him to say *'Cela leur fait si peu de mal, et à nous tant de plaisir'* ['That does them so little harm, and gives us so much pleasure'] In his eyes the rules of society are no more than *'formules banales que leurs parents sont convenus de leur répéter pour acquit de leur conscience, et les plaisanteries leur semblent renfermer la véritable secret de vie'* ['banal formulas that relations have agreed to rehearse to salve their own consciences, and jokes that seem to them to conceal the secret of life'].

The 'woman' – based on Mme de Charrière – represents the exact opposite of Adolphe's father. She is described, in very short compass, as a disappointed woman who had bowed to necessary conventions, had missed pleasure, and whose only consolation was mental analysis. It is in one sense this woman who destroys Adolphe's chances of happiness, and who leaves him in turn to destroy Ellénore. Actually Mme de Charrière died when Constant was thirty-eight; but Adolphe sees this woman die before his eyes at seventeen. It is not reading too much into the novel to suggest that Ellénore is a particularly perfect target for Adolphe because she is ten years older than himself. He cannot find anyone to love, and originally he pays court to her in imitation of a friend who has just successfully seduced a lady in waiting at the court of the principality he is visiting. He is agitated, he himself says, by *'une émotion vague'*. It is an older woman who has destroyed his illusions, who has taught him scepticism, who has reminded him that death ends everything, who has created in him these beliefs without putting anything in their place. An inevitable component of his youthful project to seduce Ellénore is therefore a desire to possess, experimentally, a surrogate of his original instructress: to revenge himself upon her by proxy, by making use of her. But as soon as he has succeeded, the situation changes: he finds himself in an even more confused state of mind.

The greatness and universitality of *Adolphe* have nowhere been better defined than by John Cruickshank. Having conceded the obvious, that in *Adolphe* Constant has been 'exploring the possibilities, and encountering the difficulties, of an *apologia pro vita sua*', and having discussed the element of moral ambiguity in Adolphe's cruel decision and subsequent ethical agonizings he points out that the book needs to be read 'primarily as a novel about human nature generally, rather than as an essay in self-disclosure.'

BIBLIOGRAPHY

Translations: J. M. Murray in *The Conquest of Death*, 1951; C. Wildman, 1959; L. W. Tancock, 1964.

Text: In A. Roulin (ed), *Oeuvres*, 1957; J. H. Bornecque (ed), 1963.

Criticism: H. Nicholson, *Benjamin Constant*, 1949; G. Poulet, *Benjamin Constant par lui-même*, 1968.

Stendhal (Henri Beyle)

Henri Beyle, who used the pseudonym 'Stendhal' for his writings from the time of his third published book (1817), was born at Grenoble in 1783. His father was a prosperous lawyer, with whom he was never in sympathy. One of the decisive events of his childhood was the death of his beloved mother, when he was only seven years old. He formed a particular loathing for his teacher, the Abbé Raillane: this accounts for much of his lifelong anti-clericalism. The chief positive influence on him in his youth was his grandfather, a Voltairean libertarian. At the age of sixteen Stendhal went to Paris with the intention of entering the École Polytechnique, but he could not be bothered to study for the entrance exam. Through the influence of his cousin Pierre Daru he obtained a commission in the dragoons; he served in Napoleon's second Italian campaign, though not as a combatant. In Italy he learned to enjoy opera, to fall in love and to fight duels. He fell in love with a lady 'not conspicuously chaste', but failed to get her into bed – for that he had to wait until eleven years later.

He was invalided out of the army in 1801, and until 1806 led a bohemian life in Paris and later in Marseilles, where he worked for an export firm. In 1806 he rejoined the government service, and served as a non-combatant officer in Germany, France, Italy, Austria and in the fatal Russian campaign (he saw Moscow burn, and was in the retreat). The fall of Napoleon broke his career, and from 1814 until 1821 he lived in Italy – the nation and culture he most loved – mostly in Milan. Eventually the Austrians, who believed him to be connected with the Carbonari movement and an 'irreligious, immoral and dangerous enemy of legitimacy', forced him to leave. For the next nine years, with little money, he lived a literary life in Paris, attaining more success in the *salons* than with his writings. After the advent of Louis Philippe in 1830 he was appointed consul, first at Trieste (Metternich refused to accept him) and then at Civitavecchia in the Papal States. He still made frequent visits to Paris, and died in the street there from a stroke, in 1842.

Stendhal began to write seriously after finally leaving the army: he wrote lives of Mozart, Haydn, Rossini, a history of Italian painting and a popular guide book on Rome (1829). His first important book, *De l'amour*, was published in 1822 and, being far ahead of its time, attracted no attention. Revealing autobiographical works such as *La Vie de Henri Brulard* and *Souvenirs d'égotisme* were posthumously published, as were his *Journal* and his *Correspondance* – the last three in the seventy-nine-volume *Oeuvres complètes* of 1927–37.

He came to the novel late, and met with little success – he himself prophesied, accurately, that he would not be taken up in earnest until fifty years after his death. Balzac, though critical, called him 'one of the superior men of our time'; his convolutedly ironic written reply is an interesting document. His first novel was *Armance* (1827); this was followed by *Le Rouge et le Noir* (1830) and the unfinished *Lucien Leuwen* (1834). Before *La Chartreuse de Parme* (1839) he wrote *Lamiel* (also unfinished). He also wrote a number of short stories, notably *L'Abbesse de Castro*.

Stendhal had a clumsy physique and a difficult temperament. He felt uncomfortable in society but, although his chief quest in life was sincere self-analysis, he knew how to play many parts. He was as often successful with women as he was unsuccessful. In his complexity, eclecticism and irony he anticipated – as he well knew – most of the problems that beset modern man.

Le Rouge et le Noir

SUMMARY Like almost all Stendhal's fiction, *Le Rouge et le Noir* has autobiographical elements. The central notion – of a debilitated upper class infiltrated by a young, energetic and intelligent member of the lower classes who, finding no outlet, is driven to criminal violence – had been in his mind for many years.

Two criminal cases gave him a basis for his plot. The earlier was a *cause célèbre* of 1827: an ambitious blacksmith's son called Antoine Berthet had become a tutor to a well-to-do family, the Michouds, in Stendhal's birthplace. He was dismissed, and entered two seminaries from both of which he was expelled; he then began to write wild letters to the wife of his former employer, with whom he had been in some way sexually involved. The husband, fearing scandal, found him another post – but he was sacked from this, too. After further threatening letters, which failed to frighten Mme Michoud, he entered the church where she was hearing mass and fired a shot at her, wounding her; he then shot himself in the jaw. Despite much public sympathy he was executed. A short time before this a young carpenter called Laffargue had shot his mistress twice and then slashed her throat; but although he was a murderer (which Berthet was not), he got only five years in gaol: his mistress was not an aristocrat. These cases, particularly the earlier, suggested the bare bones of *Le Rouge et le Noir*, although neither of the accused closely resembled the central character, Julien Sorel.

Le Rouge et le Noir traces Julien's high ambitions,

his frustrations, and his final acceptance of defeat. Its background is the France of 1825–30, when the abyss between the Liberals and the Royalists had already opened too wide to allow of any but a drastic solution. Though himself a liberal, an ex-Bonapartist and anti-clerical, Stendhal's historical accuracy has generally been judged to be fair. In fact, he distrusted the Liberal faction as much as he distrusted the Royalist – more immediately hateful though this must have seemed.

Julien Sorel, a complex mixture of sincerity, passion, deceit and recklessness, is the son of a brutal, wily carpenter. A bookworm, handsome and yet scarcely popular, he is determined to rise in the world. Napoleon having fallen, the army (the 'scarlet') is of no use to him; consequently he decides to become a priest (the 'black'). Because he is intelligent and personable, he obtains the post of tutor to the children of the pompous, heavy-handed, ultra-Royalist M de Rênal, but is dismissed when he is caught having a love affair with Mme de Rênal. He does not mind being poorly paid, but resents the fact that he has to work while people to whom he feels himself superior can idle away their time. He goes to a seminary for a short while, then secures the post of secretary to the Marquis de la Môle, whose arrogant, clever, bored and spoiled daughter Mathilde he seduces and gets with child.

Now success seems to be within his grasp: the Marquis is prepared to allow him to marry his daughter, and gives him a large sum of money, a title and an army commission. But his old mistress, Mme de Rênal, writes threatening to expose him as a seducer for money. He enters the church at which she is worshipping, and wounds her. He had intended to kill her. He is tried, and it seems as though he may be acquitted. But his statements in court are calculated to get him convicted. He is found guilty and condemned to death. He refuses to appeal. While in prison awaiting execution he is able to see himself as he really is and thus to find some measure of happiness. He is reconciled with Mme de Rênal. Mathilde buries his severed head herself; Madame de Rênal, who has threatened suicide if he will not appeal, dies only three days after his execution.

Some details of the political background require explanation. Louis XVIII's charter of 1814 tried to provide a constitution which would please both Royalists and Liberals. But the reactionary 'Ultra Royalists' wanted to return to the pre-Revolutionary situation, and the left-wing Liberals were Republican. Stendhal's attitude is pro-Liberal; but in *Le Rouge et le Noir* he is less concerned to defend the principles of the Liberals or to attack the 'Ultras' than he is to reveal the essential mediocrity of decision makers. His picture of the Church has been taken as unfair and biased; but it is a true one. Charles X's alliance of throne and altar was riddled with Jesuitry, repressive and corrupt. Stendhal was an avowed atheist, but many devout Catholics loathed the 'Ultras' as much as he did. His two decent priests are both Jansenists.

La Chartreuse de Parme

SUMMARY The exotic *La Chartreuse de Parme*, written a decade later than *Le Rouge et le Noir*, reflects Stendhal's love for Italy, whose culture he preferred to that of France. It is markedly less realistic than the earlier novel (in the sense that it is deliberately anachronistic), for the décor of the small state of Parma is in many ways deliberately sixteenth-century (it was originally planned as an historical novel set in this period), despite the contemporaneity of the action.

Fabrice de Dongo, product of a union between a French soldier and an Italian mother, leaves home to join Napoleon's army. He is sixteen. He finds himself on the field of Waterloo – through an accident – and kills

a Prussian officer. The description of the action at Waterloo – which he did not see, for he remained in Italy
throughout the Hundred Days – is one of Stendhal's most
famous passages. The vivacious but often abstracted
Fabrice's hopes are dashed by the fall of Napoleon. He
is placed on the index by the Austrians, and returns to
Parma, where he is able to solve his difficulties through
his aunt, the widowed Contessa Gina Pietranera, who
exercises a powerful influence over the liberal-hearted
conservative prime minister, Mosca della Rovere (who
is in love with her and confides diplomatic news to her).
Gina is a compellingly audacious woman, who loves
Fabrice and protects him from the jealousy of his older
(legitimate) brother and from the other dangers that
beset him. Mosca, himself married, arranges for her to
marry the old Duca Sanseverina-Taxis.

Fabrice studies theology in Naples, and an archbishop-
ric comes within his grasp. He is beginning to acquire
polish and self-confidence. But he accidentally kills a
rival who has tried to disfigure him and, after fleeing,
is caught and sentenced to twenty years in prison in
Milan. This is the result of rivalry between Gina and the
machiavellian Prince of Parma, who wishes to supplant
Mosca in her affections.

Like Julien, Fabrice finds solace in his imprisonment
in a citadel. He has long discussions with Clélia, daughter
of the governor Conti, who is his gaoler; they fall in love.
The Prince, Conti and the liberal (conservative at heart)
Fiscal-General Rassi all try to have him poisoned. But
with Clélia's connivance and under the guidance of Gina,
he escapes.

Gina plans to have the Prince assassinated – and he
does eventually die from poison. There is a revolt,
crushed by Mosca. Gina is bitterly disappointed when
she discovers that Fabrice loves Clélia; later she removes
the obstacles to the latter's marriage to a Marchese.

Fabrice, certain that his sentence will be quashed by

the new young Prince, returns voluntarily to the citadel. Gina is obliged to prostitute herself to the young Prince in order to obtain the pardon. He cheats her nevertheless; but Fabrice is pardoned, and becomes Archbishop of Parma. He is in a condition of 'elegaic resignation', goes into retreat, and becomes more pious. He meets Gina, who torments him by describing the ceremonies which attended Clélia's wedding to the Marchese Crescenzi. She and Mosca, now both widowed, marry. She dies soon after Fabrice, and at the end Mosca is left as the successful administrator of Parma.

Clélia had vowed that if Fabrice's escape from the citadel were successful she would never see him again. But the two have a three-year idyll – passed over in one sentence by Stendhal – during which she receives him in the dark. A son, Sandrino, is born – only nominally the Marchese's. The idyll is broken when Fabrice persuades Clélia to let him have charge of the boy, who is given out as dead and then removed to a secret place. Here he actually does die, and Clélia, broken hearted, soon follows him (she dies in Fabrice's arms). Fabrice resigns his office and enters a Carthusian monastery – the Charterhouse – where he too dies within a year. Gina had entertained every day at her magnificent palace in Austrian territory – and we are told that Fabrice 'never missed a day' there.

Stendhal was forced to cut drastically the last part of *La Chartreuse* by his publisher, which accounts for the sudden acceleration of the narrative. The loss is regrettable; but it has been suggested that this acceleration, even though forced on the author, confers on the final events 'something of the fascination of a phantasmagoria'. If this is the case – and it seems so to many readers – then it is witness to Stendhal's skill in turning a barbarism into an artistic triumph.

CRITICAL COMMENTARY Stendhal was unique – so much so

as to be unsuccessful in his time – in the extent to which he succeeded in infusing the rational spirit of the Enlightenment with the new romanticism. Romanticism is a notoriously difficult, although indispensable, concept; we understand it the better for studying Stendhal. His early reaction – before going to Paris – to the stuffiness and rigidity of his motherless environment was to turn to Voltaire, to logic, to the hardness of a rational approach and, in particular, to mathematics. His character (like Julien Sorel's) was of extraordinary complexity: he was (initially) violently ambitious, self-questioning, always dazzled by the personality of Napoleon and also by Parisian *salon* life. It was in this *salon* life, in the 1820s, that he enjoyed his only sustained public success – but although he only partly trusted it, he could never wholly dismiss it. He was impulsively passionate and romantic, yet afraid of women; he was at the same time profoundly self-analytical. His *superior being*, which goes some way to anticipating Nietzsche's widely misunderstood notion of the 'superman' (better rendered in English, because of its many popular associations, as *overman*), is by no means a ruthless *parvenu*. He is a man who can eventually see himself not only as he actually is but also as he is placed in society – though without sacrificing the unique qualities of his personality. The superior being is a libertarian, a freethinker, a rebel who resists all attempts to restrict his freedom; but he must also be a strict and truthful self-observer. He is one of the 'happy few' who can ignore the dictates of a *conscience* which is in fact a *superego* corrupted by the conventional and false mores of his society. The heroes of both Stendhal's masterpieces are imaginative explorations of this concept, which had been worked out in earlier writings.

Although there is much of the comic in his work, Stendhal is ultimately a tragic writer because Julien and Fabrice, romantic and yet rigorously accurate objective

correlatives for himself, find themselves unhappy except when they have become totally disillusioned or temporarily defeated by life. He was among the first of
authors to explore the themes of alienation, taken up by
Marx and subsequently other sociologists, and of the
true nature of perception. He understood, too early for
the good of his reputation within his own lifetime, that
the presence of an observer in a field – in this case that of
a writer observing his own passage through life – changes
that field: both his heroes tend to treat their environments as hostile, and learn too late that their own beings
have changed their lives.

Stendhal also realized what his predecessors could only
tentatively explore: that art and life, while inextricably
connected, are two different things; that a novel can
never be the same as the complete history of a personality
in its passage from life to death, that it was already too
late to *hold a mirror* to an artificially idealized nature.
Balzac possessed certain of the same insights, but was
more widely read because his techniques were familiar,
and because what a post-Stendhalian age calls artistic
integrity was not natural to him.

Le Rouge et le Noir was unpopular for excellent
reasons. Stendhal's 'mirror' was a truthful one, as he
asserted. Its depiction of society is highly critical. The
emphasis on individuality – as a phenomenon, let alone
a moral necessity – challenged his audience's complacent
sense of what they believed to be their unchangeable
values. Furthermore, Stendhal modified the Enlightenment sense of happiness through the exercise of reason
(in which only one side of him believed) by melancholy
and a proto-Freudian sense of erotic unfulfillability (a
famous passage in *La Vie de Henri Brulard* gives a
simple and straightforward account of what was later to
be called the 'Oedipus Complex'). His continuous self-
analysis is, as his plots reveal, an impossible project. The
future, he believed, would be different – and into this

future he rightly prophesied that his works would fit. *'Quelles seront les idées de cet ami en 1880?'* ['How will they be thinking in 1880?'] he asked in *La Vie de Henri Brulard, 'Combien différentes des nôtres!'* ['How differently from ourselves!']

Stendhal was so decidedly a proto-realist that it actually took the establishment of realism – by Flaubert – to allow him to be understood. He was among the first of novelists clear-headedly to set out to depict his characters within their social context, and to avoid idealization. But he employed a highly selective technique. In part a romantic, he destroyed his romanticism by an analytical psychological realism. He did not wish to dispense with the author's presence in the novel, but he did wish to do away with the *omniscient narrator*. Above all, social facts, which he portrays with brilliant accuracy, were under no circumstances to be manipulated in the interests of the reader's susceptibilities.

At the heart of both his masterpieces lie two painful ironies, the latter of which may be said to have anticipated the more histrionic and religious-minded Dostoievsky. First, human evil is the result of human potentiality for what existentialists call *authenticity*, the capacity to choose one's own existence, to be true to oneself (as notably explored in the novels of Sartre); thus Julien shoots Mme de Rênal more because he is a susceptible romantic, sent into a state of temporary derangement, than because she threatens his ambitions. Secondly, Stendhal sees clearly – and here he anticipates Dostoievsky – the painful paradox that evil must be perpetuated, harm done, to attain self-understanding, authenticity and peace of mind.

Beylisme, an essentially existentialist concept which might be described as a cult of egoistic energy, is a dangerous doctrine. But *beylisme* is not always properly understood. To dismiss Stendhal by asserting that his 'heroic vision of ruthless revolutionary action ... indicates little more than the disguised yearning for power in one who professed to scorn power', as one critic does, is little short of absurd. The true *beyliste* is an anti-hero; and there is no evidence in Stendhal's texts that he regards his anti-heroes as actually achieving the status of 'supreme beings'. If Julien stands above most of the other characters in *Le Rouge et le Noir* then it is not because he shoots at Mme de Rênal but because he repents of having behaved as he has on his own – and not on the world's false – terms. Fabrice is certainly no conventional hero. Even in resigning his position and undergoing privations he is making no sacrifices: he is following the dictates of his own nature. His egoism looks forward to certain aspects of that advocated by Max Stirner only three years after Stendhal's death – and only six after the publication of *La Chartreuse de Parme*. This touches on a pulse of feeling, both anarchist and right-wing-totalitarian, which can only be ignored by accepting the genteel prescription: never think dangerously. We may deplore it, or part of it, but we must acknowledge it within ourselves. To imply that the egoistic Fabrice is identical with Beyle is to fall into an all too familiar trap. Whatever Stendhal may have thought about his protagonists, both his great novels may more easily be read as tragedies illustrating the consequences of egoism than as glorifications of it. Once that is seen, his ironies may be properly appreciated.

In *Le Rouge et le Noir* the dialogue is continually and subtly revealing of character, demonstrating Stendhal's psychological detachment, and making nonsense of the claim, too frequently put forward, that he wrote *romans à thèse*. P. E. Charvet has shown how much we learn about Julien and his father from their conversation, at the beginning of Chapter 5, immediately following M de Rênal's proposition that the former should come to work for him. The father catches his son reading about Napoleon when he should have been watching the saw mill; he hits him and the book falls into the stream (a symbol of the fate of Julien's Bonapartist aspirations). He *assumes* that Julien has influenced Mme de Rênal; Julien replies that he has only seen her in church, whereupon his father accuses him of 'looking at' her (they both know what that means). Julien hypocritically states that he sees no one in church – except God. Sorel *père*, however, wants to rid himself of this bookworm son: as Charvet suggests, his aggression is calculated to make him do what he wants – to take the job.

In style the earlier novel is a model of restraint; avoiding romantic sensationalism in a romantic story, it enhances the passionate motivations of the characters. The omission of any description of Julien's execution, and the matter-of-fact way in which Mathilde's burying of his head is recorded, are both masterstrokes of delicacy. No wonder Stendhal's contemporaries were puzzled by this apparently casual treatment of such 'romantic' material.

The later book is sadder. It begins like a fairy story, then turns into a frightening account of tyranny, and finally becomes an elegy. Stendhal took for his material the life of Paul III, Alexander Farnese, rapist and murderer. But he transformed, modified and modulated this lurid tale – and brought it up to date. In both Gina – in some ways a more imposing character than her nephew – and Fabrice we are shown happiness, youth and beauty giving way to age and decay. Far from being the ferocious proto-revolutionary he is so often made out to be, Stendhal is a novelist of *rêverie* – as F. W. J. Hemmings has pointed out – whose 'purpose is just to bring a certain happiness to those few chosen spirits who resort to him'. Happiness in the Stendhalian sense is a realization of the 'inexpressible depth and richness of the individual life'. It is that happiness which only the discovery of truth by the non-materialistic imagination can bestow. He studied his own case, as all novelists must do either directly or obliquely, but illuminated that of tens of thousands of others.

BIBLIOGRAPHY

Translations: C. K. Scott-Moncrieff, *Scarlet and Black*, E, 1926; M. R. B. Shaw, *Scarlet and Black*, 1953; C. K. Scott-Moncrieff, *The Charterhouse of Parma*, 1926; L. Blair, *The Charterhouse of Parma*, 1960.

Texts: In H. Martineau (ed), *Oeuvres complètes*, 1927–37; H. Martineau (ed), *Oeuvres*, Pléiade, 1956.

Criticism: A. Billy, *Ce Cher Stendhal*, 1958; R. M. Adams, *Stendhal*, 1959; F. W. J. Hemmings, Stendhal, 1964. In R. Weingarten, *Writers and Revolution*, 1974, Weingarten is ferociously right-wing, but her criticism is intelligent and her case needs to be met. Hemmings gives the best introductory guide.

Alessandro Manzoni

Alessandro Manzoni, the leading Italian novelist of the nineteenth century, was born in Milan in 1785 and died there in 1873. *I promessi sposi* is his only novel; many regard it as second only, in the literature, to Dante's epic.

His parents were ill suited, and separated in the 1790s. He had received a good classical education by the age of sixteen, but was not satisfied with it. He came under the influence of various fiery liberals and exiles, amongst whom was the Venetian poet Ugo Foscolo, with whom he later fell out. When his mother's lover Carlo Imbonati (praised by Stendhal as a 'silent' 'genius') died in 1805, Manzoni went to Paris to join her. He remained there for five years. These were decisive to his development. Manzoni was always deeply attached to his mother; about his (putative – for he was probably the son of the poet Giovanni Verri) father he seems to have felt little. He wrote a poem (1806) on Imbonati's death, mainly in order to console his mother; and it was with her friends that he associated. These were mostly heirs of such encyclopaedists as Voltaire and Diderot; one of the chief of them was the historian Claude Fauriel, who was to remain Manzoni's intimate friend for over twenty years. In Paris Manzoni moved from confused agnosticism to Voltairian deism. Then, in 1808, he married the Swiss Henriette Blondel, a Calvinist who was already under the influence of the Jansenist group in Paris.

Alessandro followed her, as did his mother, into this form of Catholicism; as one of his biographers adds, 'though he repudiated rationalism, he never ceased clinging to reason.' Although Manzoni was not a true Jansenist, this 'heresy' was just the form of religion to appeal to a man who, terrified, swings from agnosticism to a kind of faith. Manzoni was always afraid of the rational elements in himself, always terrified of the consequences of doubt. As a man he was excessively timid, furtive and neurotic – he would adjust his clothing to the temperature by weighing it several times a day. On his death bed he wobbled about in his delirium: 'The bill's long and expensive. What will happen to me?' But he also confessed to doubts and to confusions. He even savagely denounced the Christian religion.

Jansenism, 'Catholic Calvinism', is pessimistic; but its practical advantage is that it helps to push a man into a psychologically viable faith. Men, it pronounces, cannot obey God's commandments without special grace; but the operation of grace is irresistible. So men are subject both to a kind of determinism and to God's anger. Jansenism mortifies vanity and turns free will into a scourge. Manzoni worried, as the Jansenist Pascal had worried, when he wrote: 'When we want to think about God, isn't there something that distracts us and tempts us to think of another thing? All this is evil and innate in us.' Later Manzoni became an increasingly dedicated admirer and friend of Antonio Rosmini-Serbati (1797–1855), a Catholic priest who was accused of Jansenism and who founded the Rosminians, the 'Fathers of Charity'. Rosmini's complicated and ambitious philosophical system set out to reconcile reason with faith. Manzoni was a deeply religious man tormented by doubts: a man of belief but not of enough faith to neutralize his sense of dread. Consistently opposed to all forms of mysticism, only in *I promessi sposi* did he

achieve an imaginative reconciliation of the opposites
that vied within him.

He worked on this novel from 1822 until 1827. In the
definitive reissue of 1840–42 it is mostly the language that
is revised, for by then Manzoni had become convinced of
the need for a standard language based on Tuscan – a
language anti-rhetorical, lucid and genuinely national.
His last forty years were largely taken up with the linguistic problem, to which he made the most important
contribution since Dante; but his writings on it are
mostly fragmentary (they have been admirably systematized by Barbara Reynolds in *The Linguistic Writings of
Alessandro Manzoni*, 1950).

His wife, after bearing him ten children, died in 1833.
In 1836 he married Teresa Stampa Borri. She died in
1861. He became an increasingly eminent figure, and was
visited by, among others, statesmen and writers such as
Cavour, Mazzini, Garibaldi and Balzac. Despite support
from some sections of the Church, the Papacy remained
cold towards him; at his death the Vatican had nothing
to say.

I promessi sposi

SUMMARY *I promessi sposi* is an historical novel dealing
with the period 1628–31. It is set in Milan and the surrounding district. The Duchy of Milan is ruled by the
Spaniards; the Venetian Republic lies immediately to its
east. The basis of the plot is one of the oldest in literature: the frustration of a love-marriage. But *I promessi
sposi* is not a love story, and is not meant to be. Manzoni,
though he used romantic techniques, was anti-romantic
in his refusal to bow down before *l'amore* (the concept
is an Italian illness) or before 'honour'. He claims to be
working from the 'scratched and faded manuscript' of a
seventeenth-century chronicler who, though his style has

some virtues, is 'commonplace and stiff'. He makes much use of this old device, particularly in his frequent asides to the effect that such and such an event or name or thought is 'not recorded'. He undertook painstaking historical research for the book.

Renzo Tramaglino, a silk weaver, and Lucia Mondella, of an unnamed village near Lecco (north of Milan) are to be married by the local priest, Don Abbondio, on the Sunday following 7 November 1628. It is a love match, and has the full blessing of Agnese, Lucia's mother.

A local grandee, Don Rodrigo, has become obsessed with Lucia, and is determined to prevent the match. He is in a position to do this. Manzoni portrays (with historical accuracy) a society in which the Spanish rulers issue severe edicts against such tyrants as Rodrigo, who are protected by gangsters called *bravoes* – the insignia of a bravo, besides his sinister swagger, was his quiff of hair – but take no steps to enforce them. Indeed, the Spanish are usually in secret alliance with the bravoes. There are grades of such tyrants and bullies: Rodrigo is not as powerful as the notorious 'Unnamed', the *Innominato*, whose vicious deeds have inspired terror in everyone. (Manzoni modelled his 'Unnamed' on the historical character Bernardino Visconti.) The *Innominato*'s impregnable castle lies some miles to the east of Lecco, just inside Venetian territory; he has the entire district in his grasp.

Don Abbondio is threatened by Rodrigo's bravoes and, being a weak man who only wants to continue with his pointless scriptural studies, refuses to marry the couple. Renzo, a straightforward young man, shrewd but not versed in the ways of the world, consults the local lawyer, nicknamed Azzecca-garbugli ('fastener of tangled threads' – called 'Quibble-Weaver' or 'Dr Quibbler' in translation). The lawyer at first shows him an edict which forbids priests to refuse to celebrate legitimate marriages – but then learns that Rodrigo is behind the affair, whereupon he sends Renzo packing.

After unsuccessfully trying to trick Don Abbondio into performing an irregular ceremony, Renzo, Lucia and Agnese are forced to flee. For Rodrigo has meanwhile sent a gang of bravoes led by Griso, the most accomplished criminal in his service, to kidnap Lucia; this mission fails, which further inflames him. His plans have been frustrated by Fra Cristofero, a Capuchin monk. The Capuchins enjoyed great respect, and even men such as Rodrigo had to be careful in dealings with them.

Once Cristofero himself had been a lordly young man called Lodovico, surrounded by a few bravoes; but in a street brawl he killed a man. In the course of this his faithful servant Cristofero had also died. He took sanctuary with the Capuchins, assumed his dead friend's name, and then joined the Capuchin Order: a holy, just and fearless man with a sad sense of the depravity of the world.

He manages to get Lucia and Agnese transported to a convent at Monza (a few miles north of Milan). But Renzo must continue to Milan. Cristofero gives him a letter to deliver to a monk at a Capuchin monastery there.

Now the long separation between the lovers begins. Renzo is unable to deliver his letter, as the monk is not in. He walks straight into a violent situation: the Milanese are rioting because of the lack of bread and have looted a bakery; they are now storming the house of the Commissioner of Supply. The latter is rescued by the Spanish Grand Chancellor (under the pretext that he is to be imprisoned); Renzo acts sensibly, helping to secure the safety of the Commissioner. But later he falls into the hands of a police spy, gets drunk, speechifies in a tavern about justice for the poor, and is arrested – as a much needed scapegoat. He escapes; but his name has become notorious: he helped start the riots, he is a dangerous agitator, he is to be hanged. After a long, difficult and exhausting journey he reaches his cousin Bortolo's village east of Bermago; here he is in Venetian territory. Bortolo welcomes him.

Meanwhile Don Rodrigo has, by intrigue, had Fra Cristofero sent off to Rimini. Furthermore he approaches the Unnamed. This sixty-year-old villain would lose his 'honour' if he failed to do good turns for his noble vassals (cf, the Mafia). He agrees to have Lucia kidnapped from the Convent of Monza. It so happens that he has an easy means of accomplishing this.

At this point Manzoni makes a digression of some length, to give the story of the Nun of Monza. Almost all those who advised him on the novel begged him to cut it out, but he wisely refused to listen to them. The influence of Diderot's *La Religieuse* is evident here; but the story is based mainly on historical fact, which may be found in the English translation of Mario Mazzucchelli's *The Nun of Monza* (1963).

At the Convent of Monza, Lucia and Agnese are put under the protection of the 'Signora' of Monza, 'a nun', explains a friar; 'but ... not the same as other nuns ... her father's the chief person in the town ... so she can order everyone about in the convent if she's a mind to ...'

This Gertrude (her historical original was a Suor Virginia de Leyva) is the daughter of a rich nobleman who decided that he would hand over all his wealth to his eldest son, and send the rest of his progeny to the cloister: 'his great preoccupation was to keep what there was all together in perpetuity ... so as to leave the family fortune intact for the eldest son, whose function it was ... to torture [his children] in the same way.' Gertrude had resisted, but to no avail. In attaining a privileged position she became corrupt. She became the mistress of a gangster, Egidio – and even connived at the murder of a nun who threatened to disclose the affair. (Manzoni was,

unhappily, persuaded to cut out the details of the seduction of Gertrude.) Now, at the time Lucia and Agnese are
put in her charge, this Egidio has for some time been an
outstandingly successful servant of the *Innominato*.
Through Gertrude's and his machinations Lucia is carried
off to the *Innominato*'s castle, in order to be handed over
to Rodrigo.

In her despair she vows to the Madonna to remain a
virgin if she will deliver her. This introduces a new
theme into the story: the solemn vow will impede happiness, if things turn out right. Agnese is returned to her
own village, where Renzo is eagerly sought after by the
government. Few of the villagers can believe the wild
stories that are circulating about him.

But the *Innominato*, already haunted by the terrible
misdeeds of his past, is deeply affected by Lucia and her
piteous plight. It is clear that Manzoni attached special
significance to the powers exercised by this innocent, naturally pious peasant girl; powers connected with her vir-
ginal sexuality. However, of even more importance is her
trust in God: should she give way to despair, she keeps
thinking, then she will become even more unfortunate.
Her attempts to understand the ways of providence, and
to believe correctly, are of a singular purity. It is her intervention in his life that is crucial to the direction which
the *Innominato* takes in his crisis: he determines to free
her – and he consults the saintly Cardinal Federigo Borromeo (an historical character), Archbishop of Milan,
who happens to be visiting the nearby village. To this
generous, merciful and understanding scholar he abases
himself; and to him he tells the story of Lucia. He further
confides his own spiritual anguish. The Cardinal orders
Don Abbondio to escort Lucia in a litter from the castle
to the village. The priest is frightened out of his wits,
feeling himself helplessly trapped between the powers of
the Church and those of the gangsters; but he does as he
is told. Don Abbondio, always presented with exquisite

understanding, is 'all too human': he wants a quiet life, but is ultimately irresponsible and selfish. He is the foil to Cristofero (and, at a higher level, Borromeo). But he is not a bad man.

Lucia and Agnese are lodged by a worthy tailor and his wife, and then taken back to their village, which Borromeo is visiting. A philanthropic woman, Donna Prassede, decides that she should take Lucia under her wing: how could she be truly good (ie, chaste) and be involved with a 'scapegallows' (Renzo)? This woman has benign intentions but, as Manzoni comments, 'To do good, one must know what it is ... we can only know this by means of our own passions ... which often do not amount to very much.' 'We have no positive knowledge' of Borromeo's opinion of Donna Prassede, but he agrees to her proposition because 'it was not his habit to undo things which did not concern him, in order to do them up better' (this is a supreme example of Manzoni's ironic subtlety, and an indication of one of the main themes of *I promessi sposi*). The Cardinal reproaches Don Abbondio, asking him just what his fear and love for his flock had inspired in him – and 'fell silent *as if* awaiting a reply' [my italics]. But Borromeo does not further reproach him; he merely suggests that they both offer their 'empty' hearts to God.

The *Innominato*, who has lost none of his old authority of manner, informs his entourage of his changed life, offers them his hospitality if they wish like himself to seek a new life, and sends Agnese a sum of money for Lucia's dowry – and an offer of help should she need it. Lucia goes with Donna Prassede to her Milan house.

Meanwhile Renzo disappears: the governor of Milan has made representations to the Venetian republic that the dangerous criminal Renzo Tramaglino is on its soil. But Bortolo, warned, sent Renzo off to a silk mill under the name of Antonio Rivolta, and cleverly spread a number of conflicting rumours about him.

Renzo, who can read print (with difficulty) but not handwriting, eventually finds a way of communicating with Agnese; finally he receives the news that Lucia wishes him to forget her. Renzo cannot understand – and Lucia, despite repeated prayer, cannot forget Renzo. Not even Donna Prassede can make her believe that Renzo is a criminal. After a comic and satirical passage on the astrologer and pseudo-scholar Don Ferrante, Donna Prassede's husband, Manzoni now passes on to historical events: the series of disasters which began to hit Milan soon after the bread riots. First major famine, then chaos in which even such privileged men as the bravoes were reduced to a part of the 'deplorable throng', then sickness, then – just as a good harvest might have improved the situation – the ravages through the Duchy of Milan of Wallenstein's plundering (and Lutheran) army. Throughout all this Cardinal Borromeo dispensed what charity he could.

The German army reaches the district of Lecco. Agnese decides to seek refuge in the castle of the *Innominato,* taking with her the grateful though perpetually grumbling Don Abbondio. They find their way safely and are welcomed by the *Innominato,* who has now become a kind of saint – though most of his ruffians have deserted him. The troops pass on and Agnese, Don Abbondio and his servant Perpetua return to the village – to find it devastated.

But now a new disaster reaches Milan: the plague. (The scandal of the tortures and executions of the 'annointers', wrongly supposed to have spread the disease by poisoning and sorcery, Manzoni treated in another work, which he appended to the revised version of the novel.) Both Don Rodrigo and Griso – the latter after trying to betray his master – catch the plague.

Meanwhile Renzo, safe because of the changed political situation, has returned to work for Bortolo. He too catches the rapidly spreading plague – but is one of the lucky ones, who recover. Soon he departs for his own village, avoiding Milan. He finds it devastated by plague, most of his friends dead; though Don Abbondio has survived. But Agnese has gone to Milan, and it was from her that he hoped for news of Lucia. He goes to Milan in search of her.

When he arrives he finds a devastated city. He narrowly escapes lynching when a hysterical woman accuses him of being an 'annointer'. There are piles of dead; many are dying; even nobles are purchasing their own supplies. He is terrified that Lucia has died. The city is dominated by the *monatti* – hardened, drunken men whose duty is to take away the dying. At length he encounters Fra Cristofero, who has been in Milan for three months helping at the hospital. He is dying of the disease. Renzo expresses to him his hatred of Don Rodrigo; but Cristofero shows him Rodrigo as he lies dying. He exhorts him to forgive and to pray for him. Renzo, affected by Cristofero's sincerity, finds himself impelled to do so.

At last he finds Lucia. She has recovered from the illness (Donna Prassede and her husband – who had learnedly pronounced that the plague did not exist – are dead;) but she remains agonizedly sworn to the vow she has made to the Madonna. Cristofero releases her from this vow. Later he dies. The couple return to their native village and are married by Don Abbondio. Rodrigo's successor, a Marquis, gives them financial help (the suggestion had come from Borromeo), and they are able to move, with Agnese, to Bortolo's village. (Gertrude is found out and is understood to be suffering in her penitence.) Manzoni's tale ends on a characteristic note. Renzo's life would not have been happy in this village: not all the villagers think Lucia – whose story is of course famous amongst them – is either beautiful or perfect. However, a silk mill near Bergamo is put up for sale; Bartolo and Renzo buy it. Lucia and her husband have many children; calling the first Maria in honour of Lucia's vow from which she was released by Fra Cristofero.

CRITICAL COMMENTARY Underlying all the virtues of Manzoni's *I promessi sposi* is the quality of its language. As the translator of the first good English version, Archibald Colquhoun, stated, no one 'can hope to reproduce the cadence, the subtlety, the terseness, of the original prose'. Some irony and humour are also inevitably lost. Nevertheless, much of this linguistic quality does come through. The translator can, for example, convey Manzoni's brilliant use of the colloquial (frowned upon by many conservative critics of his time). He can also convey the work's epic qualities.

The revised version of *I promessi sposi* was a triumphant success, which would not always be the case; unfortunately no comparison of the earlier and later versions exists in English. It is more suggestive, 'muted' (Bernard Wall) than the original; it has more *goro* – the Japanese term for that indefinable quality of what sounds right to a cultivated ear.

The quality of *I promessi sposi* is Shakespearean. Universally recognized as Italy's first great novel, *I promessi sposi* has naturally become the subject of much controversy. As Sergio Pacifici has written, Manzoni 'succeeded in turning what had been a much disparaged mode of expression into an art form capable of expressing the entire spectrum of human emotions'. No wonder critics confronted with this achievement have argued about both Manzoni and his novel: was he a 'paternalistic' supporter of an essentially conservative Risorgimento, or was he 'radical and progressive'? Or was he even perhaps a reactionary Roman Catholic propagandist, whose book deserved to be taken up by the Jesuits (as, curiously in view of his Jansenist connections and the Jansenists being the Jesuits' traditional enemies, it was)?

Manzoni's work was, as Pacifici has said, 'at once a product of a profound spiritual crisis and the reflection of a growing political awareness'. Of his spiritual crisis some details have already been given. His political awareness became more subtle; taking a prominent position in *I promessi sposi* – and in the positive achievements of building a national language which is part of it. Manzoni believed in the Risorgimento – and it could be argued that his contribution to the unification of Italy has been greater than that of any politician. In so far as the concept of romanticism can be acceptably defined, Manzoni became the leader of the Italian romantic movement, which coincided, and by no accident, with what is generally acknowledged to be the first historical stage of the Risorgimento, the 'period of moral and intellectual preparation' covering the years 1815–47. Manzoni held that 'literature ... should have as its purpose the useful, its subject the true, and its means the interesting', and that the writer might violate rules if impelled to do so by his personal judgement.

Marxist critics (for example Antonio Gramsci) attacked Manzoni's novel for implying that the only solution for poor folk was to resign themselves to fate and to practise Christian virtue and forgiveness. But it does not imply anything more than that immediate political action is no solution. Its 'message' is not crude, as its leftist critics have made out. Mazzini was nearer the truth when he wrote: 'Manzoni's aim, his belief, his perennial tendency, was the redemption of the people. [His followers show that they have] the high intention ... to destroy the power usurped by the aristocratic principle.'

Actually Manzoni, although he admired certain politicians at certain times and supported them because he believed that they could achieve unification, distrusted politics. His novel is not an allegory of the nineteenth-century situation; but he chose to issue it at a time when neither Italy's foreign rulers, nor most Italian politicians, nor the Vatican, had the interests of the Italian people at heart. And he is not kind, in *I promessi sposi*, to the Spaniards, to the colonialists' Italian servants, or to the vast majority of Church potentates. By going back two hundred years he washed his hands of it all – in favour, however, not of artistic disinterestedness but of eternal human values. He was no optimist; but *I promessi sposi* is an heroic attempt to demonstrate, against his own deepest convictions, that the divine order really does work in reality. It is thus a profoundly ambivalent work – not least because Manzoni avoided sentimentality or manipulation. History, public and private, shows that such saintly characters as Cristofero and Borromeo do exist, that such vipers as the *Innominato* can become truly repentant, that such humble characters as Lucia and Renzo can achieve their desires. Manzoni convinces us of the reality of this particular story. It is meticulous and exact, and it spares the reader no details of the hideousness and evil of some men, or of squalor and disease; in this aspect it is a true precursor of Verga's *verismo*.

Manzoni was yet another nineteenth-century novelist who saw that art was a form of illusion. This is perfectly clear from the deliberate gaps in his narrative. He puts these 'uncertainties' to ironic use. Unlike Walter Scott, who obviously influenced him, he looked inside as well as outside history; he was an infinitely subtler and deeper novelist. The shrewdness of his use of the device of re-telling 'history' alone makes this clear.

Exact though Manzoni is in his historical detail, we should not interpret him as taking a *political* attitude. His is a human attitude. He shows us a corrupt and murderous bureaucracy; a country maladministered by self-interested foreigners; the exploitation of poor people by tyrants; the impact of natural disaster. He shows both the naturally virtuous and those who cannot measure up to their own ideals. His psychological insight, probably his greatest strength of all, reveals motivation in a brilliant light. And all is fused together by a serene lyricism, an enchanted acceptance of life's manifestations. This lyricism is – in the most general sense – religious in tone, pervading every episode. Description of landscape is used, seemingly effortlessly, to express states of mind. The novel is within the range of the understanding of all who have lived and suffered. The question of what kind of Christianity Manzoni believed in is left open. At the very end Renzo tells Lucia that he has learned not to be a fool and to keep himself out of trouble. Lucia finds something 'missing' in this: had she not resigned herself to God? Yet, she adds, she too found troubles – in loving Renzo and promising herself to him. Manzoni adds that finally the couple agreed that some bring troubles upon themselves, while others do not and yet find them: 'when they come – whether by our own fault or not – confidence in God can lighten them and turn them to our own improvement. This conclusion, though it was reached by poor people, has seemed so just ... that we have thought of putting it down here, as the juice of the whole tale.' But did Manzoni, the supreme ironist, quite mean that it was 'the juice of the whole tale'? As Colquhoun points out, while 'Manzoni insisted on the value of kindliness and simplicity ... even amid war, foreign occupation, famine and the plague, he also hinted ... with acid irony that these scourges came largely, not from Providence, but from the folly of men.' And Colquhoun (a Marxist) sees in the book a dualism between the religion in which 'reposes all hopes of a just and happy life in the next world' and the 'rationalism which satirically, acidly, hints that the irresponsibility of a limited class not only aggravates injustice, war, famine, and plague, but in essence causes them'.

Manzoni is great enough to have been influenced by the greatest writers: Shakespeare (from whom he learned how to handle his crowd scenes), Cervantes, Goethe (his admirer), Dante, Homer. His use of irony has hardly been equalled since – irony is seldom a chief feature of Italian writing. He even anticipated certain modernist techniques: shifts into the present continuous, passages which take us into the minds of the characters in the manner practised by exponents of *stream of consciousness*. *I promessi sposi* is one of the greatest books ever to come from a human brain. It is not only a book, it is a consolation for humanity.' The verdict, given before he met Manzoni (1868), is that of Manzoni's most famous artistic contemporary, Giuseppe Verdi, whose majestic *Requiem* is for Manzoni's soul.

BIBLIOGRAPHY
Translations: A. Colquhoun, *The Betrothed*, 1951; B. Penman, *The Betrothed*, 1972. The second is preferable, though it would not be so in the absence of the first.

Text: L. Russo, 1967.

Criticism: A. Momigliano, *Alessandro Manzoni*, 1929 – in Italian; B. Wall, *Alessandro Manzoni*, 1954; A. Colquhoun, *Alessandro Manzoni*, 1954.

Mikhail Lermontov

Mikhail Lermontov was born in Moscow in 1814. His father was an impoverished nobleman of Scottish descent; his mother was less aristocratic but richer. When she died in 1817 Lermontov was put into the care of his maternal grandmother, who devoted herself to him until his death. As an adolescent he was lonely and embittered; his early poems are full of grief and a sense of frustrated hopes. He visited the Caucasus, and in its Asian landscape discovered a melancholy joy which was to remain with him for the rest of his short life. He was potentially a brilliant student, but his difficult personality, incapacity to adjust to urban manners, and contempt for his teachers put an end to his studies at Moscow University. So he became an officer in the Lifeguard Hussars (1834).

All this time he had been writing poetry; now he turned to prose and drama, producing two unfinished novels and a remarkable play, *Maskarad* [*Masquerade*], 1836, about a wife-murderer. When Pushkin was killed in a duel in 1837 he wrote an inflammatory poem, widely circulated, accusing Russian society of murdering the poet; for this he was sent to an infantry regiment in the Caucasus, which he enjoyed. He found the fighting a release from the tensions of his life (his relationship with women had been a further cause of discontent); he received recommendations for gallantry, but the Tsar would not ratify these. His grandmother soon arranged for him to return to Moscow. Here, though now famous, he was deeply unhappy. His smile was not reflected in his eyes, Turgenev noted. He could be genial; but his behaviour was wild and scandalous – one of his habits was to pursue and sarcastically to ridicule people selected at random. He struck a deliberately Byronic pose – although the influence of Byron upon him has been exaggerated.

After the appearance of *A Hero of Our Time* (in volume form) he published the separate stories in 1839–40; the complete novel, with the Foreword, appeared in 1841, when he was also involved in a duel with a Frenchman, and was once again sent off to the Caucasus. On his way he stopped at Pyatigorsk, where he seems to have deliberately gambled with death. He provoked a fellow officer Martynov, into challenging him to a duel; on the evening of 15 July 1841 he was killed instantly. (For the definitive account of this, see Laurence Kelly's excellent biography, *Lermontov: Tragedy in the Caucasus*, 1977.)

Geroi Nashego Vremeni
[A Hero of Our Time]

SUMMARY *A Hero of Our Time*, a title of debatable irony, is a highly experimental novel. There are three narrators: an *author* who is taking travel notes as he journeys northwards from Tiflis, the 'junior captain' (*shtabs*) Maxim Maximych, and the *hero* himself, Pechorin. There are five episodes: 'Bela', told by Maxim but presented to us through the traveller's view of the teller; 'Maxim Maximych', told by the traveller, and bringing together both Pechorin and Maxim in the present, and 'Taman', 'Princess Mary' and 'The Fatalist', which form part of Pechorin's journal – for, the author-traveller now tells us, Pechorin has died on his return from Persia, his destination when we met him in the second episode. The three stories told by Pechorin are incidents from his own life; but the exact chronology, and that of 'Bela', is left unclear. We may fairly take the traveller to be Lermontov as detached narrator, and Pechorin as a projection of himself (and one, moreover, allowed to speak for himself).

The novel revolves around the personality of Pechorin. Yet, apart from our short meeting with him and the four accounts of incidents in which he has been involved, his life as a whole remains a mystery.

The narrator actually possesses 'his whole life-story' in a 'thick notebook': 'there are a number of important reasons why I cannot undertake its publication, though some day this too will be presented.' Thus Lermontov implicitly questions the notion of giving the 'history' of a life: his intention is to reveal the essence of a character.

A Hero for Our Time is not merely a collection of stories: it has a unity. As Belinsky remarked, it is 'several pictures in one frame'.

'Bela' tells, in Maxim's honest but unsophisticated and puzzled terms, of how Pechorin, a young officer under Maxim's command, becomes attracted by the young daughter of a Circassian chief. He bribes her brother to aid him to kidnap the girl by turning a blind eye to the brother's theft of a splendid horse owned by the bandit Kazbich. Bela will have nothing to do with him until he promises to free her. He tells her: 'I don't suppose it will be long before I find death ... forgive me.' This has the desired effect: she confesses her love. But a few months later, while Pechorin and Maxim are out hunting, she leaves the fort, where she was safe, and is stabbed by Kazbich – who has already murdered her father – in revenge for the loss of his horse. Pechorin shows concern for her while she is dying, and even turns 'white as a sheet' when she dies. Then he seems to change his attitude: he laughs in a way that 'sent cold shivers down [Maxim's] spine'. He becomes thin and silent and is 'out of sorts'. Unlike the reader, Maxim cannot see that this coldness is simply a fashionable Byronic pose. Eventually Pechorin is posted to another regiment. The garrulous Maxim has lost touch with him since.

The traveller unexpectedly runs into Maxim again, whom he finds a bore. They hear that Pechorin has arrived; Maxim is excited at the prospect of meeting him again. Our narrator describes him ('However, these are personal views ... I have no wish to force them on other people' – one of many examples of Lermontov's early awareness of the illusory nature of conventional realism, and of his relativistic attitude): he is of average height, strong, 'proof against the turmoil of passions and the dissoluteness of city life'; he is also nervously exhausted; his eyes 'never laughed when he laughed' (as Turgenev remarked of Lermontov himself); the brilliance of his eyes is 'like the cold dazzling brilliance of smooth steel'.

Pechorin is formal but offhand with Maxim. He says he is bored. He pales when reminded of Bela. He then makes off hurriedly, displaying no interest in the papers he has deposited with Maxim years before – which our narrator easily obtains: the 'good, kindly' Maxim, because 'Pechorin had offered his hand when Maxim had wanted to embrace him' has become 'crotchety' and indifferent.

The rest is taken up with the three stories from Pechorin's journal, which the narrator *says* he is convinced are 'sincere'. (We must remember that he alone has access to Pechorin's whole life story.) Some, he remarks, might like to know his own opinion of Pechorin. His answer is in the title of the book – ' "Malicious irony" they'll retort. I don't know.'

'Taman' is brief. While Pechorin is waiting at one of the 'foulest' ports in Russia he encounters, partly owing to his innate curiosity, a group of smugglers amongst whom is a blind boy. They think Pechorin will inform on them; one of them, a watersprite of a girl, makes love to him and lures him into a boat, where she tries to drown him. She fails, and the 'honest smugglers' flee, leaving the blind boy behind them sobbing on the shore.

'Princess Mary' is the longest story and apparently reveals more of Pechorin than the others. It takes place in Pyatigorsk, near to where Lermontov himself was to die. Pechorin is on leave. He encounters his friend Dr Werner, his former mistress Vera (now married, but dying of consumption and still eager for him), a brash cadet, Grushnitsky, by whose side he has fought, and Princess Mary Ligovskoy, sought after by all the military. Grushnitsky desires her but she ignores him. Pechorin resumes his liaison with Vera at the only safe place: the Ligovskoy's house. Meanwhile he tries to make himself as obnoxious as possible to Mary, since she is popular with the others. But he saves her from humiliation at the hands of a crude dragoon captain who thinks her too high handed. Mary begins to fall in love with Pechorin, and Grushnitsky comes to look upon him as his rival; he is determined to have revenge. First he plans to dishonour Pechorin by provoking him to a duel in which the pistols will be unloaded – the dragoon captain imagines that Pechorin will 'funk it'. Pechorin overhears the plan. Then, leaving Vera's room at the Ligovskoy's at night, he is set upon by the dragoon and Grushnitsky, who imagines that he has been seeing Mary. He escapes them. Grushnitsky names him as the Princess' nocturnal visitor, so that he is forced to challenge him to a duel. Werner is able to warn him that now only his own pistol will be unloaded. The resourceful Pechorin suggests the duel be staged on a mountain ledge: whoever dies will fall as to an 'accidental' death. The antagonists meet. Pechorin wants to settle the affair amicably; Grushnitsky refuses. But then the latter has a pang of conscience: how can he kill an unarmed man? He wins first shot, but fires wildly, grazing Pechorin's knee. Now Pechorin casually points out that someone has 'accidentally' forgotten to load his pistol. The dragoon captain, Grushnitsky's second, can do nothing. Pechorin's pistol is loaded. He asks Grushnitsky to retract, but the latter cries 'Shoot! ... I despise myself and hate you.' Pechorin fires and Grushnitsky, hit, falls to his death.

When Pechorin returns he finds that Vera's husband has discovered their affair and taken her away. He chases her: 'Now that I might lose her forever Vera was dearer to me than anything.' His horse gives way beneath him. He goes back to Pyatigorsk to discover that Mary's mother will permit her to marry him. He cruelly tells Mary that he has merely been making fun of her, even though in reality he has been deeply involved with her. 'Can I be in love?' he has asked himself. Mary is devastated. Knowing that in 'another minute ... I'd have fallen at her feet' Pechorin excuses himself as unlovable, mean and despicable, and quickly leaves.

'The Fatalist', like 'Taman', is brief. Pechorin is in a Cossack village. At an inn a conversation has started on the subject of the 'Muslim belief that a man's destiny is written in heaven'. A Serbian lieutenant, Vulich, an honourable gambler whose losses spur him on to further wagers, joins the conversation. He proposes a bet: settle the argument by trying it out on the company! The others think him crazy, but Pechorin bets twenty gold pieces that there is no such thing as predestination. Vulich gets his pistol and primes it. He is calm, but Pechorin notes 'the mark of death on his pale face'. Although he has made the bet against predestination, he tells Vulich that he will die that day. Vulich replies that he might, or might not. He puts the muzzle of the pistol to his forehead; it misfires. When aimed at the wall it makes a hole in it. Pechorin pays up. The party retire. But Pechorin is awakened: a drunken Cossack has murdered Vulich. Pechorin daringly captures the killer alive, thus taking the same risk that Vulich has taken. 'I prefer to doubt everything,' is his afterthought. Later he tells Maxim

Maximych about it. At first Maxim casts doubts on the pistol. Then he adds: 'He [Vulich] should have known better than to talk to drunks after dark. Still, I suppose that's how he was meant to die.' The novel ends: 'That's all I could get out of him [Maxim] – he's not at all keen on metaphysical discussions.'

CRITICAL COMMENTARY Although Pushkin's verse novel *Evgeny Onegin* [*Eugene Onegin*, final version 1833] is as much poem as novel, and therefore outside the scope of this book, it must be discussed, along with Alexander Pushkin (1799–1837) and the contemporary political situation in Russia if *A Hero of Our Time* is to be properly understood. This will also serve as an introduction to the later Russian novels included in this book.

The Decembrist Conspiracy of 1825, designed to overthrow Tsar Nicholas I, had failed. It was badly executed, and its participants were divided amongst themselves: some were radical-conservative noblemen, others liberals or republicans, others desperados, still others mere opportunists; while some wanted the emancipation of the serfs, others wanted to preserve the social order. The result was a repressive rule (1825–55) by a wooden, fairly stupid monarch who hated reform and education and whose main object was to strengthen the autocracy. His stifling bureaucracy's chief weapon, like that of their Bolshevist successors, was the secret police. Men of decency were impotent and in despair. Nicholas's predecessor Alexander had been no reformist, and his father Paul (assassinated 1801) had been half mad; but now the situation was grimmer than ever. Yet Nicholas I, because he and his censors suspected all Westernization and all knowledge ('free thought' – which included musical notation!), was largely responsible for the pre-eminence which the Russian novel had achieved by the 1860s. Pushkin and Lermontov had precursors (notably Nikolai Karamzin, 1766–1826, Vasily Narezhny, 1780–1826, and, in the drama, Alexander Griboyedov, 1795–1829), but the process really began with them – in prose fiction, mainly with Lermontov.

In Pushkin's *Onegin* is the first vestige of the *superfluous man* of nineteenth-century Russian fiction. The term was actually first used by Turgenev in the story *Dnevnik lishnego cheoveka* [*Diary of a Superfluous Man*], 1850. This type varied greatly, but all superfluous men have one common characteristic: they are intelligent, and they are doomed to waste their lives. Bazarov of *Fathers and Sons* is typical. The *superfluous man* may lack true purpose, or he may be a strong man whose true purpose is somehow frustrated by his social or political persuasions. He is neurotic, often dandyish and deliberately irresponsible, comic, and sometimes criminal. The term is vague, implying criticism of Russian society and of the 'superfluous hero' himself; but it meant a great deal in Russian criticism after 1850.

Pushkin – gambler, womanizer and liberal without ideology – became disenchanted with the rule of Alexander I, which turned increasingly despotic after Napoleon's failure to conquer Russia. He was saved from exile or worse only because Nicholas I took him under his wing (in other words, became his censor). He felt 'superfluous' in this role and, when he was killed in a duel to defend his worthless wife's honour, intellectuals were devastated. He became the inspirer of Lermontov, Gogol and Goncharov – indeed, of the whole of Russian nineteenth-century literature. At the end of *Eugene Onegin* the hero feels 'superfluous' to society and to himself; Lermontov, a very different kind of man from Pushkin, further explored this theme.

As a poet Lermontov was, in the words of one of his own poems ('The First of January'), 'the guest who has come to the feast uninvited'. His lyricism rises from nostalgia for a rural childhood, and the beauty of nature (particularly the landscape of Asian Russia). Exiled (in 'The First of January') from paradise, he longs to 'disturb' the 'human crowd' – to throw insolent, furious poetry into their faces. Life is a 'hollow and stupid farce'. He loves Russia, but his reason cannot discover why. He dreams of himself wounded and dying in a Daghestan gorge, and in this dream he sees a young woman at a gay party, herself dreaming – of a familiar figure lying dead in a gorge. What kind of man could he be, he asks, to *feel* even as he rejects life as a farce?

A Hero of Our Time tries to answer this question. The novel is not what it seems to be: while Lermontov brings Pechorin closer and closer, so must the reader increasingly suspect Pechorin's own untruthfulness. Lermontov himself chose to be enigmatic, and to leave no diary. But is Pechorin's diary true? Or is it fiction? Stories in the form of a 'journal' casually left with a simple comrade? After all, what is Lermontov himself doing? Posing, undoubtedly, as a traveller, as Maxim, as Pechorin the diarist. 'Taman' is almost certainly an embellishment of one of Lermontov's own experiences. 'The Fatalist' is a statement of Pechorin's attitude to destiny, and foreshadows his own creator's end (Lermontov might after all have killed Martynov). In 'Princess Mary', however, Pechorin seems to reveal himself; whether he is lying or not (a man writing a novel, in a novel), whether he is always posing or not, the tale itself demonstrates his main obsession: revenge.

Revenge figured in 'Bela', in 'Taman' (the girl's attempt to drown him); and in 'Princess Mary' it figures again. The revenge seems to be the attempted one of Grushnitsky. But Pechorin only makes himself appear blameless. As Richard Freeborn points out in his penetrating analysis, 'Grushnitsky ... is the catalyst for Pechorin's philosophy. He is Pechorin's *alter ego* in several senses': his disillusionment is a 'parody of Pechorin's crippling despair', he wants to produce an effect, he causes the intrigue by which Pechorin succeeds in murdering him, he resembles all the naïve 'ordinariness' and weakness which Pechorin wishes to avoid. Pechorin, half sincere and half posing, tells Mary that he is divided, a 'moral cripple'; one part of his soul he has murdered, cut out and thrown away. The astute reader will note that in revenge for this he murders both Mary's innocence and Grushnitsky. A man of his sophistication could easily have arranged matters otherwise. Grushnitsky may be dishonourable, brash, unsubtle – but he is able to express his feelings spontaneously. For all his fine bearing, what is Pechorin? He certainly cannot be spontaneous; feeling is murdered in him: Grushnitsky (whether Pechorin's creation, or a 'real' man) must die.

Lermontov, himself a fatalist, found refuge in death. But in *A Hero of Our Time* he rose above his creature Pechorin: by the self-criticism implicit in his subtle portrait of him, by the very effort to achieve that self-criticism – and by the life-loving exuberance of the writing.

BIBLIOGRAPHY

Translations: S. Phillimore, *A Hero of Nowadays*, 1920; R. Merton, *A Hero of Our Time*, 1928; E. and C. Paul, *A Hero of Our Own Times*, 1940; V. and M. Nabokov, *A Hero of Our Time*, 1958; P. Foote, *A Hero of Our Time*, 1958; P. Longworth, *A Hero of Our Time*, 1962.

Text: In *Polnoye sobranie sochinenii* (1939–48); D. J. Richards, 1965.

Criticism: J. Mersereau, *Mikhail Lermontov*, 1962.

Nikolai Gogol

Gogol is among the most enigmatic of writers. How could such an egoistic, hypochondriacal, neurotic and finally mad reactionary produce books so full of human insight? How could his unfinished masterpiece *Mertvyye Dushi* [*Dead Souls*] (1842) amount, if only incidentally, to an indictment of a system in which, finally, he affected to believe?

He was born at Sorotchintsi in the Ukraine in 1809, when his mother was eighteen. At the age of fourteen his father, during church service, had seen the Mother of God stepping down from the altar to tell him 'Here is your wife!' at the same time indicating the seven-month-old baby of a local landlord; thirteen years later the Virgin again stepped out, indicating that he was now to marry her, which he did. So Gogol's mother told her son; the reader may draw whatever conclusion he wishes.

These facts are not strange in the context of Gogol's own life – nor even the fact that his father also wrote comedies, one of which survives. On the father's side all the men had been priests until Gogol's grandfather who, however, had been at a seminary. Gogol's mother was brought up in a wealthy household, but had little education. She was naïvely religious, as perhaps her husband was; Gogol himself regarded her as 'spiritually and intellectually ill'. She attributed to him the invention of such technological advances as the steam engine and the telegraph, much to his embarrassment. These oddities are relevant to Gogol's work.

He attended school at Nezhin, not far from his home, distinguishing himself more as comedian, mimic, actor and theatrical producer than as scholar. He was not physically prepossessing: skinny, with a long nose and tubercular swellings in the neck. At school the signs of what he later called his 'periodic' illness began to manifest themselves: he was wild and insulting at times, withdrawn and melancholy at others.

In 1828 he went to St Petersburg, where he attempted to compensate for his wretched appearance by affecting a conscientious dandyism; he hoped to become a literary success on any terms. Already he was experiencing, and expressing, the feelings of persecution which were to haunt him throughout his tormented life; the histrionic note, never absent, now becomes shriller. His literary efforts failed; he appropriated money from his mother, lied to her, travelled, accused himself – and, characteristically, left the solution of the problem of his bad character to God, in whom he fervently believed; it was not doubts but certainty which tormented him.

He was gifted as an actor, but lack of confidence led to yet further failure when he tried to enter the theatre. For a short time he worked as a civil servant; then as teacher at a girls' school; at the same time he began to write sketches of Ukrainian life.

In 1831 he met Pushkin, and in 1831–2 *Vechera na khutore bliz Dikanki* [*Evenings on the Farm near Dikanka*] appeared. Pushkin was impressed, and Gogol began to achieve a reputation. *Mirgorod* (1835), four stories, and *Arabeski* [*Arabesques*] (1835) followed. Both these contain work of genius; and Gogol's excited productivity at this time helps to explain why he failed to continue – or indeed, in any serious sense, to perform – his job as Professor of History at St Petersburg University. Turgenev, one of his students, spoke of him as missing two out of three lectures, whispering incoherently, and being ignorant of history – but Turgenev recognized his genius and importance. The influence of Pushkin was decisive, for only after his meeting with him did his true genius reveal itself. Gogol had read (or dipped into) much, but his synthesis of his influences – English Gothic, Fielding, Sterne, Cervantes, Hoffmann, De Quincey, Pushkin himself, and many others – is unique. At its best it has about it the sense of a madness under exquisitely lucid control.

His comedy *Revizor* [*The Inspector General*] (1836) was an immediate success: the reactionaries found it atrocious, but Nicholas I himself found it amusing. Pushkin supplied him with the plot for this play; he also gave him the idea on which *Dead Souls* is based, which he began to write in 1835. When he read the first chapters to Pushkin the latter laughed – but then added, 'How sad Russia is.'

Upset by the violent reactions which had been provoked by *The Inspector General*, Gogol left for Europe, where he remained (except for two brief visits to Russia) until 1848. In Paris he heard of Pushkin's death: 'My life, my highest bliss died with him,' he exclaimed in a letter. It is often asserted that after this he lost his creative powers; but, shattering to him though Pushkin's death was, this is not true. He was able to finish the first part of *Dead Souls* in Rome, and he also wrote *Shinel* [*The Overcoat*] (1842) in 1839–40. It was only after this that he experienced creative failure. He wrote the second part of *Dead Souls* and perhaps sketched out the third part; but he burned this material. Only five chapters of the second part, reconstructed by friends, survive. They contain some 'true Gogol', but show his powers on the decline; they cannot be counted as equal to the first part.

The rest of the story is one of mental disintegration with remissions. He infuriated his supporters with his *Vybrannye mesta iz perepiski s druzyami* [*Selected*

Passages from Correspondence with Friends] (1847) which, though it contains invaluable insights, is in the main a defence of the Russian system (it goes so far as to advocate the flogging of serfs). He became tiresome, advising an old friend how and when to read *The Imitation of Christ* (which, the friend rejoined, he had read before Gogol was born). He tried to fall in love with a woman, proposed, and was rejected. A visit to the Holy Land had previously failed to inspire him. He came increasingly under the influence of a semi-literate, pious, rhetorical, fanatic priest, who did him no good. In 1852, now in a continual state of religious mania, he decided to die: it was the beginning of Lent, and he stopped eating altogether. He wanted to be able to be 'found to some extent worthy of singing a hymn to divine beauty', but could not discover the capacity in himself. A team of doctors, called in by his friends, helped to kill him off more quickly by bathing him in meat broth, putting leeches up his nose, and covering him with hot bread. He died on 21 February.

Much has been written on the subject of the nature of Gogol's illness. Malaria, recurrent attacks of which are dangerous to people in nervous states, was probably a contributing factor. There were constitutional factors involved: he was incapable of forming a relationship with a woman, believed masturbation (in which he had of course indulged at school) to be a serious sin against God, and was, in Freudian terminology, a latent homosexual. His father died while he was at school, and it was largely Pushkin, his surrogate father, who changed his desire to be a successful entertainer into an ambition (suppress it though he might) to be a serious author. After Pushkin's death he formed an attachment for a very young man in Rome; Gogol nursed him devotedly, and it was in his arms that he died in 1839. 'Nights at the Villa' relates the experience, and it is significant that this account betrays a certain joy as well as sadness, and is non-religious.

It seems fairly clear, particularly in the light of what Gogol wrote about himself in letters, that he suffered – like many writers – from a form of manic depression or, more accurately, from an 'affective disorder'. He certainly suffered from deep depressions, but his manic episodes appear usually to have been modified by creative effort or to have been channelled into religious speculations. Madness, the fear of it, and its relationship to 'sanity' are predominant themes in his first mature works. Furthermore, one of the chief features of his style is that it simulates insanity. But one can no more penetrate the enigma of Gogol than one can that of Shakespeare, Dostoievsky or Tolstoy. One can only give indications.

Mertvyye Dushi
[Dead Souls]

SUMMARY In Gogol's title 'dead souls' has three meanings: a dead serf, or slave; the *morally dead* nature of the characters; and *unreal* in the sense that all these characters are inventions of, and emanate from, Gogol. The novel, the action of which covers some three weeks, is constructed around a certain type of swindle. Pushkin told Gogol about it, and both men probably knew of rare instances in which it had been practised. At the end of the nineteenth century more than ninety-five per cent of the Russian population were serfs, 'owned' by masters or the State; they were in every way slaves (but this should not mislead us into believing that every one of them suffered – some, with the connivance of their owners, could even become wealthy, and unofficially 'own' serfs themselves). Every landowner had to pay a poll tax on his serfs; the tax on those who died had to be paid until the next census year – and these years were infrequent; consequently landowners would be glad to sell off as many of their dead serfs as possible, and cheaply at that. Now if a man could buy up dead 'souls' (the official Russian term) cheaply, he could obtain a mortgage on them (a common practice) at the normal price – by pretending they were alive. Then, by fleeing before the next census, he could realize a huge profit. At the same time he could establish himself, for a while, as a real landowner.

Gogol's Chichikov is a *dvuryanin* (an official of the sixth grade in the zany 'Table of Ranks' invented by Peter I), thus a nobleman, entitled to be a landowner and to own serfs. He decides to perpetrate this type of swindle in a certain provincial town, probably somewhere between Moscow and St Petersburg and probably in 1832. Until the eleventh and last chapter we do not know what Chichikov's motives really are, nor his past history.

The story in itself is simple. Chichikov arrives at the town of NN. He is nondescript and his arrival causes no fuss. First he calls on Manilov, a depthless daydreamer who gives him what he wants – for nothing. Then, owing to his coachman's drunkenness, he finds himself at the manor of the widow Korobachka whom, with more difficulty, he persuades to part with her dead 'souls'. He falls in with the dangerous drunkard Nozdryov, with whom he fails to achieve a transaction. He now visits the bear-like, gluttonous kulak (in pre-Soviet terminology: wealthy peasant, middleman) Sobakevich. Sobakevich is shrewd, for he pretends to bring the qualities of the dead merchandise into account, and ultimately he cheats Chichikov. Finally Chichikov visits Plyushkin, a squalid miser; from him he extracts more 'dead souls'.

Now at the height of his fortunes, he returns to NN, having registered his 'serfs'. The people admire him as a rich man. The ladies seek him out. But at the governor's ball he meets disaster. He pays too much attention to the governor's daughter – for he now has sentimental dreams of marriage – and thus annoys the other women; the drunken Nozdryov arrives to denounce him as a dealer in dead serfs; the widow Korobochka, believing she has been cheated, arrives in her carriage 'hoping to discover for certain what price dead souls were going for'.

Absurd rumours about Chichikov begin to spread; the main question, and the one which terrifies the town officials most of all, is 'Who is Chichikov?' Is he a brigand whom they ought to arrest – or has he the powers to arrest *them*? Since Chichikov is a projection of Gogol himself – and *his*, the novelist's, swindle causes the action – the officials' question, though made to seem comic, is pertinent, implying: what is the nature of the artist? Chichikov remains ignorant about his notoriety until Nozdryov turns up to tell him that he is regarded as a forger and the would-be abductor of the governor's daughter. Chichikov leaves. As he does so he meets the funeral procession of the public prosecutor who, according to Nozdryov, has died of terror because of Chichikov's presence. We now learn for the first time who he is and what his motives have been.

He has been impelled throughout his life to acquire money so as to become a nobody – at any costs. He wishes no more than a comfortable but mediocre existence. In a final rhetorical passage Chichikov's troika is compared with Russia speeding into the future. The task of continuation in this vein was beyond Gogol and outside his capacity; to all intents and purposes *Dead Souls* was finished.

CRITICAL COMMENTARY The extent of the achievement of Gogol's *Dead Souls* has been complicated because it was welcomed by the influential and intelligent Russian critic Vissarion Belinsky (1811–48) as a work which was 'purely Russian, national, taken from the heart of popular life ... which mercilessly rips the covers from reality'. Belinsky, 'Furious Vissarion', despite his early death, dominated nineteenth-century Russian literature and is still, in historical terms, its most important critic. As he developed he became more radical. Though steeped in the spirit of

German idealism, he argued that literature must – by its very nature – be truthful to ordinary life: it would thus reveal social evils and lead to progress and change. He also believed that Russian literature should be truly Russian, although, by no means an unsubtle critic, he saw that this meant turning to the West. (The Mongol invasions had cut Russia off from Renaissance influences.) This was the literary philosophy of the 'natural school' the 'critical realism', of Belinsky, and he considered Gogol's *Dead Souls* to be its foundation.

Later he attacked Gogol – whom he hardly knew personally – for his reactionary pronouncements, calling him a 'lost leader'. So *Dead Souls* has come to be seen as a denunciation of the serf system and of landowners. And this, in a sense, though hardly an historical one, it happens to be.

But this is to view it superficially. The novel goes deeper. Certainly Gogol had no intention of writing a social document: the seeds of his later reactionary, anti-Western conservatism had always been within him. He was from the Ukraine, and had seen little of rural or provincial Russia (nor had Belinsky). He was a wholly subjective writer. Indeed, Belinsky himself noted this: 'in *Dead Souls* his subjectivity is everywhere and palpably apparent ... profound, all-embracing ... humane ... [forcing] him to pass the phenomena of the external world through his *living soul* and by this means to breathe a *living soul* into them.' The point is that if literature is not autonomous, then it cannot possibly be truly *social* or truly human. Humanness, in the fullest sense of the word, begets literature in order that literature may beget humanness. This sometimes happens in strange ways. *Dead Souls* is one of the strangest.

Gogol planned the work as a Dantesque trilogy; but he failed to complete the second and third parts because he was unable to depict either the positive side of life or the virtuous man – and because his genius, like that of

Cervantes, was essentially a comic one. What Gogol himself wrote about *Dead Souls* is sometimes useful, but taken as a whole it is confused. At one time he could see into the nature of his technique; at another he would agonize over his 'sin' in having failed to make the first part into a sermonizing and solemn work.

But *Dead Souls* is finished. 'After all, we are still living in the town of NN ourselves,' a critic has written. And how can we get out of it? While Gogol accepted that he was living in this town, and could not get out of it, he remained an intact artist. Chichikov's final flight may well be seen, retrospectively, as Gogol's own flight from creativity. But he had achieved more than he thought.

The structure of *Dead Souls* is simple: dramatic episodes linked by narrative and supplemented by commentary. But Gogol's own voice resembles that of a garrulous spectator continually interrupting, from the back of the stalls, a performance of a play of his own authorship. The style of the narrative, even more of the apparently irrelevant comments, is extraordinary. Unfortunately it is largely untranslatable. The nature of the Russian language when it is exploited to the full, as in Gogol, is such that it could be transformed into English only by inspired adaptation. His humour, irony, absurdity and hyperbole can be taken over into English; but his strictly linguistic devices – such as shifts of meaning achieved by use of suffixes, prefixes, special forms of address and other devices specific to the Slavonic languages – cannot.

One may therefore characterize the nature of his style only in general terms: violent oxymoron; anaphora (repetition of words at the beginning of sentences, and variations of this); extensive and intensive intrusion of the colloquial, over-familiar or vulgar; ironic, gruesome or grotesque use of the Homeric simile (the extended simile); metonymy; metalepsis (a 'far-fetched' form of metonymy) strained to its utmost limits; ambiguous use of high-flown or biblical language (parodic or in earnest or both);

use of sound to suggest sense or augment meaning; pure lyricism. It has been said that at times Gogol's prose achieves a kind of transparency that makes it 'more real than reality'.

Gogol's seemingly lunatic voice, often carrying us away from the main action, keeps reminding us that the characters *are* illusions – and yet, paradoxically, the burning sincerity of this voice causes us to reflect that they *do* have a 'life', that they are significant distillations of the qualities of real people.

The portraits of Chichikov's 'marks' are 'more like them than they themselves' (as the painter Liebermann informed a banker who complained about a portrait) by the power of Gogol's prose. They might have been no more than easily recognizable types: the dreamer; the shrewd, greedy, clumsy kulak; the decaying widow full of anxiety; the lying and sometimes menacing alcoholic; the miser. Yet, ridiculous though they undoubtedly are, they are presented with a passionate love. They are as it were 'forgiven'.

Gogol wrote that, because he wanted 'to be better', he had transferred his 'bad qualities' to his heroes: 'I began to clothe [them], over and above their own beastliness, with my own inadequacies.' He pursued his bad qualities, he said, under other names and other vocations, and depicted them to himself as mortal enemies; he chased them with malice and ridicule. And when Pushkin, after laughing, exclaimed how sad Russia was, Gogol began to see 'in what a horrifying form for a man can appear darkness and the frightening *absence of light*.' And so, he explains, he began to think about ways in which he could minimize the 'oppressive' effect of his book. The project proved to be his creative undoing, and it led to his death. But in the final analysis *Dead Souls* is not oppressive.

Gogol sought to exorcise from himself his *poshlost*. The word means something like 'mediocrity, deadness (lack of spirit or *soul*), commonplaceness, ordinariness'. To

Gogol, however, it above all connoted 'lack of responsibility towards God'. People seek to avoid *the good*
by surrounding themselves with comforting possessions
(there is an anticipation of an important feature of
Sartre's existentialism here). Such acquisitiveness is
spiritually pointless, acts as a defence against painful contact with goodness, with the living soul. This strategy, for
Gogol, is the essence, the real meaning of *poshlost*, which
Nabokov later translated as 'poshlust'.

At the end Chichikov, the author's creation but also the
chief surrogate for his own *poshlost* (a modern existentialist would call it 'bad faith'), is said to be to blame if the
reader has not liked the characters so far introduced: 'that
is Chichikov's fault; here he is completely master, and
where he thinks fit to take us there we must go.' That
Gogol sees to be his own destiny. Yet the account he finally
provides, of Chichikov's history, is compassionate. The
hope for him that is expressed is not, though some have
argued otherwise, delivered in a 'sermonizing' tone: 'And
which of you, full of Christian meekness, not in public,
but alone in private, at the moment of solitary inward
converse, asks in the depths of your own soul, the painful
question: "Is there not a bit of Chichikov in me too?"' Of
course Manilov, Korobochka, Nozdryov, Sobakevich and
Plyushkin emanated from Gogol. Of course they are not
virtuous people. Of course they are absurd. But by minute
attention to them Gogol has made them lovable: he has
explained them. Gogol died because he could not, as Manzoni so notably could, convey a sense of virtuousness and
genuine forgiveness.

Repelled by the world and by himself, Gogol pretended
merely to entertain. Hatred festered in his soul, so he
laughed ('through tears', as Belinsky rightly observed).
Knowing that he could not separate himself from his
characters, he distanced them from himself by putting
them on a stage; but while he seemed to ridicule them he
dissected them with the astonishingly flexible power of

his language; and in his dissection of them he gave them to us as an act of love. Ultimately, he could not bring these 'souls' to 'moral life'. But he undermined his own intentions by making their lives metaphors for truer lives: these characters are transformed, by his treatment, into holy ghosts of their unholy selves. And so after the first part was finished there was nothing left: no more positiveness to conjure out of negativity. Gogol's life in art was ended. His life in life dragged on; the tragedy is that he could not know – because of that very Christian meekness and modesty which he was convinced he did not possess – that he had already achieved an act of forgiveness and love. The 'unfinished' *Dead Souls* is not the *Inferno* Gogol believed it to be. It contains its own *Purgatorio*, and even hints of a *Paradiso*.

BIBLIOGRAPHY

Translations: *Dead Souls*, in C. Garnett, *Works*, 1922–8; G. Reavey, *Dead Souls*, 1948; B. Guerney, *Dead Souls*, 1948; D. Magarshack, *Dead Souls*, 1961. The first and last listed are the best.

Text: In *Sobranie sochinenii* (1966–7).

Criticism: V. Nabokov, *Nikolai Gogol*, 1944.

Honoré de Balzac

Honoré Balzac (the 'de' was his own later embellishment) was born at Tours in 1799. His father was fifty-three, his mother twenty-one. Although he maintained a relationship with his mother (who survived him) throughout his life, his accusation that she never loved him was justified. A doctor once said of her that she was not 'mad, just malicious'. His childhood was unhappy: unloved and exiled to a school from which he did not return home even in the holidays, he did badly in his lessons. But he was already reading voraciously and with a curiosity whose ambitious, greedy, rash enormity was to be characteristic of both his life and his work. In 1813 Balzac went with his family from Tours to Paris where, after receiving private tuition, he began to study law. At twenty he announced to his parents that he was going to be a writer; he met with no sympathy, but did extract a small monthly allowance. In the next ten years he continued with his prodigious reading, wrote pseudonymous 'pot boilers' and got into business difficulties. He was never out of debt for the rest of his life.

During these prentice years he fell under the influence of an unhappily married woman, Mme de Berny, twenty-two years older than himself. She was an intelligent woman who became his critic, benefactress, surrogate mother and mistress; her influence upon him was considerable. The influence of the Polish Countess Mme Hanska, whom he married a few months before his death after a seventeen-year liaison, is also crucial.

His first publishing success came in 1829, but it was not until 1833 that he conceived the plan of *La Comédie humaine*, a vast series of self-contained but interlocking novels. He published the first edition of the collection in 1842, with a famous preface. (*La Cousine Bette*, his penultimate work, was published in 1846.)

Balzac lived extravagantly, hovering between the intention of paying off his debts and escaping them. His output was huge: about 100 books and much journalism and correspondence. He deprived himself of sleep, drank inordinate amounts of coffee and died exhausted in 1850.

As a writer he was not consistent; there is much ambivalence in his work. This is aptly illustrated by the fact that although, as man and journalist, he appeared to be a conservative Catholic mystic, an admirer of Napoleon, and a legitimist royalist (a believer in an undisputed succession – Louis-Philippe's claims were weak), he is regarded by Marxist critics as a great intuitive analyst of capitalist society. He worked for the legitimist cause, believed in strong rule and established Catholicism, and had a strong nostalgia for Napoleon and the First Empire.

Balzac was fascinated by science, magic and the occult. He believed in the unity of all living things, and did not object to combining the ideas of such diverse figures as Swedenborg, Leibniz, Lavater and the naturalist Georges Buffon, one of Darwin's more important predecessors, whose *Histoire Naturelle* (1749–67) dealt with the whole animal kingdom. Balzac was always in too much of a hurry to evolve a true system, and his syncretic 'philosophy' is in itself a mishmash. He was shrewd, frenetic, well-informed, vulgar and bursting with unprecedented vitality.

La Comédie humaine

Balzac completed ninety-one out of an eventually projected series of 137 novels in the *La Comédie humaine*.
Zola was the first to give the proletariat a presence in fiction, and to pursue the history of a family; but Balzac was
the first to introduce recurring characters. His aim was to
treat human society as Buffon had treated the animal
species. From another naturalist, Geoffroy Saint-Hilaire,
he formed the notion that men as well as animals are inseparable from their environments: that the individual
and the society he lives in are interdependent. His scheme,
though pseudo-scientific, is of the utmost importance in
literary history. In this introduction to the 1842 edition
he stated that he wished to 'write the history that so many
historians have forgotten, the history of manners
[*moeurs*]'. His use of the word *moeurs* (which combines
the sense of 'behaviour' and 'conduct' with that of 'manners', 'customs') implies a realistic aim, and Balzac is sometimes still taken as the founder, with Stendhal, of modern
'realism'. But Baudelaire saw Balzac as a 'passionate
visionary' rather than an 'observer'.

The argument about whether Balzac is to be taken as a
visionary or *realist* continues unabated. There was a
visionary element in Balzac – even in his statement of his
aims. His famous definition of the writer as 'secretary' to
society sounds anything but visionary; but what he meant
by it is, in effect, visionary: Here are some relevant passages from the 1842 introduction:

At first the idea ... was as a dream ... it originated in a
comparison between Humanity and Animality.

Unity of structure ... occupied the greatest minds ... As we
read the extraordinary writings of the mystics, such as
Swedenborg ... and the works of the greatest authors on

Natural History ... we detect ... the rudiments of the great
law ... There is but one Animal. The Creator works on a
single model for every organised being. 'The Animal' ... takes
its external form, or, to be accurate, the difference in its form,
from the environment in which it is obliged to develop.

The differences between a soldier, an artisan [and other types
of men] are as great [as those between species of animals] ...
social species have always existed ... If Buffon could ...
represent ... the whole realm of zoology, was there no room
for a work of the same kind on society?

Hence the work to be written needed a threefold form – men,
women, and things ... persons and the material expression
of their minds; man, in short, and life.

But how could such a drama ... be made interesting? ... please
the poet, the philosopher, and the masses who want both
poetry and philosophy under striking imagery? ... I saw no
way ...

Then Balzac explains how he read Walter Scott and
'found the source of his genius in the infinite variety of
human nature'. 'French society would be the real author;
I should only be the secretary.' But, he continues, he cannot merely be a 'painter': 'must I not also investigate the
reasons or the cause of these social effects, detect the hidden sense of this vast assembly ... ?' This last aim is undoubtedly visionary.

His basic principles, the 'soul of this work', are: 'Man
is neither good nor bad ... society ... improves him; but
self-interest also develops his evil tendencies. Christianity,
above all, Catholicism [is] ... a complete system for the
depraved tendencies of man ...' 'Catholicism and Royalty
are twin principles.' He announces that he wishes to turn
the country back to 'Religion and Monarchy' (he did not
regard Louis-Philippe as a true monarch). He is (like

Stendhal) against universal suffrage: 'Napoleon adapted election to the spirit of the French nation with wonderful skill ... The elective system of the Empire was ... indisputably the best.'

Balzac's final aim is to establish the 'spiritual world – the sphere in which are revealed the relations of God and man'.

La Comédie humaine is divided into six main sections: scenes of Private, Provincial, Parisian, Political, Military, and Country Life. (These are the 'Studies of Manners'; there were also a number of 'Philosophical Studies'.)

Visionary, realist, or both? There is obtrusion of authorial opinion into Balzac's narrative, little into Flaubert's; in that sense Balzac is hardly a *realist* in the special sense in which mid-nineteenth-century critics understood it. Balzac does not try to detach himself from his material as Flaubert does. He is not an unobtrusive *psychologist in depth*, as Flaubert is. Nor does he possess Flaubert's awareness of the dubious status of his texts. His grand design, as revealed in most of the 'Études philosophiques', is intellectually tawdry when compared with Flaubert's tortured but subtle ideal of art. In these 'philosophical' works, which include many short stories, he attempts to show how the 'mysterious laws' reveal themselves in human actions. As a whole they fail. Balzac is a peculiarly imperfect writer. Yet, for all the vulgarity of the 'magic' ideas which fascinated him ('magnetism', phrenology and so forth), he does in his studies of manners succeed in demonstrating that there are mysterious forces in life – even for the reader who cannot allow for the existence of 'magic'. This sense of mystery is conveyed by his imagination, not by his intellectual convictions: 'Balzac constantly sought a theory of passions; it was great luck for him that he never found it,' wrote Gide.

Yet the visionary/realist argument is fundamentally misleading. There is, after all, a *vision*, a view of life, implicit in even Flaubert's fiction. And there is a *realism*, a vivid evocation of *moeurs*, in Balzac's. Every writer is trying to be realistic, in the wider sense, in his own way – even if this appears to be totally irrational. That is to say, he is faithfully depicting what he feels is the most important aspect of reality. In one important sense, then, distinction between *visionary* and *realist* is false – only a surface distinction. Martin Turnell writes that Balzac left an 'extraordinary hallucinatory vision of French life from the Revolution to the July Monarchy', both 'monstrous' and 'prodigious'. This is true in as much as his work as a whole does exercise an initially hallucinatory effect. But this is largely because his characters, however impressive, are *types*; they are, in E. M. Forster's famous distinction, *flat* rather than *round*: they 'vibrate', just as Dickens' do.

Balzac is not seriously concerned with the mixture of good and bad in *individuals*. He presents people obsessed (for example, old Goriot in *Père Goriot* obsessed with his daughters; Baron Hulot in *La Cousine Bette* obsessed with lust); his virtuous characters are too often either colourless or sentimentally heroic (arguably, Adeline in *La Cousine Bette*). Although most of his 'good' characters, like his moral asides (the longer examples of which Erich Auerbach characterizes as 'plain tripe') and his over-fanciful passages, represent serious aesthetic failings, his major creations do not. Though 'discs', they are too vigorous, too vital. And Balzac, though not a delicate psychologist, is canny when he reveals individual motivation (as in the case of Bette). He was not more fundamentally interested, however, in individual motivation than Stendhal was in description. But his assumptions about psychological motivation were seldom stupid.

But since, as Nietzsche wrote, 'all writers of all ages were convinced that they were realistic', Balzac's very visionary qualities do give his picture of society a realistic quality. His characters are not analysed, but they are rooted in their physical circumstances. Balzac, when he is not distorting his descriptions by fanciful exaggeration or feeble writing, succeeds in drawing attention to the fact that people and their immediate environments do exist *in relationship*. There is no agreement as to how historically or philosophically right he was, but there is no denying that his method as a whole works. In his best novels environment and the physical appearance of the characters, as Balzac conveys them to us, act as a significant metaphor. His geographical and topographical knowledge, and descriptive powers, are unequalled. Nor, vulgar and stylistically inelegant though he sometimes is, does he ever indulge in the vice of manipulating his plots in the interests of his avowed beliefs (even when he makes these obvious).

Balzac did succeed, in one character who figures in a number of the series, in finding an *objective correlative* for both himself and the 'guilty' artist: this is the master criminal Vautrin, whole real name is Jacques Collin. He appears in many of the books (turning up once, for a moment, in *La Cousine Bette*), but mainly in *Le Père Goriot* (1834–5), *Illusions perdues* (1837–43), (in disguise as the abbé Carlos Herrera), and in *La Dernière Incarnation de Vautrin* (title of the last volume of *Splendeurs et misères de Courtisanes*, 1839–47). Vautrin is a kind of Napoleon, an arch manipulator, a murderer and an inciter to murder. Vautrin actually replaces Bibi-Lupin as chief of police – a melodramatic touch for which Balzac had precedent, since François-Eugène Vidocq (1775–1857), a real-life criminal, had been head of a police organization consisting of criminals. Vautrin is one side of Balzac himself: for the role of the serious writer is subversive, if only because he must be a critic of his society. Thus, while Balzac separates himself from Vautrin by implying that he is homosexual, he simultaneously emphasizes his subversiveness and nonconformity. Vautrin, like Balzac, adopts masks (as a priest he even makes converts). Without Vautrin there could hardly have been Proust's Charlus, Martin Turnell observes.

As to the healing side of art: we find this in such characters, significantly both doctors, as Benassis (in *Le Médecin de campagne*, 1833) and the ever recurring Bianchon.

La Comédie humaine is as a whole one of the 'most extraordinary achievements in literature ... [it] may not be realism in the sense in which the word came finally to be understood, but its reality is unmistakable' (F. W. J. Hemmings). Other important titles in the series include the Vautrin books already mentioned, *Eugénie Grandet* (1833), *Le Cousin Pons* (1847) – classified with *La Cousine Bette* as one of *Les Parents Pauvres* section in the *Scènes de la Vie Parisienne* series of the studies of manners, the *Histoire de la Grandeur et de la Décadence de César Birotteau, Le Médecin de campagne, La Rabouilleuse* (1841–2) – and, of the philosophical studies, *La Peau de Chagrin*.

La Cousine Bette has been chosen here as representative because it is one of the masterpieces of his last years. I do not claim that it is his greatest work (which is, in any case, the uncompleted *La Comédie humaine*); but it is one of the half-dozen of his finest individual novels.

La Cousine Bette

SUMMARY In *La Cousine Bette* we come across, though only in short scenes, some of the approximately 150 characters who appear in major roles in the other novels: the crooked banker Nucingen, the successful politician Rastignac, the courtesan Jenny, and others.

The action of the novel stretches from July 1838 to February 1846. The setting is Paris. Baron Hulot is an old servant of the Empire. He is the younger brother of the irreproachable deaf seventy-two year old, Marshal Hulot, Count of 'Forzheim', as Balzac wrongly spelled it. Hulot's wife is the forty-eight-year-old, still beautiful

Adeline, née Fischer, originally a peasant from the Vosges. The marriage to Hulot had been 'like an Assumption' for her, and she has continued to admire her husband (a 'kind of God who could do no wrong') although she has for years been fully aware of his infidelities and his lavish expenditure on his women. Balzac brings out the precarious financial position of the Hulot family in the opening pages, by his careful description of the out-of-fashion, faded furnishings and flaking furniture.

The Hulots have two children: a lawyer son married to the daughter of the ex-perfume salesman Crevel, now a millionaire, and a daughter, Hortense. They also have a 'poor relation', Adeline's sister Lizbeth, the Cousin Bette of the title; though only forty-three, she looks many years older than the Baroness. Bette is an embroidress in gold and silver lace, regarded by the entire family as a paragon of virtue, yet unconsciously treated as the 'poor relation'. Bette is plain and full of resentment; the pretence of concern for the interest of the family is second nature to her – but she is motivated by envy of her sister's better looks and better fortune in marriage. For Bette's character Balzac drew on a number of real people including his mother.

Crevel, a vulgar man who would like to be regarded as a gentleman, is as obsessed with women and as driven by lust as the Baron. But he makes sure that he remains a millionaire. The Baron is an aristocrat with a notable past; even now he is head of one of the principle departments of the War Ministry. Crevel is a tradesman and Balzac, in his often comic portrait of him, never allows us to forget it: for example, when he tries to 'make an ironical bow', a 'tradesman would have recognized [in it] the gesture of a one-time commercial traveller'; his pride in his position of captain of the National Guard is simply self-satisfaction.

The Baroness wants to marry off her daughter Hortense; there is a man in the offing – but the necessary dowry is lacking. The Baron has squandered every penny.

Crevel calls. Companion in vice with Hulot, he nevertheless hates him for having taken a mistress from him. The desire for revenge, he says, doubles his 'passion'. If Adeline will become his mistress then he will provide the dowry. The Baroness indignantly refuses.

Bette half-jokingly tells Hortense that she has a lover: an artist. Hortense falls in love with the very idea of him, and virtually decides to take him over from Bette. Her behaviour in the matter is rather more than merely youthful, impetuous, or mischievous; it is viciously thoughtless. She wins and marries him.

Count Wenceslas Steinbock, a poor Pole newly arrived in Paris, has been taken up by Bette. He is an artist of genius, and under her half-tyrannical, half-protective care he does fine work. She saves him from suicide. When she discovers that the Count is to become Hortense's husband her lifelong hatred and envy of her sister reach their height: she now determines to take her revenge.

Hulot, who is never less than sincerely repentant towards his wife, is just about to lose Josépha, the singer whom he had taken off Crevel, to a Duke: a rich dwarf who 'wants her all to himself'. Hulot, whom Josépha calls an 'old dyed tomcat', as he characteristically complains to his own wife, now becomes infatuated with Mme Valérie Marneffe, the bastard daughter of one of Napoleon's most famous lieutenants, who lives in the same apartment house as Bette. Her husband is a syphilitic civil service clerk, a frequenter of low brothels; his disease is killing him. He is happy to act as Valérie's pimp, especially if he can obtain promotion by doing so. Finally he is made head of a department, when, with the connivance of Valérie, he and the police 'discover' her in bed with Hulot. (Balzac may have based this incident on an episode in the life of Victor Hugo.)

Valérie becomes Hulot's mistress. But Bette, who becomes her intimate friend, introduces her to Crevel. Soon afterwards a Brazilian lover from Valérie's past comes on the scene. Bette then succeeds in arranging for Valérie to seduce Steinbock (whose work has suffered in quality and quantity since his marriage: Bette's harsh tutelage was better, Balzac tells us in a famous passage, than a life of comparative luxury and temporary amorous pleasure). Hortense leaves the Count. Valérie now has four lovers, each of whom, with Bette's clever help, she plays off against the other. When she becomes pregnant she manages to convince each of her lovers that he is the true father.

Bette tells the family that she feigns friendship for Valérie only in their interests. She augments her own income, while Valérie takes money from both Hulot and Crevel. Bette is unmistakably Lesbian in her attitude to Valérie: she finds her 'courtesan existence strangely exciting ... adore[s] [her]'; she is the 'object of her love; and in her she [finds] ... docility ... softness ... voluptuousness ...' The two women 'count up together the accumulating interest of their respective hoards' meanwhile laughing 'over the stupidity of men'. Bette, whose chief means of gaining revenge is to encourage Hulot's crazy extravagance, gains vicarious enjoyment from Valérie's predatory *amours*.

Hulot is forced into increasingly desperate financial straits. He makes use of his wife's uncle, Johann Fischer – who is blindly devoted to him – by sending him to Africa on a crooked scheme. The affair comes to light, and Fischer kills himself in Oran. Meanwhile Hulot's wife, discovering the truth, has made the sacrifice of offering herself to Crevel in return for the two hundred thousand francs of government money which Hulot has embezzled. Crevel, involuntarily moved by her 'saintliness', agrees, without even demanding his price. But he is dissuaded from taking this course, in one of the most brilliant scenes in the novel, by the cunning wiles of Valérie.

Hulot, however, is saved from total ruin, though he is

forced to resign his position. His old brother the Marshal pays back the embezzled money – but dies from the shock. This is a severe blow to Bette, whose schemes have rebounded upon her: for she had succeeded in getting the Marshal, with the best wishes of the family, to agree to marry her. 'The peasant had, as often happens, succeeded too well.' She inherits some money from the Marshal – but her motivation in gaining money had never been other than revenge. What she had worked for was to see the Hulots in penury while she was rich.

Hulot, though rescued from out and out disaster, is still in trouble; with the aid of his former mistress, the cynical and worldly-wise Josépha, he contrives to disappear under an alias. He lives wretchedly – but continues to indulge his lustful obsessions, though at an increasingly lower social level.

After a serious illness, the Baroness is financially 'looked after', and given social work to do, by representatives of the government. Bette is still the trusted friend of everybody. She continues to visit her beloved Valérie. Financial good fortune begins to smile on the family she had determined to ruin; but Adeline laments the continued absence of her husband.

Valérie's child is stillborn, and her husband (attended, like the Baroness, by Bianchon) dies. Wenceslas continues as one of Valérie's lovers; but she and Crevel now plan to marry. Victorin, Hulot's son, is determined to destroy Valérie: he 'regards it as his duty to avenge society and the family to bring that woman to book for all her crimes'. For if Crevel does marry Valérie, then Victorin and his wife will lose most of his fortune, since this will go to the woman about whom, as Bette disingenuously says, he is 'gloriously blind', and not to his daughter. Bette, who knows of Hulot's whereabouts, has been paying him a small allowance, so as to keep him in a state of ruin – and here again 'she [went] too far in her vengeance'. She 'aroused Victorin's suspicions'. For Victorin has the support of the police in his quest to ruin Mme Marneffe. At one point he even calls on Vautrin, who assures him that while the police cannot be officially involved, the affair is in the hands of one of their criminal agents. This agent is a repulsive woman who goes under many aliases (she is in fact Mme Nourrison – her real name is Jacqueline Collin – Vautrin's aunt), tells Victorin that Mme Marneffe will be disposed of – and that he must then pay a priest, collecting for a 'pious work', the sum of forty thousand francs. Victorin is horrified, but agrees.

The old hag arranges for the Brazilian to catch Valérie and Wenceslas *in flagrante delicto*. He is driven into a frenzy and decides on vengeance. When Crevel marries Valérie he is enraged, so he poisons them both. Valérie's beauty is ruined before she dies. This is an atrocious blow to Bette. Furthermore, Crevel dies after Valérie, and thus inherits her money. Because of the complex financial manipulations which are a major feature of the book, all Crevel's money goes to the Hulot family. Victorin ends by paying an 'old monk' eighty thousand francs, 'taken from a sum of money found in Crevel's desk'. The Baron is taken home by his wife. At first he asks her, 'Can I bring the child [his teenage lover]?' He is now senile, 'broken, bowed, his expression degraded'.

Bette, seeing her life's work ruined – the people she proposed to destroy enriched, Wenceslas reunited with Hortense – quickly succumbs to consumption. But she keeps 'the secret of her hate through her painful death': all are around her bed in tears – she is the 'angel of the family'.

Hulot almost becomes himself again. Adeline is at last happy. Wenceslas is faithful – but idles his time away, although a great social success: 'he became a critic, like all weak characters who are false to their first promise.' But Hulot, his strength partly recovered, is caught in bed by his wife with the kitchenmaid, a 'Normandy wench' 'as stupid as you please'. The Baroness dies of shock. Three days later Hulot departs, and eleven months later marries the maid – who thus becomes a Baroness.

CRITICAL COMMENTARY Although some call Balzac the 'greatest of novelists', it is clear even in his finest work that he was less a novelist than a *storyteller*. (This is doubtless what led a recent critic to state that his chief vice was that he made his reader want to know what was going to happen.) But it is this that largely redeems him from his deficiencies. For it is worth repeating, Balzac never manipulated his plots in the interests of his opinions. Life remains in control. Furthermore, he possesses great skill in the art of storytelling.

Paradoxically, *La Cousine Bette* is best initially approached through its flaws. We already know that Balzac does not *analyse* characters: he presents them metaphorically by setting them in specific contexts, which he carefully describes. Some of the characters in *La Cousine Bette* have no contexts, and thus remain lifeless. The jealous Brazilian is at times a comic figure, but his final revenge is badly articulated. Hortense, at first interestingly opportunistic, is allowed to fade away into nothing. The Baroness is far too good to be true: she has nothing more to do than to remain devoted to her husband, and so becomes boring. Victorin's sense of moral uneasiness is never examined – even by Balzac's familiar means of descriptive method: facial appearance, dress and manner.

But the more important characters, though 'flat', do 'vibrate'; and they do so very largely through Balzac's special method. His descriptions of them, as they speak or dress or look, are more effective than his clumsy attempts to dissect their psychology. In the case of the real monster of the novel, Valérie Marneffe, Balzac has scarcely anything psychological to say. In Chapter XV he gives us a rather dull little lecture about depraved machiavellian courtesans with 'cash-boxes for hearts'; but the passage following this tells us much more. It is specific –

though metaphorically so; describing the way Valérie dresses, the difference between her bedroom and the rest of her apartment, and her hypocritical assumption of piety (whenever in danger of being caught out, she resorts to an indignant appeal to 'religion').

Hulot himself, whose folly gives the book its *raison d'être*, is more of a caricature than Valérie, Crevel or Bette. Although once a man of distinction – and even faithful for a while to his wife – he is by the opening of the novel shown as possessing only three traits: he must have women, he must spend too much money on them at whatever cost to himself or his family, and he is pathetically repentant when facing his adoring wife. As the Prince who has to save him and obtain his resignation tells him, he has 'ceased to be a man and become only a temperament'. Hulot, though he causes tragedy, is essentially a comic figure, a *humour* of an old lecher who might have come out of a play by Ben Jonson or, indeed, one by an author who deeply influenced Balzac: Molière. Hulot is the device upon which the novel hinges. That such scenes as the one in which Valérie's Brazilian lover is hidden in a closet, or that in which Marneffe and the police 'catch' Valérie and Hulot in bed together, are not wholly farcical is a tribute to Balzac's narrative gift and to his innate moral sense – Valérie, after all, is truly depraved, and nothing in which she is concerned could be purely hilarious.

Crevel provides a perfect example of Balzac at his best. His personality is summed up throughout the book by his pretensions of dress and behaviour: this parvenu strikes various attitudes which he imagines appropriate, and these become more extravagant as he becomes more ambitious and as he rises in the social world (at his death he is a Mayor). Yet even he has momentary pity for the wretched Adeline when she asks him for money: Balzac does not tip the scales too far over to one side.

Bette herself is essentially tragic, embodying the

author's shrewd understanding of the peasant mentality. She is in many ways also pathetic: 'thin, dark, her hair black and stringy, with thick eyebrows meeting in a tuft ... with several moles on her simian face ...' Such a person is in an emotionally vulnerable position. She did bully Adeline as a child; but the 'family had neglected the plain girl for the beautiful one'. Brought to Paris, illiterate, in 1809, no husband could be found for her; nevertheless, by 1811 she had learned to read, write and to be 'well-mannered, skilled and intelligent'. Only her obstinacy prevented her from being 'presentable' and 'acceptable'. Balzac treats us, in Chapter IV, to a dissertation on her essential brutality, although to some extent his story modifies this portrait, though not its physical details. That she is treacherous, as he asserts, is undeniable. Yet there is a touching element in her relationship with Wenceslas, whose weak character (as Balzac himself emphasizes) positively benefits from Bette's strict treatment of him.

She has found, as the novel opens, a social role that she can play through the tending of this gifted artist. True, she is envious, cunning, ready to do small mischiefs; but only when Hortense takes Wenceslas away from her is she prompted into active evil. For she has begun to establish Wenceslas as a genuine artist – and Hortense has wrenched him away from her.

Bette's fury, soon transformed into a discreetly operated cunning, is the catalyst which frees the depravity in Valérie. Hitherto she has been a comparatively small-time whore; Hulot becomes attracted to her by chance (while visiting Bette), so this leaves the way open for his sister-in-law to bring in Crevel and, later, Wenceslas. Bette's story is one of triumph and final defeat; cruelly and cunningly though she behaves, her end is tragic. She truly grieves over Valérie – and this feeling is not weaker than her frustration at failing to gain her revenge.

The strength of *La Cousine Bette* lies in the exuberance

with which most of the important points of view are put across (an exuberance of understanding amounting to compassion); in the way that 'all references cross, to form a unity not only in [the novel] but in *La Comédie humaine* itself'; and in the final triumphant double death scene near the end of the novel.

Curiously, Balzac has been criticized as having been too melodramatically cruel to Crevel and Valérie: too 'retributive'. The poisoning itself, as indeed the whole presentation of the Brazilian, could have been better managed. But the actual death scene is one of Balzac's greatest passages. It is not realistic, nor is it *visionary*; it is comi-tragic, proto-surrealist, with a zest that only Balzac and Dickens possessed. Both Crevel and Valérie are literally rotting to death: stinking, unrecognizable, 'swollen ... covered with greenish pustules'. When Bette visits her Valérie describes herself as a 'heap of mud' – and, as Balzac wryly remarks, 'repentance [has] made inroads into that perverse soul, in proportion as the wasting malady ravaged her beauty.' 'Leave me to the Church!' she begs Bianchon, who announces that he will try to cure her: her beauty, she knows, can never be restored. 'I must try to be reconciled to Him – it will be my last flirtation. Yes, I must try to *make* God' (this is the very vulgarism we have heard, at the beginning, from the venereal clerk Marneffe in a reference to her relationship with his chief). 'That is my poor Valérie's last joke,' comments the weeping Bette. It is an example of Balzac's genius at its strongest and most irresistible. Crevel is also superbly *in type* (rather than 'character'): 'Don't you worry ... death thinks twice before carrying off a Mayor of Paris! ... I still know how to pack my bags. I am an old commercial traveller.' And the young Hulot wonders sadly if 'stupidity and vanity did not perhaps possess a power as strong as true greatness of soul'. 'Can it be that the strength displayed by a great criminal is the same that upholds [one] who goes proudly to his death?' Meanwhile, Bianchon tries to devise a 'desperate remedy': 'you see me in a state of scientific enthusiasm, yet many superficial judges would pronounce me heartless'; and one of his colleagues remarks 'there will be a splendid post-mortem ... and we shall have two specimens, so that we shall be able to make comparisons.' It is one of the great scenes in fiction.

There is much to say against Balzac, but eventually most of us will, as S. B. John has put it, be 'fascinated by the possibilities of his dramatic world' and 'follow in the wake of the author's love' – his love, as Henry James wrote, 'of each seized identity'.

BIBLIOGRAPHY

Translations: Almost all *La Comédie humaine* was translated in forty volumes under the original title, G. Saintsbury, 1895–8. The translations are very unequal; most of the important novels have been re-done. K. Raine, *Cousin Bette*, 1948; M. A. Crawford, *Cousin Bette*, 1965.

Texts: For the whole of *La Comédie humaine*: M. Bouteron and H. Longnon, *Oeuvres complètes*, forty volumes, 1912–40; M. Bouteron (ed), *La Comédie humaine*, eleven volumes, 1935–58; P. Citron, seven volumes, 1965–6.

Criticism: A. Billy, *Vie de Balzac*, 1944; H. J. Hunt, *Honoré de Balzac*, 1957, and *Balzac's 'Comédie humaine'* (1959), 1964; F. Marceau, *Balzac and His World*, 1967. For Balzac and Marxism see G. Lukács, *Studies in European Realism*, 1950.

Ivan Goncharov

Ivan Goncharov was born in 1812, at Simbirsk on the
Volga, into a merchant family which lived in the style of
the gentry. He was educated at the Universities of Moscow and St Petersburg; most of his life was spent in
government service, as interpreter and censor from 1856
– a job he was, by his own account, 'obliged to take'. He
never married.

He was an associate of almost all the leading Russian
writers and critics of his time, including Belinsky, Tolstoy, and Turgenev. He wrote three novels, *Obyknoven-
naya istoriya* [*An Ordinary Story*] (1847), *Oblomov*
(1859), which had been preceded ten years earlier by the
section called 'Oblomov's dream' in the first part, and
Obryv [*The Ravine* or *The Precipice*] (1869). He also
wrote a quantity of criticism and discussion of his own
work. His last years were marred by sporadic attacks of
mental illness. Some have even suggested that his suspicions of Turgenev's plagiarism led to his collapses into
paranoia – and that these suspicions were justified. His
posthumously published *Neoby knovennaya istoriya* [*An
Extraordinary Story*] (1924) contains an unbalanced account of the affair; but Turgenev (the 'velvet knave'), although probably only heavily influenced by Goncharov's
confidences to him about his slowly gestated fiction –
rather than an actual *plagiarist* of them – seems not to
have behaved openly. Goncharov also accused Flaubert
of plagiarism.

It is common to dismiss Goncharov's first and last novels as poor ('dull, verbose and cloudy', writes one incautious critic); but Goncharov himself insisted that he wrote but a single novel, and it does him more justice to take the three works, as Richard Freeborn does, as a 'huge trilogy, or tryptych, the centrepiece of which is the undoubted masterpiece flanked by side panels that enhance by their lesser art the splendour of the central work'.

The first novel described the kind of transfer from old to new (Simbirsk to St Petersburg) that he had himself experienced. Alexander Adayev goes hopefully from country to town, and fails in his aspirations; he eventually becomes a successful official (as Goncharov did) in imitation of his uncle, whose crass example he has previously repudiated – and which, ironically, the latter himself finally rejected. Its style has been criticized as tedious but, as Belinsky was the first to see, this fault is offset by linguistic fluency and dialectical subtlety. The third novel, *Obryov*, is about Raisky, a writer and rather too much the mouthpiece of the author; it contains a distorted portrait of an 1860s-type *nihilist*, Volokhov. But its style is in parts superior to that of the first novel, and it is an indispensable guide to Goncharov's fictional techniques.

Oblomov

SUMMARY By the most scholarly calculation, the action of *Oblomov* (which includes his reveries of childhood, or 'dream') takes place between 1819 and 1856. Oblomov lives from 1812 until 1852 or 1853. He is therefore born in the same year as his creator, and dies in or about the year in which the latter began a dutiful but unenthusiastic round-the-world voyage.

Ilya Ilyitch Oblomov is found in his disgustingly untidy St Petersburg apartment – in bed. He does not actually rise until almost one third of the way through the novel. We learn that he has a country estate and is, his parents having died, the owner of 350 serfs; he has lived in St Petersburg for twelve years. At one time he worked as a government official, but an enlarged heart and dilation of his left ventricle, and 'chronic pain in the liver (*hepatitis*)' obliged his doctor to issue him a certificate forbidding him office work (which he has found excruciatingly boring). But 'sooner or later' he would have had to recover: 'Oblomov could not endure it and sent in his resignation.' He now lives in sloth with the servant – the dirty, lazy serf Zahar – who had originally been allowed to him by his parents. There is at this early stage some implicit criticism of Oblomov on the part of the narrator: as he grew older 'he reverted to a kind of childish timidity.' He has lost touch with external events, has failed to discern that his health could suffer from idleness and overfeeding; he 'grew cold faster than he developed an enthusiasm'. The deadly symbols of his self-destruction are present: the soft-folded dressing gown (patched and tattered by the end of the novel), the divan, the dust. However, it becomes clear that one component of his attitude is sheer *ennui*, and here the reader may sympathize. This section (until his friend Stolz persuades him to go out) is the most delightfully comic in the book; later this *Oblomovism (oblomovshchina)* takes on a tone both tragic and symbolic – though the novel always works triumphantly at realistic level.

For Oblomov this is a bad day. He has had a letter from the (crooked) bailiff of his estate telling him that things are going badly and that he will receive less money. Furthermore, his landlord wants him out, and he must take the unendurable step of moving. But he does nothing about it. He merely quarrels with his serf, laments his lot ('Oh, dear, life doesn't leave one alone, it gets at one everywhere!') and makes plans, but in bed: he will have time to think after breakfast – and so it goes on. He has a number of visitors: the dandy Volkov, the careerist official Sudbinsky, the journalist Penkin, the Gogolesque Alexeyev ('Nature had not bestowed upon him a single, striking, noticeable characteristic, good or bad') and the ill willed, vicious, hypocritical, 'quick, cunning' Tarantyev, who is later to cheat him as he cheats everyone else; Tarantyev is one of the nastiest characters in Russian fiction. These visitors show Oblomov to be a morally superior person as well as a valetudinarian. He cannot suspect Tarantyev's evil opportunism. And, in one of the funniest passages of the novel, Penkin wishes him to read the poem *The Love of a Bribe-taker for a Fallen Woman*, which 'shows up' 'the whole mechanism of our social life ... poetically. All the springs are touched ... The author calls up, as though before a judgement-seat ... a swarm of corrupt officials ... all the varieties of fallen women are considered ... Frenchwomen, German, Finnish ... the author is great! He reminds one of Dante and Shakespeare ...' Oblomov will have none of this ludicrous rubbish.

Oblomov then has his famous dream: an idyllic recollection of his happiness as a seven-year-old at Oblomovka, the country estate. This is nostalgic, lyrical and brings in Oblomov's childhood friend, the half-German Andrey Stolz, the schoolmaster's son; it also shows, conversely, that as a boy Oblomov had been hopelessly spoiled, 'protected like an exotic flower in a hot house', and had not been allowed to make the least effort.

Stolz then calls. There is an openness, a trust and a bond of affection between the two men. Stolz does not bore Oblomov; Oblomov's sloth and indecision appall Stolz, but he loves him. He is his opposite: the 'positive hero', the energetic man who is willing and ready to accept and exploit the consequences of the industrial revolution. We are given his early history in the opening chapter of Part Two. How he is 'all bone, muscle and nerve, like an English race-horse'. He makes 'no superfluous movements'; he balances the practical and the spiritual. He is not, as a critic has properly noted, 'very interesting'; but he is a thoroughly good fellow. He it is who now diagnoses Oblomov's state as one of 'Oblomov-ism'. And Oblomov rather helplessly asks for his aid.

Stolz goes abroad, extracting from Oblomov the (un-fulfilled) promise that he will join him. Before he leaves he introduces him to Olga Ilyinsky, an exquisitely created, loving, lovable young woman of intelligence, gaiety and innocently piercing insight. The two fall in love, a sum-mer idyll. Oblomov is guilty because he feels that he cannot ever become the man she sees in him – perhaps it is the illusion she most loves. But for some of the time she props him up in his role as lover. With the winter this idyll, this illusion on behalf of Oblomov, comes to an end.

Zahar, grumblingly loyal, slovenly, in an always fully human if sometimes brutal relationship with his master (he smashes the furniture, Oblomov kicks him in the face while his boots are being put on), does all in his power to rouse the idler. But Oblomov, although assured by Olga that she will not leave him, allows himself to be tricked by Tarantyev into taking lodgings in the house of the widowed sister of his crooked associate, Ivan Matvey-itch. The two systematically cheat him, as does the bailiff on his own estate; meanwhile he becomes utterly depend-ent on his landlady, who cares for him with a stolid, un-selfish devotion – but who is not of his class. Finally Olga renounces him. He marries Pshenitsyna and has a child by her: Andrey, named after Stolz. Stolz visits him, res-cues him from the financial trickery of Tarantyev and Matveyitch, and tells him that Olga has become his wife. Oblomov is overjoyed, 'influenced by a pure desire for [their] benefit'. He suffers a stroke and loses the use of his left leg. Olga wants to know what is going on. ' "Oblo-movism!" Andrey answered gloomily, and in spite of Olga's further questions he preserved a morose silence.'

Oblomov dies; Olga and Stolz take charge of Andrey – who will inherit the modernized estate, Oblomovska. In the final chapter Stolz is with a writer, a 'stout, apathetic-looking man with dreamy ... and sleepy eyes'. Stolz suggests that he pay a beggar for his story, which he can write and 'resell at a profit'. They come across Zahar, almost blind. Stolz promises to rescue him. Zahar exclaims: 'To think that the Lord should have taken such a man from us! He was a joy to all.' Stolz, too, had once said to Olga, who agreed with him: 'The most alluring sham cannot deceive him and nothing will make him go wrong; a regular ocean of evil and meanness may be storming around him, the whole world may be poisoned and turn upside down – Oblomov will never worship false idols and his soul will always be pure, honest, good ... His heart cannot be bribed ... Once you have known him, you cannot cease loving him.' Now the writer asks after this Ilya Ilyitch whom Zahar had mentioned, of whose name he had already heard from Stolz. ' "He is dead, and how he was wasted! ..." "But why? ..." "Oblomovism." "... What's that?" "I'll tell you directly ..." And he told him what is written here.'

CRITICAL COMMENTARY When *Oblomov* appeared it was reviewed by the radical critic Nikolai Dobrolyubov (1836–60) in a famous essay, '*Chto takoye Oblomovshchina?*' ['What is Oblomovism?']. He claimed (as Belinsky had claimed for *Dead Souls*) that the novel was a study of a contemporary Russian type: the impotent member of the decaying gentry. He related Oblomov to the *superfluous heroes* of Pushkin, Lermontov and the three earliest novels of Turgenev. Although Dobrolyubov's review is not simplistic, it is undoubtedly revolutionary in its interpretation, and it finds the character of Oblomov wanting. In a socio-historical sense – as his frustrated admirer Stolz realizes in the novel itself – of course he is; and Soviet criticism has usually taken this line. But Goncharov was not primarily a social historian, even if *Oblomov* may be seen in a socio-historical perspective (Goncharov's last novel is frankly reactionary.) Dobrolyubov's essay shows an awareness of this; but he was politically motivated. The critic D. N. Ovsyaniko-Kulikovsky saw Tyentyetnikov from the equally non-radical Gogol's abortive continuation of *Dead Souls*, as the direct forbear of Oblomov. 'In such characters we see,' he wrote, 'limp people, people who have gone to seed, incapable of managing their own affairs, devoid of will power ...'

But Oblomov is a convincing character, and so he becomes tragic. He is an extreme representative of the kind of people who were then doomed to extinction – doomed to be sucked up in the vortex created by the new commercial people, of whom Stolz is a remarkably pleasant example. This is what gives the novel a tragic dimension. 'Progress', symbolized here by among other things the idea of a railway station at Oblomovka, is not altogether beneficial to humanity. If the intelligent Dobrolyubov had to repress his misgivings in the laudable interests of his desire for reform, then Goncharov, with his imagination, could not; and he is the greater and the more tragically aware man. What is lost in 'progress' is expressed in a famous poem, 'Silentium', by Fyodor Tyutchev (1803–73), a poet who was at one time a censor like Goncharov, and whose work, again like Goncharov's, was essentially *private*. There is a remarkable affinity between the two. Here are the opening lines of 'Silentium', and they much resemble the essential details of 'Oblomov's Dream':

Quiet, hide yourself;
Hide emotions, dreams.
Let them rise and fall in silence
Like the stars
In your soul's depths.
Worship them. Quiet.

In another poem Tyutchev writes of the 'undisturbed harmony' of all things: we feel alienated from this only because we deceive ourselves that we are free. This kind of paradoxical poetic feeling and thinking, tragically not integrated into the politics of right or left, is the real climate of *Oblomov*.

Young Werther is the archetypally violent (and crude) *zerrissenheit* (disintegration) novel; *Oblomov* is a *zerrissenheit* novel in dreamy, infinitely sad slow motion. As Goncharov explained at length, he composed by 'painting' what he saw in his imagination, by not quite knowing where it was all going to lead. Oblomov, on one level obviously helpless, stagnating, sinking into the awful torpor of overeating and laziness, is on another level still the hero: his values are intact. He renounces Olga because he knows he can never become the picture of himself which she hopefully carries in her mind – and with which she is really more in love. That image combines all the humanity he now possesses with *efficiency*, the ability to 'keep up with the times': to reform Oblomovka, accept a station there, create a proper school, and so on. All these are admirable enough objectives, and neither Olga nor the more certain Stolz are presented as being bad people. Oblomov knows that he must save Olga from himself. Olga in particular is also the loser: she must share a 'modernizing' life with Stolz, and yet she has within her a desire not to have this adventure, but to share instead with Oblomov the living and radiant element in his absolute inertia. Oblomov is funny in his dirty, sordid, greedy laziness; but no one can doubt the purity of either his vision or his moral judgement. He is used; but he uses no one – for his 'victims', Zahar and Pshenitsyna, can function happily only in the kind of life he gives them. Both love him and the memory of him. He has the intuition to discern this. And if he makes Olga unhappy (Stolz he merely saddens) then this is because he recognizes his limitations.

In essence *Oblomov* is a tragic parable of the artist, one of whose functions is to dwell upon the permanent in the midst of change (Stendhal's *'rêverie'*, Flaubert's 'art', Proust's 'memory'). As a text – however Goncharov himself might have come to view it in the thirty-one years he lived after publishing it – it is by no means a 'defence' of the decaying gentry. It is an extreme statement of the plight of the poet who, willy nilly, must apprehend and love unchanging nature, and whose imagination is forced to recognize what in human nature does not and cannot change. There is one badness (one can hardly call it evil) in Oblomov. It is obvious: the cornerstone of the book and the element that makes it comic. Oblomovism. But Oblomovism is also a symbol for a staple ingredient in the make-up of the honest artist. As Henry Gifford writes, *Oblomov* was never a part of the 'natural school': 'all its abounding details serves not to document a case but to substantiate a vision.' It is one of the greatest of elegiac novels.

BIBLIOGRAPHY
Translations: C. J. Hogarth, *Oblomov*, 1915; N. Duddington, *Oblomov*, 1929; D. Magarshack, *Oblomov*, 1954. The last named is the best.

Text: In *Subraniye sochinenii*, 1952–5.

Criticism: A. G. Tseytlin, *I. A. Goncharov*, 1950 – in Russian; J. Lavrin, *Goncharov*, 1954; A. and S. Lyngstud, *Ivan Goncharov*, 1971.

Gustave Flaubert

Gustave Flaubert, son of a doctor, was born in a Rouen hospital in 1821. He was a nervous, susceptible, precocious child, drawn to the excessively romantic and the lurid and grandiosely decadent.

He was sent to study law in Paris between 1840 and 1843 – his experiences there provided him with indispensable material for *L'Éducation sentimental* – but his health became so bad that his father was forced to allow him to devote himself to literature. His illness, which continued to attack him intermittently for the rest of his life, was mysterious: it consisted of sudden seizures, apparently epileptiform, in which he would suffer unconsciousness, a vivid sense of almost hallucinatory joy, and then a profound depression.

Until 1872 Flaubert lived with his mother, to whom he was always deeply attached, at Croisset on the Seine near Rouen. His hermit-like existence, devoted to his fiction and to the education of his niece Caroline (who also lived at Croisset until her marriage), was punctuated by visits to Paris to see his friends – he knew almost every writer of account – and by more prolonged travels. Although he refused to marry, he led a full sexual life, and for long had a regular mistress – the poet Mme Louise Colet. Flaubert was generous to fellow writers, and especially encouraged the young Maupassant. His last years were clouded by financial difficulties and bad health (caused by overeating and syphilis); he died in 1880.

Flaubert is still the paradigm of the dedicated writer (Proust is the only more extreme example): the man to whom life seems worth less than art – or to whom life can have no meaning unless it be in some way shaped by art.

He has been called a romantic and a realist. He was both, but eventually neither. He tempered his excessive romanticism by technical devices which included most notably attempts to attain total impersonality (withdrawal of authorial comment), a perfect *Parnassian* style (*'le mot juste'*, artistic perfection, lofty erudition, precise objectivity), a 'harmony of the whole [novel]', and a scrupulously documented background. But, as his extensive and frequently self-contradictory correspondence reveals, the matter is not as simple as this. Historically he is a bridge between romanticism and realism, and the most influential of nineteenth-century European novelists. He was also regarded as the leader of the realistic school, although he disagreed with some of their tenets. To take one example, the true realists, inspired by Stendhal, Balzac and by the painter Courbet (who decided in 1848 to paint only the 'vulgar' and the contemporary), aimed to give a 'scrupulous reproduction of life in all its aspects'; but Flaubert, although in *Madame Bovary* (1856–7) determined to treat a 'vulgar' subject (provincial adultery) precisely and without moral intrusion, was also dedicated to producing a work of art.

The art in *Madame Bovary* was ignored by the devotees of pure realism, for whom art no longer counted; its prosecution for 'indecency' (Flaubert and his publisher were acquitted) was not. Flaubert, however, believed that life could be truly depicted only by *transforming it into art*. As he remarked, 'it was out of hatred for realism that I undertook this novel [*Madame Bovary*].' Flaubert's complex intelligence gave rise to great art; his modern detractors – who accuse him of inconsistency and pessimism – always assume, if only implicitly, that there is such a thing as human consistency. There is not; and Flaubert knew this better than they. There have been a few adequate tributes to the high degree of his achievement in reconciling – in his two greatest books and in the late *Trois Contes* [*Three Tales*] (1877) – the powerful and complex contradictions within himself.

Flaubert's juvenilia is romantic and straightforwardly autobiographical. Most of the books of his youth are seeds from which later novels grew. *Madame Bovary*, though it was the first to be published, was in fact the last of his fictional works in terms of initial conception. For some years before he set to work on *Madame Bovary*, the notion of *Salammbô* (1862) had been in his mind. This historical novel set in Carthage after the first Punic War is both over-savage and over-documented, though it has powerful passages. Here we see Flaubert's most determined effort to control his romanticism and taste for the barbarous and the exotic by means of a Parnassian *monumentalism*; he wrote it 'in order not to live'. *L'Éducation sentimentale* (1869) is a complete re-casting of a novel of the same title finished by the mid-1840s. *La Tentation de Saint Antoine* (1874) is the third rewriting of a novel Flaubert conceived as a young man, and which his close friends Maxime du Camp and Louis Bouilhet had condemned. This is concealed autobiography, in which Flaubert identifies himself as artist with Saint Anthony (its merits are disputed: 'a failure', 'dead'; 'prose poem of great power and imagination'). The posthumous and unfinished *Bouvard et Pécuchet* (1881) expresses his lifelong hatred of the bourgeois and of their 'values' – and yet Flaubert's presentation of his two comic heroes is more sympathetic than most critics allow.

Flaubert has been called 'bisexual' (by Cecil Jenkins), 'a great literary engineer rather than a great novelist' (by Martin Turnell) and 'a man sawing away at the branch he was perched on' (by Renee Winegarten). Flaubert was not 'bisexual' but, in Freudian terms, possessed a strongly accentuated *feminine* streak – which gave him acute insight into women. His grasp of psychology and his meticulous artistry dispose of the term 'engineer'. His dedication to his vocation – to depict life truthfully in his own way – absolves him of the insensitive charge of 'sawing away at the branch he was perched on'. As Robert Baldick remarked, the 'public still wants works which encourage and exalt its illusions', and so many of them abhor Flaubert; but, as he adds, Flaubert himself once wrote, 'I know nothing more noble than the contemplation of the world.'

Flaubert's immense influence on the development of the novel, his pessimism about the future of society whether in the hands of right or left, his refusal to enter into political commitments, his loathing of the bourgeois hypocrisy which he exposes with such unerring accuracy: these make him a writer difficult for many, especially dogmatists, to accept. But the negative view of him prevalent since the last war ignores his sympathy and compassion for the individual just as it ignores his intelligence and his despair, which was born out of honesty, not ill will.

Madame Bovary

SUMMARY *Madame Bovary* was published in serial form (with cuts) in the *Revue de Paris* in 1856; the full version in book form appeared in 1857. It begins by introducing the reader to Charles Bovary as a schoolboy at Tostes near Rouen. He is wearing an absurd cap, one of those objects 'deeply expressive in their dumb ugliness, like an idiot's face'. This cap, three tiered, is the image from which the novel grows: its sections represent the aristocratic (pompoms), the middle class (lozenges of fur) and the proletariat (cardboard) respectively; it is also a grotesque symbol of stupidity. Bovary is inept, clumsy and incompetent; but he is also pathetic and well meaning. He studies medicine and, at his second attempt, succeeds in qualifying. His mother marries him off to an ugly hypochondriacal forty-five-year-old shrew who spies on him and demands medicine – and sex which he does not want to give. She dies, and he is able to court and marry Emma Rouault, daughter of a farmer whose leg he has set.

As an adolescent Emma has hovered between piety and romantic dreams as evinced in the 'refuse of old lending libraries', in Sir Walter Scott and in the lives of such historical personages as Mary Queen of Scots, Joan of Arc, Héloise, and so on. She might have become a nun, but she loved the church for 'its flowers' rather than its 'discipline', and the Mother Superior is glad to see her leave. She is the natural victim of a society which Flaubert depicts as itself depraved as well as stupid, and of a poor education; she is sensitive but not intelligent; and, as George Saintsbury points out, she 'has a taste *for* men, but none *in* them'. She is presented by Flaubert not only as stupid, but also as tragic: as one who, had she but possessed the taste and the will, might have achieved an authentic existence. She is at the centre of a stifling circle, out of which she cannot escape.

Her marriage with the stupid and inept Charles soon palls. His sexual habits are as clumsy and predictable as his ugly, noisy eating. Before the marriage she had believed herself in love; now she is disillusioned. Nor is Flaubert – though always the detached rather than the *omniscient* narrator, using an imagistic and symbolic method which points towards interior monologue – unsympathetic to her predicament. The Bovarys attend the Comte de Vaubyessard's family ball; at this crucial point, when Emma finds herself in a luxurious world, her illusions evaporate. A 'yawning fissure' is opened in her life.

Charles and Emma, now pregnant (she gives birth to a daughter, Berthe), move to Yonville-l'Abbaye, some twenty miles from Rouen. Charles' mother lives with them. Here Emma becomes involved with a young notary's clerk, Léon Dupuis; she is ready to give herself to him, but he leaves for Paris. Thereupon she turns, nostalgically, to the consolations of 'religion': 'prepared to enter into any sort of devotion ... if only she might forget the external world.' She meets the Abbé Bournisien and tries to get help from him; but this religion, as Flaubert demonstrates – though always by description, never by interference in the narrative – is merely a matter of form. He cannot be bothered with a troubled woman, and ignores her. Throughout the novel Bournisien (symbol of a secularized church) is contrasted with the equally disingenuous Homais, pharmacist, voluble rationalist ('voltairien') and vicious quack. The crooked draper salesman Lheureux completes an unpleasant trio. There is only one character who is neither dishonest nor stupid: the tax collector Captain Binet – but his role is a small one.

Emma, increasingly bored and nauseated by Charles's crassness and dirtiness, and by his mother's tyrannical ignorance, now enters into a fully adulterous affair with a young landowner, Rodolphe Boulanger. Boulanger is not without scruples, but for him women are playthings – and he is tired of his present mistress. For Emma this affair, with its exciting clandestine meetings, seems at first to be the consummation of her desires. But she soon becomes filled with the dread of losing him; it is clearly implied, moreover, that she has been disillusioned by the physical aspects of the liaison. When she tries to rescue her illusions by arranging an elopement, Rodolphe – bored and not wanting to take on her child – writes her a stereo typed letter and flees. The course of the affair had been foreshadowed at the very time it began – during the Agricultural Show, the Comices Agricoles, where the lovers' declarations (Charles's calculated, Emma's ultra-romantic) are ironically interrupted by the speech of the prefect as he awards the agricultural prizes:

'I couldn't tear myself away, though I've tried a hundred times.'

'Manure!'

'And so I'd stay tonight and tomorrow and every day for all the rest of my life!'

'To Monsieur Caron ..., a gold medal!'

Meanwhile Charles, egged on by Homais, has operated on the club foot of Hippolyte, a porter and odd job man; his incompetence leads to the intervention of a superior doctor, who amputates the gangrenous leg at the thigh. Hippolyte's wooden leg is to be heard thudding throughout the rest of the book.

Madame Bovary has got into debt to Lheureux, who cunningly encourages her; Charles, while meekly agreeing with his authoritarian mother that his wife is to be prohibited from reading novels, as meekly signs Lheureux's bills. Emma, stunned by Rodolphe's faithlessness, once again returns to religion, this time hysterically; but when she re-encounters Léon Dupuis in Rouen she soon succumbs to him. After a scene in Rouen Cathedral, in which his efforts at seduction and her feeble efforts to resist are interrupted by a foolish guide, she is seduced in a cab as it races in an aimless circuit of streets, its reluctant driver angrily shouted at every time he slows down. This adultery is trite for her: she feels in it all the 'commonplaces of marriage', and she fails to discover satisfaction in brazen lust. But she indulges, with the calculated 'help' of Lheureux, in wild bursts of extravagance. Léon cools, and she finds herself on the verge of ruin. Desperate, she appeals unsuccessfully to Binet (probably to lend her the tax money he has collected: their conversation is not recorded); finally she goes to Rodolphe, but he does not possess the sum necessary ('If he had had it he would doubtless have given it her'). She steals arsenic powder from Homais' store and crams it into her mouth. At home, she dies horribly as a beggar sings an erotic ballad. Homais and Bournisien indulge in a trite argument about religion as they watch over the body, its face now hideously disfigured; they then sleep. Only Justin, Homais' wretched and bullied assistant – who has been unable to prevent her taking the poison from the shop – weeps on her grave, still devoted to her. Charles, distraught with grief, continues to sign Lheureux's bills. Eventually he discovers his wife's infidelity; soon after this he dies, a broken man. Homais, the final passage relates, ruins three more doctors in succession (they are a threat to his living as a quack), and gains a decoration.

CRITICAL COMMENTARY Not long after Louis Bouilhet and Maxime du Camp told Flaubert that his first version of *The Temptation of Saint Anthony* was fit only for the fire, Bouilhet told him of the case of Eugène Delamare, the medical officer of health of a small town, Ry, near Rouen. All we know is that this affair bore some similarities – possibly only superficial – to that recorded in *Madame Bovary*. If the influence of these now obscure events has been exaggerated, that of Bouilhet – Flaubert's friend, who until his death in 1869 acted as an invaluable catalyst – has not. It was he who, with perfect tact and insight, persuaded Flaubert to set about the task – distasteful to him, as he continually complained in letters to Louise Colet – of recording this deliberately commonplace tale.

Few great books have been subjected to such fierce attacks. All critics hostile to Flaubert know very well that it is great, and are even forced to demonstrate aspects of its greatness. The statement that Flaubert is 'the virtual inventor of the contemporary novel and the source of the most important technical advances since the middle of the nineteenth century' is indisputable. In the present climate it is necessary, if we are to gain all that this book has to offer, to answer such charges as that despite 'its superficial moral orthodoxy, it is an onslaught on the whole basis of human feeling, and on all spiritual and moral values';

that Flaubert is not a good psychologist; that Rodolphe's 'slick and shallow' 'views on love' are Flaubert's own; that he fails to 'give due weight to what was valid and genuine in Emma'; that 'what he exhibits with superb accomplishment is in fact an immature cynicism masquerading as mature vision.'

Madame Bovary cannot be described as other than a pessimistic novel, though it may also, and more significantly, be taken as a tragedy. Flaubert's famous five-year struggle to write it is not any justification of it, and cannot of itself be used to disprove the assertion that its figures fail to 'bear the weight of the symbolism that he tried to attach to them'. But if we are to put forward a view of the book contrary to the fashionable hostility to it, then its long genesis is relevant. One of the many measures of the degree of the success of a work of art is the extent to which its author resolves or overcomes his personal difficulties and conflicts through that work. We cannot judge a work by its author's avowed intentions. Finding the text satisfying, we may then refer to those intentions.

Madame Bovary is not flawless: the shifting of emphasis from Charles to Emma at the beginning is awkward, and some (though not much) of the symbolism and irony is obtrusive; there is more than a hint of artifice. Yet it remains one of the best constructed novels ever written. Its imagery is subtle and consistent. The destruction of Emma Bovary is recorded with relentless exactitude. The novel moves inexorably from phase to phase: the romantic girl at the farm at Tostes, Charles's clumsy courtship, her cherished dreams, her disillusion at the Vaubyessard ball, her interest in the mediocre Léon, her easy seduction by the casual adventurer Rodolphe, her pseudo-religious hysteria when he deserts her, her reunion with Léon and the sordidness of their adultery, her crazed extravagance, her inability to tell the unsuspecting Charles of the financial situation – and her final gesture.

Flaubert put something of himself into Madame

Bovary (there is no evidence that he said '*Madame Bovary, c'est moi*'). He also put something of his mistress Louise Colet into her: Louise's poetry was fervidly romantic (though he encouraged and helped her), and she was what anyone would reasonably regard as a nuisance with her violent demands upon him. But Emma acquires her own existence. And, although Binet (who refuses, on one occasion, to give her adultery away) is decent and Charles is pathetic as well as an inept fool, she is superior to the other characters: for all her ignorance of life and her blindly romantic idealism (its tawdriness is largely the result of her environment and education), she alone is ready to give herself to another, to risk all, for the idea of love. Flaubert himself once described her as 'naturally corrupt'; but in his book she emerges, rather, as one naturally corrupt*ed*.

Madame Bovary does not read as effortlessly as *L'Éducation sentimentale* or *Bouvard et Pécuchet*; but it was the first experiment in fiction in which the narrator deliberately withdrew himself from the action: 'Let us be magnifying mirrors of external truth,' Flaubert wrote to Louise; or again, 'I have put into it nothing of my feelings or of my experience.' But he knew too that the 'novel has been nothing but the exposition of the personality of the author'. For detachment, as he knew, is impossible: the novelist selects, he invents, and in his selections and inventions he reveals his nature. All fiction is illusion – and concealed autobiography. But new techniques enable novelists to see life from new perspectives. 'One writes with one's head. If the heart warms it, so much the better, but it doesn't do to say so. It ought to be an invisible fire.' Flaubert wanted to 'walk straight ahead on a hair hung between the double abysses of lyricism and vulgarity'. He wanted to portray life as it was 'and not seek to have more intelligence than God himself': to see the world as a work of art, a harmonious whole. This is a project noble enough.

The tragedy of Emma and her humdrum marriage and humdrum adulteries is played out against a choric background of mediocrity, trite conversation, corruption and bad faith that have been taken for granted. A part of her tragedy (and that of the dedicated Justin, a minor but important character) is that Emma's superiority is, continually, so very *un*superior, so unrealized. But moral judgement is deliberately withheld.

Is this novel, then, an 'onslaught on all human values'? Are Emma's virtues diminished by the novelist? Is it the product of 'immature cynicism'? Not all readers have found this to be the case. They sense that Flaubert meant it when he spoke of 'this ignoble reality' which 'sicken[ed his] heart ...' The style, the search for the *mot juste*, provides its own commentary: out of a 'sickening' tale arises a beautiful harmony – as Flaubert intended. But this is not 'ivory–towerism': it deliberately draws on a harsh, trivial, provincial reality. The judgement that Flaubert shared Rodolphe's views on love is grotesque; it can in no way be sustained.

As for Flaubert's sense of psychology: he sacrifices analysis in order to convey a sense of what he described as the *'moral density'* (his italics) that is to be found in the 'ugly'. But he does not put a foot wrong. Emma is wholly convincing in her moods and in her fatal moves. Is the man who wrote (about Léon, as he prepares to seduce Emma in Rouen) of 'that coward's courage that nothing can stop' a bad psychologist?

The assault on *Madame Bovary* is valid only if the critic values a starry-eyed romanticism (such as Flaubert attacked) or a vicious dogmatism above the attempt to achieve perfection in art. There are no great novels that give a straightforwardly optimistic picture of life. There are great novels that treat of its pleasures and joys. And there is a great story about a beautiful soul: *Un Coeur simple* (one of the *Trois Contes*) – by Gustave Flaubert.

L'Éducation sentimentale

SUMMARY *L'Éducation sentimentale*, composed between April 1864 and May 1869, appeared towards the end of 1869. An early version, which has been published, and translated, had been completed by 1845; this is immature work. *L'Éducation sentimentale* is an entirely different kind of novel from *Madame Bovary*. It has no real plot, no series of crucial events (though there is a rapid resolution at the end), and its canvas and cast of characters are very large: Paris in the 1840s and its social and political background and, to a lesser extent, the rural world of the anti-hero's home town, Nogent, on the Seine. The historical background (with two or three exceptions in which events are wrongly placed) is meticulous. The time covered is December 1840 until December 1851, with three unobtrusive time shifts (September 1843 to September 1844; December 1845 to January 1847; August 1848 until 1850 – this last involving Rosanette in a twenty-five-month pregnancy). A short passage at the end takes us to 1867.

It is essential to give a broad outline of the history of the period, since Flaubert refers to it in fine detail. Louis Philippe became King of the French in 1830: his reign, July 1830 to February 1848, is called the July Monarchy. It was not a success except with the commercial classes (who themselves became disillusioned, with the economic depression of 1846–7). There were revolts in the 1830s; Louis Blanc led a strong socialist opposition in the following decade. In 1848, the year of revolutions, widespread discontent led to the setting up of the barricades; the national guard turned against Louis Philippe, who abdicated and fled; his palace was stormed. The Second Republic – with Blanc a member of the basically moderate government – was proclaimed. The eloquence of the poet Lamartine (minister for foreign affairs) prevented the extreme left from taking over. By May 1848 elections had been held, and the conservatives, who had had time to regroup, inflicted a severe defeat on the radicals. A new executive council, which excluded socialists, was formed. An attempted left-wing coup failed when the national guard turned against the mob; Blanc fled. In December the authoritarian Louis Napoleon (Napoleon III) was elected President of the Second Republic; in 1851 he extended his power by a *coup d'état*; in 1852 he became Emperor, and the Second Republic became the Second Empire. (The disaster of the Franco-Prussian war, 1870, finished Napoleon III and after a period of imprisonment in Germany he went to England, where he died in 1873.)

In the second, published version of *L'Éducation sentimentale* Flaubert took out the obtrusively autobiographical elements of the first; but the protagonist, Frédéric Moreau, retains some characteristics of his inventor – though these are confined to his experiences of life rather than of art, for as an artist Frédéric is a mere dilettante. For Frédéric's central sexual experience Flaubert drew heavily on a crucial event in his own life.

When the novel opens Frédéric, the only son of a widowed mother – in somewhat reduced circumstances owing to her indebtedness to a rich and cunning neighbour, Monsieur Rocque – is returning by boat from Paris to his country home at Nogent on the Seine. Here he has a fatal encounter with Mme Marie Arnoux, with whom he falls in love, and her husband M Arnoux.

Frédéric, who soon returns to Paris, becomes a close friend of Arnoux, a shady but genial art dealer (later the owner of a factory turning out china, then a dealer in 'ecclesiastic objects') always in debt and with a number of mistresses. Mme Arnoux becomes aware of Frédéric's attachment to her, though he is slow in his approaches; but remains aloof and enigmatic. The theme of the developing relationship between her and Frédéric is one of the two main threads of the novel, and keeps reappearing. The other thread is history and social life, seen through the host of characters with whom Frédéric becomes acquainted in Paris.

A melancholy and irresolute figure (Flaubert once referred to him as *'un jeune hommet'*), Frédéric inherits a fortune from his uncle, loses some of it, but keeps enough to live comfortably. His 'sentimental education' gives the book its ironic title. But he is studied *from the outside*, in a detached manner, and in this sense represents a break with the earlier, romantic type of hero of French novels. He is not presented as an effective or a noble person, but is nevertheless more sensitive than almost every other character – like Madame Bovary, in the foreground of a less crowded canvas, he at least has the potentiality to achieve a meaningful relationship.

The chief agent of Frédéric's misfortunes is his childhood friend Deslauriers; but the book ends (1867) as it begins: with the two 'reconciled once again by that irresistible element in their nature which always united them in friendship'.

Frédéric is reunited with Deslauriers on his first visit to Nogent; the latter soon follows him to Paris, and comes to live with him in his apartment. Both study law, but while Deslauriers is for a time moderately successful, Frédéric becomes absorbed in social life – all, really, in the interests of his love for Madame Arnoux – and fails his examination. Deslauriers, a shabby go-getter, begins to embarrass him socially. After a vain sojourn at Nogent in order to purge himself of his obsession with Mme Arnoux, he moves to a new apartment where he determines to lead a 'selfish life'. The awkward Deslauriers, meanwhile, does badly – and we discern in him the development of a strong element of envy and meanness. There is even a strong suggestion of homosexuality in his attitude towards Frédéric, for he is jealous not only of the latter's independent means but also of his erotic life.

The historical events are skilfully kept in the background in the first two books, to emerge in clearer outline in the third. The destiny of all Frédéric's friends is recorded. Arnoux has great success, but his businesses gradually decline as he becomes increasingly fraudulent: he ends as a sick, poor, old failure. The always enigmatic Marie Arnoux remains with him, obsessed by her never consummated love for the younger Frédéric. The honest republican Dussardier, the pleasantest (though not the most intelligent) character in the book is killed after Louis Napoleon's 1851 *coup* – by none other than the ex-socialist, now policeman, Sénécal; the latter is one of the most perceptive portraits in all literature of the pseudo-revolutionary whose blind fanaticism leads him to support any form of strongly exercised tyranny. Hussonnet, the journalist and publicist, is a futile opportunist. M Dambreuse, aristocrat, is stupidly and wickedly dedicated to wealth; his wife is a revengeful bitch. Rosanette, the 'marshal', popular courtesan and mistress of among others Arnoux and Frédéric, turns 'fat' and 'huge'. The artist Pellerin can only talk: his painting is atrocious. The coward and fop Cisy, who has a ludicrous duel with Frédéric, becomes 'very pious'. Deslauriers, despite his scheming, fails miserably in the end. M Rocque, swindler and murderer (of a radical prisoner who asks for bread), succeeds as well as Homais in *Madame Bovary*; so does the opportunist Martinon, who becomes a senator. As for the condition of France: this becomes worse, not only because of the greed of the bourgeois but also because of the bad faith of the republicans and the socialists – symbolized by the absurd and usually drunk café talker Regimbart. There are certain crucial scenes, particularly the masked ball, in which Flaubert brings together almost every character in the novel (with the notable exception of Mme Arnoux) in a magnificent display of the exotically splendid and the corrupt. Of the revolutionary scenes the most impressive is the occupation of the Tuileries (which Flaubert himself witnessed).

Frédéric's own story is comparatively simple. Although Deslauriers is the chief agent of his last reverses, one feels that his lack of self-assertion and passivity in the face of events – as well as his sensitivity – would in any case have led to the same results. He tries and fails to free himself from his obsession with Marie Arnoux, but meanwhile pays court to Rosanette, the 'marshal' who keeps him at arm's length. He gradually becomes involved with the financier Dambreuse, whose influence his Nogent neighbour Rocque has urged him to make use of. Rocque plans to marry Frédéric off to his daughter Louise, whom he has legitimized by marrying her mother, his housekeeper. Louise falls in love with him, he vacillates, half promising to marry her, causing her great pain. Arnoux's behaviour becomes increasingly shifty, and at last it seems that his wife will yield to Frédéric. They arrange an assignation, and Frédéric rents a room for this purpose.

Mme Arnoux does not arrive. Her son becomes seriously ill with croup and seems about to die: she is forced to watch over him until his dramatic recovery. Frédéric, after waiting in despair for her arrival, rushes off into the arms of Rosanette, who now becomes his mistress. They spend a 'honeymoon' at Fontainebleau; in due course she gives birth to a child, which dies. The Arnoux's property is sold up. Deslauriers treacherously rushes off to Nogent and marries Louise.

At the point when Frédéric horrifiedly recognizes Sénécal as Dussardier's murderer, the narrative breaks off, and there comes the famous short passage, section IV of Part Three, with its compressed account of some sixteen years: 'He travelled ... He returned ... He went into society, and he had other loves ... Years went by; and he endured the idleness of his mind and the inertia of his heart.'

Marie Arnoux, now much aged, visits him. Pathetically she offers herself to him; but while he acknowledges that he has never married because of his love for her, and even while he is filled with a 'frenzied, rabid lust such as he had never known before', he is repelled: he fears 'being disgusted later'. She gives him a lock of her now grey hair and departs, never to see him again.

The last section consists of a dialogue between Deslauriers and Frédéric. Louise has long ago left the former for a singer. His career has not been successful. And the book ends when the two men agree that the 'happiest time we ever had' was when they went together into a brothel, became embarrassed, fled – and were seen leaving, thus causing a local scandal.

CRITICAL COMMENTARY When he first set to work on *L'Éducation sentimentale* Flaubert announced his intention of writing the 'moral history, or rather the sentimental history, of the men of my generation'. He also wanted to treat a theme which he had already tried out in three immature, unpublished works, the last of which had been the first attempt at *L'Éducation sentimentale*.

At Trouville, at the age of fourteen, Flaubert had seen the beautiful twenty-six-year-old Elisa, wife of a music publisher, Maurice Schlésinger. She was feeding her baby. Flaubert fell in love with her then, and again when he went to study law in Paris. But she would not reciprocate this love (though there is a possibility that she might briefly have been his mistress). There is much of Schlésinger in Arnoux. Madame Schlésinger and Flaubert did remain in contact, even after her husband had fled to Germany to escape his creditors. (What Flaubert never knew was that Schlésinger had bought Elisa from a lieutenant in return for giving him the money he needed to avoid prosecution for theft; the child was the lieutenant's, not Maurice's.) After two periods spent in mental hospitals, Elisa died insane in 1888.

The novel has three main aspects, skilfully interwoven. The first is a meticulous history of France over the period treated which, as Baldick rightly said, 'no historian or student of the period can afford to neglect'. The second is the sexual frustration of Frédéric Moreau, doomed to a failure of fulfilment through his own irresolute nature – and also, it is implied, by the moral sensitivity which despite his weaknesses he intermittently displays. The third is the characterization of the many men and women who play their parts in the book. The second theme is reflected by the first: if men of Frédéric's potentialities cannot realize themselves, then how can a whole people? And of course Frédéric's weaknesses are continually reinforced by the corruption of the society of which he becomes a part. The ineluctability of his surrender, like the stroke of fate that prevents Mme Arnoux coming to him, appealed to the naturalists, many of whom took *L'Éducation sentimentale* as a bible. But Flaubert was no proto-naturalist. His project was to tell the truth – without theoretical embellishments. That project clashed (in his own life) with his desire to elevate art over life; but in this novel, over which he worked so hard, his compulsively exact record of life is transformed into whatever art life may actually possess. It is the desperately objective exactness of the novel which gives it its 'art'. Flaubert's achievement rests on a paradox: art is 'superior' to life, but in order to be so it must nourish itself from life. As in Aeschylus and for that matter Spinoza (in his utterly different way), there is more than a hint in Flaubert's canon of the existence of an ultimately benevolent design. He probes at this by his pursuit of objective truth. After all, why loathe human *bêtise* so much if one is not haunted by a vision of something opposite to or better than it?

The 'sentimental' of Flaubert's title is an ironic pun: it refers to 'education-of-sentiments-as-it-exists', *and* alludes to Flaubert's resolutely objective treatment; his deliberate avoidance of sentimentality demonstrates that the system of the France of his day was rotten and corrupt. And systems are generated by men. Frédéric is no Flaubert, because he lacks his creator's dedication to art. But his political and sexual bad faith is a rueful commentary on Flaubert's own self-doubts as to his artistic enterprise. He was himself, after all, essentially a 'Voltairian liberal' (as P. E. Charvet has observed) as well as many other things.

Finally: one of the charges quite frequently brought against Flaubert is that his ending is disgusting. So the height of human happiness is to be traced to an abortive visit to a brothel in one's teens!

But Flaubert meant something quite different. The two young men, whose failure to achieve their object is symbolic of their failure in love (youth is curious, and visits to brothels are by no means merely to satisfy lust: they are then more 'romantic' than physical), had all before them. Now middle-aged men, they have agreed that they have failed; but they have seen the nasty, the spiteful, the murderous and the greedy succeed. Flaubert chooses to allude to a situation of intended sexual initiation. Is not his 'message' that understanding of sex and love is vital to an understanding of ourselves? Also that this life is one in which we are most happy before we have discovered that we are scarcely capable of reaching such understanding? Pessimistic, perhaps: but after two world wars and hideous tyrannies of left and right (Flaubert's view of both in *L'Éducation sentimentale* has proved correct), we still believe that one of the vital keys to a tolerable existence lies in an understanding of sex and love. There can be novels of narrow scope demonstrating the joyous aspects of existence; the wider the scope the less joyous the demonstration will be. Flaubert's scope here is very wide indeed. And our hope of survival, history seems to suggest, still lies in the intelligence (and the tenderness, of the way in which the question of how we might understand sex and love is posed. Thus Flaubert, who chose to avoid dogma and sentimentality, writing over a hundred years ago, is vindicated: as artist, as prophet, as human being, as optimist.

BIBLIOGRAPHY

Translations: G. Hopkins, *Madame Bovary*, 1948; A. Russell, *Madame Bovary*, 1950; J. L. May, *Madame Bovary*, 1953. A. Goldsmith, *Sentimental Education*, 1941; R. Baldick, *Sentimental Education*, 1964. See also D. Garman, *The First Sentimental Education*, 1964.

Texts: In A. Thibaudet and R. Dumesnil, *Oeuvres*, 1946–8. There are also a number of annotated students' editions.

Criticism: A. Thorlby, *Gustave Flaubert*, 1956; A. Fairlie, *Flaubert: 'Madame Bovary'*, 1962; V. Brombert, *The Novels of Flaubert*, 1966; P. Cortland, *The Sentimental Adventure*, 1967 and *A Reader's Guide to Flaubert*, 1968; E. Starkie, *Flaubert*, 1967–71.

Ivan Turgenev

Ivan Turgenev was born in 1818 on his wealthy mother's estate at Spasskoye in the province of Orel in central Russia. His father died in 1834. His mother was a sadistic, hateful and partly unbalanced tyrant who was nevertheless not a fool. She would have her serfs flogged or exiled for no reason; half-demented, she ignored her two sons – but might have them thrashed indiscriminately. As he grew older Turgenev learned to deal with her by refusing to meet her head-on, instead passively resisting her. In her ill treatment of the serfs she came to symbolize for him the heedless autocratic attitude that he hated. After threats to disinherit him (and his brother), she died in 1850, leaving Ivan the owner of two thousand 'souls'. He freed the domestic staff and adopted a liberal attitude to the serf farmers.

It has been suggested that he was not as 'progressive' as he 'might logically have been', but the serf–landowner problem was so complex that this is a contentious judgement. He was not in any case interested in business affairs, and made less money from his inheritance than he might have done.

Turgenev, the most adept in other European languages of his Russian contemporaries, had an excellent education. He learned to love Russian literature from his mother's household steward, Lobanov; despite the unhappiness of his childhood, he also developed the love for Russia, especially its countryside, that was to remain with him in spite of his long years of exile. Between 1833 and 1841 he studied at the Universities of Moscow, St Petersburg and Berlin. He returned to Russia an avowed liberal and Westernizer; he had met Herzen and Bakunin (not yet converted to activism), and was soaked in Hegelian idealism. Much of his early work is in verse, influenced by Pushkin and Byron; he later disowned it. Until 1860 he published in the radical magazine *Sovremennik* [*The Contemporary*], controlled by Nikolai Chernyshevsky (1828–89), the author of *Chto delat* [*What is to be Done?*], who was later to be exiled to Siberia, and Dobrolyubov; but when the latter reviewed his *Nakanune* [*On the Eve*] unfavourably he moved to a more politically moderate journal. None the less, opprobrium was poured upon him by both radicals and reactionaries for the rest of his life. He was unquestionably an irresolute man. He could see both sides of any question and also, despite his liberal conscience and his religious scepticism, was dedicated to telling the truth as he saw it. These qualities are vices in the eyes of political and clerical dogmatists.

The year 1834 was a crucial one. He met and became the devotee of Belinski, he also met Pauline Viardot-García (born in 1821), the celebrated Spanish singer. Although there is no evidence that their relationship was ever physical – it is highly unlikely – he remained in her thrall for the rest of his life and after 1847 spent much of his time following her and her husband and family wherever they went. He died in her house near Paris. (His only child, Pauline, was by a serf woman.) It was in 1843, too, that Turgenev's first published book (poetry) appeared. After this he wrote more verse, and some poor, derivative plays – the exception is the exquisite *Mesyats v derevne* [*A Month in the Country*] (1849), an improvement of Balzac's *La Marâtre* [*The Stepmother*] (1848), which anticipates Chekhov.

In 1852 Turgenev published both an obituary on Gogol

– in Moscow; the St Petersburg censor had forbidden it –
and the group of tales *Zapiski okhotnika* [known, in
various English translations, as *Sportsman's Sketches*,
Sketches from a Hunter's Album, etc]. The latter, although its contents had appeared separately, and although
written with restraint, drew attention to the unhappy
plight of the serfs and to the selfishness and ineffectuality
of their owners. The Tsar therefore had Turgenev put
into prison for a month and then exiled to his estate for
a year and a half. (The excuse was the Gogol obituary.)
These lyrical yet grim sketches were to influence Alexander II in his decision to emancipate the serfs (1861); but
he did not come to the throne until 1855. The experience
sobered Turgenev and purged him of such Westernizing
ardency as he had possessed; but it also revealed to him
the nature of the rulers of Russia, and of the malignant
bureaucracy through which they worked.

At Spasskoye Turgenev began his first novel, *Rudin*
(1856, revised 1860). He followed this with five more
novels – *Dvoyanskoe gnezo* [*Home of the Gentry*] (1859),
Nakanune [*On the Eve*] (1860), *Otsy i deti* [*Father and
Sons*] (1862) – the masterpiece, and the less successful
Dym [*Smoke*] (1867), and *Nov* [*Virgin Soil*] (1877). He
continued to write short stories, many of them of high
quality, for the rest of his life. He met Henry James (who
called him 'adorable', the 'beautiful genius'), Flaubert,
Georges Sand, the Goncourts and many others; his writings were widely regarded outside Russia as the key
to the 'Russian spirit'. 'He gave us the psychology of a
whole race,' wrote Georg Brandes. This is now generally
felt to be a limiting view since, as E. M. Forster put it
as early as 1915, we ought not to seek in novels for mere
'information' – and since Turgenev, though a realist, was
a supreme artist. He died slowly and painfully of spinal
cancer, in 1883.

Turgenev was a gentleman and a gentle man; but he
could be arrogant and evasive. Goncharov gave an

account of him which, while not entirely trustworthy, is convincing enough to show why Turgenev's fellow intellectuals came to hate him. He posed, 'making himself out to be a dandy', said Goncharov; he showed 'caressing and fawning conduct ... to all impartially'. He would forget appointments, but never one 'when it was necessary to him'. The fact is that Turgenev, irresolute and *triste*, was happier in the company of non-Russian writers. He was partly ashamed of his aristocratic origins, but knew that he could not change what he was. He quarrelled with all Russian contemporaries, who were jealous of his cosmopolitanism and international fame. He did not always behave well. But in his vivid and balanced writings he transcended his personal faults, which were not extreme. As a describer of nature and as a stylist he surpassed all the nineteenth-century Russian writers.

Otsy i deti
[Fathers and Sons]

SUMMARY The action of *Fathers and Sons* takes place over two summer months in the year 1859. As its first readers knew, the emancipation of the serfs (19 February 1861, old style) was imminent. Arkady Kirsanov returns from university to his father's estate at Marino with Evgeny Bazarov, a young doctor who has been his fellow student. Nikolai Petrovich, Arkady's father, is an old-fashioned ineffectual liberal who treats his serfs well – in return for which they cheat and abuse him. His estate is not in good condition. He has formed a liaison with a serf girl, Fenichka, by whom he has a child, Mitya. Nikolai's brother, Pavel Petrovich, is a melancholy Anglophile dandy (a type then common in Russia), whose life has been ruined by an unhappy love affair; like his brother he sees himself as a liberal, but regards the peasantry in a paternal manner, seeing their customs (it is implied) as a form of art, his conception of which he reveres in his idle way as essential to the preservation of civilization. He is secretly in love with the simple Fenichka, but is wholly honourable towards her (though his demeanour frightens her, for reasons she cannot understand).

Arkady is dedicated to the ideas of his dominating friend, the shabby, plain-speaking Bazarov. Bazarov is a *nihilist* – an exasperatingly vague term which in this context requires some explanation because it was in *Fathers and Sons* itself that it became popularized, and because it did not mean then what it means now. The word was used pejoratively in the 1820s in Russia to mean 'ignorant', 'immoral'; by 1858 it was being used to signify 'sceptic'. Turgenev, who cannot be blamed for the obtuse reaction his novel provoked, meant no more by it than 'empiricist': one who would not accept anything that could not be proved. Bazarov, however, is untidy, rude, amoral, verbally destructive, sceptical – and devoted to science. By 1870 'nihilist' was being applied (particularly by Dostoievsky) to anyone who appeared to be radical.

Nikolai is puzzled by Bazarov, but tries to understand him because he is devoted to his son. Pavel Petrovich is openly provoked by him, and their encounters become increasingly hostile.

Arkady and Bazarov visit the local provincial town, where they meet officials and progressives, who are presented as ridiculous. The main absurd official is Kolyazin: 'considered a "progressive"', he follows contemporary literature 'in the way a grown-up who meets a procession of urchins will sometimes join them'. He is sly but has 'no aptitude for handling public affairs, and no intelligence'. The main absurd 'progressives' are Sitnikov, a squeaking buffoon, and the ugly Madame Kukshin, who drinks heavily, rolls cigarettes, and discusses the *rights of women* and whether marriage is 'a prejudice or a crime' without the least knowledge of anything. While in the (unnamed) town they meet the beautiful rich widow

Anna Odintsova, who has married for money, and subsequently they visit her at her fine estate, Nikolskoye,
where she lives with her younger sister Katya.

Bazarov, to his own disgust, falls in love with Anna,
who represents all that he despises. He is forced into a
clumsy, fierce declaration; Anna, afraid of even considering action on her emotions alone, repudiates him – even
though fascinated by him. Arkady fancies himself to be in
love with her as well; he is already in love with Katya,
a fact which his immaturity will not allow him to recognize.

The two young men then proceed to the humble home
of Bazarov's old parents, who own only a few serfs and
who live little better than they. Like Arkady, Bazarov is
the object of touching parental devotion. His gentle
father, once a military doctor, does all he can to understand his son's new-fangled ways. But Bazarov cannot express his feelings for them; furthermore, it now becomes
clear that he despises the backwardness of the peasants
as much as he despises the way of the masters. After two
days, much to the grief of his parents, he leaves with
Arkady. They return to Marino, calling in at Nikolskoye
where they are coldly received. By this time the sensitive
but innately conservative Arkady is beginning involuntarily to tire of Bazarov, whom he fails to understand: he
is upset by Bazarov's harsh treatment of his own parents,
as by the casual insults he hurls at Arkady himself and at
Nikolai and Pavel Petrovich.

At Marino the estate is going from bad to worse. Only
the simple Fenichka goes on in her serene way. The hostility between Pavel Petrovich and Bazarov comes to a
head when the former catches the latter kissing the
scarcely willing – but fascinated – Fenichka in an arbour.
Pavel Petrovich challenges Bazarov to a duel, in which
ridiculous affair the former is wounded in the leg. The
two become partly reconciled in agreeing to pretend that
the affair was over politics. Pavel Petrovitch urges the

surprised Nikolai to marry Fenichka, and eventually takes himself off to a lonely exile as a 'perfect gentleman' in Dresden. Arkady discovers some old letters to Anna and, on the excuse of returning them to her, calls at Nikolskoye where he is warmly received. Here he discovers his love for Katya, proposes, and is accepted.

Bazarov, after a visit to Anna in which the two agree that 'love ... is a purely imaginary feeling' ('Was the truth, the whole truth, to be found in their words? They themselves did not know, and still less does the author'), takes his leave of Arkady: 'you were not made for our bitter, harsh, lonely existence. There's no audacity in you, no venom ... We must smash people! You're a nice lad, but you're too soft, a good little liberal gentleman.'

But Bazarov does not 'smash people'. He returns to his parents' estate and takes up work as a country doctor. Soon he falls ill: he has become infected with typhus through cutting himself while dissecting the corpse of a victim of the disease. Significantly, one cause of this is that the incompetent local practitioner has no caustic. There is now one problem left: 'to die decently.' He does this. He calls for Anna Odintsova and she comes. Seeing him in his last extremity she 'knew a feeling of sheer terror; a cold and oppressive terror; then the thought flashed instantly into her brain that she would not have felt like this if she had really loved him.' But she comforts him before he falls into his last coma.

At Marino there is a double wedding: Arkady and Katya, Nicolai and Fenichka. Father and son make the farm prosper, though Nikolai is 'too mild' for peasants or gentry. Pavel goes into his exile. We are left with a picture of Bazarov's lonely grave, attended only by his frail parents; the flowers growing over it 'speak to us not only ... of the vast repose of "indifferent" nature; they tell us of everlasting reconciliation and of life which has no end.'

CRITICAL COMMENTARY Since *Fathers and Sons* was first published there has been a tendency to judge it in polemical terms or in the light of its author's complex personality. There is an excuse for this. As in his first three novels, Turgenev is concerned with both socio-economic and erotic problems; these are not merely his overt subject matter. Further, one may infer that he was fascinated by and partly sympathetic towards, though frightened of, all kinds of revolutions and revolutionaries; a man who was anything but an activist, he was obsessed with activists (to the extent of having portraits of executed terrorists on his desk). When we analyse *Fathers and Sons* in terms of Turgenev's personality we learn something about the novel, about the man, and about the nature of artistic creation. What we shall learn in the last case is that a novel can (and therefore should) to a great extent transcend polemic and personal conflict. The truth should be more important than polemic; and in *Fathers and Sons* Turgenev gives us more of the truth about Russia (indeed, by extension, about all conservatism and revolution) than any other Russian of the 1860s, whether conservative or revolutionary. Here, then, we need to judge *Fathers and Sons* mainly as a text rather than as an index of the author's contradictory attitudes. It is a beautiful text, which reveals much about mid-nineteenth-century Russia and more about human nature. Turgenev himself said that he did not know whether to love or hate Bazarov; nor do we. But his ambiguous presence is a reality, and moreover, one that reaches into our own age.

In 1860 Turgenev published an important essay, 'Hamlet and Don Quixote' (translated by R. Nichols, 1930). There he contrasted the 'Hamlet-type' of his own generation with the 'Quixote-type' of the succeeding one. He recognizes that the two types can coexist in one man, and in varying ratio. But it is not quite true that he 'reads himself into Hamlet and sees Don Quixote as the crusading spirit he would like to be if only he were not so lucid': he was not as simple as that. He does self-critically load the scales, in the essay itself, against the egoistic, negative, introspective Hamlet-type; but he also admiringly criticizes the Quixote-type – and he does ultimately vindicate the Hamlet-type by implying that although he is sceptical and/or pessimistic, he too is willing to lay down his life for the cause of justice.

In his fiction Turgenev is subtler than in his essay, even though this provides a useful key to his approach. As Richard Freeborn so refreshingly writes, 'Turgenev's realism is to be defined, firstly, in common human terms. His novels give us pictures of real life which are true to life and acceptable in terms of a reality that every man can experience.' That is the imaginative answer to the Hamlet–Quixote dilemma which the intellectual side of Turgenev could not evade.

The non-heroes of his first two novels are *superfluous men*. Rudin is an ineffectual Westernizer, Lavretsky an equally ineffectual Slavophile; both fail with 'strong' women, who figure frequently in Turgenev's fiction. Insarov of *On the Eve* is a revolutionary and a leader – but Turgenev made him Bulgarian in order to demonstrate ironically his conviction that there neither could nor would be 'new' Russians. After his death his 'strong' Russian wife continues his work, of gathering together an army to liberate Bulgaria.

In Bazarov Turgenev at last succeeds in creating a genuinely tragic figure. At first he seems boorish and foolish, but gradually we see his integrity emerging. We also see his Quixotic qualities being undermined by just those emotions and sensations which he wishes to repudiate. Bazarov, who entirely gains our sympathy by the end of the book, is indeed a tragic demonstration of the 'superfluousness' of the Quixote-type. Rudin is too weak to go away with the woman he loves; Lavretsky is cheated of the one he loves because he has made a foolish marriage, out of ignorance. But does not Bazarov's tough in-hibiting manner also destroy his chances of happiness? Anna does marry again, 'not for love' but, at least, be-cause her husband is likely to become a 'future leader'. If Bazarov had not had a 'Hamlet-type' integrity in his Quixotic *nihilism*, he might have become a 'future leader' – and married Anna. He would have done well to understand what George Eliot understood when she commented (in *Middlemarch*) that 'scepticism ... can never be thoroughly applied, else life would come to a standstill: something we must believe in and do, and whatever that something may be called, it is virtually our own judgement.' Bazarov thinks he does believe in something – the irony of his situation is that this 'some-thing' amounts to no more than an absolute negation of everything. Yet he does, as Turgenev demonstrates, have his own 'judgement'. Perhaps critics have tended to ignore his immaturity. He possesses, despite his youthfully rough language and declared faith in scientific principles alone, emotions and sensitivity. He discerns Arkady's love for Katya before Arkady himself does. His feelings for Anna are not simply lustful: he is *in love*. He is touched by his parents' love. He behaves well towards Pavel Pavlovich, refusing to take aim at him after the other's bullet has missed him by an inch. He works as a doctor amongst people he theoretically despises. He attracts people – particularly poor people. He has a burning and quite *unscientific* passion to better humanity – but he cannot (Hamlet-like?) believe in his programme or his material: '... all our enterprises are ruined simply because there aren't enough honest people to carry them out.' He dies in the cause of scientific progress, and does not com-plain. He is intelligent but young and, as we say, *very human*: Freeborn's words are borne out: every man can understand Bazarov. *Fathers and Sons* is Turgenev's most perfect novel because it has no axe to grind. It is his final repudiation of Chernyshevsky's pronouncement (to culminate, though through no fault of Chernyshevsky, in the invidious 'socialist realism' of this century) that 'Art must exist for Life's sake, not Life for Art's.' He knew that art must be rooted in life, and his observation of Russian life is more balanced and topical than that of any of his contemporaries, even the greatest. He would have agreed with his friend Flaubert, who wrote in 1857, in a letter, that life 'is such a hideous business that the only way of bearing it is to avoid it. And one does avoid it by living in Art, in the ceaseless quest for Truth presented by Beauty ... I believe in the perpetual evolution of humanity and in its ever changing forms, and consequently I abominate all those frames which men try to cram it into by main force.' These are not in the light of history between 1857 and today pessimistic words, because Flaubert already knew that revolutions would continue to fail so long as men failed to understand themselves. We may, on the evidence of his own manifold pronouncements, call Flaubert's project *phenomenological* if we are frightened by or tired of such words as 'truth' or 'beauty'. Turgenev was more conscience-stricken than Flaubert (himself a perfectly good 'liberal') because of the truly atrocious plight of the Russian serf and because of his own aristocratic origins: his literary pronouncements show it. He is less possessed by contempt than Flaubert. But *Fathers and Sons*, the novel, bears out Flaubert's main precept. It is full of compassion, but ultimately it is detached.

Turgenev failed as a poet, but he is the most poetic of novelists: a poetic realist. His descriptions of the different settings in the novel (a dilapidated large estate, a splendid country house, a poor estate) are not at all sentimentalized; highly evocative, they are written with a uniquely melancholy nostalgic affection. Of Russian writers only Ivan Bunin has come near to such rural descriptive accuracy. The events of the novel are dramatic – though the duel is absurd – but they are neverthe-less 'staged' (Freeborn's term) against the contrasting atmospheres which Turgenev is so gifted in conveying. His vivid concise style has not been surpassed in Russian literature; his dramatically presented non-dramas are characterized – either in brief exchanges of significant dialogue or short, shrewd, objective character sketches (that of Anna early in *Fathers and Sons* offers a supreme example), or in description – by a sense of life's evanes-cence, its transitoriness, its mystery. Thus while Freeborn can perfectly reasonably speak of Bazarov as being repre-sented as the 'victor in the conflict' between nobility and peasantry, other readers can as reasonably speak of him as an eternal loser. It hardly matters what Turgenev or his polemically minded readers thought about Bazarov or about the gentle and fundamentally liberal conserva-tive Arkady. This is a story about what those who take part in, and indeed make, history are *really* like. The balance between the senses of beauty and futility is ex-quisitely maintained. 'I was needed in Russia,' says Baza-rov as he dies. 'No, it's clear I wasn't,' he adds. The author does not 'know' which of these self-judgements is true any more than he knows whether love is 'a purely imaginary feeling'. He is therefore the 'novelist's novelist' (Henry James's view): he shows us what life is, the human details that lie behind what is called 'history' in the text-books, the confusions that beset human beings. He ought to be the reader's novelist.

BIBLIOGRAPHY

Translations: C. Garnett, *Fathers and Children*, 1928; R. Hare, *Fathers and Children*, 1947; G. Reavey, *Fathers and Sons*, 1950; A. Pyman, *Fathers and Children*, 1962; R. Edmonds, *Fathers and Sons*, 1965. The first and last are the best.

Text: In *Sobraniye sochinenii*, 1949.

Criticism: H. Granjard, *Ivan Tourguénev et les courants politiques et sociaux*, 1954; R. Freeborn, *Turgenev*, 1960. Freeborn's study is outstanding.

Fyodor Dostoievsky

Fyodor Dostoievsky, son of a physician, was born in Moscow in 1821. He was one of seven. His father was strict and stuffy; after the death of his wife he went to his farm where in 1839 – by then a brutal alcholic – he was murdered by his serfs. Whatever miseries Fyodor endured as a child, his gentle mother and his elder brother Mikhail were of the greatest consolation to him. He studied at the St Petersburg Military Academy and obtained a commission in 1843, but resigned it in the following year in order to devote himself to writing. His first novel, *Bednye lyudi* [*Poor folk*] (1846), aroused the excited enthusiasm of Belinsky; but its successor, *Dvoinik* [*The Double*] (1846), disappointed him – a setback for Dostoievsky.

Dostoievsky was at this time associated with a group of mild, ineffectual liberals. Tsar Nicholas I, terrified of any kind of subversive activity, had many of the group, including Dostoievsky, arrested in 1849. They were sentenced to be shot, but were reprieved after having been led out to the scaffold (the Tsar's plan). Dostoievsky spent four years at hard labour in Siberia, and then four more as a soldier in exile there. Towards the end of this wretched period (1857), during which he conceived the notion that the salvation of the world depended on the Russian people and the spirit of the New Testament as interpreted by the Orthodox Church, he made an unhappy marriage to an hysterical and sick widow. She died in 1864. It was while he was in Siberia that he began to suffer the serious attacks of epilepsy which were to plague him for the rest of his life. His account of his prison experiences is in *Zapiski iz myortvogo doma* [*Notes from the House of the Dead*] (1860–62). This is one of his greatest books, and was Tolstoy's favourite.

Dostoievsky's first mature novel is *Zapiski iz podpolya* [*Notes from Underground*] (1864); this deals with the negative, *nihilist* type of man, who – because there was so much of him in the author – continued to obsess him for the rest of his life. In the next years Dostoievsky spent much time in Europe, deeply in debt, compulsively gambling (and losing), and engaged – with his brother Mikhail, who died in 1864 – in editing commercially unsuccessful journals. He also had a hopeless love affair with a wayward and half-demented woman, Polina Suslova. He married his young stenographer Anna Snitkini in 1867 and, after further harrowing gambling escapades in Europe, settled down in Russia in 1871. He never gambled again. Anna was not remarkably intelligent, but she was long suffering and practical, and his last ten years were spent in comparative security and comfort. Ostensibly he became a reactionary patriot who believed in 'Holy Russia' and in the missionary role of the humble people; he believed that Roman Catholicism was essentially socialistic, and was on occasions an avid anti-semite. His opinions were frenetic and can be disconcerting to admirers of his fiction, which is at its frequent best when the psychologist and artist in him overcomes the rabid polemicist. While his 'system', considered as a whole, is sociologically obtuse and confused, his non-fictional work is full of isolated insights of great value. Despite his inconsistencies and his insistence that wretchedness and poverty bring people closer to God (a God of whose existence he was in fact always agonizedly uncertain), he was a deeper thinker than Tolstoy. His strength as a novelist largely owes to his capacity to diversify himself into many characters, and to give those characters independent life; in spite of the glaring flaws in even his greatest novels, he was a master of technique – in particular of suspense and of portraying people 'from the inside'. His style is not distinguished, but he more than compensates for this by his raw power, vitality and emotional appeal. He hated Turgenev, because he saw him as an effete Europeanizing liberal; in reality he was as obsessed as Turgenev with *nihilists*, anarchists and revolutionaries. He himself can fairly be viewed as preaching a sort of primitive non-Marxist Christian communism.

His career ended in triumph, when he made a speech at an unveiling of a memorial to Pushkin in Moscow (1880). He was never rich, but his four greatest novels – though entirely separate works, they are best taken as a whole – brought him increasing fame and respect. All were first published in serial form, which accounts for their (varying) lack of organization. He died, suddenly, in 1881.

Of Dostoievsky's four major novels *Crime and Punishment* (1866) is the least flawed; the last, *The Brothers Karamazov* (1879–80), is generally regarded as his masterpiece (though a few prefer *The Devils* (1871–2)). *The Idiot* (1868–9), for all its power, is usually felt to lack balance, a 'firm centre' – a criticism also sometimes applied to *The Devils*. All four books have philosophical themes in common, although the psychological success with which these are handled varies.

Dostoievsky's chief concern was with the notion that if God does not exist – if there is not a divine, 'irrational' law – then everything is permissible (cf. the confusions of his Ivan in *Karamazov*). Though sympathetic to the anguishes of poverty, he was as far from being a humanist as it is possible to get: he passionately believed that rationalism and intellectualism were inadequate. He professed a belief in a specifically Russian messianic Christ; he was

convinced that Russia's holy mission was being ruined by
shallow European ideas, though study of his letters shows
that he was not as anti-European as he is usually made out
to have been (this also emerges in the Pushkin speech).
He was unfair in his expressions of hatred for liberals
and socialists (he badly misjudged Turgenev, towards
whom he usually behaved without charity); but he remains one of the greatest critics of *liberalism in action*.
His novels demonstrate his own doubts. While they show
no sympathy whatever with left-wing politics (which he
too easily confused with nihilism), they do show him
to be tormented not only by guilt (over his love affairs,
his gambling and, probably, a sexual interest – perhaps
not ever practised – in violating very young girls) but
also by severe doubts. His 'Russian Christ' is somewhat
of an artifact – and in his heart he knew it. It is because
he is attacking the rationalist and the unbeliever in himself, as well as the gambling reprobate, that he carries
such conviction. And, although nominally an inflamed
reactionary, he hated the bourgeois and the well heeled
(as his portrait of Luhzin in *Crime and Punishment*
clearly shows) quite as much as Flaubert did. He desired
the intelligentsia to go back to the 'people' to learn from
them – and his portraits of such people are more convincing than the aristocratic Tolstoy's. But, unlike Tolstoy, he is an urban novelist. The world of his novels is
almost exclusively that of the overcrowded oppressive
city (though *The Devils* and *Karamazov* are set in provincial towns).

Prestuplenie i Nakazanie
[Crime and Punishment]

CRITICAL SUMMARY The main plot of *Crime and Punishment* is simple: a poor student in Petersburg, Raskolnikov, who has had to leave his university studies in law,

murders a vicious old pawnbroker and, by an accident owing to his miscalculation, her half-sister. He eventually confesses his crime and is sent to Siberia for eight years. At the very end it is implied that he will repent of his deed and be redeemed by suffering.

There are two more complicated sub-plots. One concerns the misfortunes of the Marmeladov family: the father, who is run over and killed by a carriage and horses, is a masochistic drunkard who cannot keep his humble post in the civil service. A comic character; but because he drinks and sins in order to suffer and be punished, he possesses a certain kind of tragic – and characteristically Dostoievskian – dignity. His half-mad consumptive wife (who also dies) lives in a pathetic dream of the past. In a surreal scene of macabre humour she finally takes her starving children out to dance in the street in order to obtain money. Marmeladov's eldest daughter (by a previous marriage), Sonia, has become a prostitute in order to provide for the family. She is Dostoievsky's 'holy tart' who is instrumental in redeeming Raskolnikov (by prevailing upon him to confess), following him to Siberia. While Dostoievsky has the skill to make her seem convincing, it is hard in retrospect to find her so: she is the weakest aspect of the novel.

The other sub-plot deals with Raskolnikov's mother, his sister Dunya, his friend Razumikhin – and with the evil Svidrigaylov, with Luhzin (both would-be seducers of the virtuous Dunya), and with Lebezyatnikov – who plays a less important role, but who looks forward to *The Devils* because he is a nihilist.

Raskolnikov has a number of motives for his crime. The old woman is vicious, and may soon die anyway. He will use her ill gotten money in order to perform many humanitarian actions, and will improve society. At the same time he needs money to save his foolish but genuinely loving mother from having to raise it for him – and to save his sister Dunya from having to marry Luhzin, an offensive, pretentious, 'solid', 'respectable', treacherous self-made lawyer. There is a third, contradictory, motive. Raskolnikov wants to believe that there are two sorts of people: 'Napoleons' with power – and others without it. The Napoleons are 'logical' 'supermen' (but suggestions that Dostoievsky anticipated and, so to say, refuted Nietzsche are unfair to the latter), who make their own laws: they live by 'rational egoism'. But Raskolnikov is not logical. He bungles the murder, panics, and escapes simply by luck. He steals only a few articles, and hides these: he does not benefit by the crime at all. He is too weak to be a Napoleon. And so he becomes feverishly ill, makes self-incriminating remarks about the murder – which a 'Napoleon', being safe, would not do – and seeks out and eventually confesses both to Sonia and then to the police investigator. The passage describing the confrontation between these two men is amongst the most dramatic in the book.

Svidrigaylov, who has unsuccessfully attempted to seduce Dunya while she was working in his household, is just what Raskolnikov cannot be: a man devoted to his own ends. Driven primarily by lust, he is probably guilty of murder, of driving a child to suicide, of sadistic acts. He taunts Raskolnikov, who is both fascinated and repelled by him. In the end, after giving the Marmeladov children money and even saving Sonia from prostitution, he shoots himself. His 'supermanism', though it does cause pain and suffering and is relentless, is ridiculous: puny, unworthy of a 'great idea', as 'illogical', in its way, as Raskolnikov's own blundering inconsistency.

Dostoievsky's philosophical ideas are only important thanks to his powers of psychological penetration and his ability to allow his imagination to override his intellectual convictions. Thus, while Sonia herself – sickly and 'anaemic' in her saintliness – is hard to accept, as is the likelihood of Raskolnikov's redemption and discovery of God ('that might be the subject of another story', the book ends; and in this case at least it might have been a bad one), Dostoievsky does not in general interfere with his imagination, nor usually manipulate his characters. Moreover, even if they began in his mind as mere types, by the time he has finished with them they were fully rounded. As Ernest J. Simmons, resisting the notion of treating Dostoievsky as a *thinker through fiction*, has pointed out, his 'great works, it is true, are conceived in the spirit of religious and philosophical thought [but] he does not try to prove ideas by religious or philosophical argument ... What vitally concerned him was the relation of [the existence of God] to the human consciousness of his characters and how it revealed and conditioned their destinies.' Now in this Dostoievsky had got to the *existentialist* heart of the matter. For if there is no kind of spiritual law, or immortality, then men are bound – because purely rationalist-humanist arguments are inadequate and without emotional appeal – to consider, consciously or unconsciously, the question of why they should not do what they like. But they are not consistent, even when they believe themselves to be. Further, they do possess a mysterious conscience, whether they are prepared to acknowledge this or not. Dostoievsky demonstrates this with unparalleled dramatic brilliance.

Thus even the heinous Svidrigaylov is prone to self-analysis, and performs good actions – even if the general state of his being is putrid. So does the nihilist Lebezyatnikov, who frustrates Luhzin's attempt to frame Sonia by planting money on her and then accusing her of stealing it.

Above all, Dostoievsky reveals the divided state of the mind of Raskolnikov himself – and without recourse to didacticism. On one occasion he can perform a brutal murder; on another he can be full of generosity – as when he gives all the money he has to the bereaved and half-demented Mrs Marmeladov when her husband is killed. As the good, impetuous Razumikhin says of him, he 'dislikes showing his feelings, and he'd rather be cruel than put his real feelings into words'; 'two people of diametrically opposed characters [live] in him, each taking charge of him in turn.' Raskolnikov sees that he is no Napoleon, but an 'aesthetic louse'. He is his creator's first substantial 'double'; he cannot resolve the conflict within himself between his will for power and his submissiveness. He discovers that he is not powerful. Dostoievsky's demonstration of his failure is in one sense symbolic of the failure of *all* those who struggle to attain the status of 'Napoleons'; it carries greater weight than the final suggestion of Raskolnikov's future redemption and purification, that 'subject of another story'. Svidrigaylov himself, though more thoroughly committed to evil than Raskolnikov, is at bottom a pathetic figure. First he is bored; then he is terrified in a manner quite unworthy of a 'true superman' (if there is such a person); he shoots himself for no apparent reason.

The greatest achievement of *Crime and Punishment* – even greater than the tragi-comic 'scandal' scenes, such as Marmeladov's funeral and the dinner following it – is the author's depiction of Raskolnikov's state of mind and actions before, during and after the murder. He is seen 'from the inside' as few characters yet had been in fiction. His pride, boredom and excited anguish are so vividly portrayed that the reader participates in his frenzy. Although his story is sensational and melodramatic (there is murder in all four of Dostoievsky's major novels) he is, at the very least, an irrefutable demonstration of the compulsion in human beings to recognize the conscience within them.

Idiot
[The Idiot]

CRITICAL SUMMARY *The Idiot* and most of *The Devils* were

written in Europe, after Dostoievsky's second marriage. He loathed Europe – particularly the Germans – but could not return to Russia because of his debts. *The Idiot* is not as tightly constructed a novel as *Crime and Punishment*; it has been described, with justice, as a 'string of episodes'. but it attempts something more daring: the creation of a *holy fool*, a truly good character. Prince Myshkin, 'the idiot' of the title, is Dostoievsky's second serious attempt to present what he called a 'positively good character'. The first had been Sonia in *Crime and Punishment* – and the effort was a failure. Myshkin's successors in the major novels are Shatov [*The Devils*] and Father Zosima and Alyosha [*Karamazov*]. If Dostoievsky ever did succeed in creating a virtuous character, then it is Myshkin (Shatov is far more shadowy). But did he? What, despite his creator's intentions, is Myshkin really like? Certainly he is not wholly comic; is he, as Dostoievsky the polemicist might have liked him to be, wholly tragic? Is he a redeemer? Is he a 'nineteenth-century Christ'?

The plot of *The Idiot* is complex and badly organized. The main outline is simple enough, even though the central character remains an enigma. Prince Myshkin, an epileptic, is returning to Russia from Switzerland, where he has been treated for what his doctor calls 'idiocy'. It may be inferred that his disease has prevented him from relating to other people. Now, though innocent, childlike, impotent (this is obvious, as is his immunity from protracted sexual desire) and intellectually simple if not stupid or ill informed (he relies on intuition to understand people) he has been judged fit to enter society. He comes from a good family, and he inherits money. He acknowledges a base element in his nature without yielding to it: he desires to do good. The story concerns his failure to achieve this desire. He may be regarded as a bitterly comic figure – though *comic* must be understood in a specially Dostoievskian sense – or as a successful and serious portrayal of a man who is 'not of this world' or as an imaginative attack by Dostoievsky on his own polemical ideal.

The essence of the tale is Myshkin's relationship with two women: the aristocratic Aglaya Yepanchina, and Natasya Filippovna, who has been seduced and then abandoned by the rich womanizer Totsky. He becomes engaged to Aglaya, who sees his goodness but cannot help taunting him with the bad consequences it brings; finally he turns to Natasya in order to save her from the lustful villain Rogozhin. However, Natasya, who also sees Myshkin's goodness – but who revels in her dishonour and wishes to save him from her destructive personality – finally accepts Rogozhin, who marries her, murders her because he cannot possess her entirely, goes temporarily mad, and is finally tried and sent to Siberia. The final scene (there is a short epilogue) finds Rogozhin and the Prince watching over Natasya's dead body throughout the night. The Prince returns to his former madness – or probably worse. This last scene, with the body covered with 'good American cloth' and 'four uncorked bottles of ... disinfectant' (to prevent the smell), is one of Dostoievsky's most macabre and powerful. In the morning the Prince no longer recognizes those around him, or understands their questions.

The novel has many other aspects. There is the vicious Petersburg society into which Myshkin is plunged on his return, and which he mesmerizes and scandalizes by his simplicity, clumsiness and innocence. There are incomparably well realized characters such as the nihilist Ippolit, who makes a death bed 'confession' (having only a few weeks to live, he is to commit suicide at the end of making it – but he bungles this) which is at least proto-surrealist. This nightmarish document, read aloud by Ippolit, has often been described as largely 'nonsense'; those critics who regard it rather as in some mysterious way integrated are justified. The compulsive liar and drunkard General Ivolgin is a buffoon whose tragic overtones – his search for human dignity – surpass almost any character from Dickens (who profoundly influenced Dostoievsky).

However we may view the efficacy of the function of Myshkin, the episode in which he is first received by the Yepanchinas is a triumph. Even the introduction of some of Dostoievsky's least sensible and most chauvinistic ideas (which mar much of the novel) may here be justified as providing 'part of the dramatic pressures of the scene' – though only when taken in isolation.

Myshkin, as Aglaya's future fiancé, is to be introduced to the Yepanchina set, and it is vital that he behave himself. Tortured by the fact that he may not, he does not. Having anticipated that he will break a vase precious to Aglaya's mother, he does so – after a passionate attack on the 'atheistic' Roman Catholic Church and an appeal for the regeneration of all mankind by the 'Russian God and the Russian Christ'. Then, as he had dreaded, he has an epileptic fit.

As a single 'scandal' episode in the masterly Dostoievskian manner, this is magnificent. But – and this is judging the text and not Dostoievsky's polemic intentions – Myshkin's politico-religious utterances here are not in accordance either with his own character as it develops throughout the book or with any kind of Christianity (even Russian Orthodox) or, indeed, with any kind of charity or understanding. It is evident that Dostoievsky does not know what to do with Myshkin. His goodness of heart is real; but he fails completely. He can't see why Natasya and Aglaya should not allow him to love them both; he undertakes to marry them both although he has already told someone else that he can't marry because he is 'unwell' (impotent). He ends in total madness. He cannot take the suffering of others any longer. And yet the text itself tells us to accept him as *positively* good. Actually there is a case for presenting him as the cause of many of the disasters that occur in the book. Had Dostoievsky intended him simply as a bitter attack on his own idealism, he would – must – have constructed the book in an entirely different way. As a true modern Christ (he is deliberately represented as looking like the Christ of Russian ikons) he would have performed miracles – at least to the extent of controlling the suffering of others. Yet Aglaya marries a Pole and is converted to Catholicism – both terrible actions in Dostoievsky's view. Miracles are conspicuously absent from Dostoievsky's fiction. In the case of Myshkin too many contraries clash; the character is not resolved. In each of the spectacular episodes we see a slightly different Myshkin. The comic and the tragic elements in him do not coalesce. He lacks the consistency of true holiness, so that the novel as a whole offers only incidental excellencies. But it is difficult to overrate these.

Besy
[The Devils]

CRITICAL SUMMARY David Magarshack's translation of *Besy* as *The Devils* is more accurate than Constance Garnett's as *The Possessed*. But the latter title has the advantage of alluding to a central *motif* in the novel: the Russian intelligentsia (swine destined to drown) are being gradually 'possessed' of European ideas, 'devils'. In *Luke* Christ expels, into a herd of swine, the devils from a man possessed by them. The passage from the Gospel is the epigraph to the novel, and is read to Stepan Trofimovich at the end. (It should be noted that in Dostoievsky's time the Russian word *intelligentsia* – from which ours derives – meant 'educated people holding radical opinions'; thus Dostoievsky did not regard himself as a member of it.)

The intellectual genesis of *The Devils* was Dostoievsky's fierce hatred of Russian liberalism and *nihilism*, and his passionate belief in the regeneration of Russia, and then mankind, by a return to Orthodoxism. It is the blackest

and most violent of his novels, and it contains his most
savage caricatures.

In view of the flaws in the episodic and ill constructed
Idiot, caused by polemic intrusions into the text, one
might well assume therefore that *The Devils* is one of his
worst novels. In fact it is at least reasonable to argue that
it is the greatest. He remarked, 'I feel like saying everything as passionately as possible.' What he felt like saying
was polemical. But so wholehearted was his vehemence
that his imagination transcended it – or at least transcended it to a much greater degree than it had in *The
Idiot*. While many of Dostoievsky's political views are
dubious and unrealistic, and some preposterous, and almost all sociologically naïve, this intended 'message' became (among other things) transformed into a terrible
prophecy of Stalinist and post-Stalinist communism – and,
indeed, of all totalitarianism. *The Devils* is by no means
without blemishes; nor is it particularly well constructed
(especially at the end); it is diffuse. But it is certainly the
greatest fictional 'political melodrama' (as Magarshack
calls it) of all time. Dostoievsky may well not have understood political history *per se* (his notions of European
politics were erroneous); but, as *The Devils* shows, he
well understood (if only in spite of himself) how abstract
political theories can possess and turn human beings into
demons. (This is why he is a greater thinker than Tolstoy.)

Of all Dostoievsky's novels, *The Devils* has the most intact *world* of its own. It draws the reader into itself and
creates an 'unwilling suspension of disbelief'. In certain
respects it anticipates Kafka; and it is successfully expressionistic in the sense that the grotesques and violent
caricatures that people its pages are in the main portraits
of a reality which is beyond the scope of conventional
realism. An attack on the intelligentsia (as then understood: the sense of course no longer applies in Soviet
Russia) becomes a Swiftian dissection of the human condition.

The Devils hinges around four main characters: Stepan Trofimovich, his son Pyotr Verkovensky, Shatov and Stavrogin. There are a number of other important characters, such as the theorist Shigalyov, and the mad engineer, Kirillov. The garrulous narrator is not *omniscient*, as in the two previous major novels: he plays a trivial part in the action, and acts as an unconsciously ironic *persona* for Dostoievsky himself. He seems not altogether to understand what is going on, which is a strategy to enable the author to express his own artistic ambiguity. Dostoievsky's polemical spokesman, although he is much more than this, is Shatov.

Stepan is an old liberal and former university lecturer who mistakenly believes himself to be under police surveillance in 'our town'; he imagines himself to be an 'exile' there. He is at first somewhat ridiculous, given to excessive drinking and in the grip of his admirer and patroness Stavrogina (Stavrogin's mother). At the end he is converted to a vague Dostoievskyian Slavophilism, but he dies before he can accomplish a projected 'pilgrimage'. He is not portrayed with venom; this is reserved for Karmazinov (intended as a portrait of Turgenev, though the resemblance existed only in Dostoievsky's mind), a famous but absurdly vain and mediocre Russian writer who is represented as caring nothing for his country. As a character in his own right, it must be added, the 'liberal' Karmazinov is splendidly funny; perhaps too merely funny to be the spiritual father of nihilism which Dostoievsky makes him out to be.

Stepan's son Pyotr was based largely on a young disciple of the anarchist Bakunin called Nechayev, who coerced a cell of revolutionaries into murdering a student, Ivanov, in 1869. (His deed aroused horror amongst all liberals and even amongst many nihilists, and Bakunin himself disowned him. He was at large until after the publication of *The Devils*, when he was captured and imprisoned.) Pyotr in *The Devils* is the disciple of Stavrogin;

he is a predator whose real motive for arranging the killing of Shatov is not to silence him as an informer, but to
involve the members of his cell in collective guilt and thus
to gain further power over them. He is a predator without
scruple, mindlessly devoted to the destruction of all
authority. In the novel he escapes – to devote himself to
further slaughter.

Shatov, who is Dostoievsky's most convincing 'saved
character', has been another disciple of Stavrogin, and
even when he denounces him to his face he admits that he
remains under his spell. He believes in Russia, in her
Church, in the body of Christ, in the messianic role of
Russia but not, he admits, in God; 'I . . . I shall believe in
God' is all he can say. The scene in which he is murdered,
carefully led up to, is one of Dostoievsky's most horrifying and powerful.

Stavrogin is the novelist's most enigmatic creation.
Though he came late into the plan of *The Devils*, he is,
as the author wrote, 'ALL' in it. Yet he is finally 'left in
the air'. He is good looking, personable when he wishes to
be, self-possessed and capable. He has been an officer, has
lost his rank through duelling, served with distinction in
1863 in the Polish troubles, and has been decorated and
reinstated. But while people respect him, odd rumours
have surrounded him. On his return to 'our town', it is reported, he has at first lived quietly. (He does not enter
into the action proper until comparatively late; but there
is frequent and masterly reference to him – an example of
Dostoievsky's mastery of dramatic build-up.) Then he
erupts. First he pulls a respectable old man across the
floor by his nose: this character has the habit of saying
'you cannot lead me by the nose.' He bites the provincial
governor's ear. Was he not responsible for his actions, as
doctors (often ridiculous in Dostoievsky) pronounce, or
was he 'laughing at everyone'? He is certainly a debau-
chee, frequenting low haunts, seducing his mother's ward,
Dasha, whom she had officiously intended to marry off to

Stepan. He has an affair with Shatov's wife, who bears him a child just before her husband's murder. He marries a cripple, Marya, for whose murder by an escaped convict he is morally responsible. He finally seduces Liza Tushina – but cannot discover any feeling in himself through this action. Further, in a chapter which the editor of the serialized version refused to print, and which Dostoievsky left out of the final version (but it belongs to it), he confesses to a holy man, Tikhon, that he has once seduced an eleven-year-old girl who has subsequently killed herself, although he could have prevented this.

He is, above all, bored. Thus he can 'convert' Shatov to the 'Dostoievskian' views the latter finally holds (and which make him the perfect target for Pyotr's murderous plans) and at the same time infect the half-mad Kirillov (who commits suicide) with nihilist ideas. This is done out of a feeling of emptiness. Not only does he believe in nothing but, as he explains in the note he leaves before hanging himself at the end, 'even negation' has not come to him. All this shows an acute awareness: Stavrogin is Dostoievsky's proto-existentialist anti-hero who has failed to make a choice. He is further developed in the Ivan of *Karamazov*.

The Devils is spiced with 'scandal scenes', (a speciality in Dostoievsky), the most uproarious of which is the fête organized by the wife of the governor, Von Lembke (successor to the one whose ear Stavrogin has bitten). The nihilists have decided to wreck what is already an absurd project. This is sustained satirical comedy at its most masterly.

The end of *The Devils* is marred by the large number of murders and suicides which take place, yet redeemed by the final chapter, in which Stavrogin's last letter to Dasha (his mother's ward) is printed. Though resolving nothing, it suddenly humanizes Stavrogin. This suicide is not quite the aimless one of Svidrigaylov of *Crime and Punishment*, for the letter has in it an underlying note of conscience: Stavrogin confesses, for example, to having looked on 'our iconoclasts' and having been jealous of 'their hope'. To be jealous of hope is some small way towards salvation from emptiness, even in the face of a self-willed death. Hence the question, unsolved because Dostoievsky killed Stavrogin off, of what might have become of him had he not committed suicide. The fate of Ivan in *Karamazov* is similarly unresolved.

Bratya Karamazov
[The Brothers Karamazov]

CRITICAL SUMMARY It is perhaps not sensible to try to rank Dostoievsky's masterpieces in order of merit. The desire to do so is inescapable – and there is the all-important question of development. Did Dostoievsky develop? There is a case for arguing that he did, and that therefore *The Brothers Karamazov* – despite certain signs of failure of powers – is his profoundest novel. Parts of it could have been excised; the report of Dmitri's trial is too prolonged; the section called 'The Russian Monk', intended to refute Ivan's ideas, is prolix and unconvincing; Alyosha is no more successful a portrait of a saintly man than Myshkin; less of Dostoievsky's genius for comedy is displayed; the style is often less lively than it was in earlier novels. But whereas in the early works the process of transformation from bad to better is never adequately described – it is merely suggested, and sometimes disingenuously – in *Karamazov* such processes, though not to the great degree which the polemicist in the author would have wished, are traced, and with perfect psychological conviction. This is the main case for regarding *Karamazov* as Dostoievsky's *chef d'oeuvre*. Also: can it be seriously claimed that he ever created so vigorous, so terrifyingly tangible a creature as Fyodor Pavlovich Karamazov? Or, indeed, so vivid a gallery of characters?

Old Fyodor Karamazov, a widower, has been married twice. His first wife (who beat him) ran away from him, and her son Dmitry has not been brought up by his father. Nor have his other two sons, Ivan and Alyosha, by his second wife – a timid, hysterical and suicidal woman. His fourth son, the slimy epileptic Smerdyakov, is a bastard begotten by him on an idiot. Fyodor is a pursuer of lust and money. He rejoices in his wickedness and, despite his unpredictable moods, is cunning and more calculating than he seems. He will blaspheme horribly; he enjoys making hypocritical remarks, behaving preposterously, and swindling everyone. If he has a single redeeming feature, then this is his genuine zest for life. In his cups he sometimes even suggests that there is a God. Only Alyosha, the novitiate monk, tries to forgive him; the others hate him unreservedly. But all of them, even Alyosha, possess the 'Karamazov taint'. This is complex, but may best be summed up in the phrase *impulsive extremism* – in the direction of lust, of atheism, of general behaviour, even of saintliness (Alyosha).

Dmitry and his father are quarrelling over a 'loose woman', Grushenka, for whom they both lust. Dmitry, wild and reckless, has also been cheated of his inheritance by his father. He is warm-hearted, but his sensuality resembles that of his father; he lives a reprobate life. He has saved the career of the officer father of Katerina Ivanova by paying money the former has embezzled; Katerina offered herself to him, but he refused. Subsequently he becomes engaged to her. He leaves her for Grushenka, one of Dostoievsky's 'doubles': she wants to 'save Dmitry', but at the same time she wants to destroy him – even at the cost of destroying herself. Dmitry states in public that he wants to kill his father, and on one occasion actually attacks him. When he is battered to death, suspicion falls on Dmitry, who has been there on that night, and who has in fact thrashed the family's old servant Grigory in the garden. Dmitry is tried and sentenced to twenty years' penal servitude in Siberia. At his trial Ivan, who knows the truth, does not tell all of it. He is confused and heading for a mental breakdown. Katerina revengefully produces a letter from Dmitry to her saying that he will kill his father.

But Dmitry, like Grushenka, has changed. He may escape (we are not told whether he does, but a plan is afoot), and Grushenka will be with him in any case. They have both realized that their lust for each other has turned into love. Dmitry is still his old excitable self, and calls himself a sinner: though innocent, he once desired the death of his father.

The real villain is the intellectual Ivan, acting through the monster Smerdyakov. He has hinted to the latter that he might perform the crime (which he does), and he has absented himself with the clear implication that now is the time to act. Later realizing his moral responsibility, contrary to his rationalist and anti-moral intellectual views, he suffers so much that he falls into a dangerous brain fever. It is not clear at the end whether he will recover or whether, if so, he will change for the better, or become a kind of Stavrogin – a bored being, void of true life. Smerdyakov hangs himself.

Alyosha is the disciple of the holy Father Zosima. Zosima sends him out into the world: to sin and to find redemption. Dostoievsky planned a sequel telling his story, but died before he had made a satisfactory start. Alyosha is the weakest character in the book, scarcely coming alive except when he is, by Dostoievskian lights, sinning: he is convincing when he doubts the existence of God, when he is so horrified by the putrefaction of the corpse of Father Zosima that he goes off to an atheist and allows himself to be taken to the house of Grushenka to be seduced (though he is not). He thus fails to seek out Dmitry and control his actions. His response to his brother Ivan's rejection of Orthodoxy is feeble, neither here nor there.

Zosima, too, is an unsatisfactory and too holy character. In this case Dostoievsky's beliefs undermined his artistic purposes. Like Manzoni's Fra Cristofero, Zosima has once led a wicked life; but one has only to consider Cristofero to see how artificial Zosima is. He holds the existentialist thesis that all men are guilty of everything; but he is an abstraction, not flesh and blood. His answer, for this is what the section called 'The Russian Monk' is supposed to be, to Ivan's negative philosophy of life is singularly unconvincing; whereas Ivan's views, like his character, are exactly the opposite.

Ivan, talking to Alyosha, speaks of the ghastliness of the sufferings of young children (all the details were true: taken from press reports collected by Dostoievsky) and points out that he will not accept God: he will 'return Him the ticket'. It is often stated, not strictly accurately, that Ivan is an atheist. He is, rather, in the terrible predicament of rejecting a God in whose existence he appears to believe. Alyosha – like Zosima – insists that evil must exist, as well as good, so that man may exercise free will and choice. Ivan shows sensitivity and concern – a sensitivity and concern which are beyond intellectualism, and which Alyosha respects – in his feeling that the guiltless must not suffer. On another occasion he tells Alyosha the story of 'The Grand Inquisitor'*, the theme of a poem he intends to write.

*Christ returns to Seville at the time of the Inquisition. He performs miracles and is received with joy. But the Grand Inquisitor imprisons him and informs him that he is to be burned on the next day. He tells him why: Christ, he says, made the error of rejecting the temptations offered to him in the wilderness. By his refusal to turn stones into bread, and so forth, Jesus has cursed man with freedom of choice: free will. He has deprived men of an authority before which they can bow down in submission. The Roman Catholic (not of course the Orthodox) Church has 'corrected' Christ's error by entering into a league with the devil: it exercises this authority by repression and by offering men miracles and the hope of a happy after-life –

Zosima's answer, which Dostoievsky desperately wanted to make effective (for he understood Ivan's point of view – and felt it), is a pallid affair. The world is beautiful, suffering is a duty and will lead to universal harmony. Reality is ignored. All will be well when the Orthodox Church absorbs the State: there will be heaven on earth.

It seems that the Inquisitor has rejected the divine. Like Shigalov in *The Devils* he foresees a future in which nine tenths will be deprived of freedom while one tenth will enjoy absolute power.

But a curious feature of the Inquisitor is that he is *not* an atheist. He accepts Christ: he clearly implies that Christ could have performed the miracles the devil asked of him. Therefore he must be divine. Ivan himself has said that he does not disbelieve in God – only that he rejects him. (Dostoievsky once said revealingly that even if he discovered that Christ was not 'true' he would still follow him.) Clearly Dostoievsky sympathizes with Ivan's arguments; and he can never answer Ivan's objection to the suffering of even one child. Children play an important role in a sub-plot of *Karamazov*: the book ends with Alyosha employing his benign influence on a group of children, the most important of whom is Kolya Krasotkin. Beset by doubts and guilts, Dostoievsky seems in the end, if only by implication, to opt for the foundation of the kingdom of heaven *on earth*. It has been suggested that he believed in Christ but not in God. What is meant by this, perhaps, is that he believed in Christ (the Christ of the Orthodox Church) as a symbol, and that his attitude to the father (as real father, and as God) was one of

---

provided they are obedient in this one. Furthermore, he predicts a future socialism (it is clear that it is this) which will subsequently be captured by the Church when it disrupts into chaos; then the survivors will come back to the Church, and everyone except a few élitists (those in on the secret) will be happy. Christ says nothing, but kisses the ancient Inquisitor on the lips. The latter, still convinced that he is right, then allows him to go free.

hate/love. Fyodor Pavlovich himself may even be seen as a kind of terrible parody of the Creator, who gave, through his son Christ, such terrible sufferings to the world in the interests of a freedom which its inhabitants are not fitted to employ.

This frenetic Russian, whose 'views on politics could no longer be held by anyone outside a lunatic asylum' (Roland Hingley), created a world which had not, until he lived, existed. Like Shakespeare's world, it illuminates what we think we see; it demonstrates that what we think is reality is an illusion. In Dostoievsky's world men are tormented by the question of the existence of God, of purpose, of freedom.

BIBLIOGRAPHY

Translations: C. Garnett, in *The Novels*, 1912–31; D. Margarshack, *Crime and Punishment*, 1951; *The Idiot*, 1955; *The Devils*, 1953; *The Brothers Karamazov*, 1958.

Texts: in *Sobraniye sochinenii*, 1956–8.

Criticism: E. J. Simmons, *Dostoievsky*, 1950; R. Hingley, *The Undiscovered Dostoievsky*, 1962; E. Wasiolek, *Dostoievsky*, 1964; K. Muchalsky, *Dostoievsky*, 1967; R. Pearce, *Dostoievsky*, 1971.

Leo Tolstoy

Count Leo Tolstoy was born into an aristocratic family in 1828 at the estate of Yasnaya Polyana in Tula province – some 130 miles from Moscow. He had a happy childhood, but was orphaned at nine (his mother died when he was four) and brought up by aunts and private tutors. In 1844 he entered the university at Kazan. In 1847 he was treated for venereal disease, after which he returned to Yasnaya Polyana, determined to devote himself to his estate and to the care of his serfs. But in the following year he went back to Moscow and debauchery; in 1849 he moved to St Petersburg, where he contracted heavy gambling debts.

The early period of his life is marked by abrupt and frequent changes of direction: he opened a school for peasants' children on his estate, gambled, began to write seriously, and philandered. In 1851 he joined the army and saw active service in the Caucasus and later at Sevastopol (1854). In 1852 *Detsvo* [*Childhood*] was published, to be followed by sequels in 1854 and 1857. In 1855 he left the army. He met most of the leading writers, including Goncharov, Turgenev and the poet Afanasy Fet (1820–92), the closest of his literary friends. He tried unsuccessfully to free his serfs and wrote a great deal; he took a peasant woman as mistress, and a son (Timothy) was born. He travelled extensively. In 1859 he made the first of his retreats from art. He studied educational methods, and devoted himself to his peasant schools, where the teaching was Rousseauist in spirit.

In 1862 he married Sonya Behrs. The marriage was famously disharmonious; its earlier stages were the least unhappy, while he was writing *War and Peace* (1868–9) and then *Anna Karenina* (1875–7), and his wife preferred his literary to his political and social activities. He had thirteen children, most of whom survived him. His wife acted as his devoted secretary, copying and recopying his work. Under his direction they tried to practise complete confidence in each other; but this proved a strain. Matters between them did not come to a head until the late 1870s when, having finished *Anna Karenina*, Tolstoy experienced a 'conversion'. This was predictable, and to regard the publication of the banned but widely read *Ispoved* [*Confession*] (1879) as a watershed in his career is somewhat misleading. Tolstoy may subsequently have renounced all his earlier works, but he continued to write fiction and drama – and not all of this is as different as the didactic element in him would have wished.

In the last thirty years of his life he became increasingly doctrinaire and, at the same time, agonized. He preached a Christianity from which all 'superstitious' elements were eliminated (he was excommunicated in 1901), and turned himself into a prophet-anarchist. He condemned war, all orthodox religion, property and government; and he tried to give away all his own property, including the rights on his works. But his wife, who had long managed the accounts, would not stand for this. He agreed that she should publish his collected works.

In 1883 he had met Vladimir Chertkov, who became the chief 'Tolstoyan' disciple, and whose continual presence increased his wife's unhappiness (in 1910 she accused Tolstoy, then eighty-two, of having a homosexual relationship with him). Chertkov was an adherent of the didactic, not the artistic, Tolstoy, and he encouraged such highly dogmatic publications as *Chto takoye iskusstvo?*

[*What Is Art?*] (1898) in which Tolstoy renounces all art that is not both constructive and universally understandable. In 1888 he finally eschewed meat, tobacco, alcohol and hunting. He had more difficulty with sex, but preached its abolition. His didactic works have a genuine nobility of purpose, especially in the light of his anguishedly candid diaries and letters; but they do not in themselves take human nature into account. They evade problems by pretending that everyone else is like Tolstoy the moralist (which Tolstoy himself was not). Nor could Tolstoy ever conceal his aristocratic scorn for the peasants whose wisdom he held up as an example to corrupted intellectuals. His play *Vlasty Tymy* [*The Power of Darkness*] (1886) contains the negative side of his attitude, as do parts of his last full-length novel *Voskresenie* [*Resurrection*] (1899). The most perfect artistic work of his doctrinaire period is *Smert Ivana Ilyicha* [*The Death of Ivan Ilyich*] (1884–6); he never wrote more powerfully than this.

By 1910 Tolstoy's relationship with his wife, who had now been driven into full-blown hysteria, became impossible. At 4 a.m. one morning he ran away, accompanied by his personal physician and one of his daughters. But he soon caught pneumonia. He was taken in to the station master's house at Astapovo, to which hundreds of journalists, policemen and secret policemen – and Chertkov and Countess Tolstoy – flocked. Here, still reluctant to see his wife (though she was allowed brief access to him), he died.

War and Peace
[Voyna i Mir]

SUMMARY There are some 580 characters in *War and Peace* (1868–9); this alone, apart from its huge canvas, makes it impossible to give more than a broad outline.

The main action takes place between 1805 and 1812;

there is an epilogue which takes the reader up to 1820. The historical background is Napoleon's relationship with the Russians from 1805 until 1812. In June 1805 when the novel opens the War of the Third Coalition (1805–7) was imminent. In it Napoleon won Austerlitz (against the Austrians and Russians) and Jena (against the Prussians); by the secret treaties of Tilsit he forced Tsar Alexander I to recognize his conquests and to collaborate with him in a trade war against the English. But the latter policy failed; he had passed his apogee. He invaded Russia in 1812 and failed to rout her troops, under General Kutuzov, at Borodino (7 September 1812). He occupied Moscow (14 September 1812); but the Russians set fire to most of it, refused to accept peace, retreated, and left him to the mercy of an early winter. On 18 October he withdrew, chased and harried by the Russians. The withdrawal was complete on 14 December; Napoleon's army had been destroyed, mostly by the cold weather. (The dates differ slightly in the book because of the difference between the old and new calendars.)

Some of Tolstoy's characters are historical: Napoleon, Kutuzov, Murat (King of Naples), Count Speranski (Alexander's advisor who fell when Napoleon invaded and who was later responsible for the trial and conviction of the Decembrists) and several others. But most attention is given to the fictional Rostov and the Bolkonsky families, and to Pierre Bezukhov.

Pierre is the bastard son of a count. He inherits his estate and his title on the latter's death early in the novel. Natasha Rostov, daughter of Count Ilya and Countess Nataly and sister of Nicholas, is the central female character. She has another brother (Petya) and a sister, and is the close friend of a poor adopted niece, Sonya, of the Rostovs. Nicholas Bolkonsky is a retired general, a widower. His son Andrew is an important character – some would call him a co-hero. He is a member of Kutuzov's staff. His sister is Mary. Prince Andrew is unhappily

married to Lise, who dies after giving birth to his son
Nicholas – soon after Andrew, badly wounded at Auster-
litz and believed killed, returns home. There are also the
Kuragins and the Drubetskoys: Anatole Kuragin is a bad
character and so is his beautiful sister Helène; Boris
Drubetskoy is an impoverished social climber.

At the beginning Pierre and Andrew, who are friends,
both admire Napoleon, whom others call a monster and
an upstart. We are soon introduced to the Rostovs and to
the effervescent, selfish but lively Natasha, to Nicholas and
to Sonya. Sonya loves Nicholas and he may love her. But
Sonya is doomed to failure in love and ends as a 'sterile
flower'. Prince Andrew takes leave of his wife and old
father. Andrew and Nicholas take part in the fighting.
Andrew is sent by Kutuzov to the Austrian headquarters
at Brünn; but Napoleon has entered Vienna. He fights in
the battle of Schöngraben under Bagration; this ends in a
victory for the Russians, but Nicholas is injured and becomes depressed, feeling that his life is purposeless.

Pierre, now rich, marries Helène Kuragin (with grave
misgivings) but Princess Mary refuses to marry Anatole
when she catches him flirting with another woman.
Nicholas finds solace in awed admiration of Tsar Alexander. Book III ends with a vivid description of the action
at Austerlitz, and with Andrew wounded and looking up
at the sky; Napoleon, admiring his courage, puts him into
the charge of his own physician, but the reader is left to
assume that he has been fatally wounded.

Book IV finds Pierre already unhappy in his marriage;
he challenges the reckless Dolokov, whom he believes to
be his wife's lover, to a duel. He is clumsy and inexperienced; by beginner's luck he manages to wound his rival.
He separates from Helène; society takes her side. Andrew
surprisingly returns, but only to find Lise dead and himself the father of a son. Sonya declines Dolokov's proposal
of marriage. Dolokov inveigles Nicholas Rostov into
losing 43,000 roubles to him at cards; his father pays the

debt off and Nicholas rejoins his regiment. Book V sees the confused Pierre converted to freemasonry (Tolstoy sympathized with the reformist aims of the masons but considered them futile 'fools'). He tries unsuccessfully to emancipate his serfs. Then, full of zeal for his new life, he re-encounters Prince Andrew, who has been intro- ducing improvements on his own estate and tells him that the serfs will never change; Pierre passionately disagrees. But he feels that Andrew is intellectually too clever for him. There follows the famous conversation on the ferry. Pierre expounds freemasonry. Andrew remarks: 'You see a reign of goodness and truth on earth, but I don't see it.' Pierre is an idealist, and *feels*; Andrew, who *thinks*, also believes that there 'is an answer', but he is dubious as to whether it is 'God', in whom Pierre believes. 'Though outwardly [Andrew] continued to live in the same old way, inwardly he began a new life', as a result of this meeting with Pierre. Nicholas meanwhile is bewildered by Alexander's alliance with Napoleon.

Andrew's occupations at his estate are described in Book VI. Pierre continues with his freemasonry, Andrew with his search for an answer. Pierre and Helène are reconciled. Andrew falls in love with Natasha and they become engaged. Book VII concentrates on country fest- ivities and on the spontaneous nature of Natasha. Sonya's love remains frustrated when Nicholas' mother opposes her wish to marry him. Book VIII finds Pierre drinking and feeling that life is 'loathsome'. He asks himself 'what for?', and 'why?'; he has become disillusioned with the masons.

The Rostovs visit the opera and Natasha becomes prey to the fancy of Anatole Kuragin. She finds him attractive, and writes to Princess Mary breaking off her engagement to Andrew. Pierre then tells her that his brother-in-law is married; she tries to kill herself. He declares his love for her.

At the beginning of Book IX Tolstoy first mentions

his view of history: rulers and generals are 'history's slaves'.

Napoleon crosses the frontier. Nicholas distinguishes himself in action. Natasha falls ill, but improves. Pierre begins to feel that his mission in life is to end the power of Napoleon. As the French draw near old Bolkonski has a stroke and dies. Nicholas helps Princess Mary by instructing her serfs, who will not leave for a safe place, to do as she orders; she feels love for him. Pierre leaves Moscow for the front. Tolstoy now interpolates a chapter on the senselessness of the Battle of Borodino. He praises Kutuzov for realizing that by accepting battle he would lose Moscow, and he criticizes Napoleon for giving it when he already knew that he should stop. But even Kutuzov acted 'involuntarily and irrationally'. The histories are wrong. The Russian position at Borodino was not chosen by Kutuzov (in historical fact it was) and had not been foreseen: this position was unentrenched. We see Borodino from Pierre's point of view. He meets Andrew, whose thoughts are 'terrible': 'To die ... to be killed tomorrow ... That I should not exist ... That all this should still be, but no me.' He is thoroughly disillusioned: prisoners should be shot, it is all humbug, 'we have played at war', the 'aim of war is murder'. Then the battle is described. Andrew is seriously wounded: out of pride he fails to throw himself down when a shell lands beside him, though by doing so he might have saved his life. Next to him in the dressing station he finds his rival, Anatole, whose leg has been amputated; he feels pity for him. As for Napoleon; he 'imagined that the war ... came about by his will, and the horrors that occurred did not stagger his soul'; but his mind is 'darkened'.

Book XI begins with a discussion of the 'method of history', and comes to the conclusion that to discover its laws 'we must completely change the subject of our observation ... and study the common, infinitesimally small elements by which the masses are moved.' Even then we may not advance towards a true understanding. Pierre returns to Moscow and decides to kill Napoleon. The Rostovs prepare to leave Moscow, and the dying Andrew is able to travel in their train of vehicles. It is understood that if he should recover then he would after all marry Natasha who devotedly nurses him; but neither mentions this. Pierre, on his way to kill Napoleon with a dagger, is arrested as an incendiary.

Book XII first tells of Helène's illness and death (from trying to obtain an abortion), and then at more length of Prince Andrew's death. Tended by Natasha and his sister Mary, he seems to find acceptance ('death is an awakening') but it is not an altogether convincing one – rather a description of how death may come gently to a perplexed spirit.

Book XIII describes the French occupation of Moscow. Pierre, in prison, meets Platon Karataev, the peasant who accepts everything and whose simplicity and faith are to be the vehicle of Pierre's re-awakening to life. The French leave Moscow, and in Book XIV we follow the fortunes of Pierre, who is taken along as prisoner but is rescued. Petya, the youngest Rostov, is killed in a guerilla raid on the retreating French. Book XV explains the nature of Kutuzov's intuition and praises his attempts to resist moves to cut off the defeated French army. 'He alone said that *the loss of Moscow is not the loss of Russia* ... that *to carry the war beyond the frontier is useless and harmful.*' He discerned the will of Providence and submitted his personal will to it.

The final stages of the war are described. We then return to Pierre, who is ill but recovers. Now he has faith in an 'ever-living, ever-manifest God' who is 'here and everywhere'. This he learned from Karataev (who died in the retreat). He is no longer tormented by the question 'What for?' because there is this God 'without whose will not one hair falls from a man's head'. Natasha and he are now in love, though the book proper ends before their marriage.

There are two epilogues. The second is another discussion of history. Tolstoy argues in favour of predestination, but says that men cannot live except in the belief that they have free will. The first describes some of the more important events that took place after 1812. Natasha and Pierre married in 1813; they now have three daughters and a son. Natasha is robust and serene but she has lost her 'ever-glowing animation'. There is not absolute understanding between husband and wife (Natasha imagines that Pierre is jealous of Prince Andrew's memory).

Nicholas has married Princess Mary and they are bringing up young Nicholas, Andrew's son. Old Rostov dies; his wife is in decay. Nicholas becomes an excellent and just administrator – though occasionally, despite his plain wife's disapproval, he loses his temper. It is made clear that Pierre is a future Decembrist; Nicholas disagrees with his enlightened and anti-governmental views. The story ends as young Nicholas (Andrew's son) wishes to do something to please Pierre.

CRITICAL COMMENTARY *War and Peace* is often rashly described as the 'world's greatest novel'; but it is certainly one of the most ambitious and remarkable. One may object to the pronouncement that while 'fiction is a representation of life ... *War and Peace* is life' yet understand the feelings which prompted it. As its best critics have observed, the impression it gives of living *now*, and with great immediacy, is unique. Tolstoy refused to call it a novel because early in its composition he discovered that he 'did not know how to set fixed limits' to his characters: limits such as 'marriage and death, after which the interest of the marriage would cease'. Thus Pierre, we know, will be a Decembrist: perhaps his fate will be death or long years of exile. In one way the book has neither beginning, climax nor end (both Book XV and the first epilogue conclude with three dots). Life, it insists, goes on despite novels; and this successful insistence does draw attention to the self-contained nature of previous fiction: something which for Tolstoy is artificial. His kind of realism puts emphasis on the fact that people do not really – cannot – plan their lives, but are carried forward by a force which they do not understand; it tacitly criticizes *plot* – the plots of novelists and the false patterns imposed on history by historians. Tolstoy was later to exaggerate the importance of unsophistication in art – and to condemn, among others, Beethoven and Shakespeare; but ability to convey an unsophisticated awareness of the world was a vital part of his own genius from the beginning.

The Tolstoyan world, seen through the characters' eyes, is strange; reality impinges violently on each character. The Tolstoyan realism therefore incorporates an anticipation of modern *stream of consciousness*. Indeed, Tolstoy's first serious composition, *A Story of Yesterday*, posthumously published but written early in 1851, is a quite extraordinary anticipation of psychoanalysis, expressionism *and stream of consciousness*. He was forced to abandon this method only because, as may be discerned to a lesser degree in his first published work, it led him into digression – and would at that time have denied him a public. (But in the famous last chapter of Book VII of *Anna Karenina* an only slightly modified *stream of consciousness* technique is handled as well as it ever was in nineteenth-century fiction.)

The chief feature of *War and Peace* has been variously described. It is a correction of the historians' view of history. It is a 'grand valediction to the heyday of the Russian nobility', written 'because [Tolstoy] disliked the present'; it 'is concerned with spontaneity as against the fixed will'. It demonstrates that through 'what Pierre ... calls "active virtue" life may be changed for the better.'

It 'tells how Paradise may be regained by human beings'. With the exception of the last, all these views – qualified by their proponents – contain truths; all are open to some kind of challenge. In the last analysis it may be for the sense of life as it is lived and of people as they actually are that we go to *War and Peace*. For it is intensely didactic, though some claim that it is 'effortlessly' so.

Much has been written about Tolstoy's view of history. The subtlest analysis is that of Isaiah Berlin in *The Hedgehog and the Fox* (1953). The Greek poet Archilochus, from Paros, wrote in a fragment that the 'fox knows many things, the hedgehog one great thing'. Berlin divides thinkers into two sorts: eclectic ones who draw on manifold sources and systems and who have no desire to trace a simple pattern, and those who seek unity. Tolstoy, he claims, was naturally a fox, but wanted to be a hedgehog. He could find no pattern in life but none the less insisted that there was one (albeit incomprehensible).

This led him into a difficult position, for he was not, as a *thinker*, profound – at least one aspect of his personality which his wife, whatever her own material interests, instinctively understood. The weaknesses of his view of history are that he states that there are laws, but then entirely fails to enumerate them; he falls back on predestination quite unnecessarily; and he changes facts. It is not very useful to be flatly instructed that we are not free, but that we cannot exist unless we believe that we are. What is the point of Pierre's strenuous mental development – in which Tolstoy clearly believes – towards activism (the sort of Decembrist he would become would certainly seek, like Napoleon, to influence history), if this is predestined? There is in the book an unresolved confusion between *quietism* and *activism*. A man of the temperament of Tolstoy's Kutuzov – the real Kutuzov was not much like this – would certainly not have become an activist. And yet Tolstoy's creative energy is such that his Pierre and his Kutuzov appear as living figures. We believe in and are impressed by Pierre's innate goodness; and Kutuzov's philosophy is equally convincing, equally impressive. Most impressive of all is Prince Andrew's anguish: he is nearest to Tolstoy in that he is the tensest character in the book – even if Tolstoy would like to be nearer to Pierre, in whom there is much of himself too.

There is a paradox in that Tolstoy's didacticism undermines his imaginative vision – and yet we cannot think of the latter without the former. This is partly explained by his ability to diversify himself in his characters: Pierre the man who feels, Andrew the man who thinks, Kutuzov who wisely intuits, Nicholas who is a decent, fairly conventional aristocrat, and so forth.

The claim that Tolstoy wrote *War and Peace* as a *valediction* to the heyday of the old aristocracy has considerable substance, though his intention here too is somewhat undermined by his imaginative integrity. He does show the warmth and spontaneity of the Rostovs; and the consistent old Bolkonsky is by no means unlovable. Richard Freeborn points out that the Rostovs' kind of spontaneity affords a contrast to the 'essentially *imposed*, unnatural patterns of behaviour which infect men when they are institutionalized'. There are many such moments, and Natasha in particular is shown as participating in them. But the Rostovs for all their appeal are by no means perfect. Natasha is in the end disappointing: a matron without intellectual depth, prone to groundless jealousy. Nicholas is not very interesting. Petya wastes his life pointlessly. This is tribute to Tolstoy's art, and in no way invalidates Freeborn's point: for the novelist is only able to gain our sympathy for the Rostovs, to make us feel that they represent a wrongly and unjustly ravaged Russia, by presenting them as real people with real faults; they convey a true sense of corporateness. Tolstoy the sage preached family corporateness and never experienced it; and he preached peasant wisdom – but could never have invented a peasant family with the same kind of corporateness as that possessed by the aristocratic Rostovs.

The most glaring failure in the book – tiresome, unreal, a cardboard figure out of fiction of a much lower order than that of Tolstoy's best – is Platon Karataev. Such a man could not possibly exist – or, if he did, he would be a sophisticated fake; Tolstoy's invention of him demonstrates the difficulties he faced in his insistence upon the superior wisdom of peasants. It may well be that some peasants are wiser than some other men; but the Tolstoyan peasant wisdom is curiously abstract or sentimental. Tolstoy never convinced himself, and he does not convince us. Yet he can convey to us a sense of the will of a whole country when threatened – and this is a phenomenon as mysterious as it is undeniable. It did not exist in the 1860s as it had existed in 1812.

How is it that we can find Tolstoy's philosophy distracting and yet, as I have suggested, go to *War and Peace* for a sense of life as it is lived? How does the author manage it? Primarily through his technique. It used to be fashionable to follow Henry James in regarding the structure of *War and Peace* as more or less non-existent: it was formless or at least sprawling. This notion is now discredited. There are admittedly chronological errors and inconsistencies in *War and Peace*, and also anachronisms (sometimes people are made to talk as if it were the 1860s), but these do not destroy the structure. There are two main features of Tolstoy's technique. Paramount is one that has already been mentioned: the capacity to convey a sense of life in the immediate present. The characters are not 'built up' or 'explained' in terms of their heredity or environment (we hear virtually nothing of their childhoods). The emphasis is rather on the way they act *in character*; hence the sense of immediacy. This is done partly by means of a prose whose skill and subtlety defy even the best translation; a vivid prose, which makes an extensive use of the linguistic resources offered by Russian. It is also done by concentration on physical characteristics and habits, and by a method of description which eschews exact detail in favour of subjective impression – this has survived translation. Much hinges on the way people smile, on their postures and on their eyes. Napoleon's white hands are a conspicuous feature.

Secondly there is the way Tolstoy gives a unity to the book. Curiously, this arises from his intellectual didacticism about predestination. His intuition partly undermines this obtrusive element by his diversification of himself into a number of characters. But he also creates unity by his essentially intuitive modification of an unsatisfactory thesis. The vexed question of free will hardly comes into it; it is a question of careful contrasts. The 'principle on which it is composed', writes R. F. Christian, 'is to think of people and phenomena in terms of their opposites and then to contrive the juxtaposition and interaction of those opposites'. Thus there is the contrast between those who believe that they are masters of their fate and those who do not. This is quite different from the rigid theory propounded in the epilogue and in various parts of the novel (to which it does not belong). In this aspect of the novel we can recognize the kinds of people by whom we are surrounded: for example, the politicians who pretend that they can control affairs, and some of their victims who are aware of their limitations.

We may feel irritated by, for example, Pierre's series of conversions, whilst appreciating his desire to be a good man. But we are similarly irritated by people we meet in our own lives – as, possibly, by ourselves. The flaws in *War and Peace* are glaring ones, and they are the result of Tolstoy's intrusion of ideas into his material (Platon is the worst example in terms of character; Helène's death through seeking an abortion is another gratuitous detail). But an abundance of vivid and authentic detail survives these intrusions – not least the masterly battle descriptions – to which we cannot fail to respond.

Anna Karenina

SUMMARY *Anna Karenina* (1875–7), like *War and Peace*, was extensively revised. For all that the latter deals with the horrors of war, *Karenina* is a more sombre book. Although not *historical* (it is set in the 1870s), its inception lay in a real incident: the suicide (by throwing herself under a train) of a mistress of one of Tolstoy's neighbours. He saw the body. The epigraph to the novel is 'Vengeance is mine; I will repay.' This means that God – not corrupt society – repaid Anna; but also that Anna was wrong to revenge herself on Vronsky and on life. It may also mean (as Tolstoy suggested thirty years later) that the bitter consequences of a deed come not from other people but from God. R. F. Christian thinks that this leaves out of account the fact that other guilty parties get off scot-free; but perhaps Tolstoy truly meant that only people of the finest sensibility get punished (*Those whom the Gods love* ...).

The novel's main characters are Prince Steven Oblonsky ('Steve'), his wife Dolly, Anna Karenina – Steve's sister – her husband Alexis Karenin, Constantine Levin and his two brothers – Sergius, a half-brother, and Nicholas – Princess Shchbatskaya ('Kitty'), who is Dolly's sister and who becomes Levin's wife, Count Vronsky, and the vicious conscienceless Princess Elizabeth ('Betsy') who represents, to a greater extent than the philandering but agreeable Oblonsky, the hypocrisy of society. There are about ninety other characters, some of whom have important functions.

At the beginning Steve (Stiva) has upset his wife by having an affair. Levin arrives in Moscow intending to marry Kitty. He has a conversation with his half-brother and a professor about the 'meaning of life': a conversation in which Tolstoy satirizes the vacuous thinking of 'advanced' 'intellectuals'. Levin is good-naturedly puzzled by their abstractness. He is rejected by Kitty, who wants the attractive young guards officer Vronsky. Then Anna arrives; she meets Vronsky by chance, and there occurs an accident in which a railworker is crushed by a train. She feels this is a bad omen. She effects a reconciliation between the Oblonskys. She also attends a ball where, beautifully dressed and seductive, she attracts Vronsky who also attracts her. Kitty, though admiring Anna, is disillusioned by Vronsky's behaviour. Levin considers himself repulsive and when he calls on his drunken dissolute brother Nicholas all he can see in him is a grotesque version of himself. He returns to his estate where he tries without success to improve his peasants' lot.

Anna returns to St Petersburg; Vronsky is on her train. It is on the railway (again) that he declares his love for her, during a storm. She pretends to reject him; but when she meets her husband at the station she notices his 'cold and commanding figure', and especially his gristly protruding ears. She greets her son Serezha, of whom she is deeply fond – and later succumbs to her husband's lovemaking, which she finds (it is implied) unpleasant. It is not clear whether she has found it so before; all we know of her marriage to this 'correct' moralistic bureaucrat is that it had been forced upon her at a young age. We are also told that she admires her husband's moral rectitude.

In St Petersburg she visits Princess Betsy and keeps meeting Vronsky; eventually, although she has been warned by Karenin (who has noticed what is going on), she becomes his mistress. He behaves callously towards Kitty. Both are horrified: she dishonoured and haunted by shame, he feeling 'like a murderer'. She becomes pregnant by him. Not long after she has told him of her pregnancy Vronsky breaks the back of his beautiful mare in a steeplechase by making an 'unpardonable mistake'. The symbolism, sexual and otherwise, is evident.

Meanwhile Kitty is ill; Levin seeks to work happily with his peasants; but he tries to will too great a closeness between them and him, and then his happiness leaves him. In Book III the 'serious' characters feel despair and meaninglessness, all summed up by Levin's talk with the ailing Nicholas in the last chapter.

In Book IV things seem to take a turn for the better. The engagement of Levin and Kitty is contrasted with Anna's failure – after she has become reconciled with Karenin when she thought she was dying of puerperal fever having given birth to Vronsky's daughter – to keep faith: finding that she cannot bear Karenin, she runs off with Vronsky to Italy, not even at that time wishing for a divorce. From now on the Levin–Kitty relationship is the foil to the doomed Vronsky–Anna one. Levin may sometimes seem absurd – as when he cannot find his shirt on his wedding day – but never loses the reader's respect. Vronsky lives to a fixed military order. His personality does not develop; his humiliatingly clumsy attempt to shoot himself, when Karenin tells him of his (as he thinks) successful reconciliation with Anna, hardly adds to his real military stature. In Italy he tries to create a personality for himself as an artist; but what he produces is contrived and dead, and he cannot paint a successful portrait of his mistress. Yet Vronsky arouses sympathy. He cannot understand Anna, who was happy at first but now pines for her son Serezha – she visits him – and resents being a 'fallen woman', which Vronsky cannot understand. She visits the theatre, is humiliated, and then blames him for 'driving her to it'. Her predicament too arouses sympathy – for not disguising her 'fallen' condition she is thought foolish by the hypocrites. She takes to contraception and smoking. She is hardly articulate. Her liaison with Vronsky has a strong physical basis; but not much more, despite Vronsky's well intentioned, puzzled efforts. The fault lies in Vronsky's limitations as well as in Anna's possessiveness. Meanwhile Levin's brother Nicholas dies in their house; the experience is horrifying for him and for Kitty. The latter is found to be pregnant immediately after the death.

Book VI is about the false life of Vronsky and Anna at Vronsky's country estate where they are visited by Dolly; it also shows Levin in town failing – virtuously – to understand the ways of urban politicians. In Book VII Anna kills herself by throwing herself under a train: partly to revenge herself on Vronsky after a row, but mainly because she has come to reject life altogether. However, Kitty has her son and Levin feels able to communicate with God.

In the last book this mood quickly evaporates, and Levin becomes helpless and suicidal. Vronsky, desolated, seeks what is for him an honourable death in the Balkan wars. Kitty cannot understand Levin's despair: how, she asks herself, could a man of his kind be an unbeliever? We see him contrasted with his half-brother Sergey, the abstract intellectual who has now devoted himself to pan-Slavism. One of Levin's peasants, Theodore, tells him of another peasant (called Platon!) who 'lives for his soul and remembers God'. And so Levin discovers peace. The novel ends with his thoughts:

My reason will not understand why I pray, but I shall still pray ... my whole life ... has an unquestionable meaning of goodness with which I have the power to invest it.

CRITICAL COMMENTARY The virtue of *Anna Karenina*, despite the intrusion of the author's theories (as in *War and Peace*), is its compassion to transform conventional morality – which is not in itself compassionate – into an imaginative insight that is true to life. Karenin may be a pathetic cerebral bureaucrat; but he is shown to us at moments at his forgiving best; his sexual failure with Anna is not unmoving. Vronsky is in many ways shallow, his virility and sexual appeal shown to be masks: a false male code which enables him to jettison Kitty cruelly. Even he, however, finally makes the greatest effort of which he is capable. Anna, the storm at the centre, is selfish and impulsive; but her potentiality for love, though unrealized, gives her a superiority over the other characters (with the exception of Levin and Kitty). Her behaviour is certainly irrational and over-impulsive; but it stems, although only in part, from the emotional limitations of the others. Her first life was a lie, and she passionately sought to escape it. Her tragedy is that her second life also turns out to be a lie. After all, the cheerful Steve 'gets away with more' than Anna, but does not suffer for it (as she does). It is one of the book's supreme ironies that Anna meets her nemesis through being asked to patch up the quarrel between Steve and his wife – a quarrel the origin of which is his infidelity. Further, it is hard for the reader to dislike Steve, whereas he is likely to become at least irritated by the errant Anna. Thus the reader's reaction comes to mirror the prejudice of society: it easily forgives happy-go-lucky men, but is more severe and intense about women taken in adultery.

In another sense *Anna Karenina* is a successful expansion of Christ's answer when confronted with the spectacle of a woman taken in adultery. His answer avoided sexual speculation. Tolstoy, though he does not avoid the sexual issue, puts it into compassionate perspective – perhaps the greatest achievement of his novel.

It is impossible to conceive of *Anna Karenina* without Levin and Kitty; but Levin and his marriage are the weakest, the least convincing aspect of the work. Anna's story is one of pure tragedy, and this tragedy has force enough to give the novel greatness, to pull it together around her single central figure. Tolstoy is hardly 'untrue

to life' in his depiction of Levin and of his marriage; yet
it may be argued that with Levin he leaves the reader
in the air, and in a not altogether satisfactory manner.
The problem was his own. Levin, with his alternating
moods of affirmation and despair, is partly a surrogate
for Tolstoy himself – but he is also, in part, especially at
the end, an idealization of Tolstoy, who chooses to leave
him in an affirmative state. How valid, we ask, is the guess
that he will soon be once again in despair? Are we convinced that he has really learnt anything? Is his implied
spiritual success not merely poster-colour mysticism, as
vulgarly obtrusive as Karataev in *War and Peace*?

As Henry Gifford has pointed out, 'Russian writing
in the third quarter of the nineteenth century is frankly
tendentious ... Tolstoy and Dostoievsky had to move
through the element of controversy without drowning in
it. Both manage to argue their way into a larger truth.'
How, it might be asked, could Tolstoy have made Levin
into a convincing spiritual success in such an age? And
was it not therefore his duty to end on as affirmative a
note as possible? This is a question for the individual
reader. So is the matter of whether Kitty is or is not
weakly characterized; it is clear at least that Tolstoy had
more difficulty with a virtuous than with a 'lost' woman.
We feel that Kitty in a sense irritates him: she is maternal
(in contrast to Anna, whose greatest moral lapse is her
abandonment of her son), which he thinks right, but she
is not intellectual and so cannot be tormented by Levin's
terrible doubts. She simply has faith: admirable but
irritating.

Levin is less successfully portrayed in conversation with
pseudo-intellectuals than when he is describing his changing perceptions. Although he is awkward with the theorists, the dice are loaded against the latter who are too
frequently caricatured in a novel where caricature has no
place; and Levin's own spontaneous wisdom is not al-

together convincing. There is nearly always an element of manipulation present when Levin – or the Levin–Kitty relationship – is contrasted with others. But when Tolstoy describes the movements of Levin's mind he is completely successful, both stylistically and psychologically. Once again, as in *War and Peace*, the sense of *life as it is lived* is miraculously conveyed. If Levin's thoughts are not in themselves profound, the revealed *manner* of his reflection is; and that is more important. Towards the end Levin worries about 'The Church? The Church?' Can he believe in all that it professes? As he debates with himself he turns 'over, and leaning on his elbows [begins] looking at a herd of cattle in the distance approaching the river on the other side'. Again and again such natural detail adds a new dimension.

As has been demonstrated, notably by John Bayley and R. F. Christian, *Anna Karenina* is not a 'piece of life' (as Henry James believed) but an intricately and subtly structured work. It has been complained that Tolstoy's symbolism (especially the railway) is *too* professional; others find it conveys a sense of inevitability which more than redeems the occasional authorial manipulations. It is difficult to disagree with the latter view. Despite its faults, *Anna Karenina* lives up to R. F. Christian's claim: in it, he writes, Tolstoy 'demonstrated his immense range of knowledge of human nature, his breadth and understanding and an anger tempered by charity'.

BIBLIOGRAPHY

Translations: A. and L. Maude, *War and Peace*, (1922–3); R. Edmonds, *War and Peace*, 1957. A. and L. Maude, *Anna Karenina*, 1918; R. Edmonds, *Anna Karenina*, 1954.

Texts: In *Polnoye sobraniye sochinenii*, 1928–58.

Criticism: A. Maude, *Life of Tolstoy*, 1929–30; E. J. Simmons, *Leo Tolstoy*, 1946; R. F. Christian, *Tolstoy's 'War and Peace'*, 1962, and *Tolstoy*, 1969; J. Bayley, *Tolstoy and the Novel*, 1966; H. Troyat, *Tolstoy*, 1968 – biography translated from the Russian. See also I. Berlin, *The Hedgehog and the Fox*, 1953.

Giovanni Verga

Giovanni Verga was born in Catania (or possibly Vizzini) in Sicily in 1840, and died there in 1922. His parents were well-to-do. He studied law at Catania University, wrote a bad historical novel, and spent four unpleasant years in the National Guard. His father eventually agreed to buy him out and to allow him to end his studies and devote his life to writing. Sicily, though its mores interested Verga from the beginning, was primitive and isolated; in the mid-1860s he left it for Florence. In 1872 he went to Milan where he lived until 1893. After this he settled in Catania, though he made frequent visits to the mainland.

He began as a journalist and conventional, reasonably successful, novelist. He achieved fame with the skilful though sentimental *Storia di una capinera* [*The Black-cap's Story*] in 1871.

The period of his maturity begins with the transference of attention from urban to Sicilian life, which he first examines in depth in his famous short story *Nedda* (1874). But there is a considerable overlap between his two manners; for example, *Il Marito di Elena* [*Elena's Husband*], a romance in his old style, appeared in the year after *I Malavoglia* (1881).

He planned a cycle of novels which would deal with every aspect of the Italian social structure, from the humblest to the most exalted. There were to be five of them, and the overall title was to be *I vinti* [*The Conquered*]. Only two were ever completed – and a fragment of a third. These are *I Malavoglia* and *Mastro-Don Gesualdo*. They appeared, respectively, in 1881 and 1888. The third, *La Duchessa di Leyra*, was to retain the Sicilian background of the first two; but *L'onorevole Scipioni* [*The Honourable Scipione*] would treat of politics in Rome, and *L'uomo di lusso* [*The Man of Luxury*] was to be set in the Florence and Milan of rich industrialists.

Verga is a great and prolific short story writer as well as a great novelist; one of his stories, *Cavalleria Rusticana*, he turned into a highly successful drama – it later became even more famous as an opera: the basis of the libretto for Mascagni's opera of 1890. Unfortunately Verga was cheated by his publishers, and was involved in lawsuits over this for more than twenty years. Monleone later composed another version, but he too cheated Verga, who lost much of the money that was due to him. He lived well, but was not free from money troubles until the end of his life. His two great novels were failures in the eyes of the public; and he resented the phenomenal success of the vastly inferior D'Annunzio who owed him a stylistic debt. He did, however, enjoy success as a dramatist with adaptations of many of his stories.

Verga, who remained unmarried, was an accomplished adulterer – he usually found it safest to have affairs with married women, and at one time was involved with three simultaneously. He was also a depressive, which is the chief explanation of his failure to complete his great project. His last twenty years were spent in increasing solitude, and not even the recognition accorded him at the end (he was made a senator in 1920) aroused his interest. His only English biographer, Alfred Alexander, believes that his depression was 'reactive', following on the *Cavalleria Rusticana* troubles and on the failure of his major works. (But he also calls him 'cyclothymian' [meaning 'cyclothymic'], which contradicts the 'reactive' hypothesis.) There is little evidence for this view. Verga suffered from an affective disorder, a variation on the classic *manic-depression*; in his earlier years he may have had one or two attacks of mild mania – but in the main he channelled his upward swings into writing and into a busy and adventurous sexuality. As he grew older the manic phases began to fade (as is quite common), and in his old age he became simply a depressive.

I Malavoglia

SUMMARY The title of the two English translations of *I Malavoglia*, *The House by the Medlar Tree*, refers to the house by the tree to which the Tuscan family originally called Malavoglia ('ill will') are so attached. The house symbolizes for old 'Ntoni both the unity of the family and the old ways. The action takes place in the fishing town of Aci Trezza in Sicily between the years 1864 and 1876, a period of many social changes: the fishing trade – especially in anchovies – was on the decline, taxes were on the increase, steamships and railways were being built and, above all, the ways of the people were altering under the impact of these new conditions.

Old 'Ntoni is a good man, judicious and careful with money, patriarchal, attached to the old customs (rigorous in his observance of antique dress), and he is given to expressing himself – not without good sense and a certain primitive wisdom – by means of traditional saws and proverbs. He has a son, Bastianazzo, married to Maruzza; they have five children: young 'Ntoni, Luca, Mena, Alessi, and Lia.

I Malavoglia is packed with incident: we come to know almost every inhabitant of the little fishing town of Aci Trezza. Characters who play little part in the main action cannot be described as minor because they have a *choric* (in the Greek sense) function: by means of snatches of gossip, descriptions of others and political and other observations they contribute a major part of the narrative. But the main action is concerned with the family of Mastro 'Ntoni.

This upright old man's hopes and aspirations are all centred in his boat, aptly named the 'Provvidenza', his house (by the medlar tree) and his grandchildren. But disaster after disaster dogs the family. Old 'Ntoni cannot make enough profit from fishing, and so decides to speculate in lupins (not the flower, but the seed of a plant of the *genus* lupin which grows well in Sicily: it was used as winter feed for animals, and by the poor). He has to borrow money from Uncle Crocefisso (known as 'Dumbbell') in order to buy a cargo of the seed which he proposes to transport to Riposto. The ship is very severely damaged in a storm, Bastianazzo is drowned and young 'Ntoni returns badly injured. Luca is killed at Lissa, in the Italo-Austrian war – a war which he neither understands nor cares about. The matrimonial affairs of Mena are frustrated. Lia becomes a prostitute and leaves home. Only Alessi remains sensible, loyal and aware. Young 'Ntoni, having picked up bad ways during his military service, takes to drink and is eventually jailed for stabbing the local customs officer who had caught him smuggling. He too finally leaves home.

Meanwhile old 'Ntoni's sense of honour demands that he pay back his debt to Uncle Crocefisso in full. That means that he has to sell the house by the medlar tree and thus see his dearest dreams destroyed. The 'Provvidenza', refurbished, now suffers a second shipwreck.

Mastro 'Ntoni has a stroke and is taken to the hospital. But he dies only partially a broken man: Alessi is able to tell him that the house by the medlar tree has been regained.

CRITICAL COMMENTARY Verga's *Malavoglia,* as a whole

superior to its successor (itself a masterpiece) in the planned series, has had a profound effect on twentieth-century Italian fiction, especially in the period since the fascist era ended – the era in which the Italian novel seems at last to have come into its own. (Ironically, no fully satisfactory edition of the novel can yet be issued. The manuscript, together with others, was stolen from Verga's nephew by a fascist minister for the use of his 'literary' mistress, one Lina Perroni who with her brother wrote nonsense about them. This unsavoury team were not brought to book after the war.)

Verga has been profoundly misunderstood; not until three years before his death, when Luigi Rosso published his book on him, was he at all comprehended by the public or by the reviewers. His great achievement was appreciated only by a very few – notably by his fellow Sicilians Luigi Capuana and Luigi Pirandello. The polemical Capuana christened Verga's method *verismo*. This is somewhat misleading. *Verismo*, the Italian form of *naturalism*, existed as a theory and to some extent as a practice: it emphasized adherence to reality just as naturalism did, but in a particularly south-Italian manner. That is to say it concentrated zestfully on the sensual, the seamy, the primitive, the dirty, and on the horrors of poverty. An excessive and romanticized version of *verismo*, with due allowances made for thrilled bourgeois audiences, may be seen in the operas of Puccini (and indeed in Mascagni's *Cavalleria Rusticana*) – most effectively in the brief and savage *Il Tabarro*.

Now it is true that Verga was a gloomy man who wrote that 'God does not exist, or is cruel; that's all there is to be said about it.' It is also true that he had been influenced by the theories of Zola, to whom Capuana had drawn his attention. But he did not believe that the novel could become a new aspect of science – as Zola pretended to believe.

There was another side to Verga's nature. He may

often have felt convinced that human beings are at the mercy of fate (those who are the victims of affective disorders tend so to feel: the process is chemical, and could not in those days be chemically controlled) in the form of history, heredity, and every other irresistible aspect of their existence; nevertheless he possessed an innate and inviolable lyricism, a simple, uncomplicated and unadulterated love of nature, including the human beings which are part of it.

Italy had only recently become a united country, and regionalism in fiction was still predominant. This is the main reason why the nineteenth-century novel is so weak in Italy in contrast to that of France, Britain, Russia. (The same applies to Germany.) But Verga, already adept at entertaining fashionable audiences, turns this very limitation into one of the greatest triumphs of nineteenth-century literature. For *Malavoglia* – at one level as provincial a story as could possibly be conceived – is in its implications a universal comment on life.

Of his notion of *I vinti* as a whole Verga wrote: 'This story is the genuine and dispassionate study of how the first aspirations for wellbeing probably originate and develop in the humblest classes. It is the study of the perturbations brought into a family, that up to that point had led a comparatively happy existence.' The style he conceived would be consonant with the social class with which each of the novels was to deal.

In *Malavoglia*, as Verga intended, the style is inherent in the subject matter. It might just as well be put the other way around: the subject matter is inherent in the style. For Verga has created a perfectly organic work in which form and content really are inseparable.

We can appreciate why he found so few admirers amongst a public brought up on a diet of regionalist or French-influenced erotic novels (such as he himself had produced). He was truly innovatory: he departed from tradition – and did it largely on his own – by inventing a new language. Perhaps only the Polish novelist Władysław Reymount (1867–1925), author of *Chłopi* [*The Peasants*] (1904–9) and winner of the Nobel Prize (1924), and his own countryman Pavese have come near to equalling him in this respect. Certainly his influence on Pirandello was decisive, as it was on Federico de Roberto (1866–1927), author of the major Sicilian novel *I vicerè* (1894).

Verga could have employed the technique of Manzoni in *I promessi sposi*; but this would have made his treatment of such humble subject matter seem bookish. He might have been content to insert little local allusions, quotations from Sicilian lore and so forth; but that would have been even more patronizing and literary. After all, his project was to 'give a representation of reality as it actually was'. He was well aware of the limitations of the conventionalized realism which achieved 'art'. The standard literary language – particularly when 'artistically' embellished with 'local colour' – was quite inadequate to portray the primitive, harsh and even animal realities of Sicily. He could, however, have written the book entirely in Sicilian dialect. But in that case for whom would he be writing? At best, a group of patronizing Sicilian bourgeois who happened to understand that language – but little else.

So he chose the way Reymont chose (with Polish) in *The Peasants*: he invented a language comprehensible to anyone with a mastery of Italian, yet one that is never unfaithful to the spirit or essence of the Sicilian dialect. The language is thus a metaphor, a symbol. It is scarcely translatable, as D. H. Lawrence's version of *Mastro-Don Gesualdo* aptly demonstrates. And through his imaginative genius he has created a text that is superior to anything that could have been produced in the dialect itself. He loved and was identified with the material, and so was in a position to universalize it: he translated the essence of the humblest Sicilians without a trace of patronage, thus making that essence available to all readers of sensibility.

The story is told by the characters. *Omniscient* description is eschewed; so, and this is vitally important, are the impertinences of moral judgement. Verga early recognized that the time had passed for moral judgements, whether direct or implicit, for the conscientious creative writer. The old order of things was breaking down, fragmenting; the values by which people lived and in which they believed had suddenly become questionable. Verga's role in *Malavoglia*, therefore, is no more than to show his people as they are. For before one may question the values by which a people live, it is necessary truthfully to establish just what those values really are. In this respect Verga is a *modernist* as well as a *realist*: he does not question, but establishes facts.

I Malavoglia possesses universality – the point is worth emphasizing, since the novel is set in a small community – because of its integrity and because, besides showing the defeats that men and women have to endure, it also shows their courage, patience, obduracy, honour, and capacity to survive. It is also suffused with a sense of the beauty of the landscape; but this is never conveyed by rapturous description of a 'literary' sort – it is rather an exquisitely articulated rendering of the inarticulate feelings of the humble folk who people the book. It is not as pessimistic as it is often made out to be. The family ends up victorious if battered: it gets its property back. The family stands for solidarity – perhaps even for class solidarity (though in no conventional sense). In this part of *I vinti* the people are in a certain important way *unconquered*. Their name is Malavoglia; but there is an irony in this, for the family in itself is not ill willed. They defeat their very name by their natural energy and the unpretentious manner in which they accept what they are.

BIBLIOGRAPHY

Translations: M. Craig, *The House by the Medlar Tree*, 1891; E. Mosbacher, *The House by the Medlar Tree*, 1950.

Text: In *Opere*, 1955.

Criticism: L. Perroni, *Studi verghiani*, 1929 – in Italian (a fascist view of Verga, critically inane and based on stolen material; but it contains some factual information of interest – though this will need to be checked – for those who can stomach the enterprise as a whole); T. G. Bergin, *Giovanni Verga*, 1931; G. Cattaneo, *Giovanni Verga*, 1963 – in Italian; L. Rosso, *Giovanni Verga* (1919), 1966; L. Luperini, *Pessimismo e verismo in Giovanni Verga*, 1971; A. Alexander, *Giovanni Verga*, 1972 – unfortunately the only English biography of Verga, in which the biographer's main interest appears not to lie in literature.

Émile Zola

Émile Zola was born in Paris on 2 April 1840; in 1843 his family left for Aix-en-Provence (the 'Plassans' of his novels), where he spent his childhood and adolescence – and where he became friendly with Paul Cézanne. He returned to Paris in February 1858. Zola's father was an Italian civil engineer who finally settled in France. He died in 1847. Émile Zola was thus an Italian, and did not adopt French nationality until 1862. His French mother, from whom he inherited many of his neurotic traits, died in 1880.

In his early years Zola suffered extreme poverty. By 1865 he was reasonably well established as a hack journalist. *Thérèse Raquin* (1867) brought him to the notice of a wider public. In 1866 Alexandrine-Gabrielle Meley, about whose origins little is certain, became his mistress; they married in 1870. The marriage was childless, apparently by Zola's decision. In 1888 he took as mistress Jeanne Rozerot, a sempstress employed by his wife at Médan, near Paris, where he had bought a country home. By her he had two children, a girl and a boy. Eventually his wife accepted the liaison.

Henry James noted – alluding to his earliest meeting with Zola – that he was 'fairly bristling with the betrayal that nothing whatever had happened to him in life but to write *Les Rougon-Macquart*'. James even spoke of *Les Rougon-Macquart* (1871–93: *Germinal* was pub-

lished in 1885) 'as having written *him*'. This sequence of
novels was originally planned in 1867–8 as a series of ten
books which would study the whole of the Second Empire, from the *coup d'état* [of Louis-Napoléon, 1851]
down to the present day' and 'the questions of common
blood and environment'. He had only finished the first
volume and a part of the second when the Franco-Prussian
war put to an end the Second Empire and initiated the
Third Republic (1870–1940). But Zola, in what became
a twenty-novel sequence, kept chronologically within the
Second Empire.

Zola's own life was uneventful except for his affair with
Jeanne Rozerot and his involvement in the Dreyfus scandal. He early became the leader of the naturalist school,
and contributed to a volume of naturalistic short stories
Les Soirées de Médan (1880) together with J.-K. Huys-
mans, Guy de Maupassant and three others. He became
friendly with the Goncourt brothers – whose novel *Ger-
minie Lacerteux* (1864) is one of the precursors of naturalism – with Turgenev, Flaubert, whose death profoundly
distressed him, and with most of the other literary men
of his time. He agitated for a reversal of the Dreyfus
verdict and wrote *J'Accuse* (1898), a trenchant attack on
the corrupt Army. He was tried and sentenced to imprisonment but took refuge in England. When he was
able to return he continued to work on the inferior
fiction he had been writing since the completion of the
Rougon-Macquart cycle. In September 1902 he died in
his Paris apartment: the bedroom chimney had been
repaired in the summer, the workmen had left it blocked
and the fumes of the fire killed Zola. His wife survived
until 1925.

Les Rougon-Macquart

The twenty-volume sequence *Les Rougon-Macquart* is

Zola's only intrinsically important literary work, with the exception of *Thérèse Raquin* and some short stories, of which *L'Attaque au moulin* (1880) is the best.

It is generally agreed that Zola wrote only three or four masterpieces: *L'Assommoir* [*The Dram-Shop*] (1877), *Germinal* (1885), *La Débâcle* (1892) – and, for some, *La Terre* [*Earth*] (1887). The first two are most critics' choice, though James much admired *La Débâcle*. However, we cannot consider any of these out of their context which is that of the *roman-fleuve*, *Les Rougon-Macquart*. With the exception of the last novel in the series, *Le Docteur Pascal* (1893), all its parts, which are self-contained, have their moments of power and insight; all are by any standards major works. But Zola, for reasons which will become apparent, is an especially flawed major writer. When we wish to claim the status of masterpiece for a particular work by him we are, it seems, inevitably obliged to support our view by drawing attention to the ways and means by which he *transcends his shortcomings*. Admirers of Zola are uniform in their habit of apologizing (if only by implication) for his faults. This is not a common critical situation (though it does apply also to Balzac). But, at least initially, we cannot avoid it.

Zola made no secret of his intentions in *Les Rougon-Macquart*. It is not as if he only published a foolishly naïve critical book, *Le Roman expérimental* [*The Experimental Novel*] (1880); he frequently brings what he thinks he is trying to do into the body of his work, and he nags the reader with it. A coarse but powerfully imaginative writer, he keeps flawing his vital material with pseudo-scientific ideology; even to the extent of manipulating (unlike Balzac) the material in the interests of his ideas which, for a novelist of his capacity, are crude and intellectually feeble. Yet this anti-romantic devotee of a *scientific* fiction is at his best a romantic symbolist and a prophet of expressionism and surrealism; he is also a pioneer of humane sociology.

Although Zola often referred to his novels as 'poems', called himself 'only a poet' as late as 1898, and admitted that a work of art was 'a corner of Creation seen through a temperament', his plan for *Les Rougon-Macquart* was anything but *poetic*. In the preface to the 1870 edition of *Thérèse Raquin* he had already written that his aim had been 'above all scientific ... I have simply conducted on ... living bodies the work of dissection that surgeons perform on corpses.' He had reached this position from reading Hippolyte Taine (1828–93), the critic and philosopher who maintained, in a famous phrase, that vice and virtue are 'products just as are vitriol and sugar'. Zola had also read an over-confident work on heredity by Prosper Lucas, as well as the more important Claude Bernard, the physiologist who sought to put medicine on a scientific footing. He did not wholly believe in the 'laws' of heredity which Dr Lucas propounded but they served his purpose. Taine admired Lucas, and Zola now had a framework:

I want to explain how a family [he wrote in the preface to the first of the *Rougon-Macquart* series] a small group of human beings, comports itself in a society ... individuals who, at first glance, seem very dissimilar, but who upon analysis are seen to be intimately bound to one another. Heredity has its laws like weight ... I shall ... trace out the thread which leads mathematically from one man to another

Later he was to rationalize this into a 'system' by which fiction could become an experimental science: 'the experimental method, in letters as well as in science, is on its way to understanding natural phenomena, both individual and social.' Personal feelings would be allowed in 'only concerning those phenomena whose determinism is not yet fixed', and then the novelist must 'control this personal sentiment as well as he can by observation and experiment'. It is fortunate that Zola did not follow out these silly precepts.

The theory is not tenable because the novelist is forced to create: selectivity alone is a form of creativity. But Zola was torn between his temperamental pessimism and the positivist idealism which he shared with many of his contemporaries; above all he needed a method. *Les Rougon-Macquart* is inexplicable if we do not penetrate Zola's conscious intentions; but once understood we can see that, as a text, it happily fails to fulfil those intentions.

The cautiously radical Zola hated the Second Empire and wanted to revenge himself upon it. The romantic and sexually obsessed Zola – so keen to define *love* as a physiological phenomenon – refused to give up writing but wanted to make his fiction 'scientific'. These are important motivations, and they explain much. But *Les Rougon-Macquart* is not really *about* the Second Empire, or even about the way genes work themselves out through five generations. It is, rather, a whole aspect of creation (not a mere 'corner') viewed through a formidable temperament. If we allow that the sequence contains as many as four masterpieces, then we must allow one masterpiece more: the work, flawed though it is, as a whole. Its style is powerful if not eloquent; characters are never seen in depth; its ostensible 'message', as we have seen, is naïve. But it is a genuine, moving and prophetic vision of social reality. We may conveniently see how and why this is so by examining a single representative of the sequence: *Germinal*.

The background is this. The origin of the Rougon-Macquart family is Adelaïde Fouque, 'Tante Dide', born in the eighteenth century. She is the daughter of a madman, and herself half-crazy. She eventually becomes totally insane, but survives as a centenarian in an asylum until the last book. By marriage to the simple peasant Rougon she has a son, Pierre. After his death she has two bastards, Antoine and Ursule, by the alcoholic smuggler Macquart. Pierre gets hold of the property and eventually gains a position in society. His son Eugène Rougon becomes a senator of the Second Empire. Throughout the series the Rougons are represented as intelligent (though vicious) and usually successful; the Macquarts are less so. Thus Antoine is a drunkard like his father, and although he survives to an advanced age (he also conspires with Pierre, whom he hates), he marries another drunkard; their union produces offspring who are in general less fortunate than the Rougon line. His daughter Gervaise, also an alcoholic, has three more bastards: Claude, Jacques, and Étienne of *Germinal*. Later she has a daughter by a tin-smith, Coupeau: this is Nana (Anna), who is therefore Étienne's half-sister. Jacques becomes a homicidal maniac (*La Bête humaine*); Claude is a potentially great painter (here Zola suggests a connection between hereditary insanity and genius) but he cannot realize his gifts and so hangs himself.

The history is more complicated than this (at one point there is intermarriage between the Rougon and the Macquart lines), but enough has been given to make it clear that few members of the Rougon-Macquart family are less than vicious, corrupt, mad or at least unstable. There are exceptions but these are often dogged by misfortune. The degeneracy against which the members of the Rougon-Macquarts struggle, or to which they willingly succumb, is one feature of the series. Another is its scope; it explores systematically different parts of France, different classes and different milieux: the worlds of the provincial towns (Plassans; ie, Aix-en-Provence), of the big Paris department stores, of artists, of the meat markets, of the miners of Flemish France (*Germinal*), of the Paris apartment houses and slums, of high society, politics and finance, and so on. Humour, often of a Rabelaisian kind, becomes apparent from about midway in the series; perhaps Zola, torn between his lurid pessimism and his hopes for the future, found some relief in it. One possible reason for preferring *Germinal* to *L'Assommoir* (1877) is that the first has this humour (especially in dealing with the Grégoires), whereas the second almost lacks it.

Zola often disingenuously implied that conditions under the Second Republic had been better than under the Second Empire. A prime example of this is *L'Argent* [*Money*] (1891) which blames the tyranny of the Empire for stock-exchange corruption, whereas this had been quite as bad under the Second Republic. Moreover, he has been charged – not without justice – as having dealt with contemporary (Third Republic) problems under the guise of writing historical novels about Napoleon III's régime. Thus the socialism of *Germinal* was of a brand unknown in the late 1860s, when it was supposed to have taken place; likewise, the type of department-store publicity described in *Au Bonheur des dames* (1883) was also unknown at the time of the action; and so on. For a devotee of 'scientific' realism these faults are inexcusable, and they are compounded by Zola's failure to keep to a convincing chronology.

But the charge can be answered. It is not enough to point out (as L. W. Tancock does in the introduction to his excellent translation of *Germinal*) that Zola could see that the workers as well as the bosses had faults. (Had he not he would have been worthless.) His anachronistic weakness is not fatal because his work is essentially a gigantic metaphor rather than a *documentary*: a vision of masses and their exploiters. Again, everything non-human in Zola (coal mines, stores, low pubs) has a high anthropomorphic charge. It is never viewed for itself; it functions as a symbol. Zola's radical and 'scientific' intentions are important because they drove his consciousness to passionate work; we need to grasp their significance. And sometimes they do intrude into his imaginative texture. But to read him properly we must separate his intention from his imaginative achievement. This is a delicate matter: one which may be tackled, as may his anticipations of expressionism and surrealism, in *Germinal* as appropriately as elsewhere.

Germinal

SUMMARY The central character of *Germinal* (1885) is Étienne Lantier. He had been taken to Paris (previously in the sequence) from Plassans by his father, where he obtained a rudimentary education. Eventually, after witnessing the degradation of his mother Gervaise (*L'Assommoir*), he became a mechanic. The time is approximately 1867. At the beginning of *Germinal* he has just been sacked from the railways in Lille for hitting his boss while drunk.

He hated spirits with the hatred of the last child of a race of
drunkards, and his flesh was so vitiated by an ancestry
soddened and maddened by alcohol, that the least drop
had become poison to him.

He says: 'I can't swallow two little nips without wanting to go for somebody ... And afterwards I'm ill for two days.' He wanders the Flemish-French countryside in search of a job, and finally finds one in a coal mine, Le Voreaux at Montsou. The first eleven of the thirty-six chapters describe Étienne's first twenty-four hours in this mining district, thus creating an intensely detailed and atmospheric background for the action which is to follow in the rest of the novel (within the first few lines of the twelfth chapter Zola has moved the action forward by months).

Zola had spent some time studying the mines (he invariably drew on documentation and first-hand observation), but the picture he paints is less 'documentary' than a terrifying vision of squalor and hell, presided over by Étienne's impressions of the voracious pit itself, the 'beast crouching to devour the world' which continually sucks men down, extracts from them everything they have to give and disgorges them for a few hours of weary and hungry freedom. The whole district is clammy and black, the miners' houses uniformly poor and overcrowded. We are shown, usually through Étienne's eyes (for he is new to these horrors), the miners at work in the dangerously damp deep pit; we meet the rich, well disposed but comically predictable Grégoires who are, economically, parasites because they live off their big shareholding in the mines – they spend much of their cash on their daughter Cécile, whom they spoil. We also meet Hennebeau the salaried manager, his nephew Paul Négrel the engineer, the Belgian overman Dansaert, a coarse bully, and others. Indiscriminate sexual promiscuity amongst the workers is the order of the day, and is scarcely concealed; at other times they drink. The ten thousand miners of the district hardly understand who *owns* them. Zola does not give a crude portrayal of the bosses as deliberately evil – they can even be humane if their purses are not threatened. Instead he shows how the 'crushed, underfed, ill-educated' (his words, from the preliminary notes on the book) miner regards his owner: 'God knows ... People ...' explains the near-senile veteran Bonnemort, three times brought out of the mine half-dead, in answer to Étienne's question as to who owns Le Voreaux. And the voice of the old man who chokes and coughs up black mucous all the time takes on 'a kind of religious awe, as though he were speaking of some inaccessible tabernacle, where dwelt unseen the gorged and crouching deity whom they all appeased with their flesh'.

The Montsou mines are owned by a joint stock company; only one, Jean-Bart, is owned by an individual – Deneulin, a fair minded, capable and decent person who treats his men better than the cartel, who are represented by Négrel, Hennebeau and the Grégoires.

Germinal, once the scene has been set, tells the story of a strike and its disastrous consequences. Under the influence of Pluchart, a Marxist and member of the First International whom he has met in Lille and with whom he now corresponds, Étienne takes up politics. He is also somewhat influenced by Souvarine, a Russian anarchist who believes not in Marx but in the nihilistic ideas of Bakunin (though Bakunin was not expelled from the First International until 1872). Souvarine, a mysterious figure, is an engineer at Le Voreaux (and is not involved in the strike when it materializes). Étienne meets him at Rasseneur's pub where both are living. Rasseneur has long ago been sacked by the cartel for his socialist ideas – and has much annoyed them by setting up his pub and lodging house in the district. But Rasseneur is a moderate. He is the only character in the book, except for Deneulin, whose behaviour is above reproach, and we may assume that Zola himself sympathized with his position.

Étienne does not share Souvarine's nihilism, but he is presented as the victim of Marxist jargon and as a person who, although fired with a sense of justice, is of a fairly weak intellect: his mind is 'muddled', 'he found that he knew things by heart that he had not understood.' But he gradually becomes the 'undisputed leader' of the miners, who look up to him, and whose 'thick, Flemish blood' becomes fired by his political passion. He organizes a provident fund. Although he has moments of uneasiness, his popularity goes to his head. But when the strike comes he finds that he cannot control the violence it engenders. The cause of the strike is, indirectly, a recession in French industry.

The mine owners are not selling enough coal, and they have to devise a means of lowering their employees' wages. They have an excellent excuse to hand, and Négrel himself (though not the cartel) has some scruples on the matter. The miners, who work in gangs, are paid for each tub of coal they bring up. But they have to spend some time timbering up the narrow seams. Naturally, they do this carelessly: it cuts down their money. The company now proposes to pay the men for the timbering but to reduce the money paid for each tub. (It could be argued that this is not a 'disguised wage cut', since Zola himself gives no opinion on the matter; but the implication is that this is what it amounts to.) Now Étienne has his chance to persuade the miners to act. They withdraw their labour. The provident fund and the money sent from London by the International (not displayed in a favourable light) soon run out. The owners speak of bringing in Belgian workers. The miners are starving, but still determined. At a forest meeting Étienne prevails over Rasseneur, who urges caution and is shouted down, and it is decided to deal with the blacklegs of the private mine of Jean-Bart who have not gone on strike.

Meanwhile there have been developments at a more personal level. There is a memorable description of the *ducasse*, the workers' festival held on the last Sunday in July. This is brutally realistic but, as Erich Auerbach has pointed out, only the fact that the participants are miners and factory workers is unprecedented: the roots of the scene are in seventeenth-century Dutch and Flemish painting. People 'relieve themselves unashamedly', couples are copulating everywhere, everyone is drunk: it is an orgy. The workers are celebrating a temporary release from the misery of their lot. At the festival it is agreed that Étienne will go to live with the veteran miner Maheu who has befriended him from the beginning. In Maheu's tiny house live his father Bonnemort, his wife 'La Maheude' and their seven children. His son Zacharie has left the house to marry his mistress, by whom he has already had two children, so there is space. Catherine Maheu, fifteen, who works at Le Voreaux, has been friendly to Étienne from the beginning; but, though she has not reached puberty, she has become the mistress of the brutal, envious and treacherous Chaval, who has always shown hatred for Étienne. This hatred has been fanned by the fact that Étienne and Catherine have had to share the same room; a kind of tenderness has developed between them which they cannot express. Catherine, beaten and abused, nevertheless choose to stick to Chaval and eventually goes to live with him. Both go to work at Jean-Bart. Étienne has inflamed the Maheus with his revolutionary passion.

After their meeting in the forest the strikers go to Deneulin's mine, Jean-Bart, and put it out of action. The eventual result is that Deneulin is bought out by the cartel – whose offers he has steadfastly resisted for years – at a wretched price; he is forced to become their employee, though not in a menial capacity.

The strikers then go to Le Voreaux to attempt to throw out the Belgians who have now been brought in. They are met by sixty soldiers, who are eventually goaded into shooting. Maheu and others, including children, are killed. The strike is broken. Now Étienne becomes unpopular, and is only saved from being stoned by Rasseneau who takes him in. He has to go into hiding for a time. Cécile, the Gregoires' daughter, is strangled by the demented Bonnemort (who is not prosecuted) while distributing gifts.

Two other characters should be mentioned. Maigrat is an ex-miner turned shopkeeper. Protected by the cartel, his trade is greater than that of anyone else. He operates credit but often only at the price of being rewarded with the favours of a miner's wife or daughter. When the strike is at its height he is cornered by the crowd, tries to escape by climbing on a roof, falls off it and is killed. An old woman tears off his penis and parades it through the street on her stick – one of Zola's finest scenes.

Then there is Monsieure Hennebeau. He is unhappily married to a faithless woman whose affection he none the less desires. Now she is having an affair with the cynical Négrel, who is Hennebeau's nephew; at the same time she is trying to marry Négrel off to Cécile. As the strikers chant their persistent chorus of 'we want bread', Hennebeau – who has just discovered that his wife has been sleeping with Négrel – thinks only of how much happier he would have been as a toiler, copulating indiscriminately when and as he wished in the fields. 'He had food in plenty, but that did not prevent him groaning in anguish.' He does not even feel resentment against the 'famished creatures': 'only maddened by the smarting wound in his heart'.

Souvarine remains aloof from the strike and continues his work at Le Voreaux as an engineer; but he decides to act when he sees that the strike has been broken. In secret and at considerable risk to himself he descends the shaft and loosens the linings, knowing that this will cause the whole pit to become flooded, thus putting everyone's life at risk and destroying the mine for ever. He does his work and then goes up to sit on a hill to smoke his pipe and watch the outcome. When he has seen what he wants to see he departs. 'Doubtless, on that day when the last expiring bourgeois hear the very stones of the street exploding under their feet, he will be there.' No wonder Zola is not popular with Marxist critics.

Étienne reluctantly decides to join the other miners in their humiliating return to work. Both Catherine and Chaval are also returning (to Le Voreaux, as Jean-Bart is out of action); but Catherine has left her lover. They descend. Soon the lining gives way. Most of the miners escape, but some are killed; Chaval, Catherine and Étienne are trapped. Étienne, goaded by Chaval, kills him. The dead body floats up against the couple as they await rescue or death. Étienne at last makes love to Catherine (they have just eaten such of their clothes as were edible), who dies soon after. Étienne is rescued by Négrel and his team. After six weeks in hospital, during which the surviving members of the Le Voreaux disaster have gone to work at the repaired Jean-Bart pit, he sets off for Lille – and Pluchart: 'Men were springing up,' he thinks on this spring morning (hence the title of the book), 'a black avenging host was slowly germinating in the furrows, thrusting upwards for the harvests of future ages. And very soon their germination would crack the earth asunder.' (We learn from the last book of the series that Étienne took part in the Commune of 1871, and was subsequently exiled to New Caledonia.)

CRITICAL COMMENTARY Depiction of character in depth was not one of Zola's strengths (the deficiency may have influenced him in the pseudo-scientific method he evolved). *Germinal* is essentially a novel of mass action: 'Nowhere, perhaps,' Angus Wilson has written, 'have scenes of mass action been more deftly managed, nowhere the confused emotions and thoughts of simple people, treated like beasts and driven into self-defence that is often bestial, more directly made lucid without losing reality.' Zola maintains the balance between the opposing forces with great integrity and brilliance. Étienne may have high hopes as he strides away from Montsou; but there is evidence only that Zola has some sympathy with his emotional state – none that he shares these hopes, and none that Étienne has been cured of his intellectual deficiencies. He has seen the results of mob violence and been horrified by them; but Zola makes no effort to depict him as a fundamentally changed man. Transformation of character is never one of Zola's themes. His novels are of defeat – and *Germinal* tells the story of a defeat on a very large scale.

The conventional realism of *Germinal* is for the most part confined to the scenes of mass action: the *ducasse*, police brutality, the pit disaster. Zola had visited Anzin while a strike was on, and had been down a pit. He used all his documentary resources. But even here the account, while apparently presented in conventionally realistic terms, concentrates on the dramatic elements. The description of the crowded and squalid conditions in which Maheu and his family live is deliberately brutalized

Moments of genuine tenderness are few – though they have the vital function of demonstrating that decency can flickeringly exist even under the most atrocious conditions.

The novel abounds in obvious symbols: the 'devouring' mine itself; the constant references to the high temperatures under which the miners work (hell); the even more frequent references to Maheude's big slack breasts from which her youngest, Estelle, takes her food (the milk of human kindness which flows even when its giver is half-starved; the wreck of beauty by poverty and exploitation; the basic need for food – at one point Zola comments that 'these acts of revenge did not feed them'). The comfortably-off Hennebeau's sexual misery and envy of the workers' promiscuity is deliberately contrasted with the workers' material misery. If he is married to a heartless bitch, then they (and their representative Étienne) are 'married' to their terrible material lot. While they await the hungry strikers' deputation Hennebeau, the Grégoires, Deneulin, Négrel and their families eat an exquisite lunch of several courses: the careful description of this meal is, once again, clearly symbolic. Zola has been criticized for being too cruel to the Grégoires in depriving them so brutally of their beloved Cécile. But this incident is symbolic. The Grégoires' affection for Cécile is touching, and they are only gently idiotic, not unkind; but violence will occur so long as vicious abuses are not put right. Conditions that drive men like Bonnemort mad will also produce murders of innocent girls on errands of mercy. This is not an indictment of the capitalist system: it is an indictment of cruelty and injustice. (Zola's miners cannot be said to be presented as capable of owning the means of their production.)

The more crucial personal incidents of the novel cannot be considered conventionally realistic. The unrealized passion of Catherine and Étienne when they share the same room is not, it is true, unrealistic; but instead of being examined in psychological depth it is outlined in thick, Rembrandtesque lines. The consummation of their passion is wholly unrealistic, though it may pretend not to be. After more than nine days, during part of which the corpse of Chaval has persistently swirled up against them, and during which they have in the foul air eaten worm-eaten wood, the 'cloth of their garments', and Étienne's leather belt, Étienne 'took her ... in this tomb, on this bed of mud ... They loved each other in despair, in death itself.' Only an hour later Catherine dies. This episode can scarcely be judged in terms of possibility. If the falsification is not surrealist it is at least proto-surrealist. However, as Zola himself wrote, 'I ... think I falsify in the direction of truth.' This consummation, in 'hell', is clearly mythopoeic rather than 'realistic'. Although its setting is deliberately anti-romantic it points to the power of love and the spirit of life. It contrasts especially with the liaison between Négrel and Mme Hennebeau, so cynical on both sides – and so much more sordid and treacherous in spite of its comfortable setting. The corpse of Chaval significantly disappears before it happens. It is actually more affirmatory than Étienne's rising hopes as he leaves Montsou.

Zola compensates for his weakness in depicting character by the anthropomorphic descriptions of his settings. These are quasi-expressionist in that they calculatedly *express* more than realities of external appearance. By the device of viewing through eyes unused to their surroundings, Zola picks out and concentrates upon certain characteristics. When Étienne reaches Le Voreaux he is conscious of furious icy wind, the chimney 'like a menacing horn', the pump 'snoring like a monster', 'a cry of famine borne over this bleak country by the March wind', blast furnaces 'like monstrous torches'; Le Voreaux 'strikes fear into him'. Now this is not an expression of Étienne's internal state – which is never more than perfunctorily treated. But it is a picture of the hell in which a whole community, a collective, dwells. Again, the description of the festival with its emphasis on the gross drunkenness, the urination and the copulation, is an expression of social wretchedness and degradation – of hell, not of merriment. The elaborate description of the exquisite lunch enjoyed by Hennebeau and the others tells us about their collective lack of responsibility and social conscience; Zola does not allude to it. Later the cynical republican Négrel is to risk his life to save Étienne's, and when the latter is finally rescued they are to fall into each other's arms in one of those moments of shared humanity which Zola so judiciously introduces. Yet Zola's theme was not the individual, but the group; and at the lunch Négrel represents the cartel – indeed, he is just contemplating a loveless marriage with Cécile with equanimity.

Zola is frequently criticized for failing in the *Rougon-Macquart* series to observe the exact conditions of the period in which it is set. L. W. Tancock observes that the picture of events at Montsou is 'composite', containing old abuses [women were not allowed to work in the mines after 1874] long since modified or put right and modern developments of socialism unknown in 1867 ... in no sense a true account of affairs as they could ever have existed at a given time'. But he defends Zola by adding that *Germinal* gives a truly balanced picture: the workers are no better, morally, than their bosses (who also, like Hennebeau and Deneulin, suffer). This is true. Zola distrusted violent solutions, and his portraits of inflamed men defeating their own interests is deliberately terrifying. He had no wish to make 'party-political' points, and his text bears this out. Indeed, *Germinal* is in itself virtually a demonstration of the fact that politics as it was practised is no solution to social justice. But there is more to it than this. Perhaps *Germinal* is a failure in strictly historical accuracy. But why then is Zola a pioneer of humane sociology? Not only because he knows how his people talked and acted, but also because his best novels function as vivid prophetic metaphors: he sees that the lure of revolutionary action may prove fatal, that self-interest on all sides is more powerful than idealism. Yet he sees that capitalism is an imperfect system. The conditions he describes in *Germinal* no longer exist in countries where his books are read. But the *exploitation* of man by man does still exist – in the communist as in the capitalist countries, and by some workers of employers as by some employers of workers. Exploitation involves treatment of people, by people, as objects.

Germinal – and the whole of the series of which it is a part, flawed though it may be – goes beyond any purely historical circumstances by its metaphorical power. Each of its components – starvation, rage, ignorance, proneness to jargon, the impulse to destroy, foolishness, selfishness, greed and others – has a contemporary counterpart. Sociologically, internalized within groups and sub-groups, these elements persist – which is why, despite improved working conditions, violence persists. Few know, in human terms, what they are doing or why they are doing it. If only on a metaphorical level the exploited are still in the Kafkian 'Village 240', too ignorant to know how to act sensibly, and the exploiters are eating a long and delicate lunch, too ignorant to see their dismal future. It is a pessimistic vision – except that Zola allows us to see that all may become combined by their experience of suffering.

BIBLIOGRAPHY

Translations: H. Ellis, *Germinal*, 1894; L. W. Tancock, *Germinal*, 1954. *Rougon-Macquart*, twenty volumes, 1885–1907. All the important titles have been re-translated, and are available in paperback.

Texts: In *Oeuvres complètes*, 1960–67.

Criticism: A. Wilson, *Zola*, 1952; J. H. Matthews, *Les*

deux Zola, 1957; E. M. Grant, *Zola's Germinal*, 1962;
F. W. H. Hemmings, *Émile Zola* (1953) 1966. The last is
standard, and excellent. For Zola and Marxism see G.
Lukács, *Studies in European Realism.*

Benito Pérez Galdós

Benito Pérez Galdós was born in the Canary Islands in 1843. His parents were well off. He left for Madrid, where he studied law, in his youth. By the mid-1870s he had established himself as a leading literary figure. He first became famous as the chronicler in fiction of his country's history from the Battle of Trafalgar (1805) to the Restoration (December 1874): *Episodios nacionales*, the series of forty-six novels, was written between 1873 and 1912. Although these are vivid, vigorous and well documented they do not contain Pérez Galdós' best work.

Apart from his journalism, Pérez Galdós' writing may be divided into three further categories: the *novelas españolas contemporáneas* (of which *Fortunata y Jacinta*, 1886–7, is one); the modernist novels (for this is the only appropriate term); and the plays, some of them adaptations from his own fiction.

Pérez Galdós never married, but had many mistresses, most of them from the proletariat; by one of them he had children. His adventures in the slums of Madrid brought him much of his immense knowledge of the life of the city; his inveterate travelling all over Spain – and abroad – completed his sociological education. He was active in politics (in the Cortes in 1886, 1890 and 1907), on the liberal side; but he was never happy in his political position. His hatred of Church bigotry (not of the Church itself) lost him the Nobel Prize. His last years were marred by ill health; he died blind, senile and sclerotic in Madrid in 1920.

Before the revival of interest in Pérez Galdós in the 1960s he was generally assessed as a powerful, panoramic but clumsy novelist and as a 'liberal crusader' (sub-title of a misleading biography of him published in 1948). It has since been recognized that he was by no means always a clumsy stylist and that in certain books he anticipated such modernists as Miguel de Unamuno (1864–1963), the leading light of the so-called *Generation of '98*. The Generation of '98 represented a liberal reappraisal of Spain, a resurgence of properly modified nationalism, a half-tormented hope for the future. Pérez Galdós was not acknowledged as a part of this eclectic and heterogeneous phenomenon but he influenced it – and not least in his critical attitude towards the Spanish left some of whose aspirations he shared. He had at first been influenced by Dickens (whose *Pickwick Papers* he translated from French in 1868), Balzac and Zola. Later he became interested in Tolstoy. Though apparently realistic Pérez Galdós' fiction, excluding most of the *Episodios*, has in it more than the seeds of modernism. *El amigo Manso* [*The Friend Manso*] (1882), explicitly challenges all the simplistic illusionist assumptions of conventionally termed 'realist' novelists. At a less technical level Pérez Galdós is also non-conventional: his use of dreams, daydreams and morbid pathological states is all to the effective purpose of creating *character in depth*.

From Dickens Pérez Galdós learned to perfect his gift for portraying eccentrics; from Balzac he took the practice of using recurring characters; from Zola and *naturalism* he gained an interest in heredity, the effects of environment, and the sheerly sordid aspects of reality.

In matters of politics and religion Pérez Galdós was open minded, inclined to constructive scepticism, and eclectic. The constant development of his thinking makes it impossible to pin him down to any particular ideological position. When in 1907 he became the nominal head, in the Cortes, of the Republican-Socialist opposition (which involved a degree of collaboration with the Marxist Pablo Iglesias) he was not really committed. But he was consistently humanitarian, undogmatic, cultured, thoughtful, honest, anti-revolutionary, and capable of seeing particular questions from all sides. He has suffered most seriously at the hands of Marxist or quasi-Marxist critics. His 'liberalism', they assert, is due to his fear of the proletariat, towards whom he is essentially patronizing; his vein of 'fantasy' is 'childish'; *Fortunata y Jacinta* sacrifices 'some psychological realism' to the 'thesis' that the 'lower orders' could only have a serious contribution to make to society when they learned to accept the 'conventions of bourgeois society'. Fortunately there are other and subtler interpretations.

Pérez Galdós' views of religion underwent some change, particularly when he became aware of Tolstoy's unorthodox Christianity and abhorrence of its abuse in its own name, for this had some affinities with his own. It is said that he 'lacked' a 'genuine inner sense of divine transcendence'. This is true, though not a slur ('did not possess' is more appropriate than 'lacked'). But he understood the psychology of people who did feel such a 'genuine inner sense'; and he understood not only that rigid dogma and fanaticism were harmful, but also that a society cannot operate without some sort of a broad religious basis. What puzzled him was the nature of such a basis; the problem has puzzled others.

In a speech to the Spanish Royal Academy (to which he had been admitted in 1889) he managed to say very little that is specific about his own practice. The human race, to which he did not hesitate 'to ascribe the adjective *common*', is the prime author of the 'work of art'. But society is falling apart, and there is a 'terrible *ripping of the fabric*': 'the panic-stricken crowd ... invents a thousand tricks to conceal from itself its own sadness.' The middle classes are the product of the aristocracy on the way down and the common people on the way up: the end will be a 'longed-for equality of forms in all things spiritual and material' (this is ironic). 'Art,' however, 'is directed solely to giving to imaginary beings a life that is more human than social': pessimism is unnecessary. The combination of irony and cunning is evident.

Pérez Galdós was a writer cleverer and more experienced in life than any of his contemporaries (his only serious rival was his friend José María de Pereda (1833–1906) who, though gifted, lacked his scope). No single book demonstrates this more clearly than *Fortunata y Jacinta*. He remains, as is only now being realized, grotesquely underrated.

Fortunata y Jacinta

SUMMARY *Fortunata y Jacinta* has justly been described as a 'wood of interwoven novels'. It is almost as long as *War and Peace*. It would be misleading to isolate the main theme from the extraordinarily detailed picture of the Madrid life – of the bourgeoisie and the poor, but not of the aristocracy or industrial classes – of the period covered by the novel (1868–75) which serves as a massive background for that theme. But it would be impossible, except at inordinate length, to trace the various strands running through the novel. This summary must therefore be confined to the barest essentials. The story is told by an anonymous 'friend' of all the parties; he plays no action in the book.

Two well-to-do Madrid families, the Arnaíz and the Santa Cruz, have been united by the marriage of Barbarita Arnaíze to Baldomero Santa Cruz. Their union has produced, after many years of waiting, a son, Juanito (often called the Delfín). This spoiled, proud, shallow and over-indulged young man, superficially intelligent, charming and selfish, marries his cousin Jacinta, an Arnaíz. He is a glib spokesman for 'traditionalism' and 'legitimacy'; but this is to get his own way, which he never doubts is the most important subject of his life.

Before his marriage to the pretty and unsophisticated Jacinta he has taken as mistress Fortunata, a girl from the slums; she is a creature of instinct – passionate, uneducated, irresistibly fascinating to men. She had borne him a child, which died. Juanito deserted her, and she drifted into the aimless, wretched, wandering life, not of a prostitute, but of a 'loose woman' forced to use her attractiveness (without real cunning) in order to survive. But she has not lost her innocence or her passion for Juanito.

Jacinta, at first adoring, becomes suspicious of Juanito's past; eventually she (wrongly) concludes that there is a surviving child. Her own increasingly obsessive grief is apparently caused by her inability to bear a child; unconsciously she is also disenchanted by the character of her husband. She adopts a boy whom she is led to believe is Juanito's; the deception is discovered, and he is sent to an orphanage run by the philanthropic and pious Catholic Guillermina Pacheco, friend of – and indefatigable extractor of funds from – almost every character in the novel.

Juanito, now a restless idler, begins to search for Fortunata with whose sexual attractions he becomes nostalgically obsessed. He is unable, for the time being, to locate her. Meanwhile, now back in the Madrid slums, she meets Maximiliano Rubín, the youngest of three brothers who have been brought up by their aunt, Doña Lupe (widow Jáuregui), the 'turkey woman', a usurer. One brother, Juan, plays little part in the main action, though some space is devoted to him. The other is Nicolás, a gluttonous, ambitious priest: he is instrumental in having Fortunata sent to the Convent of San Micaelas, an institution 'dedicated to the reform and correction of women'. The sickly, mentally unstable Maximiliano, who is studying to become a pharmacist, has decided to marry Fortunata – who does not love him, and knows it, but is persuaded into taking the step.

After a period in San Micaelas, described in detail, she marries Rubín and sets up house. The migraine-racked Maximiliano is impotent. Fortunata pities him, feels that she must love him as husband and tries to do so; she is repelled by him.

Juanito pursues her and is successful in making her his mistress for the second time. The affair is discovered. After Maximiliano has made a frenzied attack on Juanito in the street, Fortunata is cast into disgrace in the eyes of Doña Lupe who as always takes charge of everything. Maximiliano returns to her house; Juanito, upbraided by Jacinta for his infidelity, once again deserts Fortunata – he suddenly finds her lack of breeding (she is 'witless', he tells himself) repulsive.

At this point the ageing Evaristo Feijoo, a retired colonel and 'practical philosopher', comes to Fortunata's rescue. For a time she is his mistress. Meanwhile Maximiliano turns to mystical religion; though subject to fits of extreme mental instability, he manages to hold down his position as assistant to the decent and compassionate pharmacist Ballester.

The kindly Feijoo, finding himself somewhat too old for sexual activity, now gives Fortunata a course in his 'practical philosophy', which is sensible but limited in psychological insight. She must make up with Maximiliano and resist the temptations of love. To this end he endows her with some money, to be entrusted to Doña Lupe. The usurer, who is in her own way genuinely attached to Maximiliano, is thus persuaded to take Fortunata into her house as his wife.

Maximiliano is still in the throes of his religious mania, and life for Fortunata is intolerable. She once again succumbs to Juanito whom she meets in the street. This time she becomes pregnant. Maximiliano, with the intuition often displayed by mentally disturbed people, realizes this; what she carries in her womb, he decides, 'is the child of Pure Thought ... to bring salvation to the world'. The situation becomes impossible for the mother-to-be and she leaves for the house of her aunt, the market woman Segunda. This is in the very block of slums where Juanito had first encountered her. He, meanwhile, is betraying her with the treacherous Aurora, a young widow whom Fortunata believes to be her best friend and confidant. But she does not yet know of this. Now, coming at last into direct contact with Jacinta – who often accompanies Guillermina on her charitable missions into the slums – she develops a violent puzzled jealousy of her. On one occasion she physically attacks her. However, while she is desperately unhappy because she cannot achieve Jacinta's social status and ladylike ways, she feels triumphant in one matter: she can bear a child, while Jacinta cannot.

But her puzzled anger at Juanito's wife is deliberately exacerbated by Aurora (one of Pérez Galdós' few purely malicious characters), who tells her that Jacinta is herself not a 'good woman': she is mistress to Don Manuel Moreno-Isla – Guillermina's nephew of whom Aurora has herself once been the mistress. Moreno, the most Dickensian character in the book, is as it happens obsessed with Jacinta – he dies in Dickensian style of apoplexy while in the grip of his irrational passion; but Jacinta has given no heed to him.

After the birth of the child, who is given the name of Juan (of which Juanito is the familiar diminutive), the now utterly deranged Maximiliano informs Fortunata of all the details of Aurora's deceit. Fortunata goes out much too soon after her confinement and tries to kill Aurora; a scandal results and feelings run high. The shock and effort have been too much for Fortunata. She has a fatal haemorrhage. Before dying, in confusion and distress, she dictates a note to Jacinta in which she bequeathes her the child 'so that you may be comforted for the bitterness your husband has made you undergo'. Now that she has the baby Jacinta becomes for the first time wholly disenchanted with her husband: he is reduced to a 'nobody' and feels 'empty' (he always has been, but now he feels it). The book ends with Maximiliano's monologue: 'These idiots think they're taking me in [with the tale that he is entering a monastery]! This is the asylum, Leganés. I accept it ... in silence, as testimony of my complete submission to my destiny. They can't imprison my thinking ... They can put the man they call Maximiliano Rubín in a palace or on a manure heap – it makes no difference.'

CRITICAL COMMENTARY *Fortunata y Jacinta* comes into the category of novels which Henry James called 'loose baggy monsters'; but we, at least, need not take the term as pejorative. There are many long episodes dealing with characters subsidiary to the main plot. But these do not obtrude; indeed, they are essential because they provide the vivid backcloth of Madrid life against which the psychological drama is played. The connection between Juanito and Fortunata is based, on one hand, in selfish lust and sexual curiosity and, on the other, in helpless love. Such tragically tenuous connections are reflected in the nature of certain characters who can move between the two worlds – especially Doña Guillermina. For there are two separate social worlds; yet the author points wistfully at the notion of one genuinely democratic world. Such a notion naturally led Pérez Galdós the man to ally himself with progressive political elements; but, as we know, he was bitter because (with justice) he distrusted their true motives, disliked their compromises, and simultaneously rejected revolutionary solutions. This is why his geniality of approach and remarkable insistence on psychological fairness towards his characters cannot mask his often convoluted irony and tragic sense.

Pérez Galdós is not as analytically systematic as Balzac. But his depictions of abnormal or mystical states, and his psychology, are sounder; he is not a consistent critic of society – which Balzac, if despite himself, on the whole is. It is doubtful, if people could read Pérez Galdós (not many of his novels have been translated) as extensively as they can Balzac, whether they would find him an inferior novelist. He deserves to be better known, in fact because he is superior.

Fortunata y Jacinta has been subjected to a number of interpretations. One reading is that Fortunata represents the *pueblo* (common people): she bears children to Juanito (middle-class Spain vacillating between traditionalism and *rapprochement* with the lower classes), and the second child, given to Jacinta, is the allegorical symbol of a future democratic Spain. It hardly matters whether the writer initially intended any such allegory or not; his text does not support it. The novel itself, as ambiguous as most great novels, reflects his doubts and perhaps some of his sexual guilts (he had himself met and formed a relationship with just such a girl as Fortunata in the slums; she too had been sucking a raw egg – as Fortunata is when Juanito runs across her); he led as splendidly 'democratic' a sex life as did the English painter J. M. W. Turner. It will not do to present the irresponsible Juanito as 'vacillating', even though he may (for the author) have appeared as a gloomy picture of Spain as she was – but only in the general sense that he 'suffered alternate fevers of liberty and peace'. A critic has spoken of Pérez Galdós' 'mood' when he wrote the novel as serene and never recaptured: 'Nature is the great mother ... who corrects the mistakes of her wayward children.' But these words are spoken by Rubín, who is on his way to a lunatic asylum; it is unsafe to ascribe the expressed beliefs of characters in their novels to such sophisticated novelists as Pérez Galdós.

Fortunata y Jacinta is genial, rambling and apparently

well disposed to its characters; but essentially it presents a bitter, tragic and non-ideological view of the human condition, and it contains unique psychological insights. Most of the evil in the book may be seen to stem from circumstance, and to this extent it has affinities with naturalism; only Juanito and Aurora may be said to have irremediably bad characters – though Doña Lupe comes near to it. But there is no 'reconciliation', symbolic or otherwise, between Fortunata and Jacinta – though it is usually alleged that there is. Given Juan, Jacinta soon imagines that she is a real mother, that she felt the pangs of birth; when she feels emotions 'more than pity' for the dead girl she is 'astonished'.

With death between them, it could well be that the two women, one in the visible life, the other in the invisible, were staring at each other across the void, intending and wanting to embrace [my italics].

This is not mellow. Nor do any but a hack critic and some odd friends from the *pueblo* attend Fortunata's funeral. Notably absent are Jacinta and the supposedly saintly Doña Guillermina who ('God's vicar in petticoats') is as much of an over-pious, interfering, patronizing, moralizing, tiresome busybody as she is a benevolent philanthropist. It might be argued that such things could not, socially, be; but should that be so? In any case Doña Guillermina socially can present herself anywhere, and does so frequently. Jacinta is no more intelligent than Fortunata, and her love for Juanito is less lasting, less noble, more shallow. But she is a lady and, possessing a rudimentary education, can behave like one. Fortunata cannot, and it is understandable that she wonders angrily why this is so. Ultimately this novel is a tragedy of heartless betrayal and exploitation; and the social structure is less to blame than the human depravity which generated it. To take Pérez Galdós' reticence as acquiescence is seriously to misread him.

There are many technical and other *tours de force*, of which a few outstanding examples may be given.

At the opera Jacinta – still only suspicious of Juanito, but frustrated because she cannot conceive – falls asleep. She dreams of a pretty little boy, her son, who tries to grab at her bare breasts. It is 'dirty' but 'adorable' to her. He becomes so serious that he seems to turn into a man. She tears open her buttons, exposing a breast to the 'child-man'. She slips the nipple into his mouth, but he does not react. All she now feels is the 'terrifying friction of plaster-stone'; she awakes with a shudder – all this to Wagner's music. This highly erotic episode is extraordinarily revealing. It combines her anticipation of Juanito's sexual boredom with her with her childlessness: neither man nor child will suck the nipple. It exposes her unconscious intuition that Juanito is no more than an irresponsible child. And it hints at her own sexual curiosity: why cannot a wife provide the novelty that a 'whore' can? Later, Pitusín, the boy Jacinta believes to be her husband's son, calls her 'whore' – he has been brought up to speak the language of the gutter. One night Juanito asks for Jacinta's breast. 'Not now ... nasty ... dirty,' she replies but she gives him her finger, pretending playfully that it is her breast; he sucks it and finds it 'delicious'.

The character of José Ido, who periodically suffers from mad fits in which he deludes himself that his ugly wife is an adulteress, is an example of one of Pérez Galdós' cunning questionings of conventional realism – in terms of that very realism. For this unfortunate man is a hack novelist. At one point he swears to the truth of something which is a lie: that the boy Pitusín is Fortunata's child. Jose actually believes it, but Jacinta, as yet unconvinced, exclaims: 'people have told me that you have written novels, and doing that on an empty stomach has driven you crazy ... You are mad ... You are a liar ...'

The dual nature of Doña Lupe is achieved by means of a description of her breasts, one of which is false (she has had cancer); she is 'half-flesh' to people not her creditors, 'half-cotton' to those who are.

Throughout, the psychological analyses are of a high order; Rubín is one of the best realized characters in nineteenth-century fiction; and Mauricia la Dura, who plays little part in the main action, is a most remarkable study of a psychopathic personality – one which Balzac could not, by any stretch of the imagination, have undertaken. Pérez Galdós is one of the most strangely neglected of European writers.

BIBLIOGRAPHY
Translation: L. Clark, *Fortunata and Jacinta*, 1973. This translation has been universally criticized for inaccuracies and awkwardness. But it is the only one available.

Text: in *Obrus completus*, 1941–2.

Criticism: J. Casaldnew, *Viday obru de Galdós*, 1951; S. Eoff, *The Novels of Pérez Galdós*, 1954 – now almost wholly outdated; J. F. Montesinos, *Galdós*, 1968–71 – in Spanish.

José Maria Eça de Queirós

José Maria Eça de Queirós, usually referred to as Eça, was Portugal's best and most famous novelist. Born in 1845, a magistrate's bastard, he was brought up by his grandparents. He studied law at Coimbra University and later practised it for a short while. Coimbra was the centre of the radical *Generation of 1870* movement, whose leading figure was the poet and socialist Antero de Quental (1842–92); Quental became disillusioned and killed himself – but Eça eventually decided to reconcile himself, or to seem to do so, with his disappointments. *Os Maias* [*The Maias*] was written in 1888 before this apparent change.

Eça's first work was romantic or satirical. At twenty-seven he became a diplomat and spent almost the rest of his life abroad – first in England (1874–88) and then in Paris (where he died in 1900). The years in England are the ones during which he wrote his most famous novels: *O Crimo do Padre Amaro* [*The Sin of Father Amaro*] (1875), *O Primo Basilio* [*Cousin Basilio*] (1878), and *Os Maias*. He married into an aristocratic family in 1886 and is said to have become 'a dandified snob', a 'pillar of society' 'living the comfortable life of the reformer reformed'. However, the plight of Portugal was indeed a bad one: the country had fallen into a lassitude so demoralizing that no one of intelligence could endure it. If Quental killed himself, so may – in his own way – Eça have killed himself. Yet the later, more exotic books, written with great attention to style, are not necessarily 'hollow' and full of '*fin de siècle* futility'; they may not have been looked at sympathetically enough. For Eça was an ironist, and perhaps knew what he was at. The posthumous *Contos* [*Stories*] of 1902, translated as *The Mandarin* (1966), are of particular interest.

Eça, the most cosmopolitan European novelist of his generation, was steeped in all things French; although his novels have some *naturalist* tendencies, it was Flaubert to whom he was most devoted. He deliberately used 'shocking' material: *O Crimo do Padre Amaro* is an anticlerical story about a priest who seduces a virgin – and is less compromising than *La Faute de l'abbé Mouret* [*Abbé Mouret's Transgression*], Zola's novel on a similar theme.

O Primo Basilio is a Portuguese variation on *Madame Bovary*; *Os Maias* is, as F. W. J. Hemmings has suggested, in part an equivalent of *L'Éducation sentimentale*. His late novel, *A Ilustre Casa de Ramires* [*The Illustrious House of Ramires*] (1900), is not always regarded as the book of a 'reformer reformed'; its ending is botched, and it was the work of an ailing man – but as Hemmings has pointed out 'the difference is not as great as might appear'.

Os Maias

SUMMARY   Ostensibly *Os Maias* is a novel on a melodramatic sexual theme and a merciless analysis of the apathy of the Portugal of 1875 – and particularly that of 'reformist' intellectuals. At a superficial level it is such, and it is this aspect of it which is reminiscent of Flaubert's *L'Éducation sentimentale*; but at heart it is a nonrealist, mythopoeic allegory.

The main action takes place in Lisbon in the years 1875–7; there are also a preamble and an epilogue, both important. The plot makes little pretence of being 'realistic', but there are many realistic scenes – and some fine passages describing the landscape of Portugal, which Eça loved. The style is elegant and subtle: Eça far surpasses any Portuguese novelist in this respect.

Afonso de Maia, a patriarchal figure 'older than the century itself', and his twenty-six-year-old grandson Carlos Eduardo are the sole survivors of a noble Beira family. Carlos had been brought up by Afonso, once a 'ferocious Jacobin', but now a good-humoured conservative whose advice to the radical young is: 'less liberalism, more character'. His son Pedro, Carlos' father, at first overattached to his excessively pious mother, then dissolute, committed suicide soon after Carlos' birth. For he had made an unwise marriage to a mysterious woman, Maria Montforte. She gave birth to a daughter; then after Carlos' birth she suddenly left Lisbon with an Italian. She takes her daughter but leaves her son. Pedro arrives with the boy, distraught, at his father's house, then shoots himself.

In Autumn 1875 the gifted and handsome Carlos, educated at Coimbra, a qualified physician anxious to pursue his career as doctor and progressive researcher, persuades Afonso (always presented in a fond light) to move from the family's country seat to their Lisbon house Ramalhete ('House of the Banquet') – a place Afonso associates with his son's misfortune. Carlos has many friends, the chief of whom is João de Ega, an excitable writer. Of these friends only João and the brainless bisexual narcissist Damaso Salcêde play a significant part in the plot. Carlos is much sought after by women but has never experienced love. His behaviour is sensible and balanced – 'But the blood of dilettanism flowed in his veins.' This applies even more to his group of friends, who idly hang about waiting for 'something to happen', but take no serious action.

The political background is one of corrupt stagnation: all we witness is the collapse of one administration and its replacement by an equally incompetent one.

Carlos sets up as a doctor and builds a modern laboratory. Otherwise he does little. Out of boredom he takes as mistress the English wife of the ridiculous politician Count de Gouvarinho, now in opposition but destined to become a minister in the next government. His friend João's philandering is conducted with greater intensity. He takes as mistress Rachel, wife of the Jewish banker Cohen – whose own company, however, he seeks out and whom he even praises in a newspaper. Cohen discovers the liaison and throws João, who is dressed as Mephistopheles, out of a fancy-dress party. Carlos and his English friend Craft dissuade João from taking precipitate action, and he goes home to Celorico and his wealthy mother to finish *Memoirs of an Atom* (already acclaimed by his friends as a masterpiece, but as yet mostly unwritten).

Meanwhile Carlos has fallen in love for the first time. The tiresome Damaso Salcêde, who has imitated Carlos in every particular – his homosexual motivation is obvious, though not explicitly stated – has made friends with the rich Brazilian Castro Gomes and with his supposed wife Maria Eduarda, whose daughter is called Rosa. Damaso wants to make Maria his mistress and tries to keep Carlos away; but he is able to introduce himself to her in his capacity as doctor. Castro Gomes goes to Brazil on business, and Maria is soon Carlos' lover. He sets her up in a house ('Hideaway') just outside Lisbon; an idyllic affair follows.

But Damaso writes an anonymous letter to Castro Gomes, who on returning to Lisbon informs Carlos that Maria is not his wife but merely a prostitute he picked up in Paris; Rosa is her bastard by an Irishman. Carlos is at first enraged; but he soon forgives Maria for her past, and generously offers her marriage.

João now returns to Lisbon, having accomplished nothing. With one lapse, he from this time acts as Carlos' faithful friend, confidant and go-between. When Damaso arranges to have Carlos libelled in a scandal sheet, he forces him to sign a recantation in which he declares (untruthfully) that he is a victim of hereditary alcoholism. But João, having a sexual score of his own to settle with Damaso (who is now pursuing Rachel Cohen), has this recantation published in a newspaper. He regrets this action – and it leads to tragedy.

Damaso's relative, Guimarães (who lives in Paris and pretends that he is on intimate terms with the anti-clerical French republican Gambetta) visits Lisbon. He is angry at the implication that he too must be an alcoholic. João is able to settle this matter; in the course of their conversation it emerges that Maria Eduarda is Carlos' sister: Maria Montforte, now dead after an unhappy life as a prostitute, left her papers in his keeping.

Carlos, when informed, is horrified. But he makes love to Maria instead of confronting her with the truth. This task is left to João. She then leaves for Paris, with an allowance. The aged Afonso dies of shock.

João and Carlos set off for a long journey abroad. João returns to Lisbon after some two years. Carlos settles in Paris. Occasionally the two friends meet there. At the end of 1886 Carlos visits Lisbon. He and João discuss the mundane fates of their various friends. Carlos reveals that Maria, living in Orléans, is to marry a neighbour – a 'union of two persons disillusioned by life'. The friends agree that Portugal is 'shabby and artificial'. But in the last sentences they feel a 'hope' and 'make an effort': to catch a tram.

CRITICAL COMMENTARY It is often said that in Eça 'human warmth is lacking', or that his 'major limitation is a human one'. But the treatment of Afonso (in particular), as of certain other characters such as the aimless João, is not lacking in human warmth. However, Eça does tend to produce types rather than characters. Although the unfortunate 'fallen women' in Os Maias are never patronized, they hardly emerge as vibrant human beings. It may have been that Eça could not, in his despair over

Portuguese lassitude, discern any 'character' in his com-
patriots. One must concede that the charge is not
unreasonable. Even *Os Maias* lacks a psychological dimension, and is thus weakened.

However, as an analysis of Portuguese apathy it is successful; the viciousness of some of the portraits is justified,
and is in any case fully compensated for by the scenes of
rich comedy – such as the proto-surrealist episode in which
João visits Carlos, as Mephistopheles, after his humiliation. Furthermore, Eça's love of and hopes for his country
are reflected in his lyrical descriptions of its landscape;
these are certainly not lacking in warmth.

Enough has been said of the social and satirical aspects
of *Os Maias*. More important are its mythopoeic or, at
least, allegorical aspects – all the more effective for not
being obtrusive.

Carlos is to a certain extent a representation of Eça
himself, though the biographical facts do not match
(except that Carlos is brought up by a grandfather).
Carlos is, one may say, a metaphor for Eça and therefore
for the Portuguese writer – and beyond that for the intelligent and sensitive human being in his late nineteenth-
century predicament.

As a *doctor* he has the capacity to heal; but the practice
he sets up is a failure, and he does no research work. Eça
and his friends had intended to bring about a (bloodless)
social revolution; they also failed. And where does Carlos'
medical qualification, his healing art, lead him? First,
into the arms of the frivolous Countess de Gouvarinho
(who visits his surgery on the pretext that her son is ill);
and then into a passionate and genuine affair with his own
sister (for he gets on terms with Maria when he treats her
daughter's English governess). The acute critic Hemmings, has seen that the 'thoroughly unconvincing
sequence of coincidences' in *Os Maias* 'raises doubts
about whether [it] can properly be held to qualify for

admission to the category of realist novels' and he suggests that the 'incest motif was probably intended to have some kind of allegorical significance: perhaps [Carlos'] passion for his sister is ... Eça's ... way of making manifest his chronic narcissism; or perhaps again the business is meant to represent the predicament of the old Portuguese aristocracy, condemned to inbreeding on a spiritual ... plane.' This is true enough as far as it goes; but the incest motif is itself the central issue – even though it may appear initially to be a melodramatic device.

Incest has always fascinated human beings; many modern novelists (including Hauptmann, Mann and Musil) have devoted whole novels to the theme. It is fascinating for a number of reasons: no anthropologist can fully explain the reasons for the taboo on it; this taboo is one of the features, like speech, which separate us from animals; it may have marked the point in evolution at which *homo sapiens* emerged; in societies where all forms of incest are forbidden, it often occurs between siblings who have been separated in their childhood. The possible connection between the taboo and the emergence of speech is peculiarly crucial for writers, whether they see this consciously or not.

Eça was self-critical of his own tendency towards dilettantism, a narcissistic trait which he fought to correct; and he probably thought of himself as sinking into decadence. If anything is decadent and is universally thought of (in non-primitive societies) as such, then this is incest. Yet why is it decadent? Carlos goes so far as to offer Maria marriage before he knows who she is; when he does know, he cannot resist responding to her desire for him – this consummation is one of voluptuous 'despair'. Eça is exploring a difficult area. On the one hand Carlos' action is certainly *decadent*, symbolic of the depths of narcissistic guilt to which the artist (here represented by the doctor) may sink. But the final incestuous union, conscious on

Carlos' part, has other (at least symbolic) possibilities – they are partly worked out in Musil's *Der Mann ohne Eigenschaften*. Eça is imaginatively aware of these. He is curious about just *why* Carlos has committed a terrible crime. Afonso, member of the elder generation, dies of horror; Carlos is not only destined to commit his crime, but also to fail to expiate it: he lives out an idle life in Paris. His fate is not that of the suffering Oedipus (his mother as well as his sister is called Maria). When he proposes marriage to Maria, he plans to take her away to Italy. Why, Eça must have wondered – and we, if in a strictly cerebral sense, must also wonder – did the two not go away posing as man and wife? The point is not at all that incest should be legalized (the notion is anthropologically absurd), but rather that the reason why it has never been (the ban operates everywhere in some form, and mother–son incest is universally tabooed) raises a basic mystery about human nature. We cannot claim as much for Eça's exploration of this problem, which is admittedly tentative, as we can for Musil's; but he had intimations. The theme he used was of course anything but new; what was new was his relatively sophisticated treatment of it.

Os Maias has authentic bite as a satire on the limitations of nineteenth-century notions of the function of art; it recognizes and anticipates the 'artistic–guilt' equation which concerns so many modern writers, and at least raises a fundamental question about the nature of human sexuality.

BIBLIOGRAPHY

Translation: P. M. Pinheiro and A. Stevens, 1965.

Text: in *Obras*, 1945–52.

Criticism: A. Lins, *História literária de Eça de Querós*, 1959; J. G. Simões, *Eça de Queirós*, 1961 – in Portuguese. There is no book on Eça in English, but Hemmings had an excellent passage on him in Hemmings, *The Age of Realism*, 1974.

Knut Hamsun

Knut Pedersen was born in 1859 in the upper Gudbrands-
dal, an interior mountain valley in central Norway. His
father (village tailor and crofter) moved with his family
to the Lofoten Islands, Nordlund, in 1863. The name of
their holding there was Hamsund, which Hamsun used as
a pseudonym for his first book: 'Hamsun' was a printer's
error. Knut, who spent much of his childhood being
cared for by a puritanical clergyman uncle, was an autodidact. Until 1890, when the success of his first novel *Sult*
[*Hunger*] (1890), enabled him to devote himself to writing, he led the life of a wanderer. In 1877 and 1878 he
published three pieces of fiction (never reprinted) at his
own expense under his original name of Pedersen; later
(1882-4, 1886-8) he lived in the United States, where he
performed all manner of menial tasks (including tramcar-
conductor, labourer and fisherman), and he may sometimes have been near to starvation. His first book, an
attack on American culture, brought him some reputation
as an iconoclast; this was reinforced when he toured
Norway in 1891, lecturing against Ibsen (apparently, at
Christiania, to his face) and most of the other leading
Norwegian writers (the only senior writer for whom he
professed feeling was Bjørnstjerne Bjørnson, 1832-1910,
on account of his individual style). Hamsun's iconoclasm
had its element of peasant cunning; but he was by nature
a ferocious loner. *Sult* is an original novel not merely by

Norwegian but by European standards: it tells, in an impressionistic manner and with a power reminiscent of Dostoievsky, of how starvation affects the mind of an apparently wayward hero.

At this time Bjørnson, Henrik Ibsen (1828–1906), Jonas Lie (1833–1908) and Alexander Kielland (1849–1906) dominated Norwegian literature. They all, and especially of course Ibsen, had considerable artistic virtues; but Hamsun, fiercely jealous as well as artistically convinced, disliked the attention which the literary movement they were taken to represent gave to social issues (even Bjørnson was attacked for this). Hamsun was unfair; but he had to be if he was to succeed in his own new style of fiction. *Mysteries* (1892) was, in part, a polemic demonstration of what a new and viable literature ought to be – concerned with 'secret stirrings that go on unnoticed in the mind'. It is now a commonplace that this was the general climate of thought which produced Freud, Strindberg, Nietzsche and many others.

In Hamsun's case – to which Max Stirner is also relevant – we have to try to answer the complex question: what sort of mind did he have? His mixture of brutality and stupidity on the one hand, and exquisite narrative skill and insight on the other must be unique. After *Pan* (1894) the tension in Hamsun relaxed. Through his German publishing connections he became an established popular author in Europe – he is only now coming to be fully appreciated in Great Britain though translations of all but one of his novels have been available for many years. He made a second marriage in 1909, and his *Markens Grøde* [*Growth of the Soil*] (1917) earned him the 1920 Nobel Prize; it was designed to do so. He wrote plays and bad poetry, but faded from the public eye in the 1930s; then, in 1940, he publicly supported the Quisling régime and even visited Hitler (1943), to whom he was impudent. This gained him renewed, though hostile, attention. During the war many of his readers sent their copies of his books back to him at his estate at Nørholm, where he practised as a gentleman farmer and mage *cum* recluse. After the defeat of the Nazis he and his wife were put on trial as traitors; he was partly exonerated on the grounds of mental feebleness (he posed as such), and he was fined and sent to a hospital for a time. His last book, *På Gjengrodde Stier* [*On Overgrown Paths*] (1949), is fiction, though in form it is a cunning non-fiction defence of his failure to do the 'right thing' in 1940 (no one had told him he was wrong, he complained).

Since his death Hamsun's works have regained their old reputation – the later ones even to being overrated once more – and most Norwegian intellectuals regret that he was ever brought to trial.

To penetrate to the mystery of Hamsun one needs to recognize that he was a *peasant aristocrat* rather than a humble peasant, and that peasant cunning, in the form of a slyly activated charlatanism, pervades his life and work. He is in *Sult* and *Mysteries*, and in some sections of later novels, a great writer. He is also repulsive, in his very repulsiveness. Showing us part of ourselves. The rest is mere performance, though interspersed with passages showing the old Hamsun.

Hamsun said, not long before the Nazis invaded his country, that he valued justice and fairness as the highest human qualities. How, one asks, could he then support the Nazis? The answer is that he did not mean what he said – though when on another occasion he announced in English, 'Never should I die, if I did not have to do it!' he probably meant *that*. His early struggles, which were intense, increased his natural contempt for everything that was not Hamsun or Hamsun's property (wife, children, farm); but he had to live in the world, and so he brutally projected 'Hamsun' on to certain aspects of it which he could find, or transform into being, acceptable. Despite the strangeness and charlatanism he is important, and progress into the heart of his work is, as J. W. McFarlane has written in his admirable essay on him, a 'matter of treading carefully'. *Sult* and *Mysteries* still make the strong impact they made on the young Thomas Mann who 'always loved him', even though he later spoke of him as 'broken by politics'. At the beginning, for a few years after he had established himself (the other novel that deserves special consideration is *Victoria*, 1898), Hamsun was brilliant – and might even have developed into an apostle of decency. Instead he fastidiously planned his *oeuvre*, for much of the time misusing his gifts – half cunning, half stupid. A great intuition went into the service of the ambitious writer, not of the early seeker after unconscious truths.

Mysteries

SUMMARY *Sult* had been the first-person narrative of a writer who chooses hunger rather than conventional ways out of it; who 'feeds' on it until his spirit can accept itself and, feeling morally superior, can join the crew of a ship and disappear. Johan Nagel of *Mysteries* has, fairly enough, been described as a 'reincarnation' of the hero of *Sult*; but he is at a later stage. The narrator tells us in casual fashion that 'some extraordinary things began happening in a small Norwegian coastal town. A stranger by the name of Nagel appeared, a singular character who shook the town ... and then vanished as quickly as he had come.' But this is an American translation, and is misleading. Actually the narrator does here pass his only *judgement* on Nagel: he is not merely 'strange', but 'a remarkable and peculiar charlatan'. Hamsun himself enjoyed being a 'charlatan'. This story is recounted by the use of dialogue, description, reportage of what Nagel says aloud to himself and (once) of what he thinks. Emotions, such as that 'he was astonished', are tersely described; there are no psychological analyses, and the text eschews explanations.

Johan Nilsen Nagel, dressed in a loud yellow suit and outsized corduroy cap, arrives on the evening steamer and tells the porter to take his baggage to the hotel; but he fails to disembark, and does not arrive until the next day, by carriage. On reaching the hotel he correctly senses that many years ago there had been a pharmacy on the premises. Three telegrams arrive for him referring to an offer for 62,000 crowns for a country estate. He leaves them open for all to see. Later he claims that he sent them to himself. He buys a puppy and gives it to the landlord. His behaviour baffles the town. He says he is an agronomist; it is never established if this is true. He interests himself in the recent death, apparently by suicide, of a young man called Karlsen who was about to be ordained. His body was found, wrists slashed, in a wood; nearby lay an unsharpened knife belonging to Dagny Kielland, the minister's daughter – in honour of whose engagement to a naval officer the flags have just been flying all over the town. A note clutched in the dead man's hand read: *Would that thy knife were as sharp as thy final no* (a quotation from Victor Hugo, which Nagel later frenziedly attacks as bad poetry). Nagel also becomes obsessed with Grøgaard 'Minutten', the Midget. Everyone knows the Midget. People tease him, but he is regarded as a good, trustworthy, kind fellow, even if a little wanting. A parson's son, he was born in the town. He is better educated than he pretends and is related to the Grøgaard who helped write the Norwegian constitution. He was once at sea, but fell off the rigging of his ship and sustained a hernia. Now he lives with his uncle, a coal merchant, and delivers the coal for him. Sometimes he gets drunk. Nagel meets him when Reinart, a deputy who is in the hotel bar, wants to make him drunk and offers to pay him money to gnash his teeth. Previously he has danced for him in the street for money. The Midget does 'gnash his horrible teeth', but Reinhart continues to torment him: Nagel intervenes, in the conventional role of decent fellow, and the drunken deputy is humiliated. Nagel takes the Midget to his room, presses money on him and discovers something of his past – and of Miss Dagny Kielland's part in the death of Karlsen. The Midget is evasive; it emerges that Karlsen had used him as an intermediary to take a letter to Dagny. Nagel also asks the Midget if he would accept five crowns to assume the paternity of a child that is not his; he refuses. There follows a long passage in which Nagel talks aloud to himself.

Nagel goes to the funeral of Karlsen. On the new tomb of a young girl – an 'angel', the Midget tells him – he writes obscene, (it later transpires) verses; these are mysteriously erased. Nagel gets to know some of the local bourgeoisie, including the doctor.

On the following day Nagel's characteristically abrupt changes of mood are recorded. He rises feeling in good spirits, lies in the woods, and feels a 'tremor of ecstasy'; but the sight of a peasant and thoughts of the liberal representative introducing legislation to conserve 'our national vermin' (peasants) enrages him. There is 'nothing but lice, peasant cheese and Luther's catechism'. He feels he wants to see a 'carefully planned crime ... none of your ridiculous minor transgressions!' Something with 'all the raw splendours of hell'. Then suddenly he becomes euphoric again: the town looks like 'an enchanted city'. He sees a 'boat of scented wood, with a light blue sail in the shape of a half moon'. It is Midsummer Eve. He joins some of the people he had met at Karlsen's funeral, and here meets Dagny. He describes his vision of himself in the boat of scented wood, fascinating but embarrassing his new friends and impressing Dagny.

From this point onwards Nagel's toings-and-froings become infinitely more complicated. He falls in love with Dagny but, like Werther, decides to try to be 'honourable'.

One of the features of his exhibitionism towards her is to run himself down. He puts himself in the worst possible light: he tells her that whatever he does or says is calculated, or a lie. He pretends that he does not deserve a life-saver's medal which, according to his own monologue, he has in fact earned. He poisons her dog – partly out of hatred for her because he loves her (or has decided to) and partly to test the efficacy of a bottle of poison which he carries with him. He indulges in acts of extreme generosity, but in strict secrecy. In the case of the Midget these acts may be self-protective, for Nagel senses in this man something that no one else senses: a naturally evil disposition. He tries to trick him, but the Midget will never be drawn. On the other hand the Midget successfully cheats Nagel: it was he who erased the obscene words on the 'angel's' tomb, and it is he who later substitutes water for poison in Nagel's phial. So, when the latter takes the poison and believes he is dying, he wakes up instead, after a terrifying experience in the woods. The Midget haunts his dreams (so he says) in various frightening forms. No one, until Dagny recognizes the fact (in the epilogue), realizes that he is right about the Midget.

Nagel sneers, in his mind and in his conversation, at all political activity; Mr Gladstone, and his much reported cold, afflict him with peculiar contempt as do Scandinavian affairs. He is visited by a Danish girl friend, Kamma: she calls him 'Simonsen' (which could, for all we know, be his real name), and successfully obtains money from him. It is typical of his intricate half-crazy manner of practising generosity that he should ask Kamma to call on one Martha Gude to make her an absurdly high offer for a worthless old chair. Nagel has observed this woman, who at forty-one is twelve years older than he (if both tell the truth), living in a run-down house; she is so poor that she surreptitiously sells eggs at the market. Posing as a dealer, he pretends that the chair is very valuable and makes her a high offer for it.

She is carefully distinguished from the bourgeoisie of the town (who are caricatured – simply by the device of presenting them through Nagel's not ill-natured contempt); she has an appeal – in her loneliness, simplicity and genuineness; Nagel's passionate desire to give her money nonplusses her. He is finally repudiated by Dagny (like Werther, he gives way and embraces her and, like Charlotte, she momentarily yields; in a later novel, *Redaktör Lynge* [*Editor Lynge*], 1893, where she appears in a minor role, she admits that if Nagel had persisted she would have given herself to him). He persuades the half-reluctant, bemused Martha to go away with him, and has visions of an idyllic future in the countryside. But Dagny intervenes: determined to deny Martha what she has herself renounced, she persuades her to leave town. Nagel makes his first attempt at suicide which is frustrated by the Midget's substitution of water for poison. All sorts of rumours about him are now circulating – yet only two days earlier he had taken the town by storm when he played on a borrowed violin at the summer fête (only he knew that the playing was second rate exhibitionism), and people are trying to persuade him to repeat this on the final night.

He sees the Midget dancing in front of the post office, without coat or shoes. Afterwards he accuses him of deceiving him: 'I don't trust you, Grøgaard.' Already he knows that there is some secret relationship between the Midget and Martha – something 'obscene'. He points out that while Grøgaard has acted for humane reasons, he himself is devastated: like a cat with a hook in its throat which, he pretends to Grøgaard, he has tried to poison but which now must crawl into a corner and die in 'mute terror'. Nagel then tells the cripple that while he, the cripple, is pure and irreproachable, he manages to get what he wants by silence. Full of wind and whirling words, he accuses him of being a villain with a 'secret vice'; perhaps he has murdered Karlsen (and perhaps he did): 'Your virtue brings out the brute in me.' Finally Nagel apologizes, says he is mad, and presses upon him the suicide letter he had previously written to him (the contents are not disclosed). The Midget, who has retreated into silence, refuses to accept it. Nagel joins his friends; amongst them is Dagny. He gives her a letter for Martha Gude – one written before his first suicide attempt. Dagny gives him a strange, indefinable look.

Later that night he seems to waken. He is afraid when he remembers that before attempting to poison himself he had thrown his iron ring into the sea: to rid himself forever of hypocrisy. He has to find it. He discovers a boatman, who tries to dissuade him from such a crazy project but who does begin to make plans to recover the ring. Nagel feels that without the ring life is impossible. The boatman, apparently a stranger, keeps his face turned away. He has grabbed him once when he made as if to jump out of the boat. Now he follows him: the boatman is the Midget, whose 'hideous face' 'leers' at him. Then Nagel truly awakens; it has been a dream.

'Someone is calling,' he whispers and, putting on some clothes, rushes to the end of the farthest pier and leaps into the sea. Only bubbles come to the surface.

In the brief epilogue, Dagny is walking with Martha in the following April. Mentioning the Midget's 'bad end', she asks how Nagel could have prophesied it: 'He said it a long time before you told me what the Midget had done to you.' The nature of the Midget's 'bad end' and of the (presumed) evil he did Martha are not disclosed.

CRITICAL COMMENTARY *Mysteries* is one of those modern novels (Gide's *Les Cahiers d'André Walter* [*The Note-books of André Walter*], 1891, and Rilke's *Aufzeichnun-gen des Malte Laurids Brigg* [*Notebook of Malte Laurids Brigg*], 1910, are others) which develop and refine the broad tradition of Goethe's *Werther*. The man who calls himself Nagel even wears a yellow suit (though not a blue coat); he is 'preposterous'; he kills himself, it seems, for love – and in resentment at women. Hamsun shared the misogyny of August Strindberg (1844–1912) who wrote in 1894 that women were inferior to and weaker than men, and that therefore they resorted to base tyrannical methods – 'and the man bows and sidles along, because it is a woman.' But Strindberg often tended to insanity; Hamsun did not. His chiefs debts in *Mysteries* are to Dostoievsky, to Eduard von Hartmann's *Die Philosophie des Unbewussten* [*The Philosophy of the Unconscious*] (1869), to Strindberg and to Nietzsche. The debt to Dostoievsky lies in the *otherness* of Nagel, in his rejection of the 'masses', which resembles that of Raskolnikov and which Hamsun himself felt: he called the type *en til-vaerelsens udlendung* ('social outcast'). The debt of Hart-mann is more complicated. Hamsun often referred to his admiration for Schopenhauer (1788–1860), but is more than likely that he got much or even most of his Schopen-hauer through Hartmann's popularization and adapta-tion of his thought. For Schopenhauer the conscious mind is at the service of what he calls 'will': dynamic, ir-rational, blindly striving. Schopenhauer also has a mes-sage: that man should renounce his striving, mainly through the contemplation of art, and thus become free by entering into nothing – which is not the domain of the will. The young Nietzsche took up Schopenhauer's in-sistence on the primacy of this will. But his message is different: man should not seek freedom from the will, but cultivate instead a 'will to power'. As advocated by Nietzsche this involved rejection of the weakness of con-ventional 'Christian' morality. Perhaps Hamsun got most of his Nietzsche secondhand as well: Nietzsche was first popularized in Scandinavia by Georg Brandes (whose brother Eduard had been responsible for the publication of the first chapters of *Sult* in a Danish magazine in 1888), and his ideas were taken up by Strindberg, whose version of them Hamsun accepted.

Hartmann exercised a more direct influence. In the 1917 edition of his epoch-making *Zur Psychopathologie des Alltagsleben* [*The Psychopathology of Everyday Life*] (1901) Freud assumes that Hartmann is a 'botched Schopenhauer ... turned inside out'; but he implies that Hartmann's was an important expression of the trend of the time. Hartmann, following Karl Gustav Carus, substituted for Schopenhauer's 'will' the 'unconscious', which he postulated as the source of all human behaviour. This fitted in with Hamsun's attitude, and in a form that he could easily grasp.

In 1890 Strindberg published his ostensibly most *naturalist* novel: *I havsbandet* [*By the Open Sea*]. This is the story of the destruction, by madness, of a Nietzschean *Übermensch* ('overman'). As was well known, Nietzsche himself had gone mad – almost certainly as a result of syphilis – in 1889, just at the time Brandes had succeeded in elevating his hitherto small reputation to European proportions; Hamsun did not plagiarize Strindberg's novel, but *Mysteries* is closely related to it.

Hamsun, before he went to America, had tried to gain an education at Christiania University. The combination of his own iconoclastic, ignorant and brutish personality, and the excessive academicism at the University at that time had resulted in his quick departure. His resentment is summed up in *Sult*: the 'hunger' of the protagonist is a perfect *objective correlative* for Hamsun's hunger for knowledge, for the power he vaguely but furiously felt that knowledge could confer upon him. When he came to write *Mysteries* he had succeeded in becoming famous and accepted – on his own terms. This novel is an intuitive triumph. It has no intellectual qualities: Nagel's ravings against Tolstoy, Gladstone, Ibsen and others are simply reflections of Hamsun's anger at *everyone else*. But it has incomparable value because the confused author is ultimately distanced from himself. Nagel's defeat – his puniness, the wastage of his gifts of perception, his inability to perform a *large* action (even such as a really 'big' crime), his failure to love except 'preposterously' – this is Hamsun's *creative* end prophesied, anatomized, dissected. Nagel dies; Hamsun went on, his books becoming increasingly self-conscious. He disguised the secondhand cruelty of his pantheism only by the superb skill of his *riksmål*. *Riksmål* (now called *Boksmål*: 'book language') is the Dano-Norwegian 'literary' language of Norway. *Landsmål* (now more usually called *Nynorsk*) is the 'country speech', the attempt of nineteenth-century nationalists to form a standard Norwegian from several dialects when Danish rule ended. Hamsun did not follow these; but his *riksmål* is extraordinary in its capacity to incorporate the colloquial. He never lost this ability with language.

One technical aspect of the novel should be mentioned: its pioneering use of *stream of consciousness* or *interior monologue* technique (in Chapters 4 and 18). Some *stream of consciousness* writing attempts to penetrate to pre-verbal thinking or awareness, often by use of imagery. Some merely tries to describe, in minute detail, exactly what passes through the mind. *Interior monologue* is, strictly, a form of *stream of consciousness* which uses a direct first person method (Nagel actually speaks aloud in Chapter 4; in 18 his thoughts are described, so that this is really *stream of consciousness*). The French novelist Paul Bourget used the term *monologue intérieure* in *Cosmopolis* (1893). Valéry Larbaud borrowed this to describe James Joyce's technique in *Ulysses*. Joyce himself found the first use of the method in the novel *Les Lauriers sont coupés* (1888) [translated as *We'll to the Woods No More* (1957)] of Edouard Dujardin (1861–1949). It had been suggested to Dujardin by the French critic, of Polish extraction, Teodor Wyzewa. As Joyce was aware, Dujardin's novel was only interesting for its method. Hamsun's two novels of only a few years later are quite otherwise, and one wonders if Joyce – who could write to his admired Ibsen in *riksmål* in 1901 – ever read these.

Mysteries is superior to its prototype *Werther* because the writer is able to see and to imply (if only unconsciously) that his hero is in fact *unworthy*. We share Nagel's disgust with 'news' and with inauthentic judgements. We laugh too when, fantasizing as to how he might humiliate Dagny, he hits on the idea of saying to her in public, 'Miss Kielland, I congratulate you on your clean knickers.' We sympathize with his sense of loss of self. But he is an emasculated 'authentic' man, a castrated *'Übermensch'*. He knows 'what it is about', but he can't 'do it': that he must try to create circumstances, not allow them to create him; but his efforts are notably feeble. This is in itself a criticism of both Nietzschean 'self-overcoming' and of *existentialism*. Nagel cannot defeat the Midget; he cannot push his advantage home with Dagny; he cannot even hold Martha Gude. In telling the provincials of his dreams he cheapens them. He cannot refrain from exhibitionism, even when this makes him seem absurd to himself. Yet he is sensitive, he wishes to be generous. His rejection of false values, of the arbitrary and unreal life of 'ordinary' people is sensitive. He has the intuition to create certain pictures of himself in the minds of people, and then to demonstrate that they are illusions. It doesn't matter whether or not he is rich, a good violinist, a hero who has saved someone's life, and so on: he discerns that the image people have of an individual is in any case a false one, not based on a true consideration of that person or their motives. His destruction of the images of himself that he builds up does have its truth. But within, he too feels empty. There is no substance in his love for Dagny. And he cannot better the Midget – whose frustration of his first suicide attempt drives him into superstition (the iron ring) and finally madness.

Who – what – is Minutten? He has rightly been called

a parody of Nagel. He is also, as McFarlane points out, an 'imperfect Christian': a foil to the 'deficient Nietzschean' which Nagel is.

He is known as the Midget because of an incident when several cruel, drunken 'respectable' men of the town forced him into a bath to 'baptize' him during a nocturnal orgy. The bath is full of their excrement, spittle – and cinders. One of his tormentors was a doctor who broke his rib and then treated him – free! In telling Nagel of this Minutten is full of Christian submission. But Nagel sees through him. In a way he sympathizes and even admires him: like himself, Minutten is a fraud, he practises deception – but also secretly evil, *unlike* Nagel, who is as full of Nietzschean *generositas* as he is with the desire to shock. Nagel's own 'baptism' is finally by the clean sea. The battle between him and Minutten, cryptic though it is, is one of the main strands of the novel. The false, would-be Nietzschean's final act is more 'Christian' than the false Christian's secret ill-deeds, which bring him to a 'bad end'. In so far as the Midget is Nagel's *alter ego*, he is also Hamsun's bad conscience. Hamsun, who publicly preached closeness to the soil and postulated the desirability of 'rooted' people (but he craftily introduced 'wandering' rogues into his later fiction, and yearned to be a wanderer again), also came to a 'bad end': he supported a dictatorship of madmen and mass murderers, putting all the weight of his age and authority behind his treason to decency. Later, Nagel-like (the parallel is McFarlane's), he lyingly pretended that he 'had not known'.

Hamsun was hating and hateful, always seeking revenge for the terrible humiliations of his early years. But in *Mysteries* his intuition is in full control: he can make us feel our own shortcomings in the wretched Nagel, make us laugh with him at his exposures of his own and his acquaintances' pretences – and he prophetically displays himself as the sly, secret, bottomlessly evil Minutten. The novel painfully recalls or reflects the wild feelings of youth, and demonstrates the hidden nature of the inner life that is truly vital. It is also sometimes gay: its portrayals of people enjoying the summer convey the qualities of innocence and spontaneity. It illustrates the difficulties of actually attaining *authenticity*. We willingly and often return to it, further to fathom its mysteries.

BIBLIOGRAPHY

Translation: A. G. Chater, *Mysteries*, 1927.

Text: in *Sam leele verker*, 1954–5.

Criticism: H. A. Larsen, *Knut Hamsun*, 1922; in J. W. McFarlane, *Ibsen and the Temper of Norwegian Literature*, 1960; in B. W. Downs, *Modern Norwegian Literature*, 1966.

Theodor Fontane

Theodor Fontane was born near Berlin in 1819. Both his mother and father, an apothecary, came from southern French – Huguenot – families who had settled in Prussia in the eighteenth century. He married (1850) a woman of similar origin. He spent some of his early years in a town on the Baltic; but most of his life when he was not travelling (as correspondent in the Prussian wars of 1864, 1866 and 1870; in London as a journalist) was lived in Berlin, sometimes in straitened circumstances. He worked in his father's profession until 1849, after which he lived by his pen or from petty jobs in government offices. He became fairly well known as a journalist and travel writer, and had a literary reputation as an accomplished ballad writer. At the very late age of fifty-nine he began to publish novels. The first was *Vor dem Sturm* [*Before the Storm*] in 1878, about Prussia's resistance to Napoleon in 1812–13. Fifteen more books followed before his death in Berlin in 1898.

His novels were generally well received, though his only real success was a long account of his native Brandenburg published in the 1860s. Since his death his reputation as a novelist of European stature has steadily risen. His experience was wide: he had watched the rise of Prussia and of the *Junkers* class, had worked in business and in government service, had been in the Army and had spent much time in England and Scotland;

above all he knew intimately the life of Berlin and of the Prussian small towns. He became Germany's great nineteenth-century master of ironic, shrewd, restrained realism; a novelist of poetic subtlety with a fine though unobtrusive technique. Several of his books, as well as *Effi Briest* (1894–5 – generally considered his finest), deal sensitively and perceptively with the position of women: notably *L'Adultera* [*The Adulteress*] (1882) and *Irrungen, Wirrungen* [*Trials and Tribulations*] (1893). His approach was liberal, but not in any political sense; he eschewed left-wing *naturalism* or realism, holding that true 'realism will always be full of beauty, for the beautiful belongs to life as well as the ugly'. But he was as non-doctrinaire as any major writer has been. His novels achieve his aim: they have 'intensity, clarity, lucid composition, roundness and consequent heightened intensity of feeling achieved by the transfiguration which is the task of art'.

Effi Briest

SUMMARY Frau von Briest, now married to a wealthy country gentleman, was once courted by a hussar subaltern, Baron Geert von Innstetten, who had not the means to marry her. He is now an ambitious civil servant of thirty-eight. With the best of intentions she arranges a marriage between him and her lively seventeen-year-old daughter Effi Briest. Effi is neither as potentially fine as Anna Karenina nor as victimized and impulsive as Emma Bovary; she is triumphantly *ordinary* in her suffering – and in her innate, and once again ordinary, decency. Fontane's *Effi Briest* is pitched in a much lower key than *Anna Karenina* or *Madame Bovary*.

There is no courtship. The couple honeymoon in Italy, where Effi is bored by Innstetten's earnest enthusiasm for culture. They then go to Kessin, on the Baltic. Innstetten's house is gloomy and said to be haunted. He makes no attempt to allay his wife's fears: on the contrary, he encourages them, with an unconscious sadism. Clearly Effi is for him a child-wife; he is anxious to get on, to get a post in Berlin; he is not capable of interesting his wife, or of noticing her; it is implied that she finds him sexually disappointing. Life in Kessin is dismal. The narrow, unintelligent people – with the exception of an eccentric elderly admirer, the apothecary Gieshübler – bore Effi. They are, she complains, 'strict and self-righteous'. She is afraid of the strange noises in the house and in particular of what she fears is the ghost of a Chinaman, the servant of a former foreign resident, who is buried in a little grave on the sand dunes. After the birth of her daughter Effi becomes even more bored; her husband – engrossed in his duties – more neglectful of her. When a new territorial district commander, Major von Crampas, is appointed the sexually inexperienced and dissatisfied Effi is ready to succumb to his charm – and, it must be added, to his superior understanding. Although a calculating seducer, he is a more sympathetic character than Innstetten. He has an unpleasant wife; he tries to write poetry; he can see immediately why Effi is unhappy. He is a *poseur*, but he might have been a different man in a different *milieu*. He believes politics to be vulgar, is intelligent, and appreciates Heine for good reasons. Their short affair is furtive – meeting in a hut among the same dunes where the Chinaman is buried – and Effi is relieved when Innstetten returns with the news that he has been promoted, and that they must move to Berlin. For six years Effi is happier: she is developing into an ordinary Berlin society woman. She is faithfully served by her maid Roswitha, whom she took on at Kessin while she was pregnant.

Failing to become pregnant again, Effi goes to Bad Ems to 'take the waters'. While she is away her daughter Annie cuts her forehead; the maids force a drawer open to find a bandage, and Innstetten discovers her old letters from Crampas. He challenges the Major to a duel, goes to Kessin, and kills him. He informs Effi's parents who offer to support her but refuse to receive her at home. She lives in Berlin with her maid Roswitha, and gradually becomes ill from tuberculosis. Some years afterwards Innstetten is persuaded to allow her to see her daughter, but the meeting is a failure: Effi finds that Annie has been taught to fear her as 'sinful'. Her doctor finally prevails upon her parents to allow her to live at home and after a few months of relative contentment she dies, aged twenty-seven, accepting that Innstetten had been 'correct' in all his actions, and even regretting that she had cursed him for poisoning Annie's mind against her.

CRITICAL COMMENTARY Fontane's virtues, seen to best advantage in *Effi Briest*, include balance, brilliantly selective allusion, unobtrusive irony, refusal to indulge in sensationalism or glib moral judgement, and mastery of significant dialogue. *Effi Briest* works at two levels: it demonstrates that what we take as ordinary, mundane, quotidian is in fact full of deeply human significance – this is not as familiar to readers of fiction as it might be. Less obviously, it is – not in spite of but *because* of its reticence – a terrifying and even prophetic story, though suffused with poetic colour.

There are no villains or heroes. No character attracts our strong indignation or praise. Frau Briest, who did not marry for love and who manages her husband, comes to realize that she made a mistake in marrying Effi off when she was too young – though she does not and could not recognize the insensitivity and cynicism of her move. Her husband, whose favourite phrase (it ends the novel) is 'That's *too* big a subject,' is in many ways admirable and charitable. Effi is not passionate or gifted or morally superior; she is a little spoiled; vain (she keeps Crampas' letters, perhaps from vanity rather than carelessness);

she is, as one critic has put it, 'nonchalant'. Innstetten is shrewd and, within his limitations, kind; but he is not his own master, and expects his life to conform with his wishes without making any effort. His qualities are prevented from developing by his career – a particularly marked fault amongst Germans. The dishonourable and good-willed Crampas, who by a stroke of irony is the least shallow character in the novel, is certainly malicious and opportunistic when he tells Effi that Innstetten has always posed as a believer in ghosts and the supernatural so that he can appear different and distinguished, and that he is an 'educator'; but what he says is true. Effi is horrified to learn that he has 'educated her with a ghost': she intuitively recognizes the sadistic element in him, though she cannot articulate this. Fontane here points to one of the most serious flaws in the Prussian character. It is hardly without significance that Innstetten is an anti-semite (notably, Fontane was not). But these and other nuances of character are all subdued; the narrative proceeds quietly, suggesting the pace of well ordered everyday life.

Fontane himself considered his story very commonplace. How then does he manage to invest it with such pathos and significance? In the main, by his persistent use of a symbolism and a gentle and unresentful but none the less deadly irony. There are countless dramatically ironic conversations which foreshadow future events; examples are found in the first chapter, when Effi idly meditates on the results of infidelity and, later, when Crampas and Innstetten light-heartedly banter on the subject of a duel between them before Crampas has seduced Effi. More important still are the symbols, which are all the more effective for being unobtrusive – if he so wishes, the reader may disregard them. They do not distort the 'realistic' text in any way, but add an extra dimension, one of deeper realism, to it. They are extraordinarily appropriate to the subject matter, and reveal the depths which it possesses – but which a straight-forwardly realistic novelist might well have failed to reveal. It is difficult to say how conscious Fontane's artistry was in this symbolism, much of which is sexual (he did say that he wrote the book 'as if in a dream'). Some of the symbolic material is generalized. Effi's faithful dog Rollo, always with her – after she has died he pines on her grave – stands for the element of ignorance combined with innocence in her lightweight nature, acting as a compassionate counterweight to that 'nonchalance' of which a moralist might judge her guilty. The Chinaman and his enigmatic history (he may have had a sexual relationship with the niece or granddaughter of the former owner, a sea captain, of Innstetten's Kessin house) are explicitly linked with both Effi's state of fear and with the sexual curiosity, passive though this may be, which leads her into Crampas' clutches. Ironically Innstetten practically encourages her to think that the house has a faintly sinister history. Nothing, of course, could be more 'ordinary' than the sexual fears of the ordinary young woman being represented by a *Chinaman* (or by a stuffed crocodile and a shark, left behind by the former owner). Yet Effi acknowledges the Chinaman's humanity, his reality, by wondering why he should not be buried with the others in the town cemetery. (All her neighbours are narrow-minded racists.) And so although Effi is too superficial to come to terms with her adultery – her six-year social life in Berlin is passed over in silence, the implication being that it was wholly conventional and insignificant – her capacity for humanity is revealed. Her acceptance at the end of Innstetten's behaviour is tragically ironic; because this behaviour, for all the reticence and even sympathy with which it is described, is in truly moral terms quite monstrous – even though it accords with the conventional morality of the time.

The crucial moment of the novel is when Innstetten decides to challenge Crampas. His colleague von Wüllersdorf implies that he might like to let the matter drop. Innstetten concedes that there is a question of the lapse in time; he says that he has no feelings of revenge or hatred, and that he still loves Effi. But: 'we're not isolated persons, we belong to a whole society ... If it were possible to live in isolation, then I could let it pass ... I've no choice, I must do it.' The final reason he gives is that by letting Wüllersdorf – who is to act as his second – know, 'the game has passed out of [his] hands.' Wüllersdorf is reluctant but he too finally admits that the 'world is how it is and things don't go the way that we want but the way the others want.' And so Innstetten destroys his wife's and his own happiness. For the rest of his life he feels guilty; but he had (so even Effi finally concedes) to do it.

Fontane does not attempt to diminish Innstetten's humanity. He shows how decency lives in him, imprisoned by an absurd code. With a delicate and effortlessly compassionate restraint that makes it all even more horrible, he prophesies the advent of Nazism – showing how normally decent people can be party to murder and to a misery which they condemn. Not a single person in the novel questions the 'code'; only Crampas seems, in the duel, to mock it. The modern reader must consider afresh whether the notorious excuses of ex-Nazis about 'obeying orders' and 'knowing nothing' are much different from the decent old Briest's 'That's *too* big a subject ...' – or from Innstetten's, and ultimately Wüllersdorf's, insistence that a matter must be gone through with because it is 'decreed' (whether they want it or not). *Effi Briest* remains resolutely commonplace; but it is at heart a profound and suggestive tragedy.

BIBLIOGRAPHY

Translations: W. A. Cooper, *Effie Briest*, 1913; D. Parmée, *Effie Briest*, 1967.

Text: in *Romane und Erzählungen*, 1969.

Criticism: K. Hayens, *Theodor Fontane*, 1920; in Thomas Mann, *Rede unt Antwort*, 1922; H. W. Seidel, *Fontane*, 1940 – in German; in R. Pascal, *The German Novel*, 1956; J. Renaud, *The Gentle Critic*, 1964.

Marcel Proust

Marcel Proust was born at Auteuil in 1871 and died in Paris in 1922. His father was an eminent physician; his mother came of a wealthy Jewish family. He was deeply attached to his mother, and at nine developed a severe asthma which is thought to be mainly the result of his over-intense feelings for her. He was able to do his military service (1889), and then lead the *salon* life of a charming and wealthy young man about town. He insinuated himself into the higher social circles, took a degree in law and another in literature. He supported the Dreyfus cause. In 1896 he published a collection of essays, *Les Plaisirs et les Jours* [*Pleasures and Days*]. He retained his mask of wit and dilettante, and studied the social milieu of Paris with an increasingly avid curiosity. All this time, apparently a dabbler, he was preparing for his novel; but neither *Jean Santeuil* (1925), written in the last half of the 1890s, nor *Contre Sainte-Beuve* [*Against Sainte-Beuve*] (1954), written in 1908–9 was published until the 1950s. Each is a preliminary sketch for *À la recherche du temps perdu* (1913–27).

After 1899 Proust's asthma became worse, and he began to withdraw from social life. His father died in 1903, his mother two years later. From 1910 he spent most of his time in his famous cork-lined bedroom on the Boulevard Haussmann, sleeping by day and writing by night. Though a semi-invalid, he never completely withdrew from society: Proust the absolute recluse is a myth. He had a number of homosexual affairs – preceded, however, by heterosexual ones. From 1909 until 1912 he wrote the first draft of his novel, which he spent the rest of his life revising and expanding. The first volume, *Du côté de chez Swann*, appeared at Proust's own expense in 1913 and attracted notice only from a few discerning critics, amongst them Jean Cocteau. The second, *À l'ombre des jeunes filles en fleur* which appeared in 1919, brought him fame. Further instalments appeared in 1920, 1921, 1922, 1923, 1925 and 1927. These are entitled, respectively, *Le Côté de Guermantes* (two volumes), *Sodome et Gomorrhe* (two volumes), *La Prisonnière*, *Albertine disparue*, *Le Temps retrouvé*. The last two sections were not fully revised. He died, exhausted and overdosed with medicines, in 1922, working until the end.

Proust was gentle and courteous to a fault. He was over-attached to his mother; and he was undoubtedly more neurotic than most men. His homosexuality, voyeurism and sadism tormented him greatly (he was fascinated by slaughtered animals, towards the end of his life paying to have rats beaten or tortured with hatpins, the sight of which brought him to orgasm). Unlike Gide he could never accept the strong homosexual element in his make-up. In his behaviour towards others he was not cruel but, by use of his invalidism and skill at letter-writing, he manipulated people and gained their attention. Proust was a profound self-analyst, and felt keenly the depths of degradation (doubtless not as unusual as he considered them) to which his thoughts and feelings could sink. He may have suffered from failing to outgrow a classic case of sibling rivalry. But his naked acknowledgement of his abject mental condition was heroic. It is probably most satisfactory to regard the neurotic side of him, as Roger Shattuck does, as a 'nervous child'. It is said that he never 'grew up'. But can anyone completely 'grow up' if he delves into himself as Proust deliberately did? Proust, who substituted art for life, who tried to 'become his book' had to yield to his 'infantile' impulses in order to find out about them. He caused little unhappiness – except to himself – and he gave many people great pleasure. The image of him as a monster is a false one.

À la recherche du temps perdu

SUMMARY   Reactions to Proust's *À la recherche* vary from uncritical reverence to the view that it is without interest and that people have been lying to one another about it for over fifty years. The latter view – not held by intelligent people – is stupid since the work could not have attracted the fascinated attention of so many excellent minds if it were simply boring. However, although it is always in print, it is one of the least bought of the classics, and one of the least read right through. More people have read about Proust's life than have finished his novel – even if they possess it. *À la recherche* has however been translated into sixteen languages and its prestige is immense.

Once he had found a style that was his own Proust did not find *À la recherche* hard to write. But he did find it hard to arrange what he had written, because he composed in an apparently haphazard fashion; his notebooks, Roger Shattuck has remarked, seem to be totally disordered. Yet to a large extent he succeeded in giving a structure to his material.

À la recherche has, as Proust himself recognized, no 'plot in the sense of what we rely on in most novels to carry us along in some state of expectation through a series of adventures to the necessary resolution – there just is no such thing here.' Yet a brief outline of 'what happens' – inevitably omitting many of the hundreds of characters who appear in this mammoth book (3,300 pages) is useful.

There is a narrator, twice referred to as Marcel. This Marcel is not Proust – who diversifies himself into several other main characters – but he has many Proustian characteristics. At the end of the novel he is about to write (or attempt to write) the novel that we, the readers, have just read. Since Marcel participates in the story, he possesses two identities: that of author of the book we are reading, and that of a character in it. As narrator he sees things sometimes from the point of view of the immediate present, when he does not know his fate, at others from the point of view of the older, reflective, retrospective author. Occasionally Proust himself, as author, intrudes into the narrative. (Even this account is over-simplified: at least four other *voices* have been convincingly distinguished.) The differences between Marcel and Marcel-the-narrator reflect the differences between Proust-the-man and Proust-the-writer-of-an-essay-novel (for *À la recherche*, like Musil's *Der Mann ohne Eigenschaften*, belongs to this category), and form one of the main themes of the book. The detached artist is notoriously, in one aspect, 'inhuman', cruel; Proust, although he knew that he could not do it, went as far as any man in trying to turn himself from human being into detached artist, 'user' of the sufferings of others. Yet the presence of the in many ways hapless Marcel, innocent of his future, or of any patterns in human behaviour, humanizes the book to the point of radiance – even if this radiance is not always easily discernible.

The novel begins with the as yet unnamed narrator at the point between sleep and waking. It then takes us back to his childhood (*c* 1885), when he spent his summers at Combray (an imaginary small town probably near Chartres; later in the novel its position is shifted eastwards). There are two 'ways' which Marcel's family take for their summer walks: that in the direction of the residence of the aristocratic Duc and Duchesse de Guermantes whose high-society circle Marcel will one day penetrate, and that in the direction of the home of the Jewish bohemian dilettante Swann, into whose world Marcel will also penetrate. But these memories are preceded by a single incident.

We learn of the boy Marcel's anguish when, because Swann was a dinner guest, his mother refuses to give him a goodnight kiss. Later she relents, and even spends the night in his room; he calls this a 'first abdication'. He can remember little else until the taste of a sponge cake (a *madeleine*) dipped in linden tea such as he was given as a child suddenly brings back to him an integrated sense of his childhood. Thus a leading motif of the book is introduced: the manner in which the past permeates the present.

Now we go back some years in time: the story of Swann and his infatuation for the faithless *cocotte* Odette is told, in the third person. Swann cannot understand why he is so tormented by his passion for this shallow and unpredictable girl, and his jealousies bring him close to madness before he begins to overcome them and is 'cured' of her. It is therefore surprising to discover that when they reappear in the second part, which takes us forward again in time, they have married. Marcel, not yet in his teens, admires Odette – his parents and many of Swann's former friends will not receive her – and falls in love with her daughter Gilberte in Paris. He is over-eager and her indifference causes him to withdraw himself from her rather as so many years before Swann withdrew from her mother.

Marcel, now an adolescent, goes with his grandmother to the resort of Balbec (based on Cabourg) on the English Channel. Here he meets Mme de Villeparisis, a member of the Guermantes family, and her relatives the Baron de Charlus and his nephew Robert Saint-Loup. He becomes appreciative of the work of the painter Elstir (already introduced in the episode devoted to Swann's earlier life) and through him he meets Albertine, the leader of a group of young girls who bicycle on the beach at Balbec. He is puzzled by the behaviour of the Baron de Charlus whose homosexuality he fails to recognize until later; he forms a firm friendship with Robert Saint-Loup. Most of all he is obsessed by the cryptic Albertine. He tries to kiss her in his hotel room, but she humiliates him. His future relationship with her echoes that of Swann with Odette.

Marcel and his family move into Paris property belonging to the Guermantes. Marcel begins to fall in love with the Duchesse, and intrigues to meet her. He goes to Doncières to visit Saint-Loup who is doing his military service there. Saint-Loup introduces him to his undiscerning mistress, Rachel, whose activities cause him pangs of jealousy (again echoing those of Swann and Marcel). Marcel at last meets the Duchesse at a reception given by Mme de Villeparisis; the Baron de Charlus is present, and again puzzles him.

The underlying theme of the next sections is the manner of Marcel's coming into awareness of the world. His grandmother dies in great pain; the account of this is comic (in the grand sense) but at the same time shows how an unselfish person, even in the face of the degradations imposed by dying, may retain dignity and control. Marcel becomes disenchanted with the Guermantes, with whom he gets on to social terms: he discerns their mediocrity, their hypocrisy and their snobbishness. But he is still fascinated. He finally discovers that Charlus is a depraved homosexual. Albertine succumbs to his desires, at least in part. Marcel now wants above all to possess this enigmatic creature. As soon as he begins to suspect that she is a Lesbian (which the novel strongly suggests) and is suffering from growing jealousy, he finds that he wants to marry her.

There is much on the subject of Charlus and his violent changes of mood, his snobbery and his depravity. First he is in love with the tailor Jupien, then with the violinist Morel, who is ambisexual. Marcel takes Albertine to live with him, and puts her under an intolerable and obsessed scrutiny. In order to test her he suggests that they separate; to his consternation she flees from him. Soon afterwards he hears that she has been killed in a riding accident. He receives a letter from her in which she asks permission to return. He feels guilty: if she was *not* a Lesbian, then he wronged her – but if she *was*, then he drove her to a life she hated. Even though she is dead his curiosity about her true nature continues for some time to haunt him.

Robert Saint-Loup has married Gilberte; their life is unhappy – he has discovered that his main inclinations are homosexual (hers may be, too). Marcel returns to Combray but finds it has lost its old allure for him. The war intervenes. Marcel, always delicate, retires to a sanatorium. Saint-Loup is killed at the front. Paris has been changed by the war: a perverse aristocracy is being supplanted by a vulgar middle class. Marcel returns to postwar Paris. He has long wished to be a writer but has doubted his ability to find his true voice. Now, though disillusioned and haunted by the little time he has left to live, he repudiates society and devotes himself to the recapture, in a novel – *À la recherche* – of his past. Dedication to art has supplanted life; but art could not exist without life, despite life's disillusions, corruptions and bitter comedy.

CRITICAL COMMENTARY Although Proust has a secure place as one of the great novelists, it is generally agreed that *À la recherche* has considerable faults. The difficulty is that while most readers are displeased by one or another aspect of the book, there is little agreement on what these are. Cogent cases can be made for many conflicting points of view.

The main objections to the book are that it suffers from *longeurs* (opinion differs as to which these are), that it is too evidently the product of a 'sick' personality, that it dwells to excess on homosexuality, and that the view it takes of humanity – in particular of love and friendship – is 'excessively bleak'. We should examine these objections before considering the novel's merits.

There are three main types of (alleged) *longeur*: passages about social rank and correct etiquette, passages about homosexuality (for example, Charlus' long invectives on the subject), and essay passages on *time and memory* (such as the one which closes the book). Each type has been defended. English-language readers are likely to be more interested in the revelations of the pretensions of society than in Proust's obsession with how it pretends to 'work'. Some of the descriptions of this are inordinately long and, although perhaps an important contribution to social history and in keeping with the obsessions of the narrator himself, this aspect of the novel is the one most likely to fade with time.

The amount of space devoted to homosexuality is more justifiable. This subject has always tended to upset people. Charlus, the main although not the only homosexual in the book, is one of the great creations of world literature. He is seen in a light not so much unsympathetic as, finally, compassionate. If we are to appreciate him we need to pay attention to everything reported of him; ultimately it is all fascinating and enlightening. But Proust was right – sick and neurotic as he was at the time (1921) – when he confessed to Gide that he had transposed all the 'attractive, affectionate, and charming' elements contained in his 'homosexual recollections' into heterosexual ones in the earlier Albertine episodes; that had left him with nothing, he said, 'but the grotesque and the abject' for the later episodes. There is a real mystery about Albertine; she is not altogether a real *woman* because in Proust's mind she was often really a man (with a counterpart in real life; nearly all Proust's characters are amalgams and transformations of real people). The result certainly is one of some imbalance, since the account of homosexuality (which is not excessive in itself) is unevenly balanced. It is difficult to defend Proust's initial decision not to make Marcel an ambisexual; in that sense the book may be called unrevised. But that decision is understandable: it was only towards the end of his life that Proust made some tentative (and, to him, unrewarding) efforts to justify his homosexuality to himself.

As to the so-called essay passages, some may be misplaced, but as a whole they are an intrinsic part of Proust's narrative method. Without them his entire project would have fallen to pieces. They are of exquisite quality, and they offer invaluable insights not only into Proust's own fiction but into all fiction.

Proust's approach to his material is primarily based on a distinction between what he called *voluntary* and *involuntary memory*. He saw the connection between this approach and that of his friend Bergson, but denied that Bergson acknowledged the distinction. (This was mistaken: it is essential to Bergson's philosophy.) For Proust *voluntary memory* offers only 'untruthful aspects of the past'. But *involuntary memory*, which suddenly overtakes us – like the taste of the cake soaked in tea – gives us a sense of rediscovery, shows us that the past we thought we had experienced was false: involuntary memories 'alone carry the seal of authenticity', they liberate experience from time and – if the correct, intuitive style of expressing them can be discovered – they display its essence.

This implies that we live mechanically in the present, tragically unaware of our lives' essence, which for Proust can only be enshrined in a retrospective art.

It also implies that there is no true external reality except perhaps in art. Each scene, event or experience is different for different people; each person imagines himself whole but is in strict fact a multiplicity of selves. How search for unity except through art? And the key to art is *involuntary memory*: the recapturing of something more than life itself, with its disappointments and relentless uncertainties. Bergson had written that our 'personality, which is being built up each instant with its accumulated experience, changes without ceasing'; and that 'philosophy will only know [what the multiple unity of the personality is: he acknowledges a unity, albeit unknown] when it recovers possession of the simple intuition of the self by the self.' The Marcel of Proust's *À la recherche* eventually rediscovers himself through his past – or, at least, he learns how he might do so. In an important sense the novel consists simply of a series of moments – each of these inexorably determined by the past – in Marcel's *stream of consciousness*.

Yet Proust has been accused of attacking the integrity of the personality. Actually he was searching for it. More seriously, he has been accused of degrading romantic love, and friendship, by depicting them as subjective, accidental and paradoxically inflamed by betrayal or loss. It must be admitted that there is a neurotically negative tone on these subjects running throughout *À la recherche*, but this is redeemed by his penetrating analysis of them. It is a cruel analysis, but the text alone informs us that it is as cruel to Proust himself as to anyone else.

Proust's comic gift, subtle and sometimes unobtrusive makes nonsense of the accusation that his novel is one of the bleakest ever written. He is incomparable in capturing speech habits and foibles.

By the use of the ambiguous 'I' narrator, he laughs, not ill-naturedly, at his introspective self and at the clichés with which human beings usually communicate. What seems abstract is frequently seen, upon closer examination, to be a blend of exquisite lyrical feeling and psychological profundity. Enjoyment of the comic aspects of life implies a love for it: a way of affirming that it is after all worth living. At the very least Proust offers us a diagnosis of human illness that demands our attention, and makes us laugh as well as mortifies us.

BIBLIOGRAPHY

Translation: C. K. Scott-Moncrieff: *Remembrance of Things Past*, completed by Stephen Hudson as, *Time Regained*, 1922–31. A. Mayer, *Time Regained*, 1970. Scott-Moncrieff's translation is remarkable and sympathetic, though he was forced to bowdlerize on occasion, and there are some errors. The Chater version of the last part is much better than Hudson's. There is now room for a new version – and for an introductory abridgement in French and English.

Text: There are many; the three-volume *Pléiade*, 1954, is the best yet.

Criticism: A. Maurois, *The Quest for Proust*, 1950 – the best biographical introduction; can usefully be supplemented by L. P. – Quint, *Marcel Proust* (1935), 1944, and by G. Painter, *Marcel Proust*, 1959–65; G. Deleuze, *Proust and Signs*, 1973; R. Shattuck, *Proust*, 1974 – this last is indispensable.

Italo Svevo

Italo Svevo ('Italo the Swabian'), whose real name was
Ettore Schmitz, was born in Trieste in 1861; he was thus
an Austrian citizen until 1918. Both of his parents were
Jewish or partly Jewish; his father was German-Italian,
his mother Italian. He was educated in Bavaria; later he
received a commercial training. He wrote two novels,
Una Vita [*A Life*] 1892 and *Senilità* [*Senility*] (1898), but
they failed to attract attention. After the failure of *Senilità* he gave up the idea of becoming a writer by profession. His father lost most of his money in 1880, and
Svevo was forced to be a bank clerk until 1897; after this
he worked as a partner of his father-in-law's business
(water-resistant paint). He travelled a great deal, especially to London, and his commercial success led to a sense
of boredom. In 1906 he began to go for English lessons
to an Irishman living in Trieste. This Irishman, James
Joyce, read his work and encouraged him to write more.
The war (when his paint was in constant demand) kept
him busy, but in 1923 he completed and published *La
Coscienza di Zeno*. Joyce – who took the hair of Svevo's
wife Livia Veneziani as his model for Anna Livia Plura-
belle's – saw to it that a French translation was made;
this was highly praised and made Svevo famous throughout France and Europe. The Italian poet Eugenio Montale had already recognized his genius; but most others in
Italy were still resistant to whatever came out of Trieste,

and Svevo's Italian reputation had hardly begun to bud when he was killed in a car accident in September 1928. Svevo wrote essays, plays and, notably, short stories. Today he is classed with Musil, Proust and Joyce himself among novelists.

La Coscienza di Zeno
[The Confessions of Zeno]

SUMMARY *La Coscienza di Zeno* [*coscienza* means 'conscience', 'scruple' and 'consciousness' – not, in fact, 'confessions' by which it is translated] begins with a preface by the publisher. He is 'Dr S.', Zeno Cosini's psychoanalyst, who is setting the 'confessions' before the public in order to take his revenge on his patient for having 'suddenly thrown up his cure just at the most interesting point, thus cheating me of the fruits of my long and patient analysis of these memoirs'. Dr S. hopes that Zeno will be 'duly annoyed', but says that he will be ready to share the 'financial spoils with him on condition that he resumes his treatment' (this is a characteristically involute joke: Svevo published *Zeno* – like his two previous novels at his own expense and expected no profits; further, had Dr S. intended to steal the royalties?) Zeno, writes Dr S., 'little knows what surprises lie in wait for him, if someone were to set about analysing the mass of truths and falsehoods which he has collected here'. The novel's premise is that the introduction and six sections which follow were written for the eyes of the psychoanalyst alone; but Zeno Cosini tried to make things easier for him by reading a book on psychoanalysis ('not difficult to understand, but very boring'). However, the present dominates him, the past is blotted out; trying to let himself go 'completely' he falls into a deep and refreshing sleep. The six sketches which follow are less ambitious. They are fragments of autobiography, dealing with themes in the 'patient's' life.

Chronologically they overlap, although the last recounts events that have taken place most recently in time. Zeno is writing as an old man, for his analysis began when he was old. The setting is pre-war Trieste.

The first section is called 'The Last Cigarette'. Throughout his life Zeno has suffered from an addiction to tobacco. He now succeeds in recapturing some of his past by tracing it back to his first memory of a cigarette packet (the comparison to Proust's *madeleine* is irresistible). Each cigarette was to be his last (a means, he involuntarily admits, of enjoying smoking more – since each 'last' cigarette is 'more poignant'). Eventually he has himself locked up in a sanatorium; but here, while prey to the delusion that his wife is having an affair with the doctor he gets the unattractive but sexually eager nurse drunk and tells her that it is his wife who wants him to give up smoking because after smoking ten cigarettes he becomes uncontrollably lustful. She gives him eleven, but he makes his escape, anxious to discover the doctor in his wife's bedroom – where of course he is not to be found.

In the next section, 'My Father's Death', Zeno explains how he was responsible for his father's death. The doctor instructed that the old man must keep absolutely still. Zeno zealously tried to calm him when he was restless; the old man slapped him furiously on the face and died of the effort.

'The Story of my Marriage' describes how Zeno decides to marry one of the three Malfenti sisters, Ada; he is rejected by her, and then by her younger sister Alberta. He is then tricked by Signora Malfenti into marrying the second sister, Augusta, who is plain, cross-eyed and the one he specifically does not want. But she proves to be ideal for him. In this section he meets Guido Speier, who wins Ada without difficulty. Speier upsets him by playing a Bach *chaconne* on the violin better than he can: Speier's 'slick' performance is, for Zeno, as 'unerring as fate', whereas Zeno himself cannot play correctly unless he beats time with his head and feet – this means that he is ill, for to beat time means 'goodbye to ease, serenity and music!' He even feels like murdering Speier who is an antisemite (that his name is Jewish is no accident) and a misogynist in the mould of the once influential Wagnerian Otto Weininger (1880–1903), who was himself of Jewish descent and (like Speier) killed himself.

'Wife and Mistress' tells of Zeno's affair with Carla, a girl who aspires to be a singer. He wishes both to give her up and to keep her; he pretends that Ada (whom Carla has seen in the street) is his wife; eventually he loses her when she becomes engaged to a musician, Vittorio Lali, who 'lives entirely for art', is a genius and is 'healthy' (which Zeno, a perpetual hypochondriac, feels himself never to be). Guido meanwhile marries Ada and immediately begins to deceive her with one of the maids.

'A Business Partnership' describes Guido Speier's attempt to succeed in the business of buying and selling. Zeno, whose own affairs are excellently run for him by his father's old manager, goes into partnership with him – though he is not ultimately responsible, in law, when Guido is ruined. In this episode Guido is revealed as a blunderer, a weakling and a callous womanizer (though whether Zeno is any less callous is open to question). There is much comic detail about business and stock-exchange dealings. Guido employs a secretary, Carmen, who becomes his mistress. The business goes from bad to worse, until Guido finds himself threatened with criminal bankruptcy. He fakes suicide in order to get money from his wife (who is obsessed by jealousy), gambles on the stock exchange, gets into debt, and finally dies when trying on another fake suicide. Zeno, whose role throughout has been that of equivocal adviser and protector of his friend, succeeds in salvaging a large part of Guido's lost fortune, and Ada is thus saved. She leaves for Brazil where Guido's father lives.

The last section, 'Psychoanalysis', tells of Zeno's

analysis, and of how he learned that he suffered from an Oedipus complex. It ends with an account of how he became successfully rich – by buying up all and sundry during the period immediately following Italy's entry into the war. The last six paragraphs are apocalyptic: as if the author himself has abruptly taken over from Zeno. Life is poisoned by machines; health can only belong to the beasts; man's increasing ingenuity brings with it increasing weakness; eventually some man 'weaker' than the rest will blow up the world and 'the earth will return to its nebulous state and go wandering through the sky, free at last from parasites and disease.'

CRITICAL COMMENTARY Svevo's style is ungrammatical and undistinguished; 'Merchant's Esperanto' is one critic's description of it. His German was better than his Tuscan, and he was master of only one tongue: the Triestine dialect. 'A written confession is always a lie!' Zeno wrote at the beginning of 'Psychoanalysis'. 'We lie with every word we speak in the Tuscan tongue!' And, he adds, his autobiography 'would take on quite a different aspect if I told it in our own dialect'. Svevo was thus well aware of his weakness and, like any major novelist, he turned it into a strength. His chief characters are nondescript; they lack literary or philosophical confidence. The grey, drab, alyrical style suits them perfectly.

There are three main characters in *Zeno*. One, of course, is Zeno himself, the ostensible narrator. The other is Dr S.: Dr S[vevo] or S[chmitz]. The third is Svevo himself, the creator of Zeno and Dr S. and all the other characters; this third character is conspicuous by his absence from the text – until, in the final terrible paragraphs, he merges with his creature, Zeno. The novel is one of the most sophisticated ever written, and one of the most comic. Svevo, prophetic in cast of mind as were so many other novelists of the Austro-Hungarian Empire (Musil, Kafka and Hašek are major examples), already knew very well that everything in any novel emanates from the author, that a 'photograph of reality' is impossible. In *Zeno* lyricism is sacrificed to humour: comedy is the key to this labyrinthine ultra-modernism; comedy leads the reader, laughing, into the maze. *Zeno* may be read, and read well, simply as a comic novel.

Although Svevo treats Freudian theory with irony (he saw, ahead of his time, that analysis has questionable therapeutic value, but that nevertheless Freud's formulations were of profound metaphorical value), *Zeno* is constructed on Freudian lines. According to 'classical' theory, during treatment (the entire text is apparently a result of treatment) repressed material becomes conscious. The patient, not wishing to know himself, resists; but if the unconscious material is mobilized by free association and by the emotional interplay between analyst and patient, then a 'cure' is supposed to take place. The 'cure' results from the patient's ability to recognize unconscious material and then to modify it in conscious behaviour without internal conflict. Before he can attain this stage, however, he must go through a stage of 'transference neurosis' in which he re-enacts his childhood conflicts (mainly, wanting to kill his father and possess his mother) in a less intensive form. If this induced transference neurosis is 'resolved' then the patient is 'cured'.

Dr S. writes that anyone 'familiar with psychoanalysis will know to what he should attribute my patient's hostility'. He is alluding to 'resistance'; and to 'negative transference' (the stage at which the patient becomes hostile to the analyst). But, ironically, his revenge (publishing the text – significantly a preposterous breach of medical etiquette) offers a perfect example of the phenomenon known as 'counter-transference': the situation in which the analyst reacts emotionally to the patient. (Svevo first heard of Freud in about 1910, and in 1918 started a translation of *The Interpretation of Dreams* in collaboration with a nephew who was a doctor.)

There are more ironies. Zeno begins his analysis when he is an old man (what is the point? He has already lived most of his life). He is 'cured' on his own when, taking advantage of the war, he buys up everything that is for sale (at first as he admits as a result of 'sheer lunacy'). Furthermore, Dr S., as much as Zeno, is the author himself: analysing himself, telling himself that he is cured, telling himself that he is not cured, hating himself and resisting himself. Dr S. has 'invented' Zeno, in the sense that he projects upon him his rigid theory and insists that he is less an individual than a victim of a classical Oedipus complex. Zeno has 'invented' Dr S. in going to him in the first place, and in projecting upon him a capacity to 'cure' him of his 'disease'; but he knows that his disease is life itself, and that death is its only cure. However, psycho-analysis is a deterministic theory: by seeing his past life from this perspective Zeno hopes to justify himself rather than be 'cured'.

In addition, both doctor and patient are of course the inventions of Svevo himself, and 'Svevo' – while writing *Zeno*, a 'failed writer' – is indeed the invention of the bored successful businessman Schmitz who, a pacifist, gained much of his wealth because of the most universally cataclysmic war in history.

Each of the episodes, with the exception of the end of the last, is an example of 'free association'. There is comic irony in this demonstration, since Zeno's ostensibly honest rambling account of his behaviour shows that he is inconsistent, self-deceiving, guilty of bad faith, a searcher after pointless goals. His barrenly intellectual habit of self-analysis is a means of protecting himself, even if it does not entirely succeed. He is a 'multiplicity of I's', many of whom shamelessly indulge themselves. He is like Musil's Ulrich, a 'man without qualities'. But unlike Ulrich he never even begins to search for freedom in dangerous myth. Instead (his philosophical despair in inverse proportion to his materialistic success) he ends by envisaging a purified world, emptied of human beings.

Zeno's attempt to protect and justify himself – his account is retrospective, but embodies within it the description of a similar if embryonic habit – fails because he suffers, albeit for stupid reasons (for example, over the frustrations of his desire to be loved by Ada or Carla, both mother surrogates). His self-justificatory account of his life proves to the attentive reader that he has not been justified. He protests that he was friendly towards Guido Speier, but his behaviour towards him may be interpreted as extremely hostile and unhelpful. He may even be said to have used, unconsciously, his superior knowledge of chemistry to help the hysterical Guido on his way to his presumably unplanned death: seemingly believing that he is protecting his friend, he tells him that if one wishes not to die one should take veronal alone, not veronal and sodium – Guido dies of veronal poisoning.

Why does Zeno suffer – suffer to the extent that in the closing paragraphs, at last merging with his creator, he writes one of the blackest passages in literature?

He gets his name not from one but from both of the Greek philosophers of antiquity: the pre-Socratic Zeno of Elea and the post-Socratic Zeno of Citium, originator of stoicism. Svevo establishes a (wholly arbitrary) connection between the two. The paradoxes of the first of these philosophers (almost certainly formulated to expose the fallacious arguments of his Pythagorean opponents) involved *motion*: a man, he argued, can never cross a stadium because the distance is infinite: he must cross halfway, and before that half of that, and so on *ad infinitum*. The argument, if not Zeno himself, ignores the fact that the sum of an infinite geometrical progression is infinite if the common ratio is less than one. Our progress through life is *not* composed of discontinuous 'cinematographic' units. Bergson psychologizes it thus: 'the application of the cinematographical method [the frames which give an illusion of continuity] ... leads to a perpetual recommencement, during which the mind, never able to satisfy itself and never finding where to rest, persuades itself ... that it imitates by instability the very movement of the real.' But, he later added, 'experience confronts us with becoming: that is *sensible* reality.' Zeno of Elea's fallacy (though it is really Pythagorean) is exactly what Zeno Cosini suffers from. He measures out his life in cigarettes, each one the delicious last – yet each one symbolizing the rest or sleep of death, from the perspective of which he would finally be able to see that his life had, after all, been continuous. Pure intellectualism, from which Zeno Cosini suffers, leads to the bad faith (the *mauvais foi* of the existentialists) of failing to acknowledge the reality of *becoming*, a process which is apprehended by the intuition. Zeno Cosini is writing from memory; but normal memory, Bergson maintained (writing before Freud), lets through only what may be applicable to the situation at hand: here, self-justification. By demonstrating Zeno's 'Freudian' evasions Svevo is able to trace a ghostly continuity in his creature's life: comic, yet ultimately tragic because not brought into consciousness by an *authentic intuition* (the Sartrian terminology).

The matter of the cigarettes brings us to Zeno of Citium. In the view of the stoics life was cyclic: there would be conflagration (the totally destructive machine at the end of *Zeno*), all would change to 'divine fire' and from its *ashes* (of cigarettes) another pristine world would arise, also to perish through the corruption of reason by passion, and to undergo a similar fate. The analogy with the fate of the individual is clear – and stoicism was, in practice, an individualistic philosophy.

And so in *Zeno* there is after all a hint of affirmation – a hint much reinforced by Svevo's goodnaturedly comic treatment of his material. In terms of the 'realism' it outmodes, *Zeno* is the story of a man who somehow manages, despite his bungling, to fall on his feet. At a profounder level it deals with the *obstacles*, often of an absurd triviality, to the attainment of 'authenticity', or 'consciousness' (the *coscienza* of the ironic title) of 'continuous becoming'. The contemporary novelist who has dealt most impressively with this bleak phenomenon is the Uruguayan Juan Carlos Onetti (born 1909) who, by a curious coincidence, has spoken of himself as 'solitary', 'smoking into the night'. Svevo was himself, for all but the last years of his life, unknown, lonely, a smoker, and alienated – as Jew; as Italian in the Austro-Hungarian Empire; as ex-citizen of the Austro-Hungarian Empire in Italy; as businessman (from his artistic interests); as writer in Tuscan from languages more natural to him. His vision was negative. But he wrote one of the funniest books of all time, and by his awareness of our predicament he recognized the need for alleviation.

BIBLIOGRAPHY

Translation: Beryl de Zoete: *The Confessions of Zeno* (1930), 1962.

Text: in *Opera omnia*, 1966–9.

Criticism: A. L. De Castris, *Italo Svevo*, 1959 – in Italian; P. Furbank, *Italo Svevo*, 1966; N. Lebowitz, *Italo Svevo*, 1978.

Evgeny Zamyatin

Evgeny Zamyatin was born at Lebedyan on the Don, in rural Russia, about two hundred miles south of Moscow. He studied naval engineering at St Petersburg Polytechnic, graduating in 1908. This graduation was technically illegal, as he had taken part as a Bolshevik in the 1905 Revolution, for which he was imprisoned and exiled. He taught at the Polytechnic until 1911 when he was again arrested and exiled. In 1913 he published his first book, *Uyezdnoye* [*A Provincial Tale*]; in 1914 *Na kulichkakh* [*At the World's End*] was suppressed for its criticism of the Army, and could not be republished until 1922. In 1913 Zamyatin profited by an amnesty, and took up shipbuilding. He went to Newcastle in England to supervise the building of icebreakers. In Russia Zamyatin was known as 'The Englishman' because of his reserved manner, English-style moustache, and neat tweed suits; but his two books about England are critical and satirical: *Ostrovityane* [*The Islanders*] (1918) and *Lovets chelovekov* [*The Fisher of Men*] (1921). He was a successful playwright: *Blokha* [*The Flea*] (1923) was an enormous success on the stage until suppressed, and *Atilla* (1928), upon which Zamyatin's last unfinished novel *Bich Bozhiy* [*The Scourge of the Gods*] (1938) was based, deserves performance; so does *Ogni Svyatogo Dominika* [*The Fires of St. Dominic*] (1920). He also wrote outstanding short stories.

Zamyatin, although witnessing the October Revolution

and at first supporting it, left the communist party before he went to England; his chief objection to the Bolshevik Revolution was that it was not a revolution but a realignment of *élites*. And he deplored 'socialist realism', the Soviet creed by which in effect philistines instruct writers how to write – according to the political aims of communism, the writer's task is 'the ideological transformation and education of the working people in the spirit of socialism [actually, of course, Stalinism]'. 'Socialist realism' was not actually promulgated until 1934; it was put forward by the gangster-bureaucrat Zhdanov, but the theory had been worked out by a reluctant Maxim Gorky and Stalin himself. Such a view of literature (it had its roots in the criticism of such as Belinsky) was being pushed from the time of the Revolution, and it was largely Trotsky – the only Bolshevik leader with any taste in literature – who gave the writers of the 1920s the chance to develop as they wished. Thus Zamyatin, though out of favour with the party hacks, was able in 1921 to found the Serapion Brothers, a group of writers, styled 'fellow travellers' by Trotsky (this is the origin of the phrase), who upheld the independence of art. They included Boris Pilnyak, Isaak Babel, Leonid Leonov and Victor Shklovsky. Gorky was not one of them, but he gave them protection. In 1936 Zamyatin wrote of his 'great heart'.

He wrote *We* in 1920. It was published, in a garbled Czech version and without Zamyatin's consent, in a Russian *émigré* journal in Prague in 1926; the next year a re-translation back into Russian was published, also in Prague. Previously it had appeared in an English translation made by Gregory Zilboorg in 1924. It has never appeared in Russia.

Things became increasingly difficult for Zamyatin, whose deliberately heretical views were known to the party authorities. His essays, stories and plays were suppressed, and he was attacked by 'loyal' 'critics'. He wrote personally to Stalin and through the intervention of Gorky he and his wife were allowed to emigrate to Paris in 1932. Here Zamyatin remained aloof from other *émigrés*, working at his novel and writing reminiscences of writers such as Bely and Gorky whom he had known. Ignored, poor, depressed, suffering from angina, he died in 1937.

My
[We]

We is an inverted utopia: a *dystopia*. The narrator, D-503 (men have numbers prefixed by consonants, women numbers prefixed by vowels), tells his story in the form of diary entries. The time is some one thousand years hence. The world of *We* consists of 'One State'. It is constructed of glass so that every citizen may be observed. Food is synthetic (the exact chemical formula of the ancient 'bread' is not known). The ruler of the One State is the Benefactor, who is 'elected' unopposed each year on the Day of Unanimity. The Guardians watch over all citizens, whose conversation is monitored by means of 'street membranes'. The city is surrounded by a Green Wall which cuts its inhabitants off from nature and from the hairy savages who live in the forests. Within the City the weather is always good. D-503 is working on a spaceship, the *Integral*: he is the chief, the Builder. The *Integral* will shortly 'soar into universal space' and will undertake the task of the 'endless equalization of all Creation'; those on other planets living in the 'savage state of freedom' will if necessary be compelled to be happy. Initially D-503 is an ideal citizen. He wholeheartedly accepts that 'we mono-millionedly begin work – and, when we finish it, we do so mono-millionedly'; he 'frankly' regrets that as yet 'we do not have an absolute, exact solution to the problem of happiness: twice a day ... our mighty unipersonal organism disintegrates into separate cells ... the Personal Hours.'

There is sex in the One State; it is operated through a central office: a pink ticket entitles a person desiring sex to have it with anyone of the opposite sex. Curtains may be drawn. On set days the Benefactor ritually executes on the Machine those guilty of 'disloyal' thought or action.

D-503 becomes 'corrupted'. He becomes involved with E-330, a cryptic woman of independent mind who has secret links with the world outside the Green Wall. She smokes and drinks – both forbidden. He is frustrated because he cannot reduce the emotions she arouses in him to pure mathematics. He becomes involved in subversive activities; the conspiracy between the disaffected and those who live outside the Green Wall seems likely to succeed. But the One State strikes back: it is discovered that a 'miserable little cerebral node' is the location of the sickness 'fantasy' (better translated as 'imagination'), 'the last barricade on the road to happiness'. Now the Operation, 'a triple cauterization ... with x-rays', can cure people of the disease.

Everyone is ordered to have the Operation or suffer destruction by the Benefactor's Machine, an atom smasher which reduces its victims to water. There has been revolutionary activity, and the Wall is blown up. D-503 is summoned to the presence of the Benefactor, who says to him, 'And so – *et tu?*' After listening to the Benefactor's arguments in favour of the One State, reminiscent of the Grand Inquisitor in *The Brothers Karamazov*, D-503 bursts into uncontrollable laughter and runs away. He wishes he had an ordinary mother, 'trampled upon', 'crushed'; someone for whom he could be a bit 'of common humanity', of 'her own self' – not 'the builder of the Integral'. He sees E-330 once more, makes love to her. But he is seized and given the Operation. At last he is 'happy'. Sitting beside the Benefactor he watches E-330, 'that woman', being tortured under the Glass Bell from which oxygen is slowly extracted. Unlike the others she will not talk. The revolution is by no means over. Many of those who have 'betrayed rationality' are on the rampage. But a 'temporary wall of high voltage waves' has been constructed on the 'transversal 40th Prospect'. D-503 is 'certain that we shall [conquer]. For rationality must conquer.'

CRITICAL COMMENTARY In 1923 Zamyatin wrote that 'harmful literature is more useful than useful literature' [an allusion to Belinsky's 'critical realism', but much more to the crude intensification of this – 'socialist realism'], for it is 'anti-entropic, it is a means of combatting calcification, sclerosis, crust, moss, quiescence. It is utopian, absurd ... It is right 150 years later.'

Entropy, a major theme in *We*, is a measurement of inefficiency, specifically of disorder, in a system; it is expressed as the ratio of the amount of heat present to the temperature. It must either increase or remain constant. The second law of thermodynamics has been interpreted as predicting the 'heat death of the universe'; a time must come when there will be no more energy left. The universe is 'running down' and will come to a halt. This interpretation assumes, however, that the universe is a thermodynamically closed system. The assumption is open to challenge.

For Zamyatin the heretic was the 'only (bitter tasting) remedy against the entropy of human thought'. New heresies explode 'the crush of dogma' which older heresies have become. Victims of entropy 'must not be allowed to sleep, or it will be their final sleep, death'. E-330 tells D-503 that there is no final number; that there is no final revolution; the series is infinite. Entropy, she tells him, was worshipped by the Christians as a God; it leads to 'beatific quietism, to a happy equilibrium'. Energy leads to the 'destruction of equilibrium, to excruciatingly perpetual motion'. Zamyatin uses entropy as a metaphor – for mechanical orthodoxy, acceptance of what the Benefactor calls 'true, algebraic love for humanity', which is 'infallibly inhuman'. He was also aware that the hypothesis of the eventual heat-death of the universe was not once and for all proven as a fact in physics. *We*, unlike its successors, Huxley's *Brave New World* (1930) and Orwell's *1984* (1949), is more than politico-sociological prophecy. Zamyatin's technical procedures are complex, and form an integral part of the novel.

Zamyatin had pointed out that H. G. Wells's 'socio-fantasies' were *'not* Utopias': they used the form 'in order to reveal the defects of the existing social structure', making of it a 'new and entirely original species of literary form'. He could have added that Wells's speculative fiction did more than just reveal 'defects of the existing social structure'; it revealed deep-seated ambiguities in human nature, just as Zamyatin does in *We*. (Wells's neglected *dystopia*, *Mr Blettsworthy on Rampole Island* (1928), is superior to Huxley and even Orwell, and anticipates the latter.) Zamyatin is fascinated with the One State. He appreciates D-503's 'entropic' tendencies. For all his distaste for the Soviet bureaucrats *We* has less of merely political than of existential despair in it. The Russian *émigrés* in the Paris of his exile were no more attractive to him than the Soviets.

D-503 is a self-critical self-portrait and, by extension, of the twentieth-century writer who seeks refuge in rationality because reality is too uncomfortable. In his fourth diary entry he records how he reacted to synthetic computer-produced music – a music which, curiously enough, is not at all unlike that envisaged by Hesse in *Das Glasperlenspiel*. He feels himself to be his real self in this mathematical paradise; but he is disturbed because E-330 plays some Scriabin, a *'composer'* who could 'create only by working [himself] into seizures of *inspiration* – some unknown form of epilepsy'. When she smiles it is a 'bite, aimed down here'.

He feels himself drawn into 'delectable pain'; but on the lips of the 'number' on his left, sniggering at this antique demonstration, a 'microscopic bubble of saliva' pops up and bursts. 'That bubble sobered me. I was I once more.' He settles down to enjoy the mathematic precision of the new music: 'summarizing chords of the formulae of Taylor [an "ancient" prophet of the One State – possibly Zamyatin had in mind Brook Taylor, the English mathematician who is famous for his "Calculus of Finite Differences"; Taylor's Theorem states that any function of a single variable can be expanded in powers of it. It seems to be referred to in the Eighth Entry, in which the cells of the couples having sex with the blinds down are called "cells of rhythmic Taylorized happiness"] ... the spectral analyses of planets ... What grandeur! What irrevocable regularity! And how self-willed the music of the ancients, restrained by nothing save wild fantasies.' The satirical intention is evident. But D-503 is not presented unsympathetically. His predicament is that of any modern man confronted by and torn between rationalism and the irrational. But it is cast in the terms of a phantasmagoric future. Zamyatin's 'synthetist' style ('syntax,' he wrote, 'becomes elliptic, volatile') is not a 'kind of latter-day Impressionism' – as it has been called – but expressionist; it reflects *formally* the 'negation of what everyone knows and what I knew up to this moment'. The One State has apparently only taken humanism, rationalism, the 'civilized', to its logical extreme. The world beyond the Green Wall really is dangerous and Zamyatin, though he satirizes the egalitarianism of the One State, does not minimize this.

It has been widely understood that Zamyatin in *We* was giving a 'warning' about the mechanized future and the horrors of totalitarianism. But *We* is more ambiguous and more uncertain. D-503's diary is an account of a man living in finite reality who is tempted by the dangerous extra profundities of infinite reality; an account of a potential cubist who is mesmerized by the tenets of representationalism. The link between the two worlds is mathematics.

In the sexual arrangements of the One State the 'content of sexual hormones is determined ... and a corresponding Table of Sexual Days is worked out for you'; 'the denominator of the fraction of happiness is reduced to zero – the fraction is converted into magnificent infinity.' Although the One State is ostensibly a closed system, an illusion of infinity can be created in the matter of sexual activity. Whatever happens it seems people desperately yearn for the heretical, dangerous infinity, even if they seem to submit to the comfort of what is in effect its opposite: entropy. The people of the One State are all, consciously or unconsciously, *subversives*. Even the 'double-curved' Guardian S (one of E-330's lovers) who spies on D-503, confesses to being a rebel (only he then *says* that he was joking). D-503 never knows who, apart from E-330, is in this conspiracy against the One State. It is possible that everyone except the Benefactor is in it, but will not admit it to himself. The 'struggle', and the One State, are thus pointless.

As many have claimed, rational behaviour would seem to be a human *desideratum*. D-503 believes so; but his descriptions of the One State, even at their most enthusiastic, are the opposite of dully rational: highly coloured, aesthetic, and with their ellipses and dislocations often apparently irrational. Although D-503 assumes his faith in the perfection of the One State, his true view of it, as his diary entries show, is nervous; his accounts of himself are involuntarily *phenomenological*; they are also 'subversively' metaphorical. His environment does not comfort him; yet the purpose of the One State is precisely to provide a comforting environment.

Zamyatin points to sexual feeling and activity as the factor most disturbing to the 'achievement' of total happiness by entering into a condition of rationality. D-503's expressed feeling about 'magnificent infinity' in this respect are not what he in fact experiences. He has some 'personal' feelings for 0–90, his regular mistress when the diaries begin; and when, although pronounced 'unsuitable' by the authorities, she cries and begins her 'old refrain' about having a baby, he is acutely disturbed. His last encounter with E-330 specifically correlates a sexual activity shot through with bewildering anxiety and sadistic desire ('excruciatingly perpetual motion') with an existential distress, a 'not wanting to be cured'. But Zamyatin's satire on the sexual arrangements of the One State is not really from a traditionally romantic, simplistic point of view, as it is often taken to be. None of the 'free' sexual relationships is satisfactory; on the contrary they are fraught with a sinister and unexplained tension. When E-330 first 'registers' in D-503's name (for sex), he alarmedly looks down at his 'horrible, simian hand'. His 'shaggy paws' act throughout the book as a reminder of his humanity. (The Benefactor's hands are 'stone'.)

We presents the reader with repeated images, each of which links up to certain themes. E-330's face seems to D-503 to be an 'irritating cruciform X: a crossed out face'; but then the 'wheel' begins to turn, the spokes blend together. This *motif* is taken up again in E-330's assertion of her opposition to Christianity, and in the Benefactor's references to the crucifixion, and elsewhere. While E-330 is first taking off her clothes the listening D-503 feels himself to be like one of the 'street membranes', the curvature of a new type of which he recently had occasion to calculate.

It becomes clear relatively early that *We* is not simply an exercise in horrific futurology but a portrait of the *free spirit* – most intensely expressed by women – in unhappy conflict with its own pursuit of pure rationalism. And pure rationalism is revealed as an illusion by means of translating it into the terms of a hypothetical future in which it has been as fully developed as possible – stretched to its utmost limits, as the concept of the 'happiness of *un*freedom'. That future is precisely as *convenient* a metaphor for the present predicament of the intellect (itself, conceived as separate from the organism, an imaginary entity) as $\sqrt{-1}$ is a *convenient* number to imagine for the practical purposes of certain calculations (chiefly electrical). $\sqrt{-1}$, an imaginary number (because it has a negative square), plays an important part in *We*. D-503 had wanted it 'torn out' of him at school. And when E-330's influence over him is at its greatest, when he has almost told her that he loves her and has experienced jealousy, he feels himself unwell: 'not living in our rational world but in the ancient, delirious world consisting of $\sqrt{-1}$'s.' He realizes that some solid equivalent of $\sqrt{-1}$ must 'unescapably exist'.

The whole One State is a fraud. In the first place the 'endless equalization of all Creation', supposedly the wonderful task of the spaceship *Integral*, can only mean one thing: entropy, total rest, total disorder. This enterprise of the One State is curiously similar to Freud's not altogether clearly formulated concept of *thanatos*, the 'death instinct' – which scarcely anyone has accepted, and which enraged even his most faithful disciples (but which is a meaningful formulation, as *We* shows).

But more and worse than 'hope' is offered in *We*. Disturbance and discomfort are offered. It should be noted that in this dystopia there are no sinister psychopaths; the emphasis is not on the humanly unpleasant aspects of the seizure and possession of power. If this is an anatomy of totalitarianism then it is so only incidentally. The Benefactor is a Leviathan not an ambitious human being: he has mythic qualities. In the past of the One State there has been a Two Hundred Years War. The One State has not 'won' this war. It has merely succeeded in sealing itself off from an atavistic enemy. But, as the narrative reveals, even that supposedly closed system is threatened from within. At the end 'there can be no postponement' of the execution of E-330 and others because the western districts are still 'full of chaos, roaring' and betrayers of rationality. There is no guarantee that the One State will prevail; and we already know that it is a fraud, promising happiness but offering entropy even while seeking to disguise that very fact. Not even the Operation is successful. When D-503 watches the torture of E-330 he remembers her; under torture her behaviour reminds him of 'something' (her sexual behaviour); her sharp white teeth create a 'beautiful effect' (this observation denies D-503's assertion that after the Operation he has no emotions). The sadism implicit in his irrational desire for her is activated, but under the guise of the rational.

It is true that *We* is 'on the side' of irrational romanticism against rationalism, of freedom against unfreedom. Its satirical aspects have not been missed by its readers. But its depiction of the state of freedom, of the impossibility of ever coming to rest, is not a comforting one – and has been missed by many readers. This is not a dystopia that suggests any kind of political system that might accommodate irrationality. It suggests the impossibility of all political systems, and daringly celebrates a condition of perpetual, authentic, but painful and excruciating personal revolution.

BIBLIOGRAPHY
Translations: G. Zilboorg, *We*, 1925; B. Guerney, *We*, 1970. Neither of those versions has been universally praised.

Text: *My*, 1952.

Criticism: D. J. Richards, *Zamyatin*, 1962.

André Gide

André Gide was born in 1869 in Paris. His father, a professor of law, was of Protestant stock from Cévenol; his
mother, a Protestant, came from an originally Catholic
Norman family. There was no shortage of money, and
Gide was able to pursue his literary and artistic interests
from the beginning.

He was educated at a Protestant school in Paris, but
spent much of his time in Normandy. He retained elements of his parents' puritanism but also developed a
powerfully sensual, pagan, even hedonistic, reaction to
this. He oscillated, with intelligence and honesty, between
these two poles of his nature throughout his life. He first
emancipated himself when he travelled to Africa in
1893–5.

Gide was a central figure in French letters from before
the end of the last century until his death, and was more
hated than loved by the critics: the Catholics and the
right wing abhorred his 'immorality', his liberalism, and
the confessional nature of his writings; the left became
angry with him when in 1936 he criticized Soviet Russia.
Though famous and much read, no book he wrote enjoyed unqualified critical success. But, at least in part
because of his refusal to collaborate with the Germans in
the Second World War – and because the younger existentialists then dominant in France admired him – he
received the Nobel Prize in 1947. He died in 1951.

Gide was a prolific and versatile writer. He wrote fiction, plays, travel books (usually with strong political overtones: his two books about French colonial maladministration in Africa were influential in bringing about a modicum of change; a book on courtroom procedure written in 1913 had a similar effect), prose-poetry, criticism, a huge quantity of letters, many of which have been published (to such writers as Francis Jammes, Claudel, Rilke, Edmund Gosse, Christian Beck, Valéry, and others), autobiography, dialogues – and a massive *Journal* (1889–1949). In 1908 he co-founded the important periodical *La Nouvelle Revue Française*.

Gide would only describe *Les Faux Monnayeurs* [*The Coiners*] (1926) as a novel; the rest of his fiction, which includes *Les Caves du Vatican* [*The Vatican Cellars*] (1914) and *Symphonie Pastorale* [*Pastoral Symphony*] (1919), he divided into *récits* and *soties* (satirical farces).

In 1895 he married 'Em', his cousin Madeleine Rondeaux. He loved her more than anyone else in his life, but her strict Christianity aggravated the conflict in him between the heterosexual puritan and the homosexual libertine. When she first discovered his homosexual bent she fled from him. In 1923 he had a daughter, Catherine, by Elizabeth van Rysselberghe. Mme Gide died in April 1938.

Until the end of his life whatever Gide did or wrote tended to be the subject of controversy; he insisted that his chief aim was to disturb. Although he kept up his friendship with Claudel, the latter regarded him as a satanic corruptor of youth. Georges Bernanos portrayed him as an evil monster in his own finest novel, *Monsieur Ouine* (but there is an ambiguity in the portraiture). All these were Catholics; Gide also offended Protestants and Marxists. Since his death he has attracted increasing intelligent attention: younger readers can more easily appreciate his courage, and can understand why he abominated and was concerned to analyse the disastrous fascist-nationalist streak in the French character. Further, from the evidence of the complete *Journals* it is now possible to discern his generosity of spirit, his tolerance and understanding, and his exemplary artistic integrity.

Les Faux Monnayeurs

SUMMARY *Les Faux Monnayeurs*, about a man who is writing a novel (called *Les Faux Monnayeurs*) is one of the earliest novels about people writing novels. Although nowadays usually damned with faint praise, and seldom given its due, it has been widely influential.

The outline of the plot, whose details emerge only gradually in the course of a complex and intricately arranged narrative, is as follows. The action takes place in 1896 when the Dreyfus scandal was under way. Édouard is a well known writer. He keeps a diary, often quoted from, in which he comments not only on his personal situation but also on fictional technique and on his own projected novel, *Les Faux Monnayeurs*.

Young university student Bernard Profitendieu, who has until now believed himself to be the son of a judge, discovers that he is a bastard. He leaves for the home of his university friend Olivier Molinier – who has an elder brother Vincent, and a younger, Georges, who is still at school – where he spends the night. Mme Pauline Molinier is Édouard's half-sister. Vincent has had a love affair with Laura who is pregnant by him. His mother has given him five thousand francs to start him on a career and he knows he should give this to her to see her through her confinement; she does not wish to return to her husband, Félix Douviers. But he becomes involved with the homosexual Comte Robert de Passavant and his friend Lady Lillian Griffith, who soon becomes his mistress. Subsequently it is revealed that he goes to Africa with Lillian, murders her, and goes mad – but no character in the book ever knows this.

Édouard, who is like Gide an ambisexual, and his nephew Olivier love each other, but are inhibited from expressing this. Édouard has returned from England to Paris in response to a letter from Laura. He has been reading Passavant's shallow, transiently successful new book on the train, and has struggled with his feelings of jealousy. He drops his cloakroom ticket at the station and Bernard, who has idly followed Olivier, picks it up, retrieves the case and reads Édouard's diary and Laura's letter which is a cry for help implying love. Édouard admits to himself that he 'has never written a line ... not ... indirectly inspired by her'.

In the diary Bernard reads of how Édouard has seen Olivier's thirteen-year-old brother Georges trying to steal a book; having never seen this nephew, he has been surprised to learn his identity. The school attended by Georges, a 'half-boarding house', is run by the boring old Azaïs, father of Laura's mother, who is married to the Calvinistic Pastor Prosper Vedel; they all live in the school, with Laura's sisters Rachel, Sarah and her brother Armand. The 'dazzling light of [Vedel's] faith' has blinded him to the 'surrounding world' and to himself. Édouard goes on to visit old La Pérouse, once his piano teacher, a pathetic old man who is mostly concerned with the fate of his thirteen-year-old grandson Boris who is in Switzerland.

The impetuous Bernard, having read Laura's letter to Édouard, decides that he must 'save' her (he does not know her). He calls on her, tells her that he has no surname since he is a bastard, and is about to offer his help when Édouard arrives. Bernard, using the information he has gleaned from Édouard's diary, offers to become his secretary and impudently suggests that he revisit La Pérouse. Meanwhile Olivier has visited Passavant, who also wants a secretary and who wants to seduce and corrupt Olivier – seduction and corruption being his practice. Édouard resolves to tighten the link between himself and Bernard, since the latter is Olivier's best friend. He visits La Pérouse again.

Bernard writes to Olivier to tell him that he has gone with Édouard and Laura to Switzerland (Saas-Fée) and that he is in love with Laura. In their hotel – he writes – they have met a Polish woman doctor, Sophroniska. She is treating Boris (also a bastard) for a 'kind of nervous disorder' 'according to a new method'. Boris is in love with her daughter Bronja, aged fifteen; they have a touchingly idyllic childhood love affair. The innocence of this functions as a contrast to the evil actions of which the book is full.

On receiving this news Olivier is plunged into a violent fit of jealousy – especially because Bernard is sharing a room with Édouard: he rushes to Passavant, who cynically appoints him editor of an absurdly pretentious projected new magazine – and, although it is not stated in so many words, seduces him.

Sophroniska seems emancipated and 'modern', but what she really desires is a 'complete confession' from the unhappy Boris. Her pretentiousness, sadism and the subtly sexual nature of what she wants are clearly implied; these are later made brilliantly explicit when Sophroniska refers to masturbation (mutual and solitary) as the 'most subtle – the most perfidious' form of 'laziness'. There is then an interlude in which Édouard explains his theory of the novel to the assembled company. He arranges with Sophroniska for Boris to attend the Azaïs establishment; later he also arranges for La Pérouse to teach there – he is a pathetic failure. In due course Laura returns unhappily to Douviers.

The author himself (Gide) now ironically reviews his characters. Édouard, he writes, has irritated and at times even enraged and revolted him. He treats them as real people – remarking that at first Lady Griffith had 'taken him in'. And he complains that in 'following Bernard and Olivier' he has found other characters in his path ('Laura, Douviers, La Pérouse, Azaïs') who are blunted rather than sharpened by life: 'So much the worse for me; henceforth it is my duty to attend them.'

Oscar Molinier, Olivier's father, meets Édouard and tells him of an affair he has been having with a woman for some five years; he suspects his wife Pauline of having stolen her letters to him. He also mentions a scandal in which he believes Bernard (because he is a 'natural child') has participated. Schoolboys have been taking tea in a tea shop and then going to bed ('orgies') with women in adjoining rooms; old Profitendieu has been investigating the matter, but has 'cooled down' and is now embarrassed when it is mentioned. Actually it is Molinier's own son, Georges, who was involved – and it is Georges too who has stolen the letters. He is showing them around.

We now come to the first day of term at Azaïs's, and to the schoolboys: Georges, the evil Léon Ghéridanisol, Passavant's young brother Gontran, Boris, and others. Ghéridanisol, at the instigation of his cousin Strouvilhou – an adult character friendly with Robert de Passavant – induces the boys to pass false gold ten-franc pieces. He could do it himself but the arch-corruptor Strouvilhou has instructed him to obtain accomplices. He expresses interest in Oscar Molinier's letters from the girl and tells Ghéridanisol to leave Boris alone – 'for the moment'.

Olivier has become disillusioned with Passavant and yearns again for Édouard; he cannot express his need. He tries to make a friend of Armand Vedel, who is later to become his successor as editor of Passavant's magazine. But Armand is too prematurely cynical, frivolous, self-protective and disenchanted for him (one of his poems begins 'Who'er at forty boasts no hemorrhoids'); he gives Olivier a 'pain in his heart'. None the less he agrees to join him at a dinner given by an *avant-garde* review called *The Argonauts*. Bernard takes Sarah Vedel. Afterwards Armand slams and locks the door of Sarah's room on the couple, who thereupon go to bed together.

Then follows one of the funniest chapters of the book: the account of the Argonauts' dinner. Édouard and Passavant are there, and so is Olivier, who becomes very drunk. Here Gide brings in the real-life character of Alfred Jarry, author of *Ubu Roi*. The affected, drunken Jarry 'shoots' the 'poet' Bercail – but the cartridge turns out to be a blank. Olivier quarrels with Dhurmer, a pompous pseudo-literary schoolboy, and there is talk of a duel. Édouard takes him home; during the night he tries to gas himself. Édouard saves his life, and Olivier spends some time convalescing at his home. It is suggested that their love is consummated.

The elder Profitendieu visits Édouard to warn him that Georges his nephew is involved in the circulation of counterfeit money. He also confides his grief over Bernard's departure. Bernard himself, having delayed taking his *baccalauréat*, has now passed it with flying colours. His feelings for his 'father' begin to return: he finds that he would like to tell him the news, but pride prevents him.

Bernard is led by an 'angel' to a nationalist meeting (the extreme right-wing nationalists were then anti-Dreyfusards who either believed in Dreyfus' guilt or maintained like Maurice Barrès that the injustice to him was less important than the honour of France). The angel has told him that he (Bernard) knows he wishes to serve – but what? Bernard has asked him to guide and teach him. Bernard is handed a membership form; by signing it he would dedicate himself to the 'regeneration of France'. The angel asks him what then is he waiting for? He asks the angel if he should sign. 'Certainly – if you have doubts of yourself' is the answer. Bernard throws the form away. By now someone on the platform is preaching the proto-fascist doctrine of 'obedience'. The angel suggests to Bernard that he should wrestle with the speaker, but Bernard tells him that he wishes to wrestle instead with him, the angel, that evening. The angel takes him to the wretched quarters of Paris and weeps. That night Bernard returns to his room – he is now living at the Azaïs's, sharing a room with Boris. Boris has just received a letter from Bronja telling him that she feels she has not long to live. He kneels and sobs. Bernard and the angel are busy wrestling. When the angel leaves in the morning neither has vanquished the other. But Bernard has matured: he understands 'that boldness is often achieved at the expense of other people's happiness'. He loathes the pleasure he took with Sarah, an 'emancipated' woman who despises the conventions and her family – in particular her self-sacrificing sister Rachel who looks after the accounts, sends money to the black sheep of the family (a brother in the colonies) and is going blind. He goes to Édouard for shelter, revealing that his problem is to find a rule: he cannot accept life without a rule, but he cannot accept a rule from anyone else. Édouard refuses to advise him beyond telling him that he can only find counsel in himself.

Édouard goes to the school, sees La Pérouse – who is slowly going mad – and warns Georges, at first indirectly, of the danger he is in. He shows him a passage from his own *Les Faux Monnayeurs* about a boy who is stealing – the book has for once 'been waiting' for the situation in real life. Finally he warns him directly, and Georges is able to pass on the information to the others who take the necessary precautions.

At the school Ghéridanisol, inspired by Strouvilhou, begins a cruel conspiracy against Boris who has just been informed of Bronja's death. Strouvilhou has in Switzerland got hold of an old 'talisman' written on parchment which Boris had once – before he knew Sophroniska – worn around his neck: it related to the 'magic' of the 'shameful paradise' into which he had been initiated by another boy. It reads: GAS. TELEPHONE ... ONE HUNDRED THOUSAND ROUBLES. Ghéridanisol leaves a paper bearing those words, surrounded by obscene drawings, in the classroom. Boris struggles with recollections of his 'magic' practices, 'falls', and finds in the pleasure of his 'fall' the 'stuff of his enjoyment'. For the sake of a 'little consideration' he would dare anything. Ghéridanisol forms a 'secret society' called the Brotherhood of Strong Men. Boris, 'panting for a little esteem and love', is initiated into the brotherhood by Georges, who is chosen for this task by Ghéridanisol. A 'test' is then proposed, and the ballot is rigged so that Boris will be the first to undergo it. Boris is to shoot himself in class at a certain time. Only Ghéridanisol knows that the pistol – stolen from old La Pérouse – is actually loaded. Boris shoots himself in La Pérouse's class. Only Georges guesses Ghéridanisol's responsibility; he is at last horrified – and rushes home and into his mother's arms like a little boy.

Édouard notes in his diary that he will not, in his *Les Faux Monnayeurs*, 'make use' of Boris' suicide: he can't understand it – and it is an '*indecency, for I was not expecting it*'. The school begins to break up as a result of the scandal. Bernard, following 'the impulse of his heart', returns to his father. Édouard writes that he will be dining at the Profitendieu's on the following evening. Bernard has a younger (legitimate) half-brother, Caloub. It is given to Édouard to end the novel: 'I feel very curious to know Caloub.'

CRITICAL COMMENTARY The construction of *Les Faux Monnayeurs* has more than once been compared to a 'set of Chinese boxes'. It has often been judged exclusively in the light of the author's intentions as set out in *Journal des Faux Monnayeurs*, which Gide published in 1926 and which is the counterpart of Édouard's diary. Certainly this is fascinating; but it may be detached from the text of the novel – as Gide himself acknowledged when he decided not to include it in the same volume. It can act as a guide; but it can also mislead, and perhaps not undeliberately. What Gide achieved was not quite what he consciously set out to achieve.

In English-language criticism this is a minority view, and *Les Faux Monnayeurs* is not in general highly regarded. Gide's 'preoccupation with various fictional techniques conveys an overall impression of extreme artificiality'; 'the thematic untidiness of the book is emphasized by the formal neatness of the overall structure'; the 'five or six stories ... and the links established among them remain tenuous ... We confess to a mild interest in such disquisitions when carried outside the critical seminar where they rightly belong.' These and other objections abound. But the reader with imagination, who does not love abstractions beyond idolatry, may find that the Gide of *Les Faux Monnayeurs* is not only a great critic but also, and more importantly, a great novelist. This reader must be prepared to work to fill in the deliberate ellipses; in giving him this opportunity Gide showed him the greatest respect – not many critics (there are of course exceptions) have shown him gratitude. Above all, many have missed Gide's humour; they acknowledge his irony, but it is above their heads. There is a sense in which Gide's own *Journal des Faux Monnayeurs* is a parody of Gide-as-critic and therefore of critics. A questioner of both the validity of fiction and the status of the writer, Gide succeeded in writing a major novel.

Édouard-as-writer is sometimes Gide's surrogate; but he is not Gide. Unlike Gide, who wrote a diary of a novel and a novel, he writes a diary of a novel but does not write a novel – at least he does not finish it. It seems that unlike Gide he cannot ever resolve the paradox of what he calls the 'struggle between what reality offers him [the novelist] and what he himself desires to make of it': 'the struggle

between the facts presented by reality and the ideal reality'. However even if Édouard's novel does not exist at
the end of Gide's there is always the possibility that it will
do so in the future. It will evidently deal with the same
material as Gide's, although it will not be the same. In
this sense that the novel might come into being, it is *we*,
not Gide, who 'are' Édouard. But 'our' 'novels' (various
imaginative readings of a deliberately elliptical text) will
not be identical either. Gide's method was calculated to
liberate his reader. No more open-ended novel has been
written. Édouard writes in his diary, 'The novelist does
not as a rule rely sufficiently on the reader's imagination.'
A 'deliberate avoidance of life' is 'human only in [its]
depths': 'perfectly and deeply human.' So much for
Édouard's theorizings. He wants to write what he calls a
'pure novel'.

Gide, however, while he has indeed given us an open-
ended novel with ellipses that we must fill in, simultaneously has – and with very great ingenuity and cunning –
given us *his* 'ideal reality'. He thus demonstrates that a
true novel cannot be written which does not do this, even
if willy nilly. The novelist's art is forgery. It cannot be
'pure'. But then reality is impossibly disgusting – and
hopelessly untidy. Let us see how *Les Faux Monnayeurs*
is at once 'open' and 'closed'; how it goes a long way towards resolving the paradox which Edouard gives no
sign of being able to resolve.

The form of *Les Faux Monnayeurs* has a debt to the
musical fugue, as Gide intended. Fugues have one feature
in common: they are characterized by the entry of *voices*
(melodic lines) successively in imitation of each other. The
analogy with the different *themes* in *Les Faux Monnayeurs* is obvious. The fugal form is neat as contrasted
with the disorder of life. It should be beautiful and satisfying (as in Bach, Beethoven or Verdi); life is ugly and
unsatisfying. Gide emphasizes this contrast, and thus

raises the question of the value of the counterfeit pattern which the novelist imposes upon life. Can writing aspire to the 'purity' of music?

Les Faux Monnayeurs is an 'open' novel in the sense that ends are not tied up. It has been suggested that a 'precarious order' is finally established, that the 'unhappiness' is to some extent resolved. This is unacceptable. We have no idea how Bernard will get on at home. Édouard has learned nothing – the last sentence implies that he will pursue Caloub under the guise of artistic curiosity. Olivier is stranded, unfulfilled. Laura is wretched. How will the temporarily horrified Georges develop? Will Strouvilhou and Ghéridanisol continue as nihilist destroyers, Passavant and his cronies as fakes? The narrative does not 'end': the novelist, with an ironic stroke of the knife – preposterous to devotees of the 'well made' nineteenth-century novel – severs life in mid-flux. There is no question of predicting a future for any of the participants.

In the course of the novel itself the emphasis shifts from one theme (person, relationship, situation) to another. The impact made on Gide by Dostoievsky (he published a book on him in 1923) is obvious: Strouvilhou is 'straight out of' Dostoievsky, and there are a number of darkly 'Dostoievskian' things going on. About Strouvilhou's activities and motives we are told very little. We are reminded that Vincent has gone on a voyage with Lady Griffith, who at one point writes to Passavant that she now hates him. But there is a huge gap between the last we hear of them and the perfunctory announcement that Vincent has murdered her and then gone mad. Not one of the characters is described (a point emphasized by Édouard's wondering, at the beginning, if he could have guessed from Laura's letter alone that her hair was black). We thus find ourselves speculating; and speculation changes into imagining. We are positively invited to concentrate on our own view of the characters: by dwelling on how we see Bernard, Olivier, Strouvilhou and so on, we see them more precisely (precision, Édouard writes, is obtained in the reader's imagination, 'through two or three strokes exactly at the right place') – we put the tele-scope into focus, and eventually find ourselves filling in the ellipses. Properly read, *Les Faux Monnayeurs* should make each of us his 'own novelist'. In that sense then the novel is open. Gide of course recognizes that all novels have been thus open; but his is deliberately so.

He also offers us, through a series of highly intricate technical devices, his own 'closed' version of what are after all his inventions. The charge was that the links be-tween the stories are 'tenuous' arises from a misunder-standing of the purpose of the text. Heraclitus (who like Gide was unpopular with his fellow citizens) said that an 'unapparent connection is stronger than an apparent one.' Gide demonstrates the strength of his connections by means of his *fugal* method – juggling with the 'plots' and keeping them all in the air. There are frequent and dramatic changes of perceptual perspective. Boris' death, as a critic has noted, is described by the omniscient nar-rator but 'focused in the horrified stare of ... La Pérouse'. The frame of the grotesque Argonauts' dinner is simi-larly drawn by this narrator; but the details on the Bosch-like canvas are seen from numerous points of view: Passavant's, Édouard's, Olivier's, Sarah's (for a moment). In musical terms there are innumerable 'subjects', 'answers', 'counter subjects' and 'harmonies'. The musical analogy should not be pursued too far; these features should rather be seen in psychological terms. A fugue is a 'flight' – but away from, or into, reality? That question is not answered. The 'closed' aspect of the novel depends on its technical elements; the question is whether or not these form a unity (a fugue is unified) which transcends its intellectual elements. One critic accuses Gide of failing to evoke 'human smypathy' O But another discovers an af-firmation of life and human sympathy in what he calls a 'great intellectual lyric'. To discern the lyricism – itself an affirmation of life è it is neccessary to note the moments of heightened feeling in the book. All these, with the exception of the Boris–Bronja 'idyll', are masked or distorted: Bernard's shock at learning of his bastardy and his subsequent feeling of liberation are masked by his conventional adolescent rebelliousness; Olivier's feelings for Bernard and Édouard are fatally muted by his reticence; Laura's love for Édouard is not fully expressible because of her intuition of his need to protect himself; young Gontran Passavant's grief at the death of his and Robert's father is blocked: at first, alone with the corpse, he cannot weep then later he hears a brutal voice saying 'God damn!' It fills him with horror; but it was his own voice, 'his, who until today has never uttered an oath!' Even Boris's fragile happiness is threatened by his 'shame'; only Bronja, who dies, is able to feel absolutely innocent. Naked impulse is always threatened by the intrusion of the counterfeit. Bernard comes to recognize that such falsehood is a necessity: he sees that he is a part of society. If he does not solve this problem of individualism versus duty to others then that is because the problem has by no means yet been solved. Gide offers us Bernard as a potentially 'saved character'.

In Édouard Gide views aspects of himself self-critically; but he keeps apart from him. One view of the Édouard–Passavant contrast is that it is 'good guy'–'bad guy'. This is wooden and incorrect. Édouard is sensitive and behaves 'correctly'; Passavant is a caricature of him. Passavant may even be what Édouard *really* is. Critics speak of him as a *pervertisseur*, of Édouard as a 'mature homosexual lover'. We know that Édouard thinks of himself as superior to Passavant; and so in intention he is. He is none the less a *pervertisseur*. Further, as protagonist in his own projected and in Gide's real novel, he happens to be indirectly responsible for almost every disaster that is recorded. It is he who pushes Laura into marriage – partly in order to distance her from himself. He thus sets in motion the train of events which leads to her pregnancy and unhappiness and to Vincent's murderous insanity. He is the older man who should have been able to deal with the situation between himself and Olivier; but he pushes him into the arms of the corrupt Passavant. He arranges for Boris and La Pérouse to go to the Azaïs's, an establishment of whose nature he is well aware, since he attended it and lived there; thus Boris dies. Since he fails to produce more than a few pages of his *Les Faux Monnayeurs* (and these, perhaps, for a non-artistic purpose), may he not be said to have been vicariously manipulating the lives of 'his' characters in 'real life'? This raises the questions of the novelist's and of human responsibility and the question of the nature of responsibility itself.

Gide should have the last word. In his *Journal* for 29 October 1929 he noted: '*I have never been able to invent anything.* It is by such a sentence in the *Journal d'Édouard* that I thought to separate myself from Édouard, to distinguish him ... And it is this sentence on the contrary that is used to prove that, *incapable of invention,* I have depicted myself in Édouard and that I am not a novelist.' It is forgotten that Gide invented Édouard.

BIBLIOGRAPHY

Translation: D. Bussy, *The Coiners,* (1927), 1950.

Text: in *Ouevres complètes,* 1932–9.

Criticism: D. L. Thomas, *André Gide,* 1950; A. J. Guerard, *André Gide* 1951; G. W. Ireland, *Gide,* 1963.

Franz Kafka

Franz Kafka, son of Jewish parents, was born in Prague in 1883. His father was a fairly prosperous businessman who kept a haberdashery warehouse. Hermann Kafka was dominating, commercially minded, healthy, vulgar and ill-tempered; his wife Julie was of gentler disposition. Three younger sisters all died in German concentration camps. Kafka's father played an overwhelming role in his life: he was frightened of him, sought an approval from him that he was not equipped to give, and could seldom openly express his hostile feelings towards him.

Kafka was sent to a strict school in Prague, began to read seriously towards the end of the century (he was early acquainted with Nietzsche) and to write. He studied literature and law at the German University in Prague (1901–6), during which time he met the writer Max Brod, his closest friend and the publisher of his posthumous works. His degree was in law. In 1908 he took up a position at the Workers' Accident Insurance Institute, and he remained there until ill health forced him to retire in 1922. In 1912 he met Felice Bauer, to whom he was twice engaged; the final break came in late 1917. In 1919 he was engaged to Julie Wohryzek; this was broken off in the same year. In the following year he met the most intelligent of his woman friends, the writer Milena Jesenská-Pollak; this relationship was also broken off – in great unhappiness in 1922. Both Milena – and Grete Bloch,

Felice's friend whom he met in 1913 and for whom he formed an attachment – perished at the hands of the Nazis. Only when Kafka had accepted the inevitability of his death did he settle down with a woman: Dora Dymant, a Polish girl who remained with him from July 1923 until his death from tuberculosis in a sanatorium near Vienna, in June 1924.

In his lifetime Kafka published seven small volumes of stories. He was known only to a few, but Rilke, Musil and other notables were amongst them. In 1915 he received the Fontane prize for the first chapter of *Amerika, Der Heizer* [*The Stoker*]. He left instructions to his executors that his unpublished work should be destroyed; Brod disregarded these and issued *Der Prozess* [*The Trial*] in 1925, *Das Schloss* [*The Castle*] in 1926, and *Der Verschollene* [*The Man Who Disappeared*] as *Amerika*, in 1927. Later he edited Kafka's complete works and wrote his biography. Between the wars Kafka became famous and widely translated; since 1945 he has generally been regarded as one of the greatest of European fiction writers, and is the subject of a massive body of criticism. Interpretations of his work differ sharply. His fiction is unique and inimitable: recondite, but compelling and expressed with a lucidity and serenity of style unparalleled in a nervous century. He has been described as a satirist of bureaucracy, a Cabbalist, a sick pessimist, a disguised optimist, a prophet, the victim of an acute Oedipus complex, a Christian allegorist, a symbolist, a Jewish allegorist, an atheist, an absurdist, a surrealist and much else. He is some of these but not all. He is not, for example, surrealist. The protagonists of his three novels are, respectively, *K*arl Rossmann, Josef *K*, and simply K.

None is finished. *The Castle* (written in 1922) lacks an ending. None was revised. It is important to remember then that while Kafka's quest transcends his individual 'case history', his *Collected Works* were not prepared by him or with his consent: though posterity has unanimously endorsed Brod's decision, it is doubtful if Kafka would have.

Das Schloss
[The Castle]

SUMMARY K. crosses a bridge leading from the main road and arrives at a snow-covered village which he believes has a Castle. He has made a long, difficult journey. He claims that he is the Land Surveyor whom Count West-west (implying both definitive, intensified death, 'going west' – and 'death of death': life, a new beginning), Lord of the Castle, is expecting. A young man called Schwarzer (connoting both 'death' and 'devil') arrives at the inn where he has settled for the night: the village, he tells him, belongs to the Castle and no one can spend the night in it without a permit. K. insists on staying; Schwarzer telephones the Castle. At first he is told the Castle has no knowledge of him. Then the Castle rings back: apparently the authorities do know of him. K. is disconcerted: if he has been recognized as Land Surveyor then they may be 'taking up the challenge with a smile'; on the other hand he might get more freedom of action than he had hoped for. He is defiant: 'if they expected to cow him by their recognizing him as Land Surveyor, they were mistaken.' It is thus established that so far as K.'s claims to the position of Land Surveyor are concerned he is a fraud, a confidence-man. Their apparent acceptance even made 'his skin prickle a little'.

K. claims that he has two assistants, whom he expects. Two men do arrive, apparently from the Castle; but K. has to ask them if they are indeed his former assistants (he does not recognize them). They are called Arthur and Jeremiah. K. refuses to treat them separately: 'I shall treat you as if you were one man and call you Arthur.' He telephones the Castle, pretending to be one of the assistants, and when he asks when his 'Master' can come to the Castle is told 'Never'. A messenger from the Castle, Barnabas (in biblical terms, 'Son of Consolation'), now introduces himself. He brings a letter to K. from Klamm (suggesting 'ravine', 'chasm', and 'clamp', 'lock' – which is the other meaning of 'Schloss'), 'Chief of Department X'. The letter tells him that he *has* been engaged, that the Superintendent (Mayor) of the village will instruct him in his duties, and that Barnabas will 'from time to time' 'report himself' to learn his wishes and communicate them to him: 'I desire my workers to be contented.' K. decides that this letter offers him a choice: to be a village worker with a 'distinctive but merely apparent connection with the Castle, or an ostensible village worker whose real occupation was determined through the medium of Barnabas'. He chooses to adopt the latter role, because 'then all kinds of paths would be thrown open to him.' He fails to persuade Barnabas to guide him to the Castle: instead he is taken to his home, where he meets his sisters Olga and Amalia. Invited to spend the night there, he is rude and boorish. Olga takes him to the Herrenhof, an inn where Castle officials sometimes stay. He then seduces Frieda ('peace'), the young barmaid at the Herrenhof, in the pools of beer and litter on the floor under the bar. Frieda is Klamm's mistress – or so it is assumed; but when Klamm shouts for her through the door she tells him she is with the Land Surveyor. Although she makes the first advances K. is chiefly interested in her as a means of making contact with Klamm. Thus he seeks an interview with Klamm with a view to obtaining permission to marry her.

He sees the Mayor, who tells him that although he has been acknowledged as Land Surveyor the village has no need of one: the work has already been done. The Mayor then explains to him that the Count's departments often issue contradictory orders: 'neither knows of the other.' Years ago there had been arrangements to call a Land

Surveyor in, but this couldn't have concerned K. However, the confusions of the affair had led to trouble and ill
feeling; the Mayor was relieved when it seemed to be
over but 'suddenly you appear and it begins to look as
if the whole thing must begin all over again.' He sows
doubts in K.'s mind: all his contacts 'have been illusory'.
Only the 'humming and singing' on the telephone is 'real
and reliable', 'everything else is deceptive.' The Mayor,
though not himself of the Castle, seems to know everything about K.; even that Frieda would go anywhere with
him. K. tells him that he wants no 'act of favour from the
Castle', only his 'rights'.

After this frustrating interview the wife of the landlord
of the Herrenhof, Gardena, asks to see him; she tells him
that she too has been Klamm's mistress, twenty years
before. That was a great honour. She explains to K. that
Klamm 'forgets immediately'; he refuses to accept this.
His whole hopes are now centred on Klamm. However, he
finds it increasingly difficult to come to grips with reality,
at least in terms of his own project. The villagers are
mostly hostile. They live under an inexplicable set of
rules, which they obey; no violence is applied. The village
is full of 'applicants', none of whose cases is ever resolved,
since although the officials are zealous about their files
they never read them.

The village teacher, who represents the Mayor, offers
K. the position of school janitor; he is disinclined to
accept, but Frieda persuades him to do so. At the Herrenhof he meets Pepi, the new barmaid – and probably
Klamm's new mistress. He tries again to see Klamm but
instead is interviewed by Momus, Klamm's secretary. K.
gets into trouble at the school and is dismissed; he refuses
to accept this. Frieda begs him to take her away, but he
will not. Frieda goes to Jeremiah, whom K. has angrily
thrown out and left to freeze outside. It turns out that
Barnabas' family have become social outcasts: Amalia has
refused the advances of an official, Sortini. (One of the

main features of life in the village is the Castle officials' undisputed right to take whatever women they wish.) Olga tries to regain favour by becoming a prostitute at the Herrenhof. She tells K. that Klamm is of variable appearance: he has only one consistent feature: he wears a black tail-coat. Does Klamm exist? Certainly K. sees, through a spyhole, a man whom he is told by Frieda is Klamm: he is described in some detail but no tail-coat is mentioned and his eyes are 'hidden behind glittering pince-nez'.

K. hears that he has been summoned to see a secretary at the Herrenhof. He goes into the wrong room and encounters another official, Bürgel ('little guarantor'). Bürgel tells him the secret of getting into the Castle: surprise an official when he is off his guard at night. K. goes off to sleep. Bürgel adds that the chance of getting past is really nil – but who knows? Soon after this the novel tails off, unfinished. Brod has written that Kafka told him that he would end the novel with K. on his death bed: he was there to be told that 'although his legal claims to live in the village were not valid, he was none the less to be allowed to live and work there.' This would certainly have been an ironic ending: what is the point of permission to 'live and work' being granted if one is about to die?

CRITICAL COMMENTARY An important aspect of *The Castle* is that it is not wholly interpretable. Many interpretations have, of course, been provided, which may seem to be mutually contradictory. Even though some are crude and strained to the point of absurdity, the merits of each may be seen if the novel is regarded as a series of concentric metaphors, each one narrowing into the next until a point of nothingness is reached at the centre.

Even though the novel is not an allegory or even a mixed allegory, it is *aptronymic*. An allegory hides a meaning, usually moral or religious, and often with an appealing tale. In a mixed allegory the story contains clues as to the didactic meaning. Aptronyms are names given in fiction which in themselves describe the nature of the character: Mr Butcher is a butcher and so on; 'Knecht' in Hesse's *The Glass Bead Game* is a more sophisticated aptronym. Aptronyms are evidently a feature of allegorical as well as of realistic novels; but they do not in themselves determine that the works in which they occur are allegories. If *The Castle* were an allegory it would have a single 'inner' meaning. Clearly it does not. We know that it is an 'inner autobiography'; but in it Kafka displays the opposite of the allegorist's certainty. Nor can it be said that *The Castle* is a symbolic novel, even though symbols abound in it.

At a primary level *The Castle* is an account (unavoidably satirical) of bureaucracy. The scenes in which the Mayor's files, and then later the officials' files, are revealed as hopelessly disordered are evidence of this, as is the Mayor's remark that often 'departments' are not co-ordinated. His complacent claim that while petty matters have become confused serious ones have not is typical of the claims of administrators.

This approach leads on to the next: Kafka as prophet of barbarous totalitarianism as characterized by an ever proliferating bureaucracy. We never see Count West-west and we do not know that even Klamm exists. The Castle itself may not be inhabited: it may simply be – or be used as – a symbol of terror, standing inaccessibly there. But we do see 'Castle officials' who *claim* to have access to the Castle. Barnabas is, it turns out, trying to do what his sister Olga is doing: to redeem his family from its disgrace. But he has no authority. Who really has? The villagers – almost all surly and brutish – accept their treatment, obey the absurd rules to which they are subjected, acknowledge without question their 'inferiority'. There is none of the violence which characterizes totalitarian regimes; but the cunning system of oppression acts as a peculiarly telling metaphor for it. However, everyone is guilty of complicity in this unfree state. The villagers accept the Castle's authority. There is one exception: Amalia; she resolutely resists the deliberately obscene advances of Sortini and thereby casts her whole family into disgrace. There are always such exceptions, and that Kafka should choose a woman to represent them is significant. But in general the villagers themselves are as responsible as anyone else for the drab tyranny under which they live.

Those critics such as Brod and Edwin Muir who believe that the Castle is 'good' and that K.'s real duty is to integrate himself within the community it 'administers' may object that the villagers do not live under a tyranny. In that case, nor did the happy Nazis, nor do the vast majority of Soviet Russians. They believed or believe in 'obedience' (Zamyatin's 'entropy') and find satisfaction in this; they do not see what this makes them. Kafka shows them to us as they are. Only certain *women* (Olga, Frieda, the landlady of the Herrenhof, Amalia, Pepi) are at all humanly acceptable. The men are slaves, brutes, impostors and/or liars. Here Kafka is pointing towards the masculine origins of totalitarianism and acknowledging that while it corrupts some women it can never corrupt others. In fact none of the women in *The Castle* is wholly corrupted; each shows some awareness of her own bad faith.

This suggests a yet richer level of approach: the religious. Kafka was interested in and concerned with social problems. (In 1918, for example, he conceived a project for a 'Society of Poor Workers'.) While he is unlikely to have been acquainted with the work of Émile Durkheim, it is one of Durkheim's central concepts, *anomie*, which can help us to illuminate a theme that obsessed Kafka – partially explaining why his work is so imbued with a sense of guilt. For Durkheim – a non-believer – 'God' and the sacred were *Society*: men and women should be morally involved with another; 'the image of the one who

completes me becomes inseparable from mine.' In the
absence of this moral interdependence the situation becomes 'pathological': there are conflicts (in Kafka's case
between his Jewishness and his distrust of Zionism; between his real Czech-Jew identity and his false Austro-
Hungarian status; his wish for marriage with his wish for
creative solitude) or there is nothing at all. This produces
the state of *anomie* which is obviously related to that of
alienation. Durkheim was a profound thinker, but not a
creative writer. His solution was a 'secular religion' a kind
of socialism in which Society would act as God. Kafka
went much further. He was sympathetic to both scepticism and socialism. But he questioned his scepticism, and
lost interest in socialism. Always fascinated by the Jewish
religion (he was attending lectures on Jewish Studies in
Vienna only a few months before his death), he had
strongly religious though non-orthodox apprehensions.
He saw and was aware of evil, but would not and could
not conclude that because it existed therefore God did
not exist (an atheist position). Nor was he remotely satisfied by any of the orthodox resolutions of this problem.
His approach has unmistakable resemblances to gnosticism and to (serious) Cabbalistic thinking.

In Prague before and during the war there existed a
movement called *Marcionism*. Kafka was well acquainted
with the ideas of its leading figure, the philosopher and
playwright Christian von Ehrenfels, whose seminars and
plays he attended. Marcion, a second-century 'heretic' and
precursor of Christian gnosticism, rejected the Jewish
Old Testament God – the Law-maker – as cruel, despotic
and capricious, and he described the created world as full
of 'flies, fleas and fevers': it had been made by a male-
volent demiurge. In gnostic belief the evil, material world
came into being because of the irrepressible curiosity of
Wisdom, one of the emanations of the dynamic, unknown,
unimaginable abyss of being: in her anguished desire she
gave off matter, the visible world. Man's task is to free

himself from matter by *gnosis* (knowledge, illumination) and a long since repentant Wisdom can help him in this.

Cabbalistic thinking did not crystallize as such until much later, in the thirteenth century; but it incorporates gnostic elements. Here God himself is incomplete, is involved in the 'fall', is in need of man. One aspect of God is wholly unknowable – 'the paradoxical fullness of the great divine Nothing', the so-called *En Sof*. But this nothingness turned outwards, in a primordial explosion: it began to exist, to emanate. Nothingness dramatically becomes aware of itself.

Although Kafka is not likely to have applied any consciously conceived religious plan in his writings, gnosticism and Cabbalism (and the Manicheism which bridged the gap between them) provided the intellectual and emotional air which he breathed. Such speculation was rife amongst his friends; and it is mainly in the Judaic thought with which Kafka so concerned himself (though critically) that the revival of the old 'heresies', in various forms, is to be found: it is a matter of the religious elements in men's make-up seeking a refuge from the barrennesses of positivism or the inadequacies of institutionalized religion. Kafka wrote:

> There is nothing but a spiritual world, and what we call the world of the senses is the Evil in the spiritual world . . .
> the fact that there is nothing but a spiritual world deprives us of hope and gives us certainty.

Kafka could not accept the atheist position. Atheist humanism could not give him sufficient reason to overcome his tendencies towards nihilism by finding some decent, solid, 'ordinary' way of accepting his existence without anxiety and dread. At various times he considered going to Palestine or becoming a soldier. He finally chose to be the celebrant of an absence of the divine, a sensual loather of putrid matter, a rational describer of the irrational. His concrete style is in sharp contrast to his irrational matter. This recalls the Cabbalistic paradox: it is absurd to try to think rationally about God, but that in itself is a rational premise – and so knowledge of God can only be communicated through reason. Hence the Cabbalists' rigid system. Hence Kafka's disturbingly lucid prose.

The Castle may convincingly be seen in the light of a complex network of 'heretical', uncomfortable, suppressed, hated, dualistic or mystical religious systems. *Matter* in the book is seen as disgusting. Nature is dead under the snow; it is never described. K.'s sexual encounter with Frieda takes place on a filthy floor under a bar. At the beginning K. stumbles on a 'Madonna' scene when he enters a house in the village; but its beauty is grotesque, sad, stained, sordid and ambiguous – it is, as Franz Kuna has written, a '*dislocated*' scene. The world of the village, apparently permeated by Castle officials, is bleak. When the peasants dance in the Herrenhof they are raucous, menacing, and they 'howl'. All flesh, all community life, appears as nauseating. The officials are lustful and careless – and may be impostors. 'The Castle of Kafka's novel is, as it were, the heavily fortified garrison of a company of gnostic demons, successfully holding an advanced position against the manoeuvres of an impatient soul,' writes Erich Heller.

But why is K. here, and why is he a deliberate impostor? He claims to be a Land Surveyor, a *Landvermesser*. This is a characteristically Kafkian sign for 'artist' (specifically, writer). A *Landvermesser*'s main job is to divide the land up into plots so that people shall know exactly what belongs to whom. In other words he is an accessory – and especially so in a place where the 'Castle' is believed to (and therefore does) hold absolute sway, and therefore to own or at least decide everything – to deceit and to the creation of fictions. Perhaps K. really was a *Landvermesser*: then in the world outside the Castle he could at least claim that, even if 'property is theft', still he was helping to produce a workable order and to make life go more smoothly. Here, no such excuse is possible. But the word *Landvermesser*, as Heller observes, has other connotations: hubris, audacity, spiritual pride – and most startlingly of all to 'make a mistake in measurement' (*sich vermessen*), clearly something that a Land Surveyor cannot afford to do.

Since K. will not divulge the reason why he pretends to have been engaged as *Landvermesser*, or why he is so determined to get into the Castle and to 'challenge' it, we must make our own inferences. Obviously it is not simply because he needs a job, or money, or a good time. Nor does he imagine that he can become the supreme authority: he is soon well aware of just how formidable the Castle is. His reasons are metaphysical, spiritual. He is engaged on a quest. He wants to be in a superior position to the villagers and he uses all of them to gain that end. He has been on a long journey and he has known where he was going because he apparently recognizes the village, even under snow, and he believes that the Castle is there even though it is 'veiled in mist and darkness': he gazes for a long time at the emptiness above him and knows that it is 'illusory'. But he has no respect for the Castle; he is aggressive towards it. His false claim has been made so that he can set in motion a train of events that may lead him right into it. Why?

In the person of K. Kafka is testing the status of art; he is taking it out of the 'ordinary world' and into the realms of 'truth' which it claims to inhabit. He much derided writing, and felt famously guilty about being a writer. Here he is testing his validity as a writer. After all, he was torn two ways: as he often asserted, he was nothing if not a writer. As a purveyor of fictions (his false claim; the untruthful enterprise of the *Landvermesser*) K. must force the Castle to recognize the 'truth' of his pretence. He does not even question whether or not he is acting in good faith – even if he employs 'art' (cunning, such as the contact with Frieda), to achieve his purpose. The account is undoubtedly an indictment of Kafka's kind of art, of what Kafka felt and thought about his art. K. is a cold charlatan, an exploiter of others, a man uninterested in justice (he frequently implies that he has been treated unjustly, but this is a pose), less concerned with the nature of the supposed Castle (good? bad?) than with the deceiving and the penetration of it: 'My highest, in fact my only wish is to put my affairs in order with the officials.' In any case, no one is taken in by him: if he is grudgingly tolerated then this is because the villagers have been told by the Castle officials, whose authority they accept, that they should refer to him as *Landvermesser*. Kafka's indictment of K. may not convince us; but it raises certain unavoidable questions. It shows, in Günther Anders' words, that Kafka 'was not satisfied with only *artistic* perfection'. And therein lies the dilemma of the modern writer.

But artists, writers, make larger claims (religious, sociological, philosophical). They are arrogant to do so, and aware of the fact; but then they are also impelled to do so by their sense of their own insufficiencies. To put it at its simplest, they would like to be of help. In the protagonist of *The Trial* Kafka presented us with someone who, because he was hounded, could arouse our pity (rightly or wrongly). K. of *The Castle* is an altogether less sympathetic representation of the writer – and of Kafka himself (who was not like K. at all, but full of feeling for others). Franz Kuna has put it aptly when he describes K. as one who 'has never experienced anything purer than his immediate self'. He is, in gnostic terms, a 'Wisdom' who has not yet learned to repent. In exploring the evil physical world – he may be said to have 'created' it in choosing to seek it out and to remain in it – in bad faith, he puts himself in the position of a 'material' or 'fleshly' man, the gnostic *sarkikus*, one who has no 'divine spark' in him and who can therefore never, even if he goes through the rites associated with *gnosis*, return 'home' to the 'Divine Being'.

It is at this point that the autobiographical elements must be brought into consideration. Kafka (K.) invented the world of the Castle out of arrogance, spiritual pride, hubris – and because the irrepressible curiosity of his wisdom urged him to it. This world is *sheol*: the Hebrew underworld whose meaning in the Old Testament, where it is mentioned sixty-five times, is unclear and ambiguous; certainly, however, it is a limbo of the dead. Having put K. into this position of his solitary but creative self, Kafka does not know what to do with him any more than he thought he knew what to do with himself – even when death was upon him. The world of the Castle is shot with death; but it is nearer to the mysterious *sheol* than it is to death.

The Castle itself is in fact disappointing, as K. discovers very early: a 'huddle of village houses': 'if [at a distance] K. had not known it was a castle he might have taken it for a little town.' But does K. really 'know'? Is this not a phantasm? This famous 'Castle' is not a castle at all: just a huddle of buildings with a nondescript tower and 'broken, fumbling' battlements – a tower where it 'was as if a melancholy-mad tenant who ought to have been kept locked in the topmost chamber of the house had burst through the roof and lifted himself up to the gaze of the world'. This, which so many interpreters of Kafka have taken to be 'Heaven', is yet another example of the gnostic debased spirit: evil matter. And so *this* is what the Flaubertian wisdom of artistic perfection, with its irresistible movement forwards, has created: a castle that is not a castle at all but a *lock* the pursuit of which excludes K. and his creator from salvation. But K. does not heed the warning of his disappointment – or that of the teacher, whom he meets shortly afterwards and who admonishes him, in French, for mentioning the Count: 'Please remember that there are innocent children present.' Rather, through his creator, he continues to perpetrate fictions: being intimate only with his 'immediate self' he sees people and things only from his habitually solipsist viewpoint. To him Frieda seemed 'young'; to Pepi, her successor in the taproom, and rival, she is 'oldish'. She has even confided to Pepi that she is unhappy because she is plain – as Pepi reminisces. Thus K. is not even attracted by Frieda: further confirmation of his ruthless exploitation of her in order to reach Klamm. The Klamm K. sees through the spyhole may be anyone or he may be Klamm. He is in any case both the *chasm*, ravine, that separates K. from the outside world (he crossed a bridge to get to the village) and, as representative of the Castle (in K.'s eyes), yet another lock (clamp). In the oneiric narrative Klamm appears as far more repulsively 'material' than even the Castle. But this narrative is in large part K.'s interpretation of the situation. Bürgel, who says he is a liaison secretary, offers to take his case further and even tells him that he might slip through the net by taking a secretary unawares in the middle of the night; K. has actually just done that very thing – but fails to notice it and so can never know its consequences. Kafka would like to agree with Goethe that 'by postulating the impossible . . . the artist obtains the whole of the possible'; but his neurosis, such an uncanny intensification of that of modern man, demands that his strategy shall be ceaselessly eristic. Behind all the corrupted appearances generated by the notion of the Castle, which include a non-castle, lies the unfathomable, invisible Count Westwest: extinction or rebirth? Or both? He could be reached by love.

Kafka, in January 1922, wrote in his *Diary* of his own writings as a 'secret doctrine', a Cabbala. But he, who had once seriously contemplated going to Palestine, felt that Zionism had intervened and that 'it would require genius of an unimaginable kind to strike root again.' Still, such writing (he was now working at *The Castle* itself) was only an 'assault on the last earthly frontier' but also an 'assault from above, aimed at me from above'. This, in the context of the terrible gap between the demonic world and that of the scarcely effable Count West-west which K. inhabits, speaks for itself. And there is little doubt that Kafka, in K.'s erotic exploits, was fumbling towards a use, albeit original, of some kind of Cabbalistic symbolism. He had a bad conscience about parting with his mistress Melina, and punished himself for this in his account of K.'s affair with Frieda; the metaphorical terms in which he saw this seem to have been Cabbalistic and perhaps even involved the notion of K. as destroyer of the erotically formulated 'unity within the godhead', which is the worst disaster the Cabbalist can envisage. In the Lurianic Cabbalism of the sixteenth century man was especially created in order that the demonic forces be conquered; so that God, who thus depended on man, could be restored. Now this was not at all the paternalistic God of orthodox Jewry, and here Kafka was reaching towards an expiation of his hyperneurotic dependence on the 'authority' of his father, to which he grovelled to the extent of making himself guilty by merely challenging it. K.'s task *ought* to have been to redeem the unredeemed Count West-west; but by not going straight to the 'Castle' and knocking on the door and proceeding from there, by disingenuously involving himself with the shabby idle bureaucracy which purports to represent the Castle – and by implication the Count – by his erotic ruthlessness, he fails to do so. K. exults in his alienation, and Kafka – being an honest writer – cannot see how to prevent him doing so. All this is compatible with the predicament of the European Jew: the uprooted person cut off from his past, yet rejected by his environment. The Judaic, Cabbalistic metaphors employed only emphasize this.

So Kafka in *The Castle* captures the mood of the twentieth century – and not only of the first quarter of it in which he lived. He offers no answer. Those who see a 'transformation' or a 'metamorphosis' in K. project their own hopes on to a fragment. Günther Anders considers that his work should act as a terrible warning: he was a 'good man', but his picture of the world is 'as it should not be'. The picture may, though terrible, act as more than a warning. If man exists to redeem 'God', the unnameable, then his existence is indeed, in an important sense, a curse. But by describing to us in such distressing detail how this curse operates, he at the least affirms a purpose, implies the possibility of *gnosis* (we shall not vulgarly call it 'belief'), and denies absurdity.

BIBLIOGRAPHY

Translation: W. and E. Muir, *The Castle* (1930), 1957. The 1957 version incorporates extra material.

Text: in *Gesammelte Werke*, 1950–58.

Criticism: R. Gray, *Kafka's Castle*, 1956; G. Anders, *Franz Kafka*, 1960; W. Sokel, *Franz Kafka*, 1966; P. F. Nenmayer, *20th Century Interpretation of 'The Castle'*, 1969; E. Heller, *Kafka*, 1974.

Robert Musil

Robert Musil, an only child, was born at Klagenfurt, Austria, in 1880. His father was an engineer, later a professor. Both parents were intelligent and advocates of 'enlightenment in every respect', as Musil later said; but his early years were unhappy and puzzled. He obtained a diploma of engineering (1901) from the institute at which his father was a professor. He did his military service and then put in a year as an assistant at the technical college in Stuttgart. Then he turned to experimental psychology and philosophy; his doctoral thesis for a degree in philosophy at the University of Berlin (1908) was on the epistemology of the physicist and philosopher Ernst Mach, whose positivist, anti-metaphysical, empirical approach to phenomena influenced the direction of his thinking.

Die Verwirringen des Zöglings Törless [*The Confusions of Student Törless*] (1906), set in a military academy, is the most chillingly precise of all school stories. This gained him a reputation, and he entered into some literary association in Berlin. Already he had decided to try to make his living as an author. *Der Mann ohne Eigenschaften* [*The Man Without Qualities*] (1930–33; 1952) was being planned even before *Törless*. In 1910 he married Marthe Marcovaldi, a woman older than himself (but she outlived him) who had two children by a previous marriage. From then until 1913 he worked as a librarian; then he became one of the editors of an intellectual magazine. He served as an officer in the war, and was decorated.

In 1911 he had published two stories under the title *Vereinigungen* [*Unions*]; in 1924 *Drei Frauen* [*Three women*], short stories, followed. From 1919 until 1922 he worked, first as press officer at the Foreign Ministry, then as a scientific adviser to the War Ministry. In 1922 he decided to devote himself to literature. His play *Vinzenz* (1924) was a moderate success, and he hoped soon to publish the first part of *The Man Without Qualities*, on which he was working. But this was not ready until 1930. Just as the second volume appeared the Nazis took power: he was cut off from his main market. An art historian organized the *Musil-Gesellschaft*: a group of wealthy cultured men who agreed to support him. This arrangement he felt was his due. In 1938, to escape Hitler, he left for Zurich; later he went to Geneva. Funds were largely cut off, and at the time of his sudden death he was living in straitened circumstances. He had withdrawn a third volume of his novel, when in the press, from a German publisher in Stockholm; he was not satisfied with it. There was a great deal of variant material following what Musil himself published, which takes the reader up to the thirty-eighth section of the third book, 'Into the Millennium, or The Criminals'. This unpublished material has been unsatisfactorily presented by Adolf Frisé in his edition of Musil's collected works; Musil's English translators have promised a sounder arrangement (in translation) but so far this has not appeared. Musil, although admired by, among others, Thomas Mann, Hugo von Hoffmannsthal and Albert Einstein, was for some years almost forgotten. Even when he was rediscovered after the war it took some time to interest a German publisher in the reissue of his works.

Musil was essentially a 'private' non-political man, but not one who could bear Hitler (he could have gained a temporary reputation and money by accepting the new

Nazi Austria). He bore his misfortunes with fortitude, dignity and integrity.

Der Mann ohne Eigenschaften
[The Man Without Qualities]

CRITICAL SUMMARY As Musil's translators Eithne Wilkins and Ernst Kaiser have written, 'It would be useless to attempt a synopsis of *The Man Without Qualities.* not only because of its length and complexity, but also because the real action lies not on the surface ... but within the characters' states of mind.' I have therefore here combined the outline of the plot with the exegesis.

Musil is as complex a writer as Thomas Mann; though more comic; and his irony is purer. In common with Melville, otherwise a very different writer, he had the strength of will to sacrifice his capacity to produce popular fiction in the interest of his complex and paradoxical aims.

The massiveness of scope and range of *The Man Without Qualities* has understandably not always been appreciated: the posthumous material is often contradictory and has been poorly edited. Its first sections may reasonably be interpreted as satire on Austrian society, culture and bureacracy in the year preceding the outbreak of the First World War – and as little more. But the novel becomes increasingly profound. Like Pirandello, Musil was a sceptic who refused to remain so and yet distrusted every one of the 'solutions' which our innate and indeed necessary non-scepticism forces upon us; again like Pirandello he was a relativist who saw that there are many 'realities'. Like his own Ulrich in this huge novel, Musil knew that 'A world of qualities without men [had] arisen', and that 'a whole man no longer [stood] against a whole world, but [was] a human something [moving] in a diffuse culture-medium.' Despite his acute sense of crisis, Musil was somehow able to allow his imagination autonomous free play.

He could still see his work unfold before his own eyes.

What we have of *The Man Without Qualities* is set in the year 1913–14. Musil planned to end it with the outbreak of war – which marked the end of the 'old' stable world. That world had been in process of disintegration for a long period; but the characters in the novel cannot know, as the reader does, the exact nature of its final destruction. We are still spiritually in that world, in that we have found nothing to replace it: that is why Musil sets his story on the edge of the precipice. The postwar world was a *waste land*, as Eliot termed it, an age of 'no longer, not yet', as Musil's compatriot, the novelist Hermann Broch, described it; Musil admired Rilke, and would have known his lines:

Each languorous turn of the world has such
  dispossessed children;
To whom neither the past nor yet the future belongs.

But Musil, torn apart like so many of his contemporaries by the confusions new knowledge confers, resolutely remains just inside the old world.

At the centre of the first parts of the novel is Ulrich, whose surname we never learn ('out of consideration for his father'); he is the Man Without Qualities. *Eigenschaft* means 'quality', 'feature', 'characteristic', and is not strictly translatable; but then one of Musil's more recondite themes is precisely what the word *could* or *might* mean. Ulrich, who is thirty-two, has a substantial income. His father has been a leading lawyer – a professor, adviser to aristocratic families, member of the Upper House (attached to the 'bourgeois liberal party') – and is now, at sixty-nine, a hereditary nobleman. Ulrich has had a good education (though once marred by his having suggested in an essay that 'even God probably preferred to speak of His world in the subjunctive of potentiality'); he has been a soldier, an engineer and a mathematician of distinction, and could easily have advanced himself in some branch of public or academic affairs (become a 'racehorse of genius', as he puts it); but he has chosen not to. He has awoken to sexual experience. He now lives, sardonically, in Vienna in a 'little château' which has 'three styles superimposed on each other': this mixture represents the muddled society in which Ulrich is living: he is 'taking a year off from life'. Ulrich appears to himself as a man without qualities because he 'cannot summon up any sense of reality'; but this, Musil writes, is 'by no means an unambiguous matter'. Ulrich wants the wood while the others want the trees. His ideas may only be 'unborn realities', but 'he too has a sense of reality ... a sense of possible reality.'

Musil was obsessed with *possibilities* throughout his life. Törless of the early novel is fascinated by the type of reality possessed by an 'imaginary' number which may be used in the process of making unimaginary, practical calculations. (This is not unusual: compare Zamyatin's D-503.) In philosophy the question could be boiled down to the basic problem of whether and how universals are 'real' – or 'not real'. But Musil is more than a philosopher: he brings poetic thinking to bear on the kind of question as just how, say, a 'frictionless fluid' (the example is mine), of which there is no *actual* instance, can be of *actual* scientific importance (which it is). He once described *The Man Without Qualities* as a bridge being built out into space; in that sense it is itself a certain kind of 'universal' – 'imaginary' (fictional, created), and yet of actual use. Ulrich is himself concerned with such matters: with the insidious way in which emotion (particularly in the crucial erotic area) encroaches on intellect. But he has 'no qualities'. He is not, as Musil was, a writer.

The mythopoeic element is present at the outset. If there were Utopia there would be no evil, no tension – and therefore no writing. Musil understood the tension, in writers, between a nostalgia for evil and a Utopian idealism, a longing for 'the good', and so in Ulrich he created a mythical character: a *non-artist* (he has only 'considered' being a poet – likewise pilgrim, adventurer, and disillusioned person who believes only in 'money and violence') in quest for Utopia. This was his way of attempting to solve the problem of the guilt which the twentieth-century writer feels when confronted with his lack of political or social activism. If Ulrich solves the problem, then Musil the artist (who projects himself into Ulrich) will have been useful.

Yet Musil's method is overtly realistic in the usually understood sense. 'Always begin with the concrete!' he told himself. His chief procedure is the extended aside, or essay. He or his characters comment as freely as they like and indeed as 'omnipotently' as Balzac (one of Musil's favourite authors) or George Eliot. There are some passages of lyrical description; and there is also a sustained lyrical note, at first almost totally suppressed, which becomes less and less muted as we proceed to the third book. Furthermore, the prose – unlike that of the stories – is lucid and simple. Musil was doubtless aware that effective simplicity (such as that of Blake or Wordsworth) rests on paradox. He might have chosen to express himself in an obtrusively modernistic way, as Joyce or Gertrude Stein did: to employ, for example, a *stream of consciousness* technique. But now he preferred to disguise his acute sense of the loss of coherence (resembling and related to the loss of faith in a benign God) by employing an apparently less innovatory mode. Like Svevo, he chose, with a fully conscious irony, to reject such fundamentally expressionistic techniques as *stream of consciousness* because, in his schema, they implied unearned Utopian possibilities: his narrative technique is broken down, as Burton Pike observes, into 'units' – like the flight of Zeno's famous arrow (cf. Svevo). In this way he was able to retain the element of story, of *what happens*: 'The law of this life, for which one yearns [is] ... that of *narrative order*,' says Ulrich.

Ulrich's father wants him to 'do' something; and because he is bored, sardonic and worried about his passivity, he agrees to become secretary to the newly formed *Parallelaktion* [Collateral Campaign]: this has been planned as a celebration of the Emperor Franz Josef's seventieth year (1918) on the throne of the Austro-Hungarian Empire (sometimes *Kakanien* here: a joke on the imperial-royal *kaiserlich-königlich*, 'k & k' arrangement whereby the Austrian Franz Josef was Emperor and the Hungarian monarch only King). The campaign is 'collateral' because of a similar one – to celebrate Kaiser Wilhelm II's thirtieth year on the throne in the same year – being mounted in Germany: the Austrians are anxious to prove that their Empire is of the greater cultural and political significance.

As it stands, the first (short) book of *The Man Without Qualities* is 'A Sort of Introduction', the second 'The Like of it Now Happens' and the third (unfinished) book 'Into the Millennium or The Criminals'. 'A Sort of Conclusion', which Musil planned, never got under way.

The fatuities of the Campaign give Musil room for some of his sharpest comic writing: the pretentiousness of the wife of Hans Tuzzi (Permanent Secretary of a 'feudal' ministry) whom Ulrich sarcastically calls Diotima (the priestess of Mantineia and teacher of Socrates in Plato's *Symposium*); the vacuous utterances of the members of the committee, and so forth. Underlying the satire there is a seriousness. We are able to feel Ulrich's frustration as well as his amusement. Musil is not simply trying to hold the Empire up to ridicule. There is a certain tenderness in his treatment of it.

Ulrich is only 'playing with' the people of the Campaign. But he forms certain impressions. Its initiator, Count Leinsdorf, amuses him; he comes to prefer him to Diotima and her hero Arnheim who plays an important part in the first two books. Arnheim is a Prussian Jew, a successful businessman and writer whom Diotima regards as essential to the 'cultural' aspects of the campaign. (Arnheim is a portrait of the German statesman and engineer Walter Rathenau, assassinated in 1922 by anti-semitic nationalists.) Ulrich finds Arnheim's big and impressive ideas pretentious. The exposure of the nature of this kind of enlightened, clever syncretism is an important aspect of the politico-social element in the novel. It is 'only the emergency substitute for something he had lost'. Musil cannot bring himself to believe in political solutions. Yet his portrait of Arnheim is not entirely unsympathetic. The difference between him and Diotima (intelligent if over-idealistic Utopianism as against stupid, ignorant and vain cultural aspirations) is glossed, so to say, by the affair between Soliman, Arnheim's black valet with whom he has now become bored, and Rachel, Diotima's maid. Ulrich is finally driven to call for a 'spiritual stocktaking. We must do more or less what would be necessary if what were due in 1918 were the Day of Judgement, and the old spirit had to be terminated and a higher one begun.' He knows he is being unrealistic. But he is serious. The others fail to understand him. Arnheim offers him an important job in his commercial empire. Then he hears of his father's death, and his search becomes more personal.

Meanwhile Ulrich's erotic problems remain unsolved. The 'forgotten, exceedingly important affair with the major's wife', is the suddenly injected subject of 2, 32. Ulrich recollects an early love affair: 'This beating of a twenty-year-old heart in his thirty-two-year-old breast seemed to him like the perverted kiss that a boy gives a man.' He had gone away to a small island, 'drifted into the very heart of the world' and passed into a mystical state. This is described with great exactitude and beauty, and recurs throughout the novel. It is no accident that the chapter begins with an account of Ulrich's thoughts about the 'notorious lunatic' Christian Moosbrugger, a sex-murderer.

There was a plethora of such cases as Moosbrugger's in Germany and Austria in the 1920s. He plays a vital role in the novel. He is a carpenter who has mutilated and then killed a prostitute. 'If mankind could dream collectively,' Musil writes, 'then it would dream Moosbrugger.' Musil's careful portrait of Moosbrugger is one of the shrewdest analyses of a lower-class psychopath in European literature. Musil approaches the problem from every angle. What is to be done with him? Is he mad or sane? He fascinates Ulrich, who sees in him his own criminal impulses. He represents one interpretation of the Nietzschean *Übermensch*. He also represents the bestial chaos that was to erupt in the form of Nazism and Stalinism: results of irrational energy manifested by countries at times of crisis. Yet he is surprisingly innocent, even when he thinks he is being cunning; and he enjoys the attention he receives.

Besides Arnheim, Diotima and Moosbrugger, there are other key characters. Ulrich's second mistress in the novel (the first, Leona, a pretentious and gluttonous cabaret singer, is disposed of in short compass) whom he calls Bonadea is a married woman with children who – in her sexual promiscuity – is also on a sort of quest for self-fulfilment; but this is unarticulated. Her relationship with Ulrich continues, although it is interrupted until near the end of the finished part of the novel, and provides a psychological and sometimes comic counterweight to its increasingly mythopoeic nature.

Clarisse, and above all Ulrich's sister Agathe, are more important. Clarisse is the wife of Walter, the friend of Ulrich's youth who shared conventional turn-of-the-century aspirations with him, but who is now a peevish, hostile sciolist. All she has in common with Walter is a passion for music (mainly Wagnerian) which apparently causes Ulrich to repress any feelings he has for this form of art. Clarisse is an almost psychotic Nietzschean (she represents for Musil the 'bad' side of Nietzsche's influence, as, in his way, Ulrich represents the 'good') who uncannily seeks out the 'Moosbrugger' in Ulrich; she wants Ulrich to father her a son who will be a 'saviour' and she also sees Moosbrugger as Christ (carpenter) and 'overman'. Her observations or propositions often possess the piercing exactitude of the mad or half-mad; she functions in *The Man Without Qualities* both as a psychologically convincing figure and as a suggestion that the half-crazy can see what the majority of the sane cannot. She is also under the influence of the transcendental philosopher Meingast who undergoes 'transformations' and makes Clarisse feel 'shudders of light' when he speaks ('Men with particularly fine heads are usually stupid,' Ulrich retorts).

It is Clarisse, as well as Agathe, who draws Ulrich into acquiescing in crime. While we cannot be sure how Musil would have dealt with the Ulrich–Agathe relationship, we can be reasonably certain that he would have allowed the episodes in which Moosbrugger is 'sprung' from the asylum – only to kill once more – to stand. Ulrich here allows himself, if unwillingly, to be swayed by Clarisse. Again, Clarisse's obsession with functioning as a man as well as a woman clearly reflects the situation between Ulrich and Agathe, who aspire to be 'one'.

With the third part Agathe begins to assume central importance. She is five years younger than Ulrich; their childhood was spent separately, as she has been educated in a convent. She has been married twice: first to a man who died and whose memory she cherishes (she has replaced the portrait of him she wore in a locket round her neck with poison), then to the repulsive Hagauer, whom she hates and wishes to divorce. When Ulrich and she meet at the beginning of the third book they are mysteriously attracted to each other. Ulrich condones, though under protest, her forgery of a codicil to her father's will by which she – and therefore Hagauer – is disinherited, and all the money goes to Ulrich. Agathe's innocent, con-

fident, feminine way of committing this crime fascinates
Ulrich; it is in fact the prefiguring of a later 'crime' which
both are contemplating: incest. Not much 'happens' in
the sections of the third book which Musil published; but
in a posthumously published chapter the brother and
sister go to an Adriatic island where they attempt to enter
what Ulrich has described as the 'millennium' as 'criminals' (hence the subtitle of this part).

Agathe's name means 'the Good One', and in the mid-
1920s Musil proposed to call his novel *The Twin Sister*.
For he saw that she must come to occupy its centre. But
he never reached this point, except perhaps fragmentarily,
in his actual writing. He knew (what Pasternak forgot)
that an effectively mythopoeic work cannot be created altogether consciously. Yet he had to contend with his own
extreme sophistication and his acutely self-analytic nature;
he found it difficult to fall back on lyrical procedures, but
knew he needed to return lyricism.

Burton Pike calls the novel 'three things: a gallery of
types of people, the portrayal of a society and an age, and
a primer of a new morality for mankind'. It is certainly
the first two; but to call it simply a 'primer of a new
morality' is to do scant justice to Musil's twentieth-century subtlety of mind. None of his critics has seen the full
significance of his main theme, incest – or of the difficulties he deliberately set himself. Eça de Queirós had early
seen the importance of the theme in *Os Maias* but here
he shows little more than an intelligent awareness of it.
Musil's is the most profound and least sensationalist of all
the many modern treatments.

Ulrich is driven into taking a 'year's leave from life'
because he is serious; yet in his seriousness he seems to
himself to be frivolous, guilty and reprehensibly passive.
He hides behind irony: even his uncharacteristic outburst
to the committee when he asks for a 'spiritual stocktaking' is ironic for he knows it to be a wasted effort. He
has so far been a kind of Wilhelm Meister in his passivity;

there is even a hint of Wilhelm in his sexual indifference to individuals. There are other connections with *Wilhelm Meister* which should not be overlooked. True, almost all novels in German can be related to themes to be found in Goethe; but Musil is particularly distinguished for his resolute excision of all the *romantic* elements in Goethe. In *Wilhelm Meister* the Harper praises incest and has practised it, though unknowingly, with his sister. The man-woman Mignon is his child. In *The Man Without Qualities* Clarisse is a variation on Mignon. But Musil interpolates a personal, specifically incestuous quest for truth between the 'theatrical mission' (in his novel the comedy of the Collateral Campaign) and the entrance to the order of the Renunciants (the Ulrich–Agathe relationship, however he would have treated this). He planned for the incestuous union – whether physical or merely spiritual – to fail; he thought of Agathe both as a suicide and as surviving; he had a notion of going beyond August 1914 and putting Ulrich into the war. But it seems certain that he never worked out – as Goethe, who was more self-confident and who could afford to be more optimistic, did for Wilhelm – any means of self-fulfilment for Ulrich. If the novel, as Pike claims, was to be a 'primer of morality' for mankind then first it had to be a primer of morality for Ulrich. A writer can do so much and no more. And Musil, unlike Goethe, knew that he had not begun to achieve the creation of any primer of morality. Hesse at least invented Castalia – ambiguous though the values of this mythical place are – and deliberately opposed his central character Knecht to Goethe's Meister. But Musil, whom we may feel to have been less pretentious, did not get further than Agathe, the sister; nor could he state what effect this experience would have on Ulrich in his quest for salvation.

Musil had been obsessed with the myth of Isis and Osiris over a number of years. When he published a poem on the subject in 1923 he noted that it 'contains the novel in nucleus'. The poem is both 'Freudian' and Platonic: it is concerned with 'how the gods divided the original human being, who was a whole, into two halves, man and woman' (Agathe reminds Ulrich of this, in 3, 25). All through the third book Ulrich and Agathe are contemplating the 'crime' of *physical* incest. This is perfectly clear. Agathe's voice becomes 'suddenly husky' when she reminds Ulrich of Plato's retelling of the old myth; and throughout the Ulrich–Agathe scenes Musil implies the struggle of the two to evade their increasing desire for each other. Agathe puts her garter into their father's coffin; in another passage Moosbrugger thinks of women as creatures with garters.

There is critical controversy about whether, in the posthumously published section, Ulrich and Agathe actually 'commit' incest or not. Yvonne Isitt, near to the mark here, points out that while no one (including Musil himself) can be certain, 'the spiritual relationship of Ulrich with his *Eigenliebe* [self-love: which is how, at one point, he has described what Agathe is to him] must ultimately be regarded as incestuous'. However, Kaiser and Wilkins have a point, for in the simplest form of the Isis–Osiris myth (this has almost infinite ramifications as it becomes transformed in later mythologies) Osiris (fourth divine Pharaoh, abolisher of cannibalism and institutor of civilization and justice) is cut up into fourteen pieces, which are dispersed. Isis finds all these pieces except for the penis, which has been devoured by a crab. One may thus postulate a desexualized Osiris; and therefore suggest that Musil – at one point – might have intended Ulrich to overcome his physical desire for his sister. However, it is not without point that Clarisse, as she becomes more and more obsessed with her role as hermaphrodite, becomes increasingly insane.

Musil failed to finish at least in part because of his truly heroic effort to defy the Teutonic tradition of paradox too easily resolved by abstraction or deliberately enigmatic and therefore evasive ending (as in *The Glass Bead Game*). He was determined, as the published section of the third part demonstrates, to give Agathe the full attributes of a human being: for all the enormous mythopoeic weight she has to bear, she must also exist in a realist mode. She must be shown to adjust to her Isis-role which is, after all, to 'reassemble' her brother and (possibly) to renounce her criminal desire for him in order to subdue his for her. There is a revealing passage in 3, 30. The confused Ulrich pompously tells Agathe that the 'moment you shift out of harmony with everyone else [incest would be a paradigmatic case] you commit yourself to everlastingly not knowing what's good or what's bad ... We live in a time when morality is either dissolving or in convulsions ... for the sake of a world that may yet come, one must keep oneself pure.' And (though the narrator does not say so) he weakly falls back on the idea of 'duty': he is after all confronted with the impulse to perform with full consciousness the most criminal of all actions. Agathe protests that he 'does his duty' because that's the way he is and he enjoys it; and she throws her arms around him to avoid his seeing her sobs. He is consumed with a 'troublesome embarrassment'; his physical desire is stilled. And Agathe, discerning his coldness (which makes her 'quite beside herself') realizes 'that she must deal with her troubles all on her own'. Her troubles are mostly his.

As far as Musil gets (in the published portion) Agathe is seen as a full human being rather than as the symbolic figure she also is. The treatment is exquisite and moving. (It is pertinent that St Agatha was a Sicilian martyr who, if only according to legend, had her breasts sheared off by order of the man to whom she would not yield.) Beyond that point Musil falters. But he had achieved much, and if in the last nine years of his life he failed to satisfy himself, then this was because of his unique integrity.

He achieved a novel in which myth operates at a realistic level; he doggedly observed Goethe's epigram: 'If you want to enter the infinite, pursue the finite in every direction.'

He saw that modern man must dare to rediscover himself by the creation of personal myth – that thought had *not* been 'emancipated from myth'. And he saw the difficulties. He was pragmatic enough (in the best, [William] Jamesian sense) to understand that technological advances could not simply be thrown aside, and that political revolutions solved no fundamental problems.

And he saw, as his treatment of the tormented Agathe shows, that although women have or would have a key role to play in a 'world that may yet come' they are still desperately alone. He is the least male-centred of the major twentieth-century novelists, and in certain respects unsurpassed.

BIBLIOGRAPHY
Translation: E. Wilkins and E. Kaiser, *The Man Without Qualities*, three volumes, 1953–65.

Text: *Gesammelte Werke*, 1952–7. A new edition is necessary.

Criticism: B. Pike, *Robert Musil*, 1961; E. Kaiser and E. Wilkins, *Robert Musil, Eine Einführung in das Werk*, 1962 – indispensable; some of the material is in the introduction to the English version, volumes 1 and 3.

Jean-Paul Sartre

Jean-Paul Sartre, a great-nephew of Albert Schweitzer, was born in Paris in 1905. His sailor father died when he was young, and he was brought up by his mother and his grandfather. He was a student of philosophy at the École Normale Supérieure; in 1933-4 he studied in Germany where he absorbed the ideas of Martin Heidegger and Heidegger's teacher Husserl. From these and from his early conviction that 'sadness and boredom' lie at 'the bottom of nature' (1929) he derived the bases of his philosophy. Sartrian existentialism was the culmination of a philosophical tendency that went back to Max Stirner, Nietzsche and Kierkegaard, to Unamuno and Ortega y Gasset in Spain, to many literary works of the past – in particular to Tolstoy's *The Death of Ivan Ilyich* – to Pascal and St Augustine before that, and to gnosticism before Augustine. But existentialism became associated exclusively with Sartre and with his lifelong companion Simone de Beauvoir; it was immensely influential in the years immediately after the war. It excited the young and enraged the conventional. Sartre, who taught at Le Havre, Laon and Paris after his return from Germany, then joined the army, and was taken prisoner in 1940. Released in 1941, he joined the Resistance. In 1945 he founded the magazine *Les Temps Modernes*. His major philosophical work, *L'Être et le néant* [*Being and Noth-*

ingness], appeared in 1943. His first novel, *La Nausée* [*Nausea*], had appeared in 1938. The unfinished three-volume *Les Chemins de la liberté* appeared in 1945–50. The fourth book, *La Dernière Chance,* was not completed. Sartre has written some dozen plays and film scripts; he has also partly completed both an attempt to reify Marx, *Critique de la raison dialectique,* and a study of Flaubert. *Les Mots* [*Words*] (1964) is about his childhood. There are many important essays in the *Situations* series of volumes, of which there are now ten. Most of his work, which also includes studies of Baudelaire and Jean Genet, has been translated. Over the last twenty years he has published nothing creative. Sartre has never been a member of the French communist party, and has never been a true Marxist. Existentialist freedom has come first; and Sartre is philosophically critical of Marx's attitude towards the future. But he has supported a succession of left-wing and anti-Stalinist causes. He supported the Hungarians in 1956 and the Czechs in 1968. Today, blind and ailing but as genial and aggressive as ever (a recent essay is splendidly entitled *'Élections, piège à cons'* [*'Elections, trap for cunts'*]) he has taken up a position hardly distinguishable from that of a nineteenth-century anarchist. In 1964 he was awarded the Nobel Prize, which he declined. He is the only person to have done so.

For much of his life Sartre lived in hotel rooms, accumulating as little personal property as possible. He is a self-acknowledged 'café philosopher'. Since 1945 he has devoted himself solely to writing, editing – and some political action. He will be remembered primarily for his novels and plays, and for his contributions to man's phenomenological understanding of himself. Even his detractors and those who regard him as unrealistic acknowledge that he is a brave and, as one of his English critics has admitted, 'strangely impressive' man.

La Nausée

SUMMARY *La Nausée*, first entitled *Mélancholie* by the author, was written before Sartre asserted the principle of *littérature engagée*: that the writer should be 'committed' to a definite, 'chosen' project of action which will further the liberation of men. Sartre has found it difficult to commit himself for long to any cause except that of his own freedom; thus *La Nausée*, a more purely phenomenological novel than any work by Sartre which has followed it, is not only his best but his most revealing creative work. It expresses his brand of atheist existentialism in an emotional rather than a philosophical manner. *Les Chemins de la liberté*, though excellent, is more of a demonstration. We need not here be concerned with whether Sartre is philosophically 'right' in his gloomy view of the absolute contingency of existence: we meet a man who *feels* this, as most serious readers of books have articulately felt it at one time or another. Ways of thinking and feeling do not need to be 'true' to be experienced.

La Nausée purports to be edited: the 'editors' write in a preliminary note that the notebooks to follow are being published 'without any alterations'. They were 'found among Antoine Roquentin's papers' – which implies that Roquentin is dead, or that he has completely abandoned his former self.

Roquentin is an historian. He has travelled in central Europe, north Africa and the Far East; since the 'beginning of January 1932 at the latest' he has been living for three years at Bouville ('Filthtown', *boue* being French for mud, mire, slush, ooze, or filth – the notion of stickiness is vital in Sartre's thinking), 'where he was completing his historical research on the Marquis de Rollebon'. The diary runs from 29 January 1932 until a short time afterwards. All the headings after the first refer simply to days or times. Bouville closely resembles Le Havre, where Sartre taught philosophy after his military service.

La Nausée describes the *nausea* experienced by Roquentin as he contemplates himself and Bouville, and finally explains the reasons for it.

Roquentin – thirty, a bourgeois with red hair, some money of his own and a mistress, Anny, in Paris – is writing the life of the Marquis de Rollebon, a native of Bouville who went into exile in 1789, travelled in Russia and became a secret agent of the Tsar; a smuggler, spy and assassin, he was eventually imprisoned on a charge of treason by Louis XVIII and he died before being brought to trial. Roquentin works in the town library, where he encounters 'the Autodidact' Ogier P—, a bailiff's clerk who is building up his knowledge by working his way alphabetically through all the books. Roquentin is bored with the Marquis and feels that he would like to write a novel rather than a biography – for 'nothing can ever be proved' and the characters in a novel would appear more realistic or at least more amusing. He suffers from 'that filthy thing, the Nausea'. He goes to a café owned by a woman with whom he casually goes to bed when he feels like it: this time 'I had come along for a fuck' – but the *patronne* is out shopping. 'I felt a sharp disappointment in my prick ... the Nausea seized me ... I wanted to vomit.' He contemplates the mauve braces of the waiter, whose blue cotton shirt standing out 'cheerfully against a chocolate-coloured wall' also brings on the nausea. But he dissolves it by asking a waitress to play a record, 'Some of these days/You'll miss me honey!'

Roquentin's pointless, bored existence sickens him; the only 'purity' he can experience is 'empty'. Both he and the objects which surround him are absurd (in French the word suggests 'insufferability' as well as pointlessness), contingent, superfluous (*de trop*). There is no logical justification for existence, and the citizens of Bouville who attempt to justify their lives are *salauds* ('swine', 'filthy stinkers', 'bastards') – a key word in Sartre:

Everything is gratuitous, that park, this town, and myself ... that is what the Bastards [*salauds*] ... try to hide from themselves with their idea of rights ... nobody has any rights; they are entirely gratuitous, like other men, they cannot succeed in not feeling superfluous ... secretly, they *are superfluous* ... amorphous and vague, sad.

Roquentin only gradually becomes aware of the reasons for his nausea. A fair proportion of the novel, which is never solemn, is devoted to brilliantly comic satire of provincial life: the Autodidact (who has foul breath), the bronze statue of the town's celebrity, Impétraz – a school inspector who painted and also wrote three books, among them *Popularity among the Ancient Greeks* (1887) – the Bouville citizenry's Sunday perambulation, the tour of the museum. Roquentin's dreams are irreverently comic: he and two soldiers spank Maurice Barrès on the bare bottom; he shouts to the park-keeper, 'This park smells of vomit!'

With increasing acrimony, aggression and vehemence (sometimes bitterly humorous) Roquentin rejects the prevailing code. No one understands him. When he tells the Autodidact in the course of a long conversation over lunch that there is absolutely no reason for existing, the latter tells him that a few years ago he has read a book by an American called *Is Life Worth Living?* in which the author had come to an optimistic conclusion. And then there are 'people', he is reminded; but at this stage Roquentin is not a humanist (although Sartre himself was later to write a book claiming that existentialism is humanist). Left-wing humanists want to preserve human values, he sneers to himself. They are widowers with beautiful eyes who weep at anniversaries and love the higher animals. All the humanists are locked up in the Autodidact, 'tearing one another to pieces without his noticing it'. He is infuriated when the Autodidact insists that he must write 'for someone'. As the Autodidact goes on nagging him about loving people he has a 'really bad attack' of the nausea. He now thinks he knows what it is: 'I know: I exist – the world exists – and I know that the world exists. That's all. But I don't care.' His not caring frightens him. He flees the restaurant, thinking that the people still in there saw a crab 'escaping backwards from that all too human room'. During this attack things alarmingly break free from their names; words become useless, ridiculous.

Roquentin goes to the park and suddenly the 'veil is torn away'. Now he sees that the nausea *is* him; he can stand it more easily. The occasion of his insight is his contemplation (famous in post-war literature) of the root of a chestnut tree. Up until now he supposes that he has looked at objects as *appurtenances*: he would have said that existence was nothing, 'an empty form which added itself to external things'; the individuality of things was a veneer. Now this veneer is stripped away: 'leaving soft, monstrous masses, in disorder – naked, with a frightening, obscene nakedness.' And so the 'word Absurdity is now born beneath my pen'. The root is beyond explanation because it is individual: it is, amazingly, itself – just as was the pebble he picked up on the beach, or the Auto-didact's hand which he touched and thought of as a 'fat maggot', which it was not. Roquentin is in 'horrible ecstasy', 'possessing' his nausea, because he understands that the world, though it exists, 'lets itself be encountered' and cannot be *deduced*. It is 'absolute, and consequently perfect gratuitousness'. He wants to get rid of the 'sticky dirt' or 'tons and tons of existence', but is trapped in its contingency. Faced with this he decides to stop writing his book and go permanently to Paris. Meanwhile he visits his mistress Anny in Paris. She laughs at him and he feels false. They discuss their relationship, and Anny, who has been an actress, tries to explain what she means by 'privileged situations' such as being a king, going to look at your dead father, or making love. She had once felt (she explains) that her duty was to transform 'privileged situations' into 'perfect moments'. When she first kissed him, Anny tells Roquentin, her dress had been hitched up and her thighs covered with nettle stings; but it was 'necessary not to suffer' because the kiss (though she felt no desire) was 'an engagement, a pact': stoicism was not enough.

But now she is disillusioned: there are no 'privileged situations'. Roquentin, who records that he loves her, believes that she now feels as he does: he tells her of his 'adventures'. But she is not happy. He mentions the rag-time song which dissolved his nausea, and wonders 'if we couldn't find something in that direction, or at least look for it'. She is not very interested in what he is saying; but despite the lack of communication her own train of thought is similar, for she speaks of pictures and statues as not being of use: of use, we must infer, in the overcoming of nausea. Her project is to 'outlive herself': she states this twice. As an actress she has obtained 'perfect moments', but only for other people. She finds Loyola's *Spiritual Exercises* useful. He leaves, having failed, as she puts it, to 'find' her. She has said she is leaving for England with another man on the next evening. Roquentin spies on her at the station: he sees her, with the man and she sees him, 'with expressionless eyes'. He returns to Bouville, reflecting that he is afraid of towns, but 'you mustn't leave them', for outside them is Vegetation, a 'great mass of hair' threatening to engulf everything.

Back at Bouville he feels free, and therefore peculiar. He has no reason to live: Rollebon is dead; his past is dead; Anny has taken away all hope from him; he is 'alone and free' but 'this freedom is rather like death'. He has learned that 'you lose'; only the *salauds* 'think they win'. His thoughts move to the *salauds*: everything for them obeys fixed laws, tomorrow is just another today.

For him laws may change, and he wishes that they would for the others too: a child's cheek may crack to reveal a laughing third eye, clothes may suddenly come alive, a man may go to his comfortable bed and wake 'naked on a bluish patch of earth, in a forest of rustling pricks'. Then they will be plunged into solitude and horror, and he will shout 'Where is your dignity as a thinking reed?'

On his last day in Bouville he searches for the Autodidact. He goes to the library. The Autodidact enters, as do two boys. The Autodidact comes up to speak to them. He begins to stroke the hand of one of the boys. The Corsican librarian spots him, inveighs against him, and punches him with 'a little whine of pleasure'. His nose begins to 'piss blood'. Roquentin angrily grasps the Corsican and holds him up in the air. The Autodidact leaves, refusing his offers of help.

Roquentin again feels his existence as a 'consciousness of being superfluous'; but he thinks of the Autodidact, weeping, bleeding, bent, walking through a ferocious town which has not forgotten him, a gentle and hunted soul saying to himself 'Oh, God, if only I hadn't done that, if only I could not have done that, if only it could not be true!' He wonders what he will do in Paris and feels sorry for himself. He is in the café with whose *patronne* he sometimes goes to bed. He thinks he is going to have an attack of the nausea. But the waitress puts on the jazz record of 'Some of These Days': 'I myself am going to leave ... behind the existence which falls from one present to the next, without a past, without a future, behind these sounds which decompose from day to day, peels away and slips towards death, the melody stays the same, young and firm, like a pitiless witness'. He thinks of the 'Jew with coal-black eyebrows' who wrote the tune and asks himself why it could not have been he who was 'chosen so that the miracle could be performed' instead of that 'fat lout full of stale beer and spirits'. He asks for

the record to be played again, finding himself moved by
the sufferings of the composer, who had bills to pay and
perhaps woman trouble – the first time for years that he
has felt sympathy for another man. No one, he reflects,
can think of him as he thinks of the composer: 'gently.'

'So can you justify your existence? Just a little? I feel
extraordinarily intimidated.' He considers by what creative act he might justify his own life, so that men will
think 'gently' of him. He cannot write songs: it would
have to be a book. But not a history book: 'history talks
about what has existed – an existent can never justify the
existence of another existent.' The book he writes will
have to be 'beautiful and hard as steel and make people
ashamed of their existence'. The readers would think of
him as something 'precious and almost legendary'. Perhaps one day he'll be able to remember: on 'that day ...
it all started'. He might succeed in accepting himself. Tomorrow, he thinks, 'it will rain in Bouville.'

CRITICAL COMMENTARY Sartre has become a polemicist
who 'justifies his existence' by 'involvement'. But *La
Nausée*, a great novel – and a great comic one at that – is
first of all a work of imagination; only secondarily is it
'philosophy'. Much of it strikes a familiar note; but this is
not only because of the post-war vogue for Sartrian existentialism. It is also because it perfectly captures the spirit
of sensitive youthful rebellion. Roquentin's nausea, a
floating feeling of *anxiety* which abstracts from *every*
object (fear, on the contrary, is directed to one particular
object), was not philosophical. Only later did Sartre seek
to systemize it into a kind of category. In view of all we
know of Sartre, however, we must approach *La Nausée*
first from the philosophical point of view.

The message of the German philosopher Husserl, the
founder of the movement called *phenomenology* was
Back to the things themselves! Sartre objects to what he
calls the tradition of 'subjective idealism' in French philo-

sophy. Descartes doubted whether the objects he perceived, including his own body, existed; but his own doubting was 'immune from doubt'; therefore he was *thinking* – his reflections presupposed his existence; *cogito ergo sum*. If he was a thinking being, then – he argued – he must be a substance whose essential attribute is thought.

Sartre calls this a strategy of self-deception: it involves the false notion that a self-reflectively realized consciousness is immune to deception. For Sartre the immediate, pre-reflexive experience of things is primary. The contingency of which we hear so much in *La Nausée* cannot be rationalized as disguised necessity; but, as one may fairly put it, since Sartre (like Roquentin) yearns for grounds for necessity, contingent existence is obscene. Sartre was excited by Husserl's original project of 'going back to the things'. Husserl believed that the mind was 'intentionalist': *directed to an object*. However, that 'object' might be hell fire or a flat earth; such notions achieve equal status with mauve neckties or roots – and for the very good reason that they are as 'real' to the mind. Rejecting both a search for the 'reality behind appearances' and a 'cause–effect' philosophy, Husserl claimed for immediate pre-reflective recognition the status of *fundamental* knowledge. But because he wished boldly to see things as they actually are, he was forced to 'bracket', suspend his judgement about the actual world. This process is called the 'phenomenological reduction', or *epoché*. He then argues that consciousness has a unique 'being of its own': since it is intentionalist it is full of 'immanent acts'. From there we can return to the actual world: we now consider 'real' objects as they depend on, 'declare themselves' to, consciousness, which is the one absolute – a 'transcendental ego'. A Husserlian investigation into the sociology of religion would lead (hopefully) to an account of its *structure in consciousness*: this is, philosophically, idealist.

Sartre was fascinated by the *epoché*, but violently rejected it as yet another form of self-deception. Accepting the intentionalist nature of consciousness, he claims that self-consciousness is not a consciousness of pre-reflective consciousness, but of the 'intentional object': in other words – and this explains how Roquentin feels – self-consciousness is a trick. It leads us to believe that something – anything – in the self enjoys a higher status than the objects of its contemplation. But the self, and all selves ('mankind'), are as gratuitous as the object – all objects; this Roquentin realizes when he contemplates the root of the chestnut tree. Hence the nausea. In much simpler terms: we are no more important than litter; we are not important at all. *La Nausée* reflects Sartre's refutation – heroic in terms of his temperament – of the 'privileged status of the self'. As Robert Cumming has put it: nausea is the true protagonist; the 'discrepancy between the necessary structure of the story as told (as a work of art) and the sense of ... the indeterminacy of the future'. Self-consciousness: 'obscures by its loquacity' this discrepancy. Proust had, *à la* Husserl, 'finished' *his* novel within his novel (invented a 'transcendental ego'); it is important that Roquentin does not finish his within his. The use of the lyric 'Some of These Days' as an analogue for Roquentin's future novel parodies – with deliberate coarseness – Proust's use of music: in one celebrated passage Marcel hears the septet by the composer Vinteuil as 'ineffable' and as a call away from emptiness.

Cumming has also pointed out that Sartre in *La Nausée* wants to dispose of the traditional analogy between thinking and seeing: 'visual consciousness ... encourages reflection to undermine the real world by "bracketing" the thing as it really exists.' Sight, Roquentin thinks as he looks at the root, 'is an abstract invention, a cleaned-up, simplified idea, a human idea'. To *touch* something – as Roquentin is frequently doing – is not so passive: it is an action, and it more clearly reveals the solid resistant weight of objects on the toucher.

Roquentin gives up history when he realizes that behind the past (which he once thought of as full of 'honor-
ary events') as in boxes, 'there is nothing'. There is some
hope for him because now he understands that people's
'nature' consists of no more and no less than their choice
of a future. We can seek rest in false stability (like *les
salauds*) or exercise our absolute freedom by, in Sartre's
words, 'putting [our own] past[s] out of action by secret-
ing [our] own nothingness'. We create our own necessity.

We have seen Roquentin as philosophical being. What
of him as a character in fiction? True, Sartre already rejects the traditional novel's insistence on characters whose
actions can be 'explained'. In this sense *La Nausée* is an
anti-novel. But he has (as he always does) disrupted his
own project by telling a story; and he has created a character. At the very least he has shown us the phenomenological structure of Roquentin's intentionality. But this
is not the book of a *philosopher as novelist*. It is the first,
and last complete, novel by a novelist who subsequently
turned into a philosopher; and it is about a man who
thinks he is an historian but discovers that he wants to be
a novelist. We shall never know if Roquentin too became
a philosopher. Sartre tells us that he 'was' Roquentin,
and we know that he has several things in common with
him: his Anny is like a girl Sartre knew in Paris; he lives
in a town like Le Havre; his imaginings are similar to
hallucinations suffered by Sartre after a dose of mescalin
(he saw crabs and polyps, and was followed by a gigantic
lobster in Venice; a most endearing story). Yet we are not
told that Sartre's *La Nausée* is Roquentin's novel; it can
hardly be. Sartre's imagination here, in the main comic,
has sufficient power of empathy to create a character different from himself: one whose choice might have been
(as Sartre's was not) to be a novelist. This is another
reason why we never see his novel – and why we must not
take *La Nausée* to be it. All we have is a diary he (pre-

sumably) left behind him in Bouville: not worth taking. Did Sartre sense within himself the future corruption of a novelist, and the generation of a philosopher? Or was he contemptuous of *La Nausée* and hopeful of producing something better? He spoke disparagingly of it for many years – not as weighty as a baby starved to death, he said; only now does he recognize it as his best work.

Whatever Sartre's intentions, *La Nausée* amounts to a *story*, the unerringly convincing story of a man who feels nauseated by all the objects with which he is surrounded, including his own body (his own hand often seems like a crab), but whose aggressive attitude to *les salauds* is furiously energetic and therefore creative. And it is here that the story slips away from the philosophy. For Roquentin possesses empathy as well as energy. He can identify with the composer and the singer of 'Some of These Days' and, in particular, with the wretched Autodidact. This feeling, which is indubitably necessary to the creation of a novel, is in no way justified by the Sartrian philosophy of that period – or indeed by Roquentin's nihilism. The Autodidact, it will seem to those familiar with Sartre's thinking, has been 'set up' throughout the novel as a typically Sartrian example of self-deception and bad faith, a grotesquely unauthentic scholar. But if he is a 'farcical creature' then the last we see of him is by no means farcical. Some readers seem to think his pederasty is but one more dimension of his ridiculousness. On the contrary: there is genuine compassion in the description of his misfortune. Those who angrily mutter platitudes at him are now less dignified than he is – in his dejection. 'People' do after all count for Roquentin: he picks up the loathsome Corsican – whose only feeling is pleasure at being able to express conventional moral indignation. There is a mellowness in Sartre's treatment of this episode, as there is in the sadness of Roquentin at not being able to communicate with Anny.

The other great quality of the novel is its salutory humour. That we are not important, that our seriousness is absurd, that our solemn projects to benefit society or to perform public services are no more than elaborate systems of self-deception, that we have no rights and no dignity: such insights are not only comic but joyful to attain: a release from cant; a hopeful state of mind. *La Nausée*, in its boisterous explosion of the pretensions of 'good citizens' and 'patriots', and its brilliant psychological analysis of that feeling of gratuitousness, known to many of us at some time or another, does for our time what Flaubert did for his. However much we may have come to disagree with Sartre, we cannot deny that here he prepares the way for something better than the kind of public life we are so preposterously expected to share by *les salauds*.

BIBLIOGRAPHY

Translations: L. Alexander, *The Diary of Antoine Roquentin*, 1949; R. Baldich, *Nausea*, 1965.

Text: *La Nausée*, 1938.

Criticism: P. Thudy, *Sartre*, 1960; C. Audry, *Sartre*, 1966; A. Stern, *Sartre*, 1967.

Hermann Hesse

Hermann Hesse was born in 1877, in Calw (Württemberg). His parents were Pietists with experience of missionary work in the East. He was an unruly boy, quite uncontrollable: he was sent to various schools, and vacillated between various jobs (clockmaker's apprentice, bookseller) before settling down; but he always read voraciously. After producing some competent, derivative writing in the post-romantic style of the period he achieved success with the novel *Peter Camenzind* (1904). He married, had three sons, and appeared to have found tranquillity. But the outbreak of the war and his wife's mental illness exposed the nerve of restlessness within him (already, in 1911, he had made a journey to the East); in *Rosshalde* (1914) he directly poses the problem of whether an artist should marry – and he comes down against marriage. He violently opposed the war – thus losing his popularity with the German public – and went to Switzerland. The next years were ones of crisis. He fell under the influence of one of Jung's disciples and was analysed; he felt he owed much to this experience, but did not believe that psychoanalysis alone could solve human problems.

In 1919 he published the novel *Demian* under the pseudonym of Emil Sinclair, its narrator. Once again he gained the attention of the German public, especially of the young. Later he acknowledged his authorship. In 1923 he became a Swiss citizen. He was still restless (in 1924 he made a brief, disastrous new marriage; he married again in 1931), and the culmination of this period is the 'crisis' or *Zerrissenheit* novel, *Der Steppenwolf* (1927), which was not a critical success at the time. He had in the meanwhile been prolific: writing essays, tales, poetry, novellas and the novel *Siddhartha* (1922). Soon after the beginning of the 1930s he began work on what is generally regarded as his masterpiece, *Das Glasperlenspiel* [*The Glass Bead Game*]; it was published in 1943. In 1946 he received the Nobel Prize. Although he wrote stories, poetry and many letters after this, he remained in seclusion in rural Switzerland (Montagnola) behind a notice requesting 'No Visitors Please'. He died in 1962, not long after his eighty-fifth birthday. His work has remained immensely popular all over the world, especially with the young.

The Glass Bead Game

SUMMARY The bulk of *The Glass Bead Game* is ficticiously narrated by a meticulous historian of about the year 2400 A.D., with the full title: *A tentative sketch of the life of Magister Ludi Joseph Knecht together with Knecht's posthumous writings, edited by Hermann Hesse.* The period of which the historian writes is indeterminate: it is best taken as lying between our own time and 2400.

Castalia is an imagined province forming a separate part of an unnamed country. The narrator is himself a Castalian. In a long introduction it is explained that Castalia came into existence after our own age of artistic triviality and exhausting wars. A period of political consolidation is said to have followed (the details are vague, except that the focus of power has shifted from West to East). Castalia is an intellectual, élitist community, secular but not atheist, dedicated to artistic tradition, most particularly to music and mathematics. Nineteenth-century music is never mentioned; literature is pointedly omitted. The country encourages and supports the Castalian province. Some, called 'hospitants', are allowed to receive their education in Castalia, and then go back into the 'world'. Members of the Castalian order possess some authority over the educational system of the country. If the country represents the State, then Castalia represents Culture. A consciously conceived triad is completed by Religion, the Church, which is termed Roman Catholic, but which mysteriously seems more Pietistic than Roman Catholic in its ideals. The country is dotted with monasteries. Admission to the Castalian élite – to its school and then to the community at Waldzell – is by selection from the country's own schools; it depends on scholastic brilliance, a capacity for music and mathematics, and a certain ascetic cast of character. Amongst this élite, sensuality is sublimated by meditation; it is admitted that young Castalians can have sexual relationships but there is, rather curiously, no 'involvement'. The Order is exclusively male.

Its aspirations and ideals are summed up in the Glass Bead Game, which Hesse never fully describes. The game has some analogies with chess and with serious astrology. It is a kind of 'world language of intellectuals'; its subject matter is the relationship between seemingly randomly paired art forms (for example, Caesar's Latin and intervals in Byzantine hymn tunes) and it is played with beads strung on a frame. At times such content and techniques of the game evoke strong suspicions of authorial ironic mockery. It seems to be a kind of non-electronic computer devoted to the eternalizing or 'freezing' of the highest art forms: it is thus anti-historical, synchronous as distinct from diachronous. It is an 'approach to the spirit that is unified in itself beyond all images', and it seeks cerebral perfection and timelessness, a 'direct route into the interior of the cosmic mystery'; a 'single plant should be able to talk with Linnaeus in Latin [who classified plants]'.

The twelve central chapters are cast in the form of a traditional German *Bildungsroman*; but the narrator does not have all the facts at his disposal. The end of the story is 'legend'. There are four appendices: the poems the protagonist Joseph Knecht wrote (against the rules) as a student, and three tales which he wrote as exercises in the same period of his life.

The events in themselves are of the simplest. Joseph Knecht (*Knecht* means 'servant'), of unknown parentage, is selected by the Old Music Master, a Castalian, as a suitable candidate for the Order. He goes to the school at Eschholz and thence to Waldzell where his abilities soon become the object of attention both to the Magister Ludi (Master of the Games: the most important post in the hierarchy, though not invested with more authority than the president and council) and to his fellow students. He makes three particular friends, one of whom is the 'hospitant' Plinio Designori who is fascinated by the ideals of the 'Pedagogic Province' but none the less mocks it as a 'priestly caste ... a pack of spoon-fed eunuchs'. Knecht disputes with him, and is acclaimed; but he admits to the then Magister Ludi, Thomas von der Trave (a somewhat malicious allusion to Hesse's admirer and friend Thomas Mann, hinting that he is a 'master of travesty'), that he has some sympathy with Designori's position. Yet despite his doubts, poems and exercises, Knecht devotes himself to the game. At the age of thirty-four he is sent to the Catholic monastery of Mariafels for the purpose of helping to improve the relationship between Castalia and the Church. He succeeds in this task to the extent that the narrator gives him credit for helping to establish a *détente* that 'still' exists. He also meets Father Jacobus, a portrait of the cultural historian Jacob Burckhardt whose relativist ideas influenced Hesse in 1899 and then more powerfully during the Nazi era. The Father is friendly but anti-Castalian: 'You ... have distilled a kind of world history to suit your own tastes ... To study history means submitting to chaos and nevertheless retaining faith in order and meaning. It is a very serious task ... and possibly a tragic one.' The old music master and Jacobus are two of Knecht's teachers; the third is an enigmatic Chinese scholar, Elder Brother, who lives in isolation in the Bamboo Grove, speaks little, and devotes himself to study of the *I Ching*; he is clearly intended as an ironic portrait of Hesse himself. Before he visits Mariafels Elder Brother grants Knecht the rare privilege of spending time with him.

On his return to Waldzell Knecht is given first prize in the annual Glass Bead Game; Magister Thomas dies and he is elected Magister Ludi (the youngest in Castalian history).

But after less than a decade in office Knecht decides to leave his post for 'the world'. His wish is to be an educator of (servant to) young boys. To the council and president of the Order – who, as he has known all along, will refuse his request and force him to depart without their approval – he explains that Castalia is in danger: because of its élitism, he says in effect, its value will be lost, for there will be eras in the future when it will no longer exist. 'The average Castalian ... does not regard [the unscholarly man] as a brother ... Most of us ... lack ... respect for history. We fail to do it justice.'

Meanwhile Plinio Designori, who has succeeded in 'the world', has none the less decided that he was wrong in his former attitude to Castalia. His marriage is not satisfactory and he has trouble with his rebellious son Tito. Knecht helps Designori in his personal conflicts, and arranges to become Tito's tutor.

Tito has gone to a house by a mountainous lake; Knecht follows him there. That night he feels ill, unable to control his heartbeats. The next morning he goes out to the lakeside; Tito performs a strange pagan dance, and then challenges Knecht to a race across the lake. He plunges in. Knecht follows him; but the water is icy, and he drowns. Tito feels guilt and responsibility. This is 'the legend', written perhaps by 'some of his favourite students'.

The appended thirteen poems of Knecht express his divided soul. Of the three biographies the first is of a rainmaker (called Knecht) in a primitive community who has to sacrifice his life when he fails in his task. The second concerns a patristic Christian, Josephus, who finds fulfilment by seeking out and learning from another desert 'confessor' – who turns out to have been seeking him out to learn from him. The third tells of Dasa, an Indian prince who, deprived of his royal rights, 'dreams' a whole life of lurid experience only to learn that all has been *maya*: illusion.

CRITICAL COMMENTARY The fiction of Hesse deliberately lends itself to over-ingenious exegesis. A hostile critic might, indeed, make a convincing claim that all his work is reducible to literary history, philosophy and symbolic, quasi-Jungian autobiography. He was a master of pastiche; and though a private and good-hearted man, was also ironic and cunning. There are a number of conflicting opinions about the meaning of his work. The question of his gifts is not in doubt. The question of whether the 'strange and haunted old man ever learned anything worth knowing' (James Wright, translator of Hesse's lucid poems) remains open.

Although Hesse detested much in the German personality – and even tried to escape from it by becoming a Swiss – he is none the less quintessentially German. His work is full of highly conscious oppositions of such concepts as *Natur* and *Geist* (approximately, 'spirit'), or *Geist* and *Seele* (approximately, in this context, 'sensuality plus responsible acceptance of its existence') and so on.

Hesse's main preoccupations, which run throughout his work, are not difficult to grasp (though they have been made to seem so). His fundamental problem is commonplace. It has been well stated by Emerson: 'The human mind stands ever in perplexity, demanding intellect, demanding sanctity, impatient of each without the other.' Hesse's works before *Demian* demonstrate great gifts; but they are not of a major calibre. It was during the First World War that he began to devise, or to try to devise, solutions. He was influenced by Nietzsche, especially by his pronouncement that 'God is dead', by Burckhardt, by mystical, eclectic Christianity, by Buddhism, by Hölderlin (also from Württemberg), by Goethe, Schiller and German romantics such as Jean Paul (1763–1825) and Novalis (1772–1801) – to whom he owed stylistic debts. His mature novels explore the possibility of the *rebirth* through *awakening* of men (or Man). The relevance of such a notion, whether it be at a political or theological level, is not in question. But the way in which it is presented is in question. Did Hesse state it usefully? It must be conceded that in *Der Steppenwolf* he succeeded in posing the problem in a powerful and convincing manner. Many believe it to be his best novel. Others, convinced that such systems as Jung's are meaningful, find Hesse meaningful; his novels are often interpreted in Jungian terms – for example, the drowning of Knecht has been seen as reflecting the 'Jungian primordial matrix of life'. *Steppenwolf*, his most original and yet a desperate novel, is the least derivative. 'If man can look into the mirror of his own self and laugh at the image, ie, not take himself seriously, then he can enter this magic theatre, this "picture gallery of his soul". There, set free from time, reality and space he will find a multiplicity of souls' (Eva J. Engel). By the time of *The Glass Bead Game* Steppenwolf's Magic Theatre (itself a variation on the theatre in *Wilhelm Meister*) is being described by the Castalian narrator as a particular phenomenon of our own century – the presentation of which, in the long introductory section, is as quietly satirical and shrewd as anything in Hesse's writing.

To take *The Glass Bead Game* – despite its undeniable readability, fascination and limpid prose style – as a satisfactory book it is necessary first to grant that the special category of *lyrical novel* exists and is viable, and secondly to accept 'transcendental' explanations of its meaning.

The *lyrical novel*, a useful category, is a product of late romanticism: the 'tendency to telescope poetry and narrative in the novel'. It offers a writer special means of exploring the relationship between the inner life and the external world. The lyrical novel has always, writes Ralph Freedman (its expositor), 'suffered from a certain anemia ... underemphasis on character ... overemphasis on image, dream-like encounter, or allegory ... [but] at its best [it] can be a voyage of discovery on to a strange subterranean sea in ... the lyrical mood ...' What is 'discovered' by Hesse?

The mood of *The Glass Bead Game*, written at the time of the Nazi ascendancy and deeply affected by it, is, as it were, anti-*Zerrissenheit*: it deliberately elevates themes of personal anguish to metaphorical – some would say symbolic – heights. Hesse, though insisting upon the necessity of story telling gifts (which he had in abundance), had no interest in psychology. Knecht cannot be interpreted as anything but an *allegorical* figure: his sublimation of his sexual instincts by meditation and by his ideal of humble service (a key motif in Hesse) is simply taken for granted. Women – apart from Designori's sketchily drawn wife, the 'tribal mothers' of the rainmaker story, and Dasa's wife – are entirely absent. This omission is odd. Why are there no women in the Castalian Order? After all, one of Hesse's earlier themes had been the need for 'the mothers'. Was this simply an artful Jungian rationalization of an essentially patriarchal attitude? The exclusively masculine ambience of this novel generates a sense of disturbance which can be diminished only by the postulation of the existence in it of various 'feminine symbols' of a mystical kind.

It is, basically, an expression of three hardly unfamiliar problems: that individual fulfilment vitiates social obligation, or vice versa; that perfect art itself eventually becomes imperfect through lack of contact with or contempt for the imperfect, 'bestial' 'world' (in *Steppenwolf* half of the protagonist Harry Haller is a 'wolf'); that 'rebirth' is necessary. The most common view taken of the story of Knecht's defection from Castalia and his later death is that it is exemplary: '... the true beneficiary of Knecht's death is not Tito ... the later Castalia ... is one that has profited from Knecht's criticism and ... example; it is far removed from pure aestheticism, a realm of Culture that exists in a tension of interaction with State and Religion' (Theodore Ziolkowski). His death is a paradigm of 'service': 'he leaves behind a Tito for whom this sacrificial death of a man vastly superior to him will remain forever an admonition and an example' (Hesse himself, in a letter of 1947).

Since the novel is so accomplished and fascinating, there must be merit in such a view. Its expression of basic problems has undeniable beauty. But Hesse's own opinion of the meaning of Knecht's death amounts to no more than a personal claim, made in an ironic mood; is this justified by the text he produced? Many readers find hardly a hint of this 'improved' Castalia in the narrative. Careful attention to the account of Knecht's drowning suggests that it is either a stupid waste, the indulgence of a boy's thoughtless whim, or that it is a pretentious trick: an embarrassingly symbolic escape from answering a question Hesse could not answer. Certainly the description of Tito's rapturous dance 'under the sign of Pan' is embarrassing, and only those who inflate Hesse's philosophical achievements, as is a common habit, could find it otherwise.

In contrast Stephen Koch wrote of Hesse that his 'thought is irretrievably adolescent ... in his chosen role of artist of ideas, he is invariably second-rate'. But he adds: 'he is never *less* than second-rate ... never cheap, never trashy.' Although his ideas are 'derivative, schoolboyish ... boringly correct', although in 'book after book, the Great Ideas [chase] the Terrific Experiences home to their all too-obvious destinations', yet his 'aesthetic sense is different and better than this; it does transform itself into "something else", as the kids say.' This, quoted approvingly by James Wright in the introduction to his selection of translations from Hesse's poems of homesickness (*Poems*, 1970), represents a reasonable compromise – and it accounts, without unnecessary patronage, for Hesse's continuing appeal to the young.

Thus for some readers the best feature in *The Glass Bead Game* are Knecht's poems: here a true tension, a true dialectic, is maintained – and there is no strained attempt to arrive at a solution. But as Koch has implied this work is, at the least, on a very high *aesthetic* level. Those to whom Jungian-type 'solutions', such as 'individuation', appeal may find the work full of meaning – inevitably of a 'higher' sort. Others, painfully unable like Hesse except perhaps in his role of 'adolescent', erudite 'thinker') to resolve their tensions will undoubtedly appreciate the aesthetic necessity of the whole context, but will reserve the greatest admiration for the poems (and, possibly, for the tales).

BIBLIOGRAPHY
Translations: M. Savill, *Magister Ludi*, 1949; R. and C. Winston, *The Glass Bead Game* (1960), 1972.

Text: in *Gesammalte Schriften*, 1957.

Criticism: in R. Freedman, *The Lyrical Novel*, 1963; T. Ziolkowski, *The Novels of Hermann Hesse*, 1965 and *Hermann Hesse*, 1966.

Thomas Mann

Thomas Mann was born in Lübeck in 1875. His elder brother Heinrich Mann (1871–1950) was also a celebrated writer. Mann's father was a wealthy grain merchant and a senator of Lübeck; his mother was German-Brazilian, born in Brazil. In 1891 his father died, and two years later Mann went to Munich, where he lived – with some interruptions – until 1933. He started writing at school and published some stories. *Buddenbrooks* (1901), a long novel describing the decay of a German merchant family, brought him popular success, and is regarded by some as his greatest achievement. In 1905 he made a marriage which turned out to be remarkably happy. He supported the German cause, and militarism, in the First World War, but thereafter became more liberal in his views; he resisted the rise of the Nazis, and went into exile when they gained power. In 1912 he published *Der Tod in Venedig* [*Death in Venice*], and in 1924 *Der Zauberberg* [*The Magic Mountain*]. In 1929 he received the Nobel Prize. From 1933 until 1938 he lived near Zürich; he spent the next fourteen years in America, and acquired American citizenship in 1944. The *Joseph* tetralogy appeared 1933–43; *Doktor Faustus* in 1947; *Der Erwählte* [*The Holy Sinner*] in 1951; an expanded fragment of 1911, *Die Bekenntnisse des Hochstaplers Felix Krull* [*The Confessions of Felix Krull, Confidence Man*] appeared as the first volume of a novel in 1954.

Mann had been a public figure since the 1920s, and in America he became the natural leader of the German exiles there. He wrote at least a dozen volumes of political speeches, literary essays and studies. There are almost as many volumes of stories. While in America Mann attacked the Nazis so vehemently that he was accused of being not merely anti-Nazi but anti-German. He was much distressed by the attacks directed against him in Germany after the war, and felt compelled to issue a detailed polemical rebuttal in 1952. He left America in 1952 at least partly because the anti-communist hysteria worked up by Senator Joseph McCarthy reminded him of Nazism, and although he remained a liberal he advocated the tolerance of communism. After leaving America Mann settled in Switzerland, where he died in 1955.

Doktor Faustus

SUMMARY The garrulous narrator of *Doktor Faustus*, Serenus Zeitblom ('Serene Time-flower'), writes down the life story of his friend, the composer Adrian Leverkühn ('Livebold': an allusion to Nietzsche's famous dictum, *Live dangerously*), between 1943 and 1945. The events of his friend's life are thus paralleled by those of the latter phase of the Second World War. Zeitblom is a liberal humanist of Catholic origins who has given up his profession of teaching because of his hatred of the Nazi order, which intensifies as the narrative proceeds. He begins by disclaiming any artistic capability. The demonic is foreign to his nature, he tells us; and he doubts whether he is truly called to his present task. Yet he loved Leverkühn. His bookish, pedantic, humourless and slow style pervades his narrative which does not make it any easier to read. Details of his own life are not included except where relevant to those of Leverkühn's.

Adrian Leverkühn, born in 1885, has a Lutheran background; the town of his birth, Kaisersaschern, is full of associations with the Middle Ages. These are reinforced by the teaching he receives as a theology student in Halle from Kumpf – who is preoccupied with the devil and who uses Lutheran terminology – and from Schleppfuss ('Dragfoot': a devilish figure) – whose conception of God is demonic, and who declares 'the vicious to be a necessary ... concomitant of the holy'. Leverkühn – cold, distant, reserved – eventually decides to abandon theology for music. His teacher Wendall Kretzschmar (the spelling of his name, not preserved in the English translation, is an allusion to Nietzsche), an advanced analyst of Beethoven, is the chief influence here; but Leverkühn is terrified of the consequences of his decision. So is his mother. He studies under Kretzschmar in Leipzig, and finds a friend in the writer Rüdiger Schildknapp. He feels that 'almost all, no, all the methods and conventions of art today *are good for parody only*': all his compositions except the last are parodic.

Leverkühn writes a letter to Zeitblom telling him of how a guide (looking like Schleppfuss), really a pimp, took him to a Leipzig brothel where he met a prostitute called Esmeralda; he sat down at the piano, played a chord, and left. This letter is mostly pastiche of sixteenth-century Lutheran prose; quotations from the original *Faustbook* (1587) are incorporated in the text. We have met *hetaera esmeralda* before: as an exotic butterfly in the collection of Adrian's father. All Adrian's music is to be based on a note sequence derived from the phrase. One year later he seeks out this Esmeralda – now in Hungary – and despite her own warnings contracts syphilis from her. There is every reason to believe that this woman is none other than the rich Frau von Tolna who later turns up as Adrian's patroness and whom he never sees (as Tchaikovsky never saw Frau von Meck). This deliberate contracting of syphilis carries with it the suggestion of a pact with the devil – especially as it occurs twenty-four years before his collapse: twenty-four years was the time Mephistopheles gave Faust. However, Adrian tries to get his condition treated; but one doctor dies and the other is arrested (for reasons not given). Later Adrian goes to Italy where, during an attack of migraine, he discusses the possibility of a pact with a (presumably) hallucinatory, Lutheran devil. Leverkühn draws the devil's attention to the possibility of a salvation achieved by a 'sinfulness so graceless that it makes a man utterly despair of grace' (this is orthodox Lutheranism in the sense that no man can know salvation until he has felt himself to be damned). No formal pact is concluded, although the arrangement is ratified by Leverkühn. (The incident in which Leverkühn is taken to the brothel is from a book by Paul Deussen about Nietzsche, who is recorded as having had this experience in Cologne. The idea of deliberate self-infection is based on remarks made by Nietzsche after he went mad. There is no further evidence to support either story. But Nietzsche probably became insane as a result of syphilis.)

Leverkühn returns to Germany, to a farm near Munich. He succeeds with his music, but in his attempts to love he fails. He asks his friend the violinist Schwerdtfeger to woo Marie Godeau for him; but Schwerdtfeger goes off with her and is shot by a jealous woman, Innes Roddes, with whom both men have been involved. He loves his little nephew Nepomuk Schneidewein, but he dies of meningitis at the age of five. This event makes him wish to 'take back' Beethoven's Ninth Symphony: the 'good and noble ... what we call the human ... is not to be ... I will take it back.'

The artistic circles in Munich before the First World War and immediately after it are characterized; these are the most comic and satirical parts of the novel. Most of the characters have been identified. The Kridwiss circle of the 1920s is depicted as potentially fascist. Before his final collapse Leverkühn composes the symphonic cantata *The Lamentation of Dr Faustus,* 'fearful', 'cynical' and 'awful' – yet, according to Zeitblom, possibly redolent of a 'hope beyond hopelessness'. He summons his friends to hear some parts of it on the piano. He accuses himself – once again he uses archaic language – of the murders of Schwerdtfeger and Nepomuk, of incest with his sister (the only time this is ever mentioned), and of having made a pact with the devil. He then collapses into insanity, to be eventually cared for by his mother until his death ten years later in 1940. A 'veiled unknown' attends his funeral – Frau von Tolna?

CRITICAL COMMENTARY *Doktor Faustus* cost Mann more effort than any of his other novels; so much so that he wrote a book about it: *Die Entstehung des 'Doktor Faustus'* [translated as *Genesis of a Novel,* 1961] (1949). Mann stated that Zeitblom and Leverkühn are 'identical', but this is so difficult to accept at its face value that we must take it to mean that he intended to portray two main sides of himself as well as two sides of Germany. Leverkühn is not modelled on any single person. Mann drew on anecdotes about Hugo Wolf (who died mad) as well as Nietzsche; he certainly had some aspects of Mahler in mind; and the musical technique he uses is the dodecaphonic one systematized by Arnold Schoenberg (who was enraged by the book), as Mann eventually acknowledged in a note. There are three ingeniously counterpointed time levels: the sixteenth century, the age of Luther and of the Faust legend recorded in the *First Faustbook* of 1587 upon which *Doktor Faustus* draws; the lifetime of Leverkühn; and the time, 1943–5, in which Zeitblom is writing.

Usually taken to be a masterpiece and a successful portrait of a genius, *Doktor Faustus* is both an attempt to diagnose the sickness of Germany and to comment on the predicament of the modern artist. Music provides the link between Leverkühn and Germany. Music which frightened as well as attracted Mann, he saw as something irrational and degenerate. Germany also frightened him, and he conceived of it as having made a pact with the devil; having sold its soul in blood. The character of Adrian is above all concerned with 'break-through' (*Durchbruch*), which is a central theme. 'Whoever,' he asserts, 'succeeded in the break-through from intellectual coldness into a touch-and-go world of new feeling, him one should call the saviour of art.' And he adds that art will change and will become 'without anguish, psychologically healthy, not solemn, unsadly confiding, an art *per du* with humanity'. This is not at all like his final piece of music, which grieves Zeitblom; so, curiously, does his feeling about the future of art: what Adrian says he writes 'did not fit with' his 'arrogance': art 'is mind, and mind does not at all need to feel itself obligated to the community.' Yet Zeitblom feels like pressing Adrian's hand because he has shown feeling. It is somewhat confusing. For Adrian's 'break-through' is not into any warmth, but into a 'polyphonic objectivity', a rigidly mathematical type of music whose being is in a totalitarian world of strict rules. Germany also aspires to this condition, and has sold its soul for the gift of temporary domination over other countries. Adrian and Germany desired to make contact with others; but they chose a fascistic way to do this. As Zeitblom records Adrian's final collapse Germany is being overrun by its enemies; and in the last sentence he asks for God's mercy for Leverkühn's soul and the fatherland.

But Adrian is also the modern artist who seeks isolation, accepting the 'absurdity' of existence and seeking, Nietzsche-like, to conquer it by discovering originality – he may even achieve this in his music. Mann always connected artistic inspiration with disease, and this is presumably why Adrian infects himself with syphilis: his music will be heightened by his secret terror of madness and his enforced solitude.

Leverkühn is often seen, as by Andrew White, as the Lutheran 'elect sinner': 'Adrian *uses* parody as an artistic means to self-redemption and the redemption of art.' He extends 'the kingdom of the banal', and the last cantata is (for White) what Zeitblom fumblingly calls it, a 'transcendence of despair – not betrayed to her, but the miracle that passes belief'. This approach ignores Zeitblom's ambivalence – it even ignores Mann's own deliberately ambivalent approach. It is true that the devil tells Adrian that future generations will gain health through the products of his illness; but if that is true and if, as so many critics assert, this devil is 'no liar', then why not represent the whole matter in a more positive light: as an heroic sacrifice?

Erich Heller, who better understands the difficulties inherent in accepting Mann as a great novelist, also believes in the final cantata: 'the Devil has done his work and granted a soul. The deepest feeling has found authentic expression.' This assumes that the reader, like Heller, is convinced of the musical greatness of *Lamentation* – although it does not exist.

Heller is perhaps on more solid ground when he draws special attention to the function of parody in *Doktor Faustus* and in Mann's own work: 'Having been deserted by the suffering God and His promise of redemption, agony no longer permits the lie of "meaning" with which the play of art molests and mocks it: only its "undistinguished and untransfigured expression" may still be permissible.' When the 'real thing' becomes impossible then only 'higher parody' is left; only the devil can help. For Heller the *Lamentation*, 'albeit on the margin of silence', does achieve the 'seemingly impossible'. Those who cannot hear this music, this subjective expression of 'final despair' conceived within a technically unbreakable, paradoxically objective framework, can only see *Doktor Faustus* as a fiercely negative work.

In his earliest phase Mann had been thoroughly deca-

dent (naturally enough), and under the spell of Schopenhauer's philosophy. Arthur Schopenhauer (1788–1860)
saw man's irrational will – his emotions and, in particular,
his sexual drives – as being more powerful than his intellect. Indeed, this *will* is beyond man: it is an anticipation of the blind, destructive Freudian Id. Life is
suffering; this can be mitigated, although only in part, by
art (and philosophic knowledge and compassion), which
involves understanding of the will (so that it may be renounced). Either the intellect is an unwitting instrument
of the will or, by use of its capacity to understand the will,
it can provide a limited solace. Schopenhauer hated
women, Jews, other philosophers – in fact most people; his
system is contradictory and very far from being meta-
physically sound; but he anticipated the pessimistic mood
of the mid-nineteenth century and lived to see his work
become famous. Mann the writer was intoxicated (as he
put it) with Schopenhauer because Schopenhauer's picture of the artist is one of a person who has the ecstatic
bravery to demonstrate that the only thing in which man
may have faith is *nothing*. There is something exciting
about imparting such a horrible truth to one's readers;
furthermore, Schopenrauer embodied his pessimism
with persuasive and often exquisite prose. Nietzsche, the
next influence on Mann, never challenged Schopenhauer's
basic belief; but he insisted on the necessity of man's
asserting his will – even in the face of nothing'. It is often
claimed that Mann outgrew Schopenhauer and came to
terms with (his idea of) Nietzsche. But, as an artist, did he?
Or are his fictions a series of disguised affirmations of
Schopenhauer's attitude? As a good citizen Mann sincerely
deplored the demonic irrationality of art; as an artist he
began by plunging himself into decadence and irrationality: he was divided. Did he later really resolve his conflicts, as is usually claimed? His liberal-humanist polemic
is not of a high quality, as has been noted by a number of

critics (such as Michael Hamburger). It is pompous, rhetorical, muddled and stilted; his admirers seldom choose to quote from it. It is not consistent and will not stand up to examination.

However, his fiction should, if his admirers are right, be a different matter. Either it should contain a refutation of his earlier, pre-*Buddenbrooks*, gleeful amorality and contempt for the weakness of compassion or decency, or it should embody an essentially negative vision (it is no argument against a negative vision, such as that 'human destiny is tragic' – words used by Mann himself in his anti-democratic phase– that it *is* negative).

There is a third possibility: that this writer was both unilluminating and self-indulgent; that he harnessed his undoubted intelligence and superb literary ability to the barren project of being both a respectable citizen (*Bürgher*) – though in bad faith – and a successful writer. The case for this has been put most persuasively by Ronald Gray, who writes of his need to express a ' "yes" and a "no" in rapid alternation'; of the key, in narcissistic self-indulgence, that he found to 'permanent self-enjoyment'. A careful reading of Mann reveals (to some) a vacillation between a creatively immature decadence – to contempt for decency on the grounds of its pointlessness – and a mechanical regard for conventional proprieties. It is not suggested that Mann was insincere in his perplexity; only that he was an illusionist whose own style (as apart from his ability as pasticheur and perpetrator of the purple passage) has been overrated; that, intelligently aware of profound conflicts, he was unable to resolve them profoundly.

As Gray writes, Aschenbach of the famous *Death in Venice* is a 'born deceiver', an ingratiating writer, a cheat whose style is 'supreme' only in the eyes of a bourgeoisie he despises – and he represents no writer unless it be Mann himself. His writing is calculated to impress his public by its 'deliberate imprint of mastery and classicizing style' (Mann's description of Aschenbach's writing). Is this not how most of Mann's adulators take him: as 'the wise master', impeccably liberal and noble? One cannot accuse Mann of lack of subtlety or unawareness – like his brother Heinrich, he was obsessed with the notion of the artist as confidence trickster. Perhaps one cannot accuse him of lack of artistic integrity: what is wrong in winking knowingly at the initiates as you subtly show contempt for mere admirers – as Gray demonstrates, by close analysis, he is doing even as early as *Buddenbrooks*? But one can accuse his admirers of overrating the degree of his accomplishment. If his nihilistic message was that ruthlessness is justified because there is no morality (arguably a misinterpretation of Nietzsche, even if Nietzsche is partly responsible for the misunderstanding) then he had no right to mislead his readers (by his liberal stance) into thinking that it was not. From the time when the Nazi threat became manifest Mann publicly opposed it; yet in his creative works he, as it were, contains it. And *Doktor Faustus* is the most confusedly ambivalent of all his novels. Taken as an indictment not merely of German music but also of Germany, it in fact contains and even sometimes glorifies the Nazi myth which it by declaration seeks to condemn. Its premise is that Adrian Leverkühn's disposal of his soul to an internal devil (for there is nothing supernatural involved, despite the pretentious implication that there is) is parallel to Germany's abandonment of itself to a raging psychopath. Yet the *Lamentation*, terrible though it may be, is a phoenix arisen from ashes – future people will gain riches from it, Leverkühn tells himself through his devil.

Leverkühn is still presented as a 'holy sinner', and as a much more interesting character than the fussy Zeitblom whose absolute incapacity for artistry – which he keeps emphasizing – throws his own artistry into bold relief. Zeitblom's general and conventional attitude of horror at what his friend has done is interrupted by bursts of specious admiration and conjecture of a positive kind, such as that in infecting himself Adrian may have been taking upon himself the burdens of a sickness shared by all. But in fact we are told nothing about why he infected himself. The question is evaded. Likewise, we cannot know if he is actually guilty of the crimes of which he accuses himself when he lapses into insanity. Did he plan Schwerdtfeger's death? Can we really seriously believe that a devilish venom in his eyes killed his nephew? He is as likely to have led a harmless life. As for his incest with his sister: Nietzsche thought that Cosima Wagner had brought him to the mental hospital and that she was his wife. Is there any more truth in Leverkühn's assertion? We are not informed. Zeitblom sees Leverkühn in his last years of sanity both as Christ-like *and* diabolical. Which is he? Both, or neither? Mann, although he plainly wants his reader to assume the existence of a colossal and absolute evil, actually continuously 'veers away' (Gray) from it. Are we, despite the use of the first *Faustbook* as source, dealing with diabolical matters at all? Or are we only being lured into thinking that we are? In this case – particularly because the word 'diabolical' is surely appropriate at least as a metaphor for Nazidom – *Doktor Faustus* is not only less sensational and less interesting than it seems: it carries within it a basic artistic *indifference* to Nazidom.

Mann tricks us, again, into the delusion that music can be described in words. He incorporates a quantity of tiresome technical discussion – much of it lifted from what his fellow exile Teodor Adorno, a composer and musicologist as well as literary critic and phenomenological analyst of totalitarianism, told him. He gives further credence to the reality of Leverkühn's music by having it performed by real conductors, such as Klemperer and Walter (also fellow exiles in America). It has been asked, with proper awe, why Mann did not himself

compose Leverkühn's music. The answer is that he was incapable of it – and that it is doubtful if he had more than
the haziest notion of what it sounded like. This music is a
disingenuous fiction. Certainly it could not have resembled Nietzsche's own rather charming but inexorably minor
music; nor could it, despite its serial nature, be anything
like that of Schoenberg (or of J. M. Hauer, an Austrian
composer who invented a twelve-tone method independ-
ently of Schoenberg, and probably a little before him).
One is tempted in fact to dismiss Zeitblom's description
of it as pretentious bosh – and to suggest that Mann knew
less about music than his discussions of it in *Doktor
Faustus* imply.

Zeitblom, having suggested that the *Lamentation* contains the seeds of hope (this is reinforced by the 'devil's'
promise to Leverkühn that his works will eventually provide health), ends by asking when there will be 'dawn' for
Germany, a 'miracle transcending faith, the light of hope'.
What does this mean? Is it simply bad thinking and bad
writing? What are we to make of Zeitblom's inconsistencies? He condemns evil, yet suggests that in it lies the
seed of good. A book which 'seems to be written in
condemnation of a whole tradition ... can also be read as
a seeming justification for the same tradition'. Gray suggests that this is 'horrible' and 'oppressive'. Mann had
every right to present the destiny of humanity as being
symbolized by Nazism, if that was the tragic conclusion
of his imagination. But one would then expect a sense of
tragedy to be present in the work – and for that sense to
be unequivocal. Instead we are confronted by a garrulous
bore of a narrator, a series of linguistically dead, pious
and platitudinous condemnations of evil, and a 'Faust'
who has no coherence as a personality but is rather a
concatenation of anecdotes, ideas, associations and symbols. Even Heller calls the novel 'stupendous' rather
than 'great'; and, if only as a piece of inspired playing to

the gallery by a man of impoverished imagination, it is indeed stupendous.

In *Doktor Faustus* the link between art and evil is sensationalized to the point of absurdity by the device of symbolizing it in terms of the basic equation Nazism = art. Not a single truly gifted German writer joined the Nazi party – not even the authoritarian militarist Ernst Jünger or the nihilistic Gottfried Benn. The parallel is strained; and that Mann should insist upon it – even appearing to find hope in it – is indicative of his own true stature as a writer. Leverkühn is an unconvincing puppet who tells us nothing about the origins of great music – because the great music he is supposed to have written does not exist. Heller and other critics, however, take a different view. The novel will continue to be discussed.

BIBLIOGRAPHY

Translation: H. T. Lowe Porter, *Doktor Faustus*, 1949.

Text: in *Gesammelte Werke*, 1956–60.

Criticism: H. Hatfield, *Thomas Mann*, 1951; E. Heller, *The Ironic German*, 1958; A. White, *Thomas Mann*, 1965; R. Gray in *The German Tradition in Literature 1871–1945*, 1965; L. Voss, *Die Entstehung von Thomas Manns Roman 'Doktor Faustus'*, 1975.

Cesare Pavese

Cesare Pavese, the son of a judiciary official, was born in 1908 on a farm in the rural Piedmontese region of Cuneo, south of Turin, the city where he was educated and where he spent almost all his life. His teacher was Augusto Monti, who influenced two generations of Torinese anti-fascists. He specialized in American literature and after graduating with a thesis on Whitman he began (about 1930) to write critical articles about him and make translations from him and other American writers. He was a noted translator of Melville, Faulkner, Twain, Defoe, Dickens and Joyce. Anglo-Saxon literature influenced him deeply, but he remained quintessentially Italian in his own work.

In 1935 he was imprisoned for 'anti-fascist activities', and spent some time on a lonely coastal island. After his release he went to work for the Milan publishing house, Einaudi, and stayed there as a valued editor for the rest of his life. His first book was of poetry, which he continued to write. His letters and diary are important; the latter has been translated as *This Business of Living* (1961). His major work, however, was in prose fiction; nearly all this has been translated.

Asthmatic, shy, wearer of pebble-lensed spectacles, sexually without confidence, Pavese failed dismally in his relations with women. He could be 'good friends' with them, but could not gain love from them – though he longed for it. But he understood women very well, and they liked him.

Towards the end of his life he formed a desperate habit of attaching himself to increasingly impossible love-objects: one of the last was an American film-star, now dead, who might have been invented by him for the purpose of rejecting his needs and hopes. Towards the end of 1950, at the peak of his fame and having just completed his masterpiece *La luna e i falò* [*The Moon and the Bonfires*] he checked in at a hotel in Turin, made a few telephone calls, and took a fatal overdose of sleeping pills.

Pavese's suicide was a traumatic event in the minds of most Italian intellectuals. There are a number of reasons for this. He was the leading young writer of Italy. He had become politically disillusioned, as his letters and diaries make clear: in a country that had been ravaged by fascism, this was a matter of importance to those who love freedom and are devoted to the notion of realizing their national character in democratic and peaceful ways. If this gifted man decided to kill himself then the outlook seemed to be confirmed as bleak (his prognosis has not proved altogether wrong). Further, his decision to end his life – he had been obsessed by suicide from childhood – brought up the agonizing questions of the personal price the writer has to pay for his art, and of what use are art and culture to life?

And yet *The Moon and the Bonfires* is the most perfect and comprehensive of his many fine novels. He uses it to resolve his problems as perfectly as he ever could have resolved them. It is a tragic novel – although no more without affirmatory qualities than is Verga's *I Malavoglia* – and it is possible that the ultimate factor in Pavese's decision was that he felt he had said all he had to say. Though he was not a Christian his dominant message is that life is not worth living unless it is lived for others. But there were larger reasons; among the last words of his diary are: 'All this is sickening.' Who but a bigot or politician could deny the force (if not necessarily the validity) of this judgement? So that, in a certain sense, Pavese's choice may be regarded as a part of his last novel, one of the greatest and widest in scope – short though it is – to be written in our time.

La luna e i falo ò
[The Moon and the Bonfires]

Pavese described *The Moon and the Bonfires* as the 'historical saga of [my] own time'. He weaves together many themes and makes use of many symbols – all of which are integrated into the story. The narrative convinces on a purely realistic level. Like *I Malavoglia*, whose influence Pavese's work reflects, the novel is organic in that the different parts, though functioning separately, also function together to create a living whole. No modern novel can surpass it in technical skill: it is of extreme complexity – its depth becomes apparent with each re-reading – and yet it appears simple. Indeed, ultimately, when the experience of reading it has been fully assimilated it has the virtues of simplicity.

The narrator, Anguilla (the word means 'eel': the eel travels back, in the face of great obstacles, to its birthplace – the subject of a well known poem by the Italian poet Eugene Montale), returns after the end of the Second World War from America, to which he had emigrated – indeed, escaped in desperation – twenty years before, to the mountain village in the Langhe hills where he was brought up. (There is a personal allusion here to Pavese's own 'escape' – as he saw it – into translation, mainly from the American, during the fascist era.) He returns as a comparatively rich man, and is referred to as 'American'. The main theme of the novel is that of the return to origins, the impulse to discover who one really is. It is of significance therefore that Anguilla, a bastard, does not know who his parents were, or indeed exactly where he was born – he was dumped on the steps of Alba Cathedral. He can only go back to where he grew up, fostered by a couple anxious for the money provided by the orphanage.

Most of the narrative is retrospective: Anguilla's reminiscences of his childhood and of his years in America, and his old friend Nuto's accounts of what has happened while he was away. Anguilla is trying to recapture his childhood and so discover himself; but he cannot do this, even though he can understand what is driving him – and he eventually leaves. In the crippled and undernourished boy Cinto he sees his earlier self. The bonfires of the title are those kindled at midsummer. They are the product of superstition, but Nuto tells Anguilla that the people are right to make them: 'They're awakening the earth.' Despite Anguilla's protests he affirms his belief in the moon: 'we must believe in the moon.' To understand, he tells Anguilla, he would have to 'become a countryman again'. This is Pavese's way of mourning the loss of simplicity.

Anguilla learns what has happened to the people he knew as a child. Some are still alive: the embittered farmer Valino, who can scarcely make a living from his parched land and who beats his sister-in-law, his dead wife's mother and his son Cinto – not because he is crippled but because of the 'utter misery and ... rage at his life which never gave him a break'. But Valino finally goes berserk: he kills the two women, burns down his farm, and hangs himself. Cinto survives.

Anguilla is most anxious of all to learn of the fate of Santa and Irene of La Mora, the large farm where he had worked twenty years earlier. What has happened to them is only gradually disclosed throughout the novel. Santa was only a child in Anguilla's childhood, but her two elder sisters Irene and Silvia had fascinated him with their nubility and their awe-inspiring, distancing superiority as the daughters of Sor Matteo, the owner ('They pissed, too,' he once told himself). When he recollects his sexual life in Genoa as a soldier, and then in America, it is by reference to the memory of those two. He never saw Santa (Santina) when she was grown up; but he comes to realize that the two elder girls 'weren't the prettiest after all ... [they] weren't peasants any more and they weren't real ladies, either. They didn't manage very well, poor things – that's how they died.' Both girls had a disastrous set of adventures with various men. Silvia became pregnant, had an abortion – and died of it before Anguilla left. Irene married a no-good, Arturo, who beat her. She too is dead. The book ends with Nuto's account of Santa's death. At twenty she had become beautiful. She had cheated both Partisans and Germans, and Nuto himself was there when she was shot by the Partisans. Her body was burned: 'You can't cover a woman like her with earth ... There are too many men who wanted her.' He describes the burning, ending, 'Last year the mark was still there, like the bed of a bonfire.'

CRITICAL COMMENTARY The four time settings of *The Moon and the Bonfires* – Anguilla's childhood, his history after that, the events in Italy in his absence (Nuto's 'time'), and the present – are deliberately intertwined. Pavese thus shows that though Anguilla seeks return he does not find it. This is a return that is no return. Gian-Paolo Biasin has drawn attention to a passage in Pavese's diary:

In life, there is no return. As the seasons come around, the passing years colour the same theme in ever-different ways. The beauty of our own discordant rhythm – moderation and invention, stability and discovery – is that age is an accumulation of equally important things, growing wider and deeper all the time.

The unchanging seasons and the human rituals that they generate can teach men wisdom, but there can be no return to childhood. The Bergsonian *durée* (phenomenological time) is real; but so, after all, is 'clock time'.

Anguilla has 'forgotten', he tells us, the use of the rituals (the moon and the bonfires) in the countryside. He has been in America (where, he concludes, everyone is like him, a bastard – used in the literal sense, not as an insult), and has dealt in manure wholesale in the city. He is uninvolved. He leaves. He has become sophisticated, but the price has been renunciation of his roots. Nuto on the other hand accepts life calmly. In Nuto Pavese is undoubtedly expressing a personal regret that he was ever a writer or a city man at all: as an urban thinker, he felt, he was condemned to be useless to others. But *The Moon and the Bonfires*, though its author's self-willed death is built into it, rises above personal considerations. It is an elegy for a stability based on the so-called 'primitive'. Life is not really any easier for Nuto than it is for Anguilla – except that the former carries his responsibilities whereas the latter only wants to find some to carry. The new generation is represented by Cinto: crippled, his chances of love cruelly diminished from the start. Nuto expresses his disgust at this injustice. And Anguilla and he agree to give him a chance after Valino's final gesture against life. Again, Nuto – like Pavese – could not commit himself politically. He did not fight in the Resistance, though he harboured a fugitive.

The affirmatory quality of the novel lies in its lyrical description of the countryside and its rituals, and in the mythopoeic vision which unites it. Santa ('saint') dies in white, having served neither party. True, at a mundane level she is a whore and a traitor; her behaviour is ignoble. But there is a tragic irony in the discrepancy between her mythical function, as sacrificed and consecrated moon-figure (moonlight and whiteness persist throughout Pavese's prose and poetry), and her squalid function at the realistic level. As early as 1942 Pavese wrote in a letter of 'places' being 'as much alive as people are, each with its own personality. They are mythical. That great hill [it figures in *The Moon and the Bonfires*] shaped like a woman's breast, is the very body of the goddess to whom, on St John's Night, the traditional bonfires of stubble will rise.'

The epigraph is from *King Lear*: 'Man must endure/ His going hence e'en as his coming hither./Ripeness is all.' This, as Biasin writes, 'contains the hidden meaning': 'acceptance of the mystery behind life ... destiny as seen in history, recognition of others, compassion.' In the last words of the novel its two main symbols are fused. The moon: female, immortal in relation to the evanescence of human existence (as are the brain cells to those of the rest of the body). The bonfires: sacred or obscene (such as Valino's fire) moments, festivals, luridly beautiful significations of the inevitability of 'clock time'. Pavese could not accept himself, and could find no public cause to which to give himself. No woman, he was convinced, would have him. But he left behind him an affirmation of *life as myth* so powerful that it gives his own death a mythical and noble quality.

BIBLIOGRAPHY

Translations: M. Ceconi: *The Moon and the Bonfires*, 1961; L. Sinclair, *The Moon and the Bonfire* (*sic*: *i faló* is plural) (1952), 1963.

Text: *La luna e i faló*, 1950.

Criticism: D. Fernandez, *L'Echec de Pavese*, 1968 – in French; G.-P. Biasin, *The Smile of the Gods*, 1968.

Alain Robbe-Grillet

Alain Robbe-Grillet was born in 1922 at Brest. He trained as an agronomic engineer and, after being forced to work in a German tank factory during the war, became an agronomist: first an employee of the National Institute of Statistics and then a specialist in exotic fruits. But he abandoned this work for literature, and published *Les Gommes* in 1953. Since 1955 he has worked as literary director at Éditions de Minuit, who publish his books. He and Jérôme Lindon, the owner of the press, established the *nouveau roman*, or 'new novel', as a genre. Other exponents include Claude Simon and Nathalie Sarraute – both of whom, older than Robbe-Grillet, had published their first novels many years earlier – Michel Butor, Claude Ollier and Samuel Beckett's collaborator Robert Pinget. Samuel Beckett is usually regarded as a precursor. Robbe-Grillet is also well known as a critic and publicist, and as a film maker: the *ciné-roman L'Année dernière à Marienbad* [*Last Year at Marienbad*] (1961) is, in its filmed form, his most celebrated work. His novels, which include *Les Gommes* [*The Erasers*] (1953), *Le Voyeur* [*The Voyeur*] (1955), and *La Jalousie* [*Jealousy*] (1957), have been very widely translated. He may well not be the best of those novelists whose work has been categorized as *nouveau*, but he is the most widely known in that particular capacity, and his practice is as theoretically 'pure' as possible. He thus has considerable historical importance, as well as undoubted ability, and has exercised a wide influence both in and outside France.

Nouveau roman

The term *nouveau roman* resembles *existentialism* in that it describes a tendency in fiction writing rather than a fixed genre. Its theorists are often fiercely polemical and, as often, self-contradictory. One should not seek for consistency in their critical writings. Thus, Roland Barthes, an apologist for Robbe-Grillet, has fairly been termed both a behaviourist and a romantic idealist. At the heart of the theory is the recognition that, in Barthes' words, literature 'must signify something other than its content and its individual forms'.

Sartre had revived the term *anti-novel* in 1947, in introducing a novel by Nathalie Sarraute. Here he meant to convey little more than the notion of a fiction which questioned its own validity and honesty. The purveyors of the *nouveau roman* refined this considerably – to the extent of setting up models.

In *La Prisonnière*, the fifth part of Proust's *À la recherche du temps perdu*, Marcel puts forward the notion of the 'private signature' of nineteenth-century writers (in particular of Hardy and Dostoievsky); they are the authors, essentially, of one book, he says: for throughout all their books they are really trying to express their secret world. They do this by means of *style*. Proust loads the term here with its maximum of meanings, and implies all the features of the writing itself: choice of words and syntax, imagery, and so on. Barthes, too, is interested in the discovery of this *style*, this element which underlies everything else – and which the author even seeks to deny, to efface and negate. It is this style or structure which is independent of content or individual form. In this essentially *structuralist* approach the work is not taken for granted. The fiction favoured is that which sets out to examine the process by which fictions come into being. Particularly praised are self-destructing books: novels that undermine their own validity.

Husserl's phenomenology has also been of importance to theorists and exponents of the *nouveau roman*. Reality is extended to accommodate all the data of consciousness, even when this is not realistic in the conventional sense.

Barthes, here closely followed (or paralleled) by Robbe-Grillet, has also called for a 'zero degree' style: an anti-humanist and non-moralistic approach in which the writer functions neutrally, as a camera lens. This had been achieved, without resort to theory – and more effectively – in such novels as Camus' *L'Étranger*. But Robbe-Grillet and others sought to give this 'neutralism' a philosophical basis. (Arguably they thus weakened it.) It is significant that Robbe-Grillet was originally an agronomic engineer and statistician, for his novels have scarcely concealed scientific aspirations; and, at least as polemicist, he is open to the charge that he fails to discern the mythological status of science, which he tends to regard as a valid absolute ('Science is the only honest means available to man for deriving advantage from the world around him': an oddly insensitive remark from a novelist). Robbe-Grillet has posited a universe of the novel in which 'gestures and objects will be "there" before being "something"; and they will still be there afterwards, hard, unalterable, eternally present, mocking their own meaning, which tries in vain to reduce them to the role of precarious tools between a formless past and an indeterminate future.' (The notion of objects 'mocking their own meaning' is singularly anthropomorphic, especially when it comes from an alleged enemy of anthropomorphism.) This is reminiscent of Sartre, and the point of departure is that of Sartre; but Robbe-Grillet has taken Sartre to task for glorifying 'to the utmost the ideas of nature and tragedy'. He is able, apparently, to envisage a future in which man, by 're-fusing communion' with a world that 'does not return his glance', 'also refuses tragedy'. For 'nature and tragedy' Robbe-Grillet seeks to substitute an emotionless geometry: a *grille*, suggests Bruce Morrissette, 'that converts any locale into a portion of his personal universe'.

The *nouveau roman* as such exhausted itself by about the mid-1960s. At about the time Georges Perec's crushingly dull *Les Choses* [*The Things*] (1965) appeared it became apparent that if the *theory* were pursued any further then no one would read novels advertised as 'new' – only, at best, pretend to. But it continues to exert a strong influence – as it should, for it raises fundamental questions even though it does not solve them. Meanwhile *Les Gommes* remains the paradigm of the early *nouveau roman*.

Les Gommes
[The Erasers]

SUMMARY   Robbe-Grillet is as much against 'plot' as he is against 'ideas', 'characters', 'symbols' or 'humanism'. *Les Gommes* therefore has a plot so intricate as to be unsusceptible to certain interpretation; and it abounds in symbols. It is thus intended as a parody of the conventional techniques, the 'myths', with which Robbe-Grillet wishes to dispense. *Les Gommes* is essentially a transformation of the Oedipus myth into terms of the detective story. The title, however, ironically 'erases' any such link! Four main sources are literary: Simenon, for the crime tale structure and some features of the style, and the atmosphere (Pierre Mac Orlan, 1883–1970, painter, thriller writer, romancer and evoker of the sensations produced by ports, also seems to be drawn upon in this respect); James Joyce, for the story-myth parallelism; Kafka, for the element of mystery; Sartre's *La Nausée* for the many *chosiste* passages (descriptions of objects which emphasize their 'neutrality': their refusal to be 'appropriated' by man). A fifth source, acknowledged by the author, is anti-literary: an aura of pulp thrillers and supporting feature films pervades the book. Clearly this is the kind of writing Robbe-Grillet most enjoys. A sixth is the science of geometry.

Since Robbe-Grillet plays with time as he likes (though the events take place classically in a twenty-four-hour period), interposes false scenes (which?) and *chosiste* descriptions of things, and since he uses many other distracting techniques with great skill, it is not possible to describe the plot in more than general terms. It is deliberately a plot which defeats itself: it defies meaning. Yet the attention paid to the story line is meticulous.

In some anonymous low-country port resembling Amsterdam Professor Daniel Dupont has supposedly been assassinated by a secret group. There is some confusion on this point, as a man called Albert Dupont has also died. Central Intelligence send their agent Wallas to investigate this 'plot'. He soon discovers that some of the clues are merely misleading while others appear to point to him (he might, it is sometimes suggested, be Daniel Dupont's son). Actually Dupont, who has suffered only a flesh wound in the arm, is not dead but lying low. Wallas, after trying to solve a sphinxian riddle asked by a drunkard, decides that the murderer will return to the scene of his crime, and goes to await him. Dupont returns. Wallas, thinking he is the murderer, shoots him. The telephone, supposed not to be working, rings: Wallas is told by the chief commissioner Laurent that Dupont is alive. He is now pursued by other agents. He finds his feet 'swollen with too much walking' (an allusion to Oedipus, 'Swell-foot'). He ends in woebegone confusion.

This framework is supported and yet challenged by a plethora of detail. The Oedipus theme is obsessively and obtrusively pushed: flotsam in a canal takes on the shape of the Sphinx, a motif on curtains recalls the classical myth, as do the names of streets. Wallas tries to buy a certain kind of eraser which, both a sexual object and one 'containing the idea of its own negation', arouses him erotically – perhaps, at one point, towards his own step-mother. The novelist himself appears as a minister who sees 'plots' everywhere. For Robbe-Grillet geometry is at once an analogue of the novel and a pole of dialectic, the other pole being what John Sturrock calls the 'elaboration of extravagant and banal myths, the usually erotic fantasies of the popular imagination'. Thus *chosiste* descriptions alternate with 'myth-making'. Robbe-Grillet's purpose, in his *chosisme*, is didactic and prescriptive. Not only does he tell us that the 'world is not for us', but also he asserts that our myth-making – which, however, he clearly acknowledges as inevitable, even if one suspects him of wanting everyone to be a machine – is irrelevant: myths, imagination itself, have no part in the structure of human existence.

In Robbe-Grillet this assertion is dogmatic. It does not faithfully describe an attitude of mind, as it does in *La Nausée*. The result, unless one is content to follow the convolutions of his enormous ingenuity is that Robbe-Grillet's fiction is oddly insubstantial. Though intellectually admirable it remains at bottom polemic. Convinced of contingency, Robbe-Grillet refuses to look at other possibilities: anyone who anthropomorphizes or exercises his imagination in a mythopoeic manner is seen as deluded. This is small minded – and not really very audacious. What is audacious is on a more superficial level, recalling the bright depthless promise of an inexperienced prodigy in putting shapes together: the brilliantly arranged mixture of modernist techniques, of pastiche of various procedures and styles, the vulgar, 'smutty' and pervasive eroticism, the intelligence with which feeling is mimicked. Robbe-Grillet's rejection of 'character' is founded on a proper refusal to conform to the *now* inadequate assumptions – the so-called 'naïve realism' – of (most) nineteenth-century novelists; but in him it reflects an inability to come to terms with the puzzle 'character' sets. This was a challenge Pirandello took up. Sartre's Roquentin assumes, in the reader's mind, a personality: an illusion, certainly, but fiction must deal in illusion all the time. Having rightly claimed that the novel changes, Robbe-Grillet has tried to freeze it – thus arrogantly but ironically denying his own premise. In effect he denies flux. It is salutary to be reminded that all mechanical *habits* of thinking, all comforting assumptions, should be discontinued. As William James wrote, we ought to know that when we think we are thinking we are usually 're-arranging our prejudices'. But Robbe-Grillet brings no warmth or psychological insight to bear upon the problem of why and how we continue to fall into bad habits – only an intellectually conceited atheistic positivism which alternates between the sullen, the exasperated (illustrated in the novelist's obsession with 'tiny flaws') and the breezily self-assured. The Sartre of *La Nausée* writes as one involved in 'bad habits', as one not able to be 'engaged'; Robbe-Grillet is far less serious in as much as he writes somewhat casually as one who knows the answers to 'tragedy'. Our intellectual attention is glibly engaged. But only this. A whole dimension is missing: the grain of life, the feeling of it as it is actually lived, warmth, decency.

The plot of *Les Gommes* may be interpreted in a number of conflicting ways. Its very open-endedness may suggest that all plots are naïve: that there are no plots in real life, which is contingent. It may, however, be interpreted as an illustration of what happens when someone tries to impose 'meaning on reality': Wallas recreates 'in modern form a parallel of classical tragedy' (the epigraph to the novel is from Sophocles: 'Time which sees all has found you out against your will'). 'Unaware of the inverted and hidden relationships that tie his actions to the past legend, Wallas has relived an archetypal myth.' On a different if not irreconcilable view the false murder which exists only in the assumptions of some of the characters, in particular of Wallas, becomes objectively true at the end.

If we treat the text as independent of Robbe-Grillet's critical polemic it quickly loses force and falls to pieces. And so we must accept it as buttressed by all this philosophical polemic, this synthesis of preceding tendencies. And we are bound to conclude either that Dupont is *not* Wallas' father – or that it doesn't matter if he is, that it has no relevance. But this raises the question of the nature of what we call 'chance'. Is it aleatory, as Robbe-Grillet seems to think? None of this is resolved. If only Wallas were alive enough to arouse our non-philosophical interest (for the *novel as philosophy* distorts the non-philosophical way readers will continue, willy nilly, to read novels), this plot might help to demonstrate tensions actually experienced by the reader. As it is *Les Gommes* is less efficient in this sense than Wilkie Collins' *Armadale* (1866), a sensationalist but fascinating novel describing a man's attempts to avoid what he is horrifiedly convinced must be his guilty destiny. As Paul West has written, 'to present people as if they were unknown animals in an observation-chamber' is an 'arresting trick' but a 'wilful distortion of what most of us ... think we *know*'. The good fiction of the future, immune from prescription, will take into account the tendencies summed up in the lucid though journalistic criticism of Robbe-Grillet, and even of the literary criticism implicit in his novels; but it will also convey a direct sense of the psychology of men and women. It will be phenomenological, but not didactic. Sartre's remarkably theological atheism does not seem shallow because it is tormentedly and continuously affirmed; Robbe-Grillet's does: because it is merely the complacent refuge of a man whose trade just happens to be novel writing instead of statistical investigation, the construction of 'flawless' geometrical models or the analysis of tropical fruits.

BIBLIOGRAPHY

Translation: R. Howard, *The Erasers*, 1964.

Text: *Les Gommes*, 1953.

Criticism: B. Morrisette, *Les Romans de Robbe-Grillet*, 1962; A. Robbe-Grillet, *Snapshots and Towards a New Novel*, 1965.

Albert Camus

Albert Camus was born at Mondovi near Constantine in Algeria in 1913. His father, a cellarman in the wine trade, was of Alsatian origin; he was killed at the Battle of the Marne in 1914. His mother, of Spanish origin, moved to a two-room apartment in a working-class district of Algiers and kept a large family by working as a charwoman. She was illiterate; but Albert was an eager and precocious reader and a promising pupil, and he won a scholarship to the Lycée in Algiers. He was also devoted to sport, and became a strong swimmer, a boxer and a footballer. His childhood poverty and his status as an Algerian Frenchman were decisive factors in his life.

In 1930 Camus, attacked by tuberculosis, left home. For a while he lived with an uncle. He worked in many odd jobs, studied philosophy and literature assiduously, and attended the University of Algiers. A marriage he made at twenty broke up within a year. From 1934 until about 1937 he was in the communist party. In the mid-1930s he founded a theatre company, acted, and wrote plays; in 1937 he became a journalist. He also worked on his first novel and on essays. His 1939 report on the destitute Kabyle region is markedly non-political and humane in its approach. In 1940 he made another marriage. (To use Henri Peyre's quaint phraseology, throughout his life he 'had some reason to incriminate himself for not having always observed the commands of marital fidelity'.) By 1942 he was actively involved in France in the resistance against the Nazi occupation. From the autumn of 1943 he edited the underground newsheet *Combat*; at the liberation this appeared with his name on its masthead, and he continued to edit it until 1947. He was by then famous as the author of two novels, *L'Étranger* [*The Stranger*] (1942) and *La Peste* [*The Plague*] (1947) as well as of the long essay *Le Mythe de Sisyphe* [*The Myth of Sisyphus*] (1943), an attempt to 'find a means to go beyond' the sense of nihilism which had pervaded European thinking at least since Nietzsche. Essentially this points to the joy of being alive as an antidote to the pointlessness of life and the inevitability of death; it is more 'sweet and exhilarating' (Conor Cruise O'Brien) than philosophically coherent or revolutionary.

Camus became the most celebrated figure on the non-communist left (some would say that he was on the right) in France. In 1951 he published *L'Homme révolté* [*The Rebel*], an indictment of Marxism, as well as of the Soviet Union. This led to the famous quarrel with his friend Sartre in 1952 – a quarrel that has been misrepresented in Camus' favour in journalistic English-language accounts of it (one does not have wholly to agree with O'Brien to appreciate that his account is a valuable corrective). Sartre later wrote a moving obituary essay on him.

Camus' position seemed to be the honourable but difficult one of genuine liberal humanist. He was a confused thinker, who could not accept that anti-Marxist motives might on occasion be as bad as Marxist. His identification of Soviet communism with all Marxism was perhaps facile. It is interesting that the section of *L'Homme révolté* devoted to Max Stirner – the name assumed by Caspar Schmidt (1806–56), whose *Der Einzige und sein Eigenthum* [*The Ego and His Own*] (1846) is one of the most nakedly and frightening egoistic books ever written, and one which has been called a precursor

of anarchism and fascism as well as of the *new left* manifestations of recent years – is missing from the English
translation, *The Rebel*. For Stirner influenced Camus
in his distinction between *revolution*, which he deplored,
and the more egoistic notion of *rebellion*, of which he
approved.

Camus had excellent reasons for being political: he
realized that if he put himself above politics he would be
guilty of complicity in whatever might follow. And his
feeling, surely correct, that in revolutions 'Prometheus
always turns into Caesar' was deeply felt.

As a French Algerian Camus wanted absolutely fair
treatment for the Arabs, and he deplored repression – but
he could not bring himself to embrace the cause of, or to
see any reason for, Arab independence. He unequivocally
backed the presence of the French army in Algeria. This
was an unrealistic attitude, as General de Gaulle himself
soon saw.

Camus' real devotion was to artistic truth, and although
his non-fiction contains many insights, and is clearly the
work of a noble-minded if muddled man, it is in his
fiction that his genius fully emerges. In 1956 he published
La Chute [*The Fall*], his most revealing novel; this was
followed in 1957 by *L'Exil et le royaume* [*Exile and the
Kingdom*], six stories. Of his plays the brilliant adaptations of works by others – for example, *The Possessed*
(1959) – are the best. His *Carnets* [*Notebooks*] were published in two volumes after his death. In 1957 he was
awarded the Nobel Prize – the youngest writer, with
Kipling, ever to receive it. On 4 January 1960 he was
killed instantly in a car accident (he was not driving).
He left behind him the first draft of a new novel; he had
well developed plans for a new theatrical venture and
for a book on Don Juan. His senseless death came as a
severe shock to the literate world, for he seemed to have
been cut off at the height of his creative powers.

La Chute
[The Fall]

SUMMARY *La Chute* is the monologue, begun in a low-class bar called the Mexico City in the harbour of Amsterdam, of a once successful Paris lawyer who now calls himself Jean-Baptiste Clamence (suggesting John the Baptist, the precursor: the *vox clamantis in deserto* – voice crying in the wilderness – of Matthew 3, iii). Jean-Baptiste Clamence is not his real name. There is apparently an interlocutor, but his speech is not reported; it is only echoed in the monologue. Clamence has certain features in common with the enigmatic Pechorin of Lermontov's *A Hero of Our Time*, and Camus prefaced the English translation with a quotation from Lermontov: 'Some were dreadfully insulted, and quite seriously, to have held up as a model such an immoral character as [Pechorin]; others shrewdly noticed that the author had portrayed himself and his acquaintances ... *A Hero of Our Time*, gentlemen, is in fact a portrait but not of an individual; it is the aggregate of the vices of our whole generation in their fullest expression.'

Clamence's monologue, which parodies Camus' own convoluted elegance of style, is intense and bitterly sarcastic. He is now, he says, practising the profession of 'judge-penitent'. He also has a sideline: admiring criminals. He enjoyed his life as a lawyer, celebrated for his passionate defence of 'victims'; he specialized in 'noble cases'; he had 'peace of conscience'; he was charitable and delighted with himself; he lived in Eden – 'no intermediary between life and me'. Then one evening he heard behind him a 'good, hearty, almost friendly laugh'. He could not see who laughed, but when he went home he looked at his smiling reflection in the mirror: 'it seemed to me that my smile was double.' After this he became prone to dejection. He began to discover things about himself, mainly that he was a vain play-actor (for his own benefit). He lived 'without any other continuity than that, from day to day, of I, I, I'. He was hit and insulted in the street by a stranger; resentment gnawed at him for days. He now realized that his dream of being 'half Cerdan [French world middleweight boxing champion, one of the lovers of Edith Piaf; killed in a plane crash], half de Gaulle', of dominating 'in all things' 'had not stood up to facts'. He describes how as a bachelor he successfully played 'games' with women, not experiencing love but enjoying himself until he became bored. One woman with whom he had had a 'shabby experience' had reported his 'deficiencies to a third person'. And so he charmed her, won her back – and mortified her in every possible manner until she 'paid a tribute aloud' to his mastery of her, whereupon he lost interest.

Then Clamence comes to the apogee of his 'confession': once, two or three years before he thought he heard the laughter, he had failed to prevent a 'slim young woman dressed in black' from jumping to her death off a bridge over the Seine: he had walked on, even when he heard her body striking the water.

He goes on to confess that it seemed to him that everyone was laughing at him: judging him. He began to think of death. Instead of helping people, he began to contemplate behaving aggressively to indulge his vanity: jostling the blind on the street, smacking children in subways, shouting 'lousy proletarian' at workers. He did not actually make these gestures, but he did change from his former habits. He announced a manifesto exposing the 'oppression that the oppressed inflict on decent people', began an *Ode to the Police* and an *Apotheosis of the Guillotine*, said 'My God!' at atheist meetings. He resisted his 'flattering reputation' by 'pleasant indiscretions'. He took to debauchery and drink. But even this did not help him: his liver troubled him, and he became very tired. One day a piece of flotsam reminded him of the body of the girl in the Seine which would 'continue to await me ... everywhere ... where lies the bitter water of my baptism'. He realized that he was not cured, and could not be: that he 'had to live in little-ease'.

Clamence begins to succumb to fever. He inveighs against religion. Christ himself felt guilty: he heard every night the voice of Rachel calling for her children who were slaughtered for him. But Clamence loves him; he was not superhuman: 'he cried aloud his agony'. But unfortunately he 'left us alone'.

Now in his bed and suffering from malaria he tells of how, when in Africa in the war – a neutral but interned in a camp – he was made 'Pope'. A young Frenchman in the camp had declared the need for a 'Pope of the wretched', and asked who had the most failings. Clamence had raised his hand, for a joke. So he became Pope: group leader with responsibility for distribution of water. 'I closed the circle the day I drank the water of a dying comrade.'

He reveals that he has in his cupboard one of the panels of the Van Eyck altarpiece at Ghent, *The Adoration of the Lamb*; this panel is *The Just Judges*. It was stolen – not by Clamence – in 1934 and replaced by a copy. For a time it hung on the wall on the Mexico City bar; Clamence regards it as still the property of the proprietor. At the end he asks if his interlocutor will arrest him. Is he a policeman? Ah no, he is a lawyer. He suspected as much. Clamence says that he will continue to preach slavery, even though it is not immediately realizable, at the Mexico City: he must present it as 'true freedom'.

He briefly tells the story of how he came to be in Amsterdam. He closed his office in Paris and travelled. He ended up in this limbo, 'corseted by canals', practising the 'profession of penitent to be able to end up as a judge':

I accuse myself up hill and down dale ... But at the same time the portrait I hold out to my contemporaries becomes a mirror.

His project is to convince everyone that 'we are in the soup together'; but, he says to whoever he is speaking to, '*You* are not only intelligent, you look polished by use.' Nevertheless he feels sure his interlocutor will return. He will see Clamence teaching others that they are vile, and thus himself 'grow taller ... How intoxicating to feel like God the Father.' What happened to you one night, he asks, on the banks of the Seine? 'I shall at last say through your mouth: "O young woman, throw yourself into the water again so that I may a second time have the chance of saving both of us!"' If taken literally 'we'd have to go through with it', but,

It'll always be too late. Fortunately!

CRITICAL COMMENTARY *La Chute*, which Sartre and most other critics regard as Camus' best novel, has been very variously interpreted. Some have seen it simply as a satire on Marxists or quasi-Marxist fellow travellers. Nathan A. Scott interprets it as an exhibition of the 'morbid perversion of *solidarité* that may be promoted by a soured Manichaeism': Jean-Baptiste does not himself submit to the slavery he preaches, and represents for Camus 'the absolute antithesis of the true rebel'. Other Christian critics believe that Camus was entering a phase of 'neo-Jansenism', and therefore look upon Clamence with more charitable eyes. Henri Peyre, although he mistakenly states that Clamence is the owner of the Mexico City bar, sees the novel as anti-existentialist, anti-Christian and an indictment of those writers who 'secure the complicity of their readers while exorcising their own demons' – and as Camus' denunciation of the 'egotist' he might otherwise have become. Conor Cruise O'Brien accepts that there is a measure of satire of Sartre and his colleagues, but insists that this is partially self-critical. He finds *La Chute* has Christian 'tendencies' (Camus himself approved of this approach though he denied having become a Christian) but interprets it as in essence a symbolic statement of Camus' uneasy political position.

O'Brien's is the subtlest approach. Camus, O'Brien believes, found through the Algerian crisis that there was something he preferred to justice. 'Essentially Camus is beginning to take the side of his own tribe against the abstract entities.' Two calls were pressing on him: that of the Arabs and that of his mother (who needed, as he very truthfully said, the protection of the French army). Clamence's paralysis on the bridge 'corresponds to that of his creator'. The laughter he hears is provoked by the discrepancy between what he says and what he does. The 'two calls' fuse into one: Rachel's voice calling her children. In this ideological interpretation – O'Brien calls Camus a tragic figure who should have joined Sartre in his denunciation of neo-colonialism – 'artistic truth ... reveals justice as a complex and self-flattering illusion.' In these terms *La Chute* must ultimately be a failure, a statement of defeat: artistic truth, being itself a 'form of justice', has been betrayed – even if as O'Brien acknowledges it is an 'heroic achievement' in which Camus left us a 'mirror'.

There is no doubt that *La Chute* contains satirical elements. Francis Jeanson had written the offensive review of *L'Homme révolté* in Sartre's magazine *Les Temps Modernes*. Camus replied, over Jeanson's head, to Sartre personally. This reply was printed, and Sartre's answer followed in the same issue (August 1952). The charges that he combined 'dreary conceit and vulnerability', that he was the victim of 'a dismal self-importance' which obscured his 'inner problems' but which he himself would call 'Mediterranean moderation', and that he was revolting not so much against the 'Communist state' as against himself, cut Camus to the quick. Hence the jokes: about the atheistic novelist who prayed every night, but 'how he gave it to God in his books! What a dusting off ...'; and about Clamence's *Ode to the Police*. The Frenchman Clamence meets in Africa must be an allusion to Jeanson for, as Sartre told Camus in his reply, Jeanson had like this Frenchman been in a Spanish concentration camp for trying to join the French army in Africa.

But this satire is incidental and not, I think, ill natured. In *La Chute* Camus had, if in spite of his feelings, digested and accepted Sartre's basic criticism of him: 'You need a guilty party; if it isn't you, then it must be the universe.' The novel is not an 'answer' to Sartre: it is an explanation, made on a high artistic level – and perhaps not voluntarily, since no truly serious literature can be the product of wholly conscious thinking or feeling. Nor, however, must it be seen as an endorsement of Sartre: it is successful because it draws attention to the predicament of the writer in his political role. Sartre is as much involved here as Camus. This is not a question, as O'Brien rather reluctantly implies, of agreeing with Sartre's political position and condemning Camus'; no one should read *La Chute* without reading Sartre's reply to Camus (translated in *Situations*, 1965): it illuminates the novel, for it is in a sense a portrait of, or at least a sketch for, Clamence. Regardless of the political questions at issue, Sartre was right in his *psychological* diagnosis of how Camus had reacted: 'You decided against history, and rather than interpret its course, you preferred to see it as one more absurdity ... while condemning mankind, you stood next to it, but outside its ranks ...' Sartre did not have to be 'politically correct' to be psychologically correct. Camus' search, in *L'Homme révolté* and in the play *Les Justes* [*The Just*] (1950), for the limits of the permissible in relation to ideological murder may have been muddled, but it was made in good enough intellectual faith; however, it was an evasion, as Sartre implied, of a profounder search for the truth about Camus' self. (Much the same charge, though in a different form, could be made against Sartre himself.)

In 1954 the Algerians revolted. In 1962 the French army began to leave and Algeria became independent. It was easy for non-Algerians to condemn the oppression of the Moslems as obscene; but it was not so easy for intelligent Europeans who were also Algerians. A man cannot help feeling what he feels – or not feeling what he thinks he ought to feel; and Camus knew that he felt a certain solidarity with the European Algerians – and that he could not emotionally identify with the Moslem cause. When the Moslems rose he condemned them. His first novel, *L'Étranger*, is about a European killing an Arab and, as O'Brien has shown, it sustains the myth of French colonialism (for example, in pretending that the courts of law made no distinction between European and Moslem). Camus' keen conscience was stretched to the limit by the difficulties of his position over Algeria as well as by the nihilistic and Olympian tendencies in himself which had so shrewdly been exposed by Sartre. Furthermore, he was more sensitive than Sartre was (or has ever been) over the question of terrorism: both the torture of Algerians by the French and the murderous tactics of the Moslem FLN deeply upset him. In *La Chute* he went perhaps as far as any imaginative writer could go in the way of honest self-examination and self-criticism.

The novel consequently transcends Camus' political confusions; and Clamence is thus not Camus, but rather anyone who has the pretensions of a writer and a prophet and a man of political conscience. O'Brien, however uneasily, makes of political 'rightness' an absolute, and seems to argue from the position that the writer must be 'committed'. But can an abstract 'rightness', held by a man, ever be *true*? O'Brien is optimistic to think so. Camus was forced, by the question, to withdraw into a hubristic solitude. (He remained silent after his attempt to intervene in Algeria had made him unpopular with both sides.) He tried in *La Chute* to purge himself of his *hubris,* his 'artistic detachment'. When O'Brien remarks that Camus was beginning to take the side 'of his own tribe' against the 'abstract entities', does he mean by 'tribe' 'writers' – or 'European Algerians'? There is no evidence that *in the novel* he was taking the side of the European Algerians. He seems rather to have been taking no side at all. He was 'committed' to common decency (which is more difficult than political correctitude, whatever that may be); otherwise, as he saw, he was doomed to mere hedonism; but this commitment involved looking at himself as he really was, which is ultimately a more important enterprise even than being 'wrong' or 'right' about Algeria. O'Brien finds that Camus through Clamence is discovering that there is something he prefers to justice: the 'emergence of the ironical *juge péni-tent* prepared the way for a different view of life, more conservative and more organic'. But what greater justice can there ever be than to know oneself, or failing this to try to do so? Sartre wrote of *La Chute* as 'perhaps the most beautiful and least understood' of Camus' books. 'Rarely,' he added, 'have the qualities of a work and the conditions of the historical moment so clearly required that a writer live.' However ironic (but irony is above all a gesture of self-despair), however elated in its often Stirner-like egoism, the monologue that is *La Chute* is a step on the way to self-discovery in a way that *L'Étranger* and *La Peste* were not. In these terms it is not a failure. It is strangely compelling, a statement uninhibited by abstract considerations.

We should not fall into the error of taking Clamence as 'good' or 'bad', for this distracts us from seeing him as he is. We are hoodwinked into speaking of an 'interlocutor'. There is none. Clamence is speaking to himself, as he finally admits when he recognizes his 'listener' as one of his own kind: a lawyer. 'Are we not all alike, constantly talking and to no one ... ?' Clamence continually craves his own patience ('I am indeed grateful to you ... for your curiosity'; 'I now run the risk of really interesting you'), because he is bored with himself. He talks to himself because no one else will seriously listen to him: imagine a 'man in the street' making more than a polite gesture to this monologue (or reading *La Chute*). Yet the 'listener' is supposed to keep four assignations with Clamence after their first meeting in order to hear out his tale.

A fall suggests a rise; a John the Baptist suggests a Christ to come. Clamence is interpreted by a number of critics, all of whom suppose Camus to have been depicting him as a sinister Marxist, as a cunning trickster pure and simple. But how? He suffers, as he admits; and he 'cons' only himself. He has (he says) changed his name. This seems to be merely blasphemous irony. But is it altogether? His attitude to Christ himself is at least as reverent as Nietzsche's – and this was summed up in the latter's remark that in truth the only Christian died on the cross. Clamence's talk about Christ is far too serious, too earnest: he recognizes him, even as he accuses him of leaving 'us alone'.

Clamence led a conventionally virtuous life until he discovered that he was a hypocrite; sophisticated self-analysis led him to self-contempt, and self-contempt led him to contempt for all men. Perhaps his vivacious, gleeful monologue is 'rhetoric disguised as a confession'; perhaps he does suffer from bad faith; but he also suffers in having to make his confession in this foggy city. *He* is a slave: to his need to talk. Nor does his rhetoric conceal lies. He is lonely and sterile. Yet he is not wholly diabolical: an 'aggregate of the vices of our whole generation in their fullest expression,' he says 'we have lost track of the light, the mornings, the holy innocence of those who forgive themselves.' Not the remark of an absolute charlatan. He is yearning for a more innocent and simple life. But in leaving the girl to drown he has missed his chance – and he really has, even if he does dramatize the matter, and make an exhibition of himself.

Germaine Brée sees Clamence as 'sure of his ultimate mastery', the 'inspired perpetrator of a colossal fraud'. This wholly negative view ignores his patent suffering. Surely convoluted irony does not intimate certainty of 'mastery'? Germaine Brée's own statements, that he is frustrated and 'cannot break the charmed circle of his isolation', contradict her interpretation. In Clamence Camus presents *himself as writer*: guilty, if sometimes happily so.

The note of elation in the monologue has puzzled critics; but this is simply the animal pleasure gained by writers from the exercise of their verbal energy and, as such, it is healthy rather than sick. *La Chute* is Camus' sardonic apology for having been, for being, a *moraliste*, a judge. It is also an apology for his fiercest critics.

BIBLIOGRAPHY

Translation: J. O'Brien *The Fall*, 1957.

Text: in *Oeuvres complètes*, 1965.

Criticism: G. Brée, *Camus* (1961), 1964; N. A. Scott, *Albert Camus*, 1962; C. C. O'Brien, 1970.

Boris Pasternak

Boris Pasternak was born in Moscow in 1890. His father, Leonid, was a well known painter; his mother was a pianist. Both parents were Jewish. He first studied music, and fell under the influence of the mystical ideas of the composer Scriabin. He studied philosophy in Germany (1912) and eventually obtained a degree from Moscow University. He began writing in 1912, and had achieved full success as a poet by the early 1920s. In 1918 he wrote what many critics describe as his prose masterpiece, *Destvo Luvers* [*The Childhood of Luvers*].

As poet Pasternak began as a 'futurist', under the influence of Mayakovsky; he also absorbed the visionary poetry of Blok. Between 1917 and 1922 he characteristically refused to attach himself to any group; nor did he show any apparent concern with politics. In a dense, sharp, lyrical and yet not always easy-to-follow style he explored love through nature and nature through love. His verse, written in regular forms, always had an especially musical quality. His underlying theme is often that of poetic creation: how and why it happens and what it means. He keeps the 'I' hidden, submerged in natural metaphor. In 1927 he published two long poems in praise of the Revolution, but in 1934 he stopped writing original poetry for some years: he could not accept the dictates of 'socialist realism'. He concentrated mainly on translations from Shakespeare – including a version of *Hamlet*. He also began, in 1934, to plan *Zhivago*, parts of drafts for which were published in a magazine in 1938. In the war he brought out some inferior poetry; but Zhdanov's notorious attacks on 'deviationist' writers of 1946 forced him into silence until after Stalin's death. In 1954 ten of the twenty-five poems with which *Zhivago* closes were published in the Soviet Union, and the projected novel was mentioned as being almost completed; two years later another eight poems – from what eventually became a different group – appeared. His later poetry is simpler than his earlier, and is more concerned with religious themes and imagery.

In May 1956 *Novy Mir*, the leading Soviet literary periodical, refused to publish the novel unless some cuts and revisions were made. Pasternak had meanwhile agreed with the Italian publisher Feltrinelli for a European publication. Despite Pasternak's request to him to return the script, Feltrinelli went ahead and published (in Russian) in 1957. He claimed that Pasternak had previously instructed him to do so, and had told him that any further communication could be understood as having been made under duress. (The standard Russian text appeared in Austria in 1959.) In 1958 he was awarded the Nobel Prize, but was forced to decline it – and to write to *Pravda* to 'apologize' for his 'error'. His life was shortened by the mean persecution from which he henceforth suffered: expulsion from the Writers' Union, abandonment by many old friends, attacks in the Press. He died at his country house at Peredelkino in 1960. A number of writers and artists, including the pianist Richter, defiantly attended his funeral. *Zhivago* has not appeared in the Soviet Union.

Doctor Zhivago

SUMMARY *Doctor Zhivago* is told in an apparently haphazard and, at the beginning, rapidly accelerating manner,

with abrupt transitions. Its central motif is the relationship between the personality of Zhivago (a word which
suggests 'living') and the twenty-five poems, written by
him, of which the seventeenth and last section of the
novel consists. *Zhivago* is at bottom an attempt at a statement about the relationship between experience (life)
and poetry (art); the latter is seen as constituting the
meaning, the essence, of the former. It is advisable to
read the poems first.

For Pasternak the prose narrative was as important as
the poems, and certain critics accept this. For others the
sixteen prose sections fail to carry the poetry's weight.

The action spans the life of Yura (later usually addres-
sed as Yury) Zhivago (1891–1929) from the age of ten,
when his mother dies, until his own death in Moscow.
His father, once rich, has dissipated a considerable fortune
and abandoned the family to poverty long ago. Reduced
to alcoholism and despair, he throws himself off a train
soon after his wife's death.

We are introduced to Lara Guishar, young daughter
of a Russianized Frenchwoman who has survived through
the advice of Komarovsky, a 'lawyer ... a cold-blooded
businessman'. Komarovsky, who has seduced and corrupted her mother as well as advised her, now has his eye
on Lara, and succeeds in making her his mistress while
she is still a schoolgirl; she loathes him, and feels herself
enslaved by him. At one point she unsuccessfully tries to
shoot him. Eventually she marries Pasha Antipov, the
son of a socialist railway worker, in order to escape from
Komarovsky.

Zhivago grows up in the Moscow home of the brothers
Gromeko, professors of chemistry; later he marries Tonya,
the daughter of one of them. Drawn to art, he nevertheless
decides to become a doctor: he believes that a 'man should
do something useful in his practical life'. He meets Lara
(on the occasion of the attempted shooting), and is greatly
fascinated by her.

Pasha Antipov leaves Lara, though she begs him not to, for the army: his wife, he decides, does not love him. We have now passed through the 1905 uprising and reached the First World War. Russia is fighting Germany; Antipov, who has been obliged to give himself up as a prisoner of war, is believed to have been killed.

There are descriptions of action between the Russians and Germans. Lara has pursued Antipov to the front, as a nurse; she does not believe a brother-officer's story to the effect that he has been captured – by a stroke of irony this officer thinks he is lying for her comfort. Yury, at the front as a doctor, has been wounded and is recovering in hospital. He meets Lara at the moment she receives the news about her husband.

Yury and Lara are often brought together in their work, and eventually against the background of the turmoil brought about by the Revolution they become lovers. But the same Revolution forces them to part when Zhivago has to return to Moscow – where he sees his little boy and his wife. Soon the civil war begins. Yury catches typhus, nearly dies, and then decides to take his family to the Varykino estate near Yuryatin. On the journey he is captured by revolutionaries. He is taken to see Commissar Strelnikov ('Shooter'), the 'pride and terror' of the region who has committed a number of atrocities. Strelnikov frees him, though he accuses him of being a 'White' and a 'deserter'.

At Varykino Zhivago begins to keep a diary; he has made his peace with the Yuryatin Soviet, but is already privately critical of it. He is more shaken (as was his creator) by the presence of art in *Crime and Punishment* than by Raskolnikov's crime: 'art,' he writes in a key passage,

is an idea, a statement about life, so all-embracing that it can't be split up into separate words ... [it] ... turns out to be the essence, the heart and soul of the work.

He realizes at this time that he has a hereditary heart defect. He meets Lara again, and she tells him that 'Strelnikov' is none other than her husband, Pasha Antipov. Shortly after this Yury is captured by partisans and conscripted to serve with them as a doctor. He remains in the hands of this 'forest brotherhood' for two years. Then the Whites attack, and in the ensuing bloody turmoil Zhivago escapes to Yuryatin. He hears that Tanya and his children have reached Moscow. He meets Lara once again, and their love finds its fullest expression. It transpires that Komarovsky, the ruiner of Lara's life, had driven Yury's father to suicide. Lara and Yury become acquainted with Sima Tuntseva, a seemingly half-mad, ecstatic old lay-preacher. Zhivago believes her to be 'intelligent' and 'gifted'. Her preaching is intimately connected with the 'Mary Magdalen' poems at the end of the book. Yury receives a letter from Tanya in Moscow telling him that she and the family are to be deported.

Then Lara and Yury are separated again. Komarovsky turns up and offers to save them from the vengeance of the Soviets, who 'are sharpening their claws', by taking them to an autonomous region. Lara firmly believes that Yury will accompany them, but he deliberately renounces her – although allowing her to imagine that he will follow them to safety. At this time he is absorbed in his poems and writings; without quite knowing what he is doing, he is 'working on his lament for Lara'. He feels a tragic joy; he rejects the 'god' of the Revolution and dedicates himself to art which 'always serves beauty', which is the 'joy of possessing form', which is the 'key to organic life'.

Shortly afterwards Strelnikov (alias Pasha Antipov) turns up. He has fled, as he is now to be court martialled on a trumped-up charge. Wildly and incoherently he confesses his terrorist crimes. He warns Zhivago to leave. He then shoots himself.

Zhivago reaches Moscow, where he gradually 'goes to seed'. His heart disease worsens. At first he publishes a few pamphlets and poems; the views expressed in them resemble those of Sima. But he becomes increasingly depressed and ill, suffers from 'grumbling ... tempers and ... nerves', and takes up with a woman, a telegraphist called Marina, by whom he has two children. He is reduced to doing odd jobs.

In the early summer of 1929 Yury talks with two of his old schoolfriends, Gordon and Dudorov. The latter suffer from 'average taste'; they accept the Soviet system in hackneyed terms; they shower the dissenting Yury with 'sermons'. But they are anxious for him, and help Marina when he disappears. He has deserted her: gone 'into hiding' under the protection of Yevgraf (implying 'to write well'), who tries to get him a job in a hospital. Meanwhile he takes up writing again. It is implied that 'Hamlet' the first of his poems given at the end, expresses his state of mind at the time.

One day he gets on a tram. Feeling stifled, he tries to open the window. The passengers are angry, telling him that it is nailed down. He rushes out of the tram, runs down the street, and falls dead. By one of the coincidences with which the novel is studded, Lara arrives and mourns him; she then vanishes again – into, the narrator suggests, a concentration camp and subsequent death.

A brief epilogue tells of Gordon and Dudorov, first as convicts, sentenced for 'political crimes', then as officers in the army in 1943 (Yevgraf is now a general), and finally, 'some five or ten years later', as 'ageing friends' feeling a 'peaceful joy for this holy city [Moscow] ... And it seemed that the book in their hands knew what they were feeling and gave them its support and confirmation.' The book (presumably a typescript) referred to is of Yury's writing, and it has been compiled by Yevgraf.

CRITICAL COMMENTARY Opinions on *Doctor Zhivago* differ sharply. Few if any critics deny Pasternak's prowess as a poet; few fail to admire his earlier published prose, which is cast in short forms. But *Zhivago* has evoked widely differing responses: it is a great poetic novel; such a novel as Shakespeare would have written had he lived today; a flawed novel; a 'sentimental' and over-ambitious work or a 'failed epic' – as Isaac Deutscher called it, using *War and Peace* as his battering-ram.

Henry Gifford argues that the prose of *Zhivago*, a poet's novel, 'cleanses the doors of perception'. It is a 'great valedictory work, a singing of "eternal memory" not to a social order but to a moment of promise, in the summer of 1917, which was never fulfilled ... The poet – like Russia itself – must pass through the darkness of the grave to achieve resurrection.' Thus Zhivago, who should not in Gifford's view be identified with Hamlet or Christ, is wayward, weak, without will – but a 'Christian hero, strong in his weakness'. He is passive, not concerned with the remaking of life, but with resurrection.

As poet Pasternak was at his best when writing about nature, into which he projected himself. To 'become' nature is for him to enter into eternity. The erotic too is seen as a part of this process of becoming. Pasternak, though seldom explicit about sex, and never in *Zhivago*, is an exceedingly erotic poet. From the time he started to plan *Zhivago* in 1934 he gradually began to feel, as he put it, like an 'atheist who has lost his faith'. The Christian – specifically Orthodox – symbolism upon which his novel is constructed does not imply a conventional 'conversion'. He merely accepted, as George Katkov writes in his commentary to Kamen's translations of his poems, the 'story and legend of Christianity as a system of symbols which, when applied to everyday life, changes it beyond recognition'. This was consistent in a man who believed 'metaphor to be the shorthand of genius'; he had not discovered a 'belief', but a metaphorical system which was inseparable from the Russian landscape. He was less concerned with 'belief' than with the continuous *process* of dying into nature and thus being resurrected.

Now *Zhivago* can be interpreted as a successful attempt to demonstrate this process, which in his poetry Pasternak seldom cheapens or over-simplifies. But it can also be taken as a failure to fuse fiction and poetry – a failure begotten by Pasternak's mistaken desire to become, in Katkov's (approving) words, a 'witness to his time', an apostle of freedom and Russian resurrection. In the poem 'Hamlet' Pasternak identifies Hamlet with Christ: both were 'sent' by their fathers. Hamlet, wrote Pasternak in 1956, gave up his position in society 'to do the will of Him that sent him'. Yet Katkov apparently finds no difficulty in stating that though the poem is 'by Zhivago' the 'mission' is Pasternak's. Others may find in this contradiction the key to Pasternak's failure to fuse fiction and poetry.

Some of the material in *Zhivago* is vaguely autobiographical; the poems are specifically autobiographical (if only in Pasternak's reticent way), even though many are related to episodes in the prose narrative. For 'Hamlet', though a beautifully wrought poem with a magnificent last line (a Russian proverb), seems in this context to presage a self-conscious role of martyr on Pasternak's part. This is not to his discredit: he had endured much, and he had been filled with horror at the degeneration of hope into bestiality. In his proper role as poet he had every right to feel as he did. But, even though he did not wish to take a 'seat at the table of the greats' (as has been suggested), he may have made a serious error in abandoning his natural genre as writer of poetry and sensitively autobiographical prose.

If we ignore Pasternak's intricate symbolic/metaphorical *intentions*, which are highly obtrusive, then we may find the text of *Zhivago* less ponderously impressive than these high intentions. There are beautiful fragments about landscape and the role it plays in relationships and events. The atmosphere of Moscow is powerfully conveyed. But some of the battle scenes are, as A. F. Boyd has noted, 'strangely overwritten'. When Zhivago con-

templates Lara in metaphorical terms we are presented
with a moving picture of a nature/love poet just such as
Pasternak himself was. But Zhivago himself, as a personality moving through time, is unreal. Pasternak has
unquestionably set himself, among other things, the task
of writing an historical novel about Russia in the first
three decades of this century; thus his hero needs to be
felt as 'real' in an historical sense. If life is 'about' transcending history, then the successful 'biographer' of
Zhivago would demonstrate, in psychological terms, how
he discovers this. Yet while the notion of a metaphorical
art being superior to and more permanent than history
is implicit in passages of the novel, there is a confusion –
for at the end, and in the key poem 'Hamlet', there is a
suggestion that Yury's writings have the power to redeem
history itself. *Zhivago* is Pasternak's confused attempt to
atone to himself for his indifferences to social matters (a
gesture common to poets); but he will not and cannot
abandon his sense of poetic mission, and so, in an epic
form in which he is not happy, he disingenuously trans-
forms this sense of mission into something almost embarrassingly messianic.

The difference between Marcel Proust and Marcel his
narrator is functional in *À la recherche du temps perdu*;
in *Zhivago* the difference between Yury Zhivago and
Pasternak points to a fatal flaw. Pasternak committed
himself in this project to a type of realism which was
alien to his natural manner of apprehending existence.
The 'Judas' Komarovsky is a hopefully Dostoievskian
creation, but is in fact 'frankly atrocious' (A. F. Boyd),
a ridiculous figure from Victorian melodrama. Antipov-
Strelnikov is 'wooden' and flat. Lara-as-Lara is never alive
except as a metaphor or symbol (for, among other things
Mary Magdalen) in Zhivago's mind. Sima is a puppet: a
vehicle for the expression of a series of liturgical metaphors. There are frequent passages of weak and sentimental writing. As a long sustained work, Zhivago is

jerry-built. Favourable judgements of it depend too heavily on Pasternak's own finger pointing unerringly at his symbolic structure. But his language does not support this structure, and his conventionally realist intentions undermine it. Readers should pay attention to the high claims made for the novel. They should also pay attention to the other view, well expressed by Renato Poggioli in his *The Theory of the Avant Garde*: 'With [Zhivago] ... Pasternak who until recently, especially as poet, was the last *avant-garde* artist surviving in Soviet Russia, returned to traditional literary and artistic forms, even pre-revolutionary ones, to express a conscientious objection which was not that of an artist but that of a man.' In other words in *Zhivago* Pasternak's Symbolist procedures are over-obtrusive, old fashioned and over-conscious.

Though his genius is apparent in it, the form he should have chosen was that of a sequence of poems interspersed with prose passages, and the central character should have been the 'I-less' Pasternak of the poems, and not Zhivago – the nature of whose existence 'in reality' is aptly demonstrated by the notoriously vulgar 'film epic' that was made, under the title of *Doctor Zhivago*, in the West.

Totalitarian pressure was more responsible for this failure than any defect in Pasternak himself; totalitarian pressure practically distorted his image of himself into a missionary martyr; totalitarian pressure made him into a real martyr.

BIBLIOGRAPHY
Translation: M. Hayward and M. Harari, *Doctor Zhivago* (1958), 1961. The Zhivago sequence of poems is well translated in H. Kaman, *In the Interlude*, 1962.

Text: *Doktur Zhivago*, 1959.

Criticism: B. Pasternak, *An Essay in Autobiography*,

1959; H. Munchnic, *From Gorky to Pasternak*, 1961; A. F. Boyd in *Aspects of the Russian Novel*, 1972.

Günter Grass

Günter Grass was born of Polish-German parents in 1927 in the then Free State of Danzig, which was seized by the Nazis in 1939. He spent a year in the German army during which he was wounded and captured by the Americans; then he worked as a labourer and stonemason's apprentice. He studied art in Düsseldorf, Berlin and Paris (he is a sculptor and draughtsman) during the 1950s. He began his literary career as a 'nonsense' poet and post-expressionist playwright. *Die Blechtrommel* [*The Tin Drum*] (1959) made him famous – the influential *Gruppe 47* awarded him a prize for it before he had finished it – and was translated into many languages. Establishment critics regarded it as pornographic. Five more novels followed: *Katz und Maus* [*Cat and Mouse*] (1961) – really a novella – *Hundejahre* [*Dog Years*] (1963), *Örtlich Betaupt* [*Local Anaesthetic*] (1969), *Aus dem Tagebuch einer Schnecke* [*From a Snail's Notebook*] (1972) and *Die Flunder* [*The Flounder*] (1978). In 1960 Grass moved from Paris back to West Berlin. He has been a committed and active supporter of the SPD, in particular of Willy Brandt (who resigned as party leader in 1974). He calls himself a 'revisionist'.

Die Blechtrommel
[The Tin Drum]

SUMMARY *The Tin Drum* is told, 'drummed', in the first

person by the Danzig-born dwarf Oskar Matzerath, from a lunatic asylum to which he has been confined for the murder of a nurse (a murder he did not commit). Sometimes he calls himself Oskar and 'I' in the same sentence. He has a voice which can break glass at long range. In order to get tin drums to beat he has used the threat of this voice. He arranged to be a dwarf at the age of three, by contriving to fall down some cellar steps: he wished to avoid growing, which he regarded as absurd. The action covers the years 1899–1955, since Oskar traces the history of his family back to his grandparents. But the main narrative spans Oskar's lifetime: 1925–55. Oskar could, if he wanted to, clear himself of murder; but he prefers the comfort and security of the madhouse. The narrative often embraces the present: Oskar is visited in the hospital – where he is allowed to beat his drum for a certain time each day – by various friends and doctors.

The Tin Drum is an audacious mixture of accurate historical fact, given as meticulous background, and grotesque fantasy, written in a wildly energetic prose influenced by surrealism but never quite surrealist; the influence of *Simplicissimus*, set against a similarly war-torn background, is always apparent.

Oskar's grandfather, who has been wanted by the police for setting fires and who has taken on another identity, blushes when he is discovered some years later: it is not a 'blush of shame, but the lingering glow of the sawmills he had set on fire'. It is not clear whether he drowns or becomes Joe Colchic in the USA, 'founder of fire insurance companies'.

Oskar is born; his 'mental development is completed at birth and after that merely needs a certain amount of filling in'. He is the product of adultery, and is not the son of his mother's second husband, Alfred Matzerath, or of her first, Jan Bronski – though in 1925, while Matzerath's wife, she is Bronski's mistress. Matzerath, however, is his 'German' 'father', Bronski his 'Polish' one.

Oskar is at first amoral and non-political; he is given to screaming if he does not get his own way.

His first thirteen years are spent in Danzig, which Grass often evokes vividly, in a perfectly realistic manner. Was he, he asks himself in 1955 in his hospital, a member of the Resistance? Did he 'drum for the people'? 'No,' is his answer. His drumming in those days was 'destructive' and 'evil'. By the use of his voice – he can shatter shop windows – he tempts people into becoming thieves. In this period Oskar's mother 'gets religion', and there is a long and brilliantly written section of what Roman Catholics regarded as blasphemy against their Church (Grass is not impartial on the subject of Roman Catholicism). Oskar becomes increasingly obsessed with nuns. His mother dies of a surfeit of fish. He meets the waiter, Herbert Truczinski, his associate in a burglary campaign. The first of the three books ends with an identification of the (Catholic) Christ with the heavenly gasman (of the gas chambers). The SA expel the drunken trumpeter Meyn for cruelty to his four cats, while they arrange the Crystal Night (*Kristallnacht*) pogrom, driving the toy seller (needed by Oskar for drums) to suicide. Meyn ends up in the Waffen SS. Oskar's 'German' father, a member of the Nazi party, warms his hands at the blazing synagogue.

The Germans invade. Jan Bronski is executed for having been in the post office, which had held out against the Nazis. This contaminates Oskar 'for all time with the taste of perishability'. At sixteen he impregnates Herbert Truczinski's young sister Maria – now married to Matzerath – when both succumb to the aphrodisiac qualities of fizz powder. A son, Kurt, is born. Greff, a Nazi greengrocer, builds Oskar a drumming machine out of a pair of scales. Greff hangs himself, in his old uniform of boy-scout leader, on the shop scales: he has been summoned to appear in court on a morals charge. Oskar – who has (while hidden) interrupted Nazi mass meetings by his drumming, causing the crowds to break into his rhythm and into dancing – tours the Atlantic Wall as a drummer, taking with him his selections from Rasputin and Goethe, his two mentors. He joins an armed band of thugs called the Dusters (these, particularly the Edel-weiss Pirates of Cologne, became a feature of German city life towards the end of the war). For the Dusters, Oskar is 'Jesus', whom he now follows although he does not believe in him.

The Russians are now advancing towards Danzig. Mat-zerath chokes himself in attempting to swallow his Nazi party badge. Oskar begins, although slowly, to grow: it happened, apparently, when his four-year-old son Kurt threw a stone at him at Matzerath's funeral, whereupon he leapt into the grave after throwing his drum and drum-sticks into it. He continues to grow, and suffers from fever and swellings. The Russians are now in Danzig. Mr Fajngold, Maria's new lover, applies liberal quantities of disinfectant, which he has learned to do at Treblinka concentration camp (eventually he put down kerosene instead, and applied a match). He proposes to Maria, but she refuses him; she sets out with Oskar for the Rhine-land. Oskar is still growing; with his swollen joints he can no longer hold his drumsticks. The final section of the second book, 'Growth in a Freight Car' (going to the Rhineland) is narrated by Bruno Mästerberg, Oskar's male nurse in the mental hospital. The constant vibra-tions of the train to Stettin have further promoted the dwarf's growth, which results in the formation of a hump. His voice has lost the power to demolish glass.

The third book takes us into the postwar world of Gerresheim, near Düsseldorf: the bad years of shortages and the black market, the currency reforms, night clubs, the 'economic miracle', and the creation of an affluent society which is, however, riddled with guilt. Oskar's son Kurt proves himself to be an expert on the black market. But Oskar decides to become an assistant to a stonemason with chronic boils instead of a black marketeer. The stonemason carves tombstones; Oskar is increasingly pre-occupied by death.

With the currency reforms (generally taken as the beginning of the 'economic miracle') Oskar has to remember 'his hump and [fall] victim to art'. He becomes a successful artist's model; eventually he poses naked. The 'sons and daughters of the Muses ... have recognized the Rasputin in you', he tells himself; 'but will they ever discover the Goethe who lies dormant in your soul ... ?' He decides to be a drummer in a jazz band. Eventually he becomes a government-sponsored solo drummer, and achieves immense success: his tin drum has become a gold mine. He is regarded as a healer, and 'Oskarism' becomes a catchword; what he cures best of all is loss of memory.

But he becomes a suspect in a murder case. A nurse, Dorothea, with whom he had once tried to make love while wrapped in coconut matting, was murdered by another nurse jealous of her because she was loved by a Dr Werner (later she also kills Werner). Oskar incriminates himself by showing an obsession with Dorothea's ring finger – brought to him by his dog while in the ryefield where she was murdered. He is convicted, but deemed not fully responsible for his actions. While under observation, he flees. He is apprehended in Paris, and tells the French Interpol detectives that he is Jesus. He finishes his recollections, written in the hospital, with the realization that the 'Black Witch' is forever in front of him, 'coming closer'.

CRITICAL COMMENTARY Grass was the first German novelist to approach the question of 'collective guilt' – discussion of which had become conventional, self-justificatory, cliché-ridden – in purely imaginative terms. Thus his overall tone is never far from comic; at the least, it is never earnest. *The Tin Drum* has been called neo-baroque, neo-picaresque and mannerist (this connotes 'marked by peculiarities', and is related to 'baroque', even to the extent that certain critics have misleadingly confused the two). In the wider sense, it is certainly expressionist: even the graphic descriptions, let alone the fantastic detail, tell us about the inner states of the participants, most particularly about that of Oskar who carries the weight (in large part autobiographical) of his own narrative.

Oskar is a multi-levelled figure; but he exists in his own right as fantastic clown, buffoon and quasi-picaresque anti-hero. His considerable autonomy as an individual gives the novel a unity. But it is inevitable that the reader, because of the chaotic historical background and because of the implications of Oskar, should assault this unity in his quest for meaning. The inevitability of this process is reflected and thus acknowledged in the hybrid style. The author knew that allegories and symbolic meanings must be found in his text; but in the composition of this text he eschewed allegorical or even symbolic intention. The background is meticulous, and is based on Grass's own experience, while its vividness draws from the energy of his invention. Thus, while we may and should analyse the work in terms of its political and other implications, we must do so in the knowledge of its artistic integrity. This is the story of Oskar, and Grass is devoted to it; whatever of himself gets into Oskar (and it is a good deal, although often distorted in the time-honoured expressionist manner) has clearly not been consciously planned. Oskar is a true and uncalculated *objective correlative*, a child of imagination. The sheer exuberance of the narrative allows us to respond to him, first of all, with *our* imaginations.

Oskar's drumming, which has at times a benevolent magic about it (breaking up Nazi meetings and causing people to dance naturally and joyfully), is the equivalent of artistic creation. At the same time he is what he is:

German-Polish – and therefore neither German nor
Polish. He is also representative of the 'guilty artist', a
theme which has obsessed modern writers, and none (for
obvious enough reasons) more than the Germans (Kafka
was oppressed by it, and it is the central *motif* of all
Thomas Mann's fiction – as it was of that of the Austrian
novelist Hermann Broch). The artist feels guilty because
he is in grave and sometimes agonizing doubt about – to
put it at its simplest – the usefulness of his work. Oskar is
'mad' (as artists are often supposed to be, and indeed
often, in one valid sense, are) and he is at first a rogue.
He is also deformed: as a result of allowing himself to
grow after the death of the pathetic Matzerath. It is not
without significance that for a very short time he considers
becoming a doctor (as an immediately useful man, the
apparent opposite of an artist).

Oskar is not, as he has sometimes been taken to be,
'Germany'. Rather, as an artist, employing his drumming
as 'technique' for acknowledged artistic purposes – in-
direct polemic (breaking up fascist meetings), subversion
of the existing order, exhibitionism, entertainment (a
necessary concomitant of creation), control, recollection
of the past – he is an inevitably compromised victim of a
corrupt political order, one which, in his unhappy case,
is one of the most barbaric and evil of all time.

The gift of artistic creation, we may infer from *The Tin
Drum*, is simultaneously a punishment, a crime, and a
responsibility. It has been suggested that the 'lack of a
unifying allegory' weakens the novel. But had Grass
consciously tried to make a unified allegory he would
have destroyed its power. Undoubtedly it is symbolic –
but then symbols *are* what they represent, whereas allegories are not what they represent. Grass left his novel
open-ended – Oskar still comfortably inside the madhouse, his book finished, his future entirely uncertain,
his main fear of the not altogether explicit 'Black Witch'
– but he took it as far as, at that point, he honestly could.

Oskar, although he has his hump, wills himself to grow up – mentally as well as physically. He therefore undergoes a change of heart, a conversion. And even before this conversion (bizarre though its form may be) Oskar has been as much a representation, if a lopsided one, of 'inner emigration' (term for the mental reservations, or ironic or disguised protests of those who stayed in Nazi Germany but rejected the system) as he has been of the infantilism, the deliberate regression to the world of the Id, of Nazism.

Now Grass, while clearly influenced by the baroque and the picaresque, and by Rabelais, Grimmelshausen, Sterne and his eccentric comic German predecessor Jean Paul (whose real name was Johann Paul Richter, 1763–1825) and Thomas Mann, was writing in the tradition of the specifically German movement, Expressionism, which flourished between 1910 and the early 1920s (this should not be confused with the anti-mimetic technique of expressionism 'with a small "e"', even though the term itself derives from the practices of post-impressionistic painters who just preceded the German precursors of the Expressionist movement). Expressionism, which eventually sobered down into the so-called *Neue Sachlichkeit* ('New Objectivity') tendency of the mid-1920s, had usually been exclamatory, ecstatic, grotesque, violent: at its best it contained legitimate protest and a valid apprehension of reality which looked like a denial of external reality, but it also contained the seeds of a totalitarian attitude (several Expressionists – such as Johst and Becher – became declamatory fascists or Stalinists). In Oskar Grass retrospectively captures the ambivalence of Expressionism: its search for a truth beyond a mimesis which had become materialistic, in conflict with its sinister features of barbarity and nihilism. One of the emblems of the Expressionists had been the Norwegian Edvard Munch's woodcut 'The Shriek' – and Oskar begins by screaming. Later he uses his magic voice to smash glass objects and to tempt people to thievery. But although he keeps up his drumming, he loses his destructive vocal powers.

It is hard not to see Oskar as a kind of justification of the continuation of creative activities, even in the madhouse of the contemporary world. He loses his drumming powers when he decides to grow (the artist as a child). After renouncing black market activity in favour of work for a stonemason, he regains this power. He is even prepared to take on the responsibility for a murder which he did not commit. His peculiar strident voice, the destructive 'shriek', has, however, disappeared. Thus, while creative activity is not justified, it is seen to continue. Nor does Oskar lose moral stature. On the contrary, he gains it, even if he also retains a certain grotesque distinction: his hump. This, paradoxically, is his freedom. Not from responsibility – but from that false conventional morality which all the major writers have rejected in their writings if not in their lives.

While Grass may be defended from the charge of failing to provide a self-conscious allegory, it must be admitted that his explosive material slips from time to time out of his control. While in general outline the novel has a coherence, both in its unobtrusive but meticulous drawing-in of the historical background, and in its concentration on Oskar's development, some of the images are unassimilable. Whether this is gain or loss must depend on the reader: on whether he admires the coherence of art as truthful, or whether he prefers to be 'authentically' disconcerted by what he reads. But Grass's concentration on small and apparently trivial objects (for example, Dorothea's comb, examined in such detail by Oskar) undoubtedly compensates for this failing (if it is a failing). As Arrigo Subiotto has pointed out, there is an interesting distinction between his contemplation of objects and that of the *nouveaux romanciers* (one of whom is Robbe-Grillet): the latter want to de-anthropomorphize objects, but Grass uses them to enhance emotion.

Perhaps the most successful aspect of *The Tin Drum*, apart from its wide scope, is the way in which Grass has been able to subjugate such complex material, so sophisticatedly treated, to a vision (that of Oskar) which, although it is by no means 'naïve' (as it has been characterized), is imaginatively pure. The avoidance of conventional attacks on Nazism and the insistence on the necessity of understanding – involving phantasmagoric comedy and a satire that emerges of its own accord – are exemplary.

BIBLIOGRAPHY
Translation: R. Manheim, *The Tin Drum*, 1962.

Text: *Die Blechtrommel*, 1959.

Criticism: in B. Keith-Smith (ed), *Essays in Contemporary German Literature*, 1966.

Alexander Solzhenitsyn

Alexander Solzhenitsyn was born at Rostov-on-Don in 1918. He graduated in physics and mathematics at Rostov University. Called up in 1941, he had a distinguished war record; by 1945 he was a captain and had received two decorations. But his correspondence was intercepted, and an impolite reference to Stalin resulted in a sentence of eight years in a corrective labour camp (the setting of *Ivan Denisovich*). He remained in exile until 1956; in 1957 he was 'rehabilitated' after it was found that there had been no case against him. He taught physics and mathematics until 1962, when *Novy Mir* published *Ivan Denisovich*; he continued to publish shorter pieces in Russia until 1966. But he could not get clearance to publish *V kruge pervom* [*The First Circle*] (1968) about a 'privileged' labour camp for specialist scientists, or *Rakovy korpus* [*Cancer Ward*] (1968) based on his experiences in a cancer ward in Tashkent. These were published (in Russian) in Italy, and then widely translated. The first part of his historical novel, *Avgust chetyrnadtsatogo* [*August 1914*] (1971) appeared in Paris.

In 1970 Solzhenitsyn was awarded the Nobel Prize; but he was not then allowed to go to Stockholm to receive it. Instead, he was subjected to increasing persecution, including expulsion from the Writers' Union. He replied with a courageous campaign of running criticism of the Soviet government. He would not leave the country, which the authorities wanted him to do – so that they could refuse him re-entry. The publication in Paris in 1974 of the first two parts of his seven-part study of the Russian prison camp system from 1918 onwards, *Gulag Archipelago* ('Gulag' is an acronym – it crops up in Pasternak's *Zhivago* for Glavnoye Upravleniye Lagerei: Chief Directorate of Camps) was too much for the foolish and dazed Soviet authorities. They suddenly forced him out of Russia (October 1974); later his second wife and children were allowed to join him. He lived in Switzerland until 1976, when he went to America. He has kept up his attack on the Soviet system from outside. He has also, perhaps unfortunately, indulged himself in certain naïve pronouncements about the affairs of other countries, of whose history he is ignorant. For the present he is functioning more as an anti-communist polemicist preacher and exposer of Soviet infamy than as a creative writer.

Odin den v zhizni Ivan Denisovicha
[One Day in the Life of Ivan Denisovich]

SUMMARY *Ivan Denisovich* describes a single day, from reveille to lights-out, in the life of Ivan Denisovich Shukhov in a corrective labour camp. Just one January day in the only slightly under 4,000 days of his sentence. It is 1951, and Stalin is still dictator. Shukhov was called up in 1941; subsequently he was taken prisoner by the Germans, but escaped. For surrendering 'to the enemy, intending to betray his country [and returning] in order to carry out instructions given by the Germans' he received ten years. He signed the 'confession' because it was a 'simple calculation: if he didn't sign, he'd be shot; if he did, he would live on for a while.' (Such sentences were and are common.)

Shukhov does not occupy a top place in the prison hierarchy, but after eight years in various camps he has learned to look after himself. On this morning, however, he feels ill. He fails to get an interview with the doctor: the (unofficially) statutory number (two men) have got in before him. The medical orderly is not really a medical orderly at all, but an ex-arts student who spends his time writing poetry: the doctor 'was keen that he should write in prison what he had not been in a position to write as a free man'.

This is a 'good' day for Ivan. His feelings of illness wear off. He gets extra rations at dinner and at supper by doing favours. The harassment by guards and the freezing weather are no worse than usual. The prisoners are searched in the icy wind when being marched to their work. But the leader of Ivan's gang, 104, manages to fix a 'good percentage' (a few extra rations); the gang has avoided being sent to build the Socialist Community Centre, where there is no protection at all from the cold; he has been happy building a wall – there is a bril-liant description of this – which is to be part of a new power station. He finds a bit of hacksaw blade and slips it through the search on the return march; it will make a useful knife. He has done a favour and has thus earned himself a bit of food from the recipient of a parcel. He has been able to buy some tobacco. And be-fore lights out there has only been one recount of the prisoners in the icy cold – there are often more. He goes to sleep satisfied, not caring about the two more years he has to serve or the next Sunday that the prisoners are going to lose.

Ivan gets no parcels – the private enterprise currency of the camp – but he is experienced, and earns a little by making slippers and doing favours. His gang boss, an old inmate of camps, has singled him out as a reliable man, and this confers upon him a certain authority.

There are concise portraits of some of the inmates: a pious Baptist who will pray for nothing for himself but his daily bread; two fine, closely bound Estonians: Ivan

has never known a bad Estonian; the sea captain Buinov-
sky, who is serving a twenty-five-year sentence because an
English admiral to whose convoy he had been attached
as liaison officer in the war had sent him a souvenir gift
inscribed 'As a token of gratitude'; Yetyukov the perpetual cadger, who gets himself beaten up – will not survive
because he doesn't understand how to; Tyurin the gang
leader, whose troubles began in the 1930s when it was
discovered that he was the 'son of a kulak', and who
tells tales of his sufferings as though he were speaking
of someone else.

Little attention is given to the individual guards,
and in this simple eye-witness narrative the commandant
is never even glimpsed. We merely hear that he is pot
bellied. Some guards are brutal, some are less so. But all
are dehumanized; as are some of the prisoners: Khromoi
('Lame'), the cowardly mess-hall orderly who beats his
fellow prisoners with a stick when they try to get their
food; the squealers; the camp trusties; 'bastards of the
first water'.

Hunger and cold are omnipresent. Happiness is
measured by the weight of bread, and varies according to
the temperature. Most of the narration is concerned with
the means by which Shukhov survives: apparently trivial, but in this context not so. The struggle to obtain
the right number of bowls at meals; the great effort to
retain a trowel; the preservation of bread – some of
which has to be sewn up in his mattress; the need for a
smoke, even one drag from a cigarette someone has all
but finished; the constant watchfulness on his and his
gang's behalf. And on this one day, having just avoided
the dreaded cells – the windowless stone centre of this
hell, where the heat of the stove is just enough to melt
the ice so that the prisoner must lie in a puddle of water
– Ivan is actually happy.

CRITICAL COMMENTARY *Ivan Denisovich* has great documentary value – as an accurate description of a Siberian labour camp towards the end of the Stalinist era – and great literary merit. It is a straightforward account, seen through the eyes of a man so charmingly unsophisticated that he half believes the new moon really is new (he asks the sea captain what happens to the old one: does it form stars?). Remarkable authorial restraint (Solzhenitsyn's use of Ivan as a *persona* is completely successful) gives the novella an extra-political dimension. Although incidentally a damning indictment of a barbarous and at the same time stupid system of terror, *Ivan Denisovich* is an affirmative book. The style is indivisible from the content, a feat which Solzhenitsyn has not repeated. It is clipped, colloquial, and full of the unfamiliar idiom of the camps (a fact that its translators can hardly bring out. Since they have no Anglo-Saxon parallels to draw upon – prisons are unpleasant but they are not like the Russian camps – they are driven to employ slang phrases familiar to English speakers). It is the courageous, irrepressible, vital lingua franca of the oppressed, the victims of a tyranny which can confine and torment men, but which cannot wholly numb all of them.

The conditions are terrible. It is universally accepted that all camp food and the contents of parcels will be progressively diminished as they are handed down – each person in the chain, guards and prisoners alike, taking his cut. Although some of the inmates are real criminals and traitors – some served with Bendera, the Soviet general who collaborated with the Nazis – as many are not; their 'crime' is that they were captured by Germans, as often as not because of Russia's state of unpreparedness in 1941. As a critic has put it, the 'tiniest details of camp life, and the most marginal personal ups and downs, become almost fantastically magnified and acquire the status of major human events.' Yet human values persist. The captain is getting a little old for the harsh conditions and the hard work but, knowing that he will ultimately be able to adapt, the gang looks after him in the period of transition. Everyone has to steal and graft in order to survive: the system makes that inevitable. Even in this framework a spontaneous morality generally prevails over anarchy. Solzhenitsyn is adept at showing how in general the men will not go beyond a certain line. The gang leader gets his privileges, but no one begrudges him because he negotiates for the gang and thus looks after its welfare. People, like the cadger Yetyukov, who do cross the line don't get on so well.

There is a hideous irony here, all the more painful for not being openly stated. These men are supposedly in prison for not being 'good communists', or for being 'traitors' to communism. Their guards run a brutal, non-communist system. And yet they themselves, with exceptions, survive by pulling together: by being communistic (in the primitive sense). A paranoid totalitarian system is seen to generate a kind of genuine (non-Marxist, but rather Christian) communism. Humanity is generated by suffering. Ivan enjoys building a wall fast, for the gang's sake, much more than any dutiful communist lackey would.

The one aspect of prison life that Solzhenitsyn does not deal with is the sexual, even though the language in the book is of the coarsest.

Solzhenitsyn's later work, although of great documentary value, and containing some memorable passages (including the caricature of Stalin in *First Circle*) is more diffuse, and is often spoiled by philosophical asides which intrude into an already doughy texture. Solzhenitsyn is not especially gifted as a philosopher or as a political commentator. *1914* is feeble, and even the journalists who exploit the ill treated Solzhenitsyn for ideological purposes were hard put to it to praise it. Unlike the quieter Andrey Sinyavsky – eight years younger – who published abroad under the name of 'Abram Tertz' and underwent six years of hard labour for it (he is now living in Paris), Solzhenitsyn has tried to continue the *realist* tradition of the nineteenth-century Russian novel. Sinyavsky, who is the more important and imaginative writer, is a modernist in the tradition of Zamyatin. Pasternak decided to abandon, for *Zhivago*, the modernistic style of *The Childhood of Luvers*, which the percipient Zamyatin praised for belonging 'entirely to contemporary art'; the result did not reach anywhere near the level of his best poetry – or prose. For all their virtues Solzhenitsyn's subsequent works do not give as profound a description of the reality of Soviet Russia as do Sinyavsky's novels. But *Ivan Denisovich* could hardly be improved upon.

BIBLIOGRAPHY
Translations: R. Parker, *One Day in the Life of Ivan Denisovich*, 1963; M. Hayward and R. Hingley, *ibid*, 1963; G. Aitken, *ibid*, 1970.

General Bibliography

The following list consists of general books. All of them have useful passages dealing with the novelists represented herein; they also contain bibliographies.

General

A. J. Krailsheimer, *The Continental Renaissance*, 1971.
F. W. J. Hemmings, *The Age of Realism*, 1974.
M. Bradbury and J. McFarlane, *Modernism*, 1976.

These are the only three volumes so far available of the *Pelican Guides to European Literature*. The first is excellent, the second indispensable, and the third useful but markedly below the standard set by its predecessors. It is only fair to warn the reader against the article on Svevo (and Joyce), as this author has been dealt with more competently in the books listed in my bibliography for him.

French

P. E. Charvet (ed), *A Literary History of France*, six volumes, 1967–74.
J. Cruickshank (ed), *French Literature and its Background*, six volumes, 1967–70.

German

A. Closs (ed), *Introduction to German Literature*, four volumes, 1967–70.

Spanish

R. O. Jones (ed), *A Literary History of Spain*, eight volumes, 1970–73.

Italian

There is no long and comprehensive work on Italian literature in English. But F. de Sanctis, *History of Italian Literature*, a highly suggestive nineteenth-century classic, has been translated (1931), 1959. J. H. Whitfield's *A Short History of Italian Literature* (1960) is good, as is the collection of essays edited by S. Pacifici, *From Verismo to Experimentalism*, 1969. There is a plethora of material for those who read Italian.

Russian

H. Gicord, *The Novel in Russia*, 1964.
A. F. Boyd, *Aspects of the Russian Novel*, 1972.
R. Freeborn, *The Rise of the Russian Novel*, 1973.

Portuguese

There is nothing in English on Portuguese literature except A. Bell's *Portuguese Literature* (1922), 1970, which is instructive but dated and dull. Eça, however, is well dealt with in *The Age of Realism* (above).

Scandinavian

Hamsun is dealt with in A. Gustafson, *Six Scandinavian Novelists*, 1968.

Index

Fictional characters have been indexed only where reference has been made to them other than in the section devoted to the particular novel in which they appear